Nursing Law in

Nursing Law in Ireland

By

John Lombard
LLB, LLM, GDip, PhD

Published by
Clarus Press Ltd,
Griffith Campus,
South Circular Road,
Dublin 8
www.claruspress.ie

Typeset by
Manila Typesetting Company

Printed by
SprintPrint Ltd,
Dublin

ISBN
978-1-911611-34-9

All rights reserved
No part of this publication may be reproduced, or transmitted in any form or by any means, including recording and photocopying or any digital means, without the written permission of the copyright holder, application for which should be addressed to the publisher. Written permission should also be obtained before any part of the publication is stored in a retrieval system of any nature.

Disclaimer
Whilst every effort has been made to ensure that the contents of this book are accurate, neither the publisher nor author can accept responsibility for any errors or omissions or loss occasioned to any person acting or refraining from acting as result of any material in this publication.

© John Lombard 2021

For Mom, Dad, Eileen and Lydia.

Thank you for your constant support and encouragement, not only in the writing of this book, but in every endeavour that I undertake.

Preface

The role of the nurse and midwife has expanded and evolved over the years. This is a point that echoes throughout this work. Very few aspects of nursing practice have gone unchanged in the past 30 years. During this time there have been changes in education, greater professional autonomy, increased competencies, and a broader scope of practice. Although such developments are to be welcomed, they raise a host of challenges for the nurse and midwife, not least of which is the need to be informed and aware of the legal framework which shapes medical treatment and care. This served as a key motivating factor behind this book. *Nursing Law in Ireland* is intended to provide an accessible yet comprehensive overview of the key legal and ethical issues arising in nursing practice. This book addresses a wide range of topics including: negligence; decision-making; confidentiality; the role of the nurse prescriber; the regulation of reproduction; end-of-life issues; and clinical research ethics. This reflects the breadth and scope of nursing practice. It follows that not all areas could be addressed within the confines of this text. For instance, distinct legal and ethical issues arising in the context of children's nursing, psychiatric nursing, intellectual disability, or public health nursing are not covered.

Nursing Law in Ireland is written with healthcare practice in mind. It is hoped that it can provide a guide to the legal framework for the registered nurse and midwife. As the book aims to deliver a practical, accessible, and critical analysis of the relevant law it is hoped that it will also provide undergraduate and postgraduate students with a solid grounding in the relevant legal principles. This text may also prove beneficial to students and practitioners in allied health professions.

Tracing the evolution of the nursing profession and the related legal developments has made this an enjoyable book to write. However, the shifting legal framework coupled with the absence of consolidated legislation in Ireland can make it challenging to precisely define the parameters of practice. Every effort has been made to ensure this book reflects the most recent developments in Irish law and accurately depicts the legal framework as it stood in September 2020. Nonetheless, I bear responsibility for any errors or mistakes within this work.

I would like to thank everyone who has supported the writing of this book. I am particularly grateful to David McCartney of Clarus Press for his patience, advice and enthusiasm throughout the writing and publication process. I am thankful to my colleagues in the School of Law University of Limerick. Their collegiality and kindness have created an enjoyable and productive space within which to teach and research. I have also had the benefit of working with, and learning from, many inspirational mentors and friends over the years and so I thank all of those who have shaped my understanding and knowledge of the law to date.

John Lombard
17th November 2020

Contents

Preface vii
Table of Cases xi
Table of Legislation xv
Abbreviations xxxi

1. Introduction 1
2. An Introduction to the Irish Legal System 7
3. The Nursing and Midwifery Board of Ireland 33
4. Negligent Practice in Nursing 67
5. Patient Autonomy and Decision-Making 93
6. Confidentiality and Access to Personal Health
   Information 141
7. The Administration of Medicines 183
8. Legal Aspects of Pregnancy 209
9. Legal Aspects of End-of-Life Treatment and Care 239
10. Clinical Research Ethics 289

Index 329

Table of Cases

A, B, and C v Ireland [2010] ECHR 2032 ....227, 228
A and B v Eastern Health Board, Judge Mary Fahy and C, and
 the Attorney General (the C Case) [1998] 1 IR 464 .... 226n
Aintree University Hospital's NHS Foundation Trust v James
 [2013] UKSC 67 ....258, 275
Airedale NHS Trust v Bland [1993] AC 789 ....258, 275
An Irish Hospital v RF [2015] 2 IR 377..260
Attorney General v X [1992] IESC 1; [1992] 1 IR 1 ...... 223, 224n, 225
Attorney General (SPUC) v Open Door Counselling Ltd [1988]
 IR 593..223n, 225n
Ava Kiernan v Health Service Executive [2015] IEHC 141 77

Barnett v Chelsea and Kensington Hospital Management
 Committee [1969] 1 QB 428...83
Bensaid v United Kingdom (2001) ECHR 82............................. 266n
Blyth v The Company of Proprietors of the Birmingham
 Waterworks (1956) 11 Ex Ch 781..70
Bolton v Blackrock Clinic (23 January 1997)
Brennan v An Bord Altranais [2010] IEHC 193..............................62
Burke v John Paul & Co Ltd [1967] IR 277 89
Byrne v Ireland [1972] IR 241.. 15n

Canterbury v Spence 464 F.2d 772 (1972) 112
Chatterton v Gerson [1981] QB 432 102
Child and Family Agency v A [2018] IEHC 112, [2018]
 3 IR 531..157, 159, 160
Coco v AN Clark (Engineers) [1968] FSR 415 143
Collins v Mid-Western Health Board [2000] 2 IR 154 80
Conole v Redbank Oyster Co [1976] IR 191 87
Corbally v The Medical Council [2015] 2 IR 304 .... 50, 50n, 51
Cosgrave v Ryan and the Electricity Supply Board [2003] 1
 ILRM 544 .... 82, 83n
Crowley v Allied Irish Banks and O'Flynn [1988] ILRM 225 86

D v Ireland App No 26499/02 (ECtHR, 28 June 2006) 226
D v United Kingdom (1997) 24 EHRR 423 266
D (A Minor) v District Judge Brennan, the Health Services
 Executive, Ireland and the Attorney General (HC 9 May 2007) 226
David Noel McCandless v The General Medical Council (1996)
 7 Med LR 37 49

Donoghue v Stevenson [1932] AC 562 71
Dowling v An Bord Altranais [2017] IEHC 62 .... 49n, 64
Dunne v National Maternity Hospital [1989] ILRM 735 78

Fairchild v Glenhaven Funeral Services [2002] 3 All ER 305 .... 84, 85
Fitzpatrick v FK [2008] IEHC 104, [2009] 2 IR 7 99,
 .... 118, 125, 136, 237, 254
Fitzpatrick v National Maternity Hospital [2008] IEHC 62 220
Fitzpatrick v White [2007] IESC 51 .... 114, 115
Fitzpatrick and Another v K and Another [2008] IEHC 104;
 [2009] 2 IR 7 .... 106, 107, 108, 110n, 120
Fleming v Ireland & Ors [2013] IEHC 2; [2013] IESC 19 268,
 .... 269n, 270n, 271

Geoghegan v Harris [2000] IEHC 129; [2000] 3 IR 536 .... 113, 114
*Gillick v West Norfolk and Wisbech Area Health Authority and
 another* [1986] 1 AC 112 .... 234n
Glass v United Kingdom (2004) 39 EHRR 15
Glencar Explorations v Mayo County Council [2002] 1 IR 84 72
Governor of X Prison v McD [2015] IEHC 259 136

HE v A Hospital NHS Trust [2003] EWHC 1017 138
Health Service Executive v JM A Ward of Court [2017]
 IEHC 399 .... 257, 258, 275
Healy v Buckley [2015] IECA 251 116
Herczegfalvy v Austria (1992) 15 EHRR 437
Hickey v McGowan [2017] IESC 6 92
House of Spring Gardens v Point Blank Ltd [1984] IR 611 148
HSE v B [2016] IEHC 605; [2016] 2 IR 350 237
HSE v Information Commissioner [2008] IEHC 298 174
Hunter v Mann [1974] QB 767 153

JM v Board of Management of St Vincent's Hospital
 [2003] 1 IR 321 .... 99, 118, 119, 254

Keane (an infant) v HSE & Ors [2011] IEHC 213 .... 92n
Keenan v United Kingdom (2001) EHRR 913 .... 266n
Kelly v St Laurence's Hospital [1989] ILRM 437 .... 74, 75, 77
Kennedy v Ireland [1987] IR 587 .... 15n, 149
Kenny v O'Rourke [1972] IR 339 84
Kirby v Burke & Holloway [1944] IR 207 73
Kruse v Johnson [1898] 1 2 QB 91
Kudelska v An Bord Altranais [2009] IEHC 68 .... 50n

L v Lithuania App no 27527/03 (ECtHR, 11 September 2007) 266
Le Lievre v Gould [1893] 1 QB 491 71

Malette v Shulman (1990) 67 D.L.R. (4th) 321 ....102, 136
McCarthy v Murphy [1998] IEHC 23..90
Mellet v Ireland Comm. No. 2324/2013, UN Doc. CCPR/
    C/116/D/2324/2013 (2016)..228
McGee v Attorney General [1974] IR 284.......................15, 148, 223
McGrory v Electricity Supply Board [2004] 3 IR 407..................... 149n
McK v Information Commission [2006] IESC 2..... 151, 152n, 173, 174
Mooney v Terrett [1939] Ir Jur Rep 56... 92n
Murray v Miller and Brady (14 November 2001) CC
    (Roscommon)..86

North Western Health Board v HW & CW [2001] 3 IR 622.............237
Nursing and Midwifery Board of Ireland v OCM [2016]
    IEHC 780..65

O'Brien v. Cunard S.S. Co. 28 N.E. 266 (1891)............................ 103n
O'Brien v South Western Area Health Board [2003]
    IESC 56...214, 215
O'Ceallaigh v An Bord Altranais [2009] IEHC 470..........................58
O'Connor and Tormey v Lenihan [2005] IEHC 176.........................178
O'Donovan v The Cork County Council [1967] IR 173 75
O'Laoire v Medical Council (27 January 1995) HC...........................48
Open Door Counselling and Dublin Well Woman v Ireland
    (1993) 15 EHRR 244.. 223n
Overseas Tankship (UK) Ltd v Morts Dock & Engineering
    [1961] AC 388...88

People (AG) v O'Brien [1965] IR 142... 15n
Perez v An Bord Altranais [2005] IEHC 400 .... 49, 50n
PP v HSE [2014] IEHC 622 ....254, 279
Pretty v United Kingdom [2002] ECHR 423; (2002) 35
    EHRR 1 ....100, 117, 270

Quinn v Mid Western Health Board [2005] IESC 19.................. 83n, 85

R v Bourne [1938] 3 All ER 615..222
R(Burke) v General Medical Council [2006] QB 273............. 120, 121n
R (on the application of Tracey) v Cambridge University
    Hospitals NHS Foundation Trust [2014] EWCA Civ 822........273,
    .... 274n
R(Purdy) v DPP [2009] UKHL 45...270
Re a Ward of Court [1996] 2 IR 79..........................15n, 16n, 99, 118,
    .... 135, 136n, 254, 255, 258, 275
Re C (Adult: refusal of treatment) [1994] 1 All ER 819....106, 107, 108

Re T (Adult: Refusal of Medical Treatment) [1992] 4 All ER
  649..98, 136
Roe v Wade 410 U.S. 113 (1973)...223
Rosenberg v Percival [2001] HCA 18...115
Rotunda Hospital v Information Commissioner [2011] IESC 26... 149n
Ryan v Attorney General [1965] IR 294 .... 14, 252n

Schloendoff v Society of New York Hospital 105 N.E. 92
  (N.Y. 1914) 98
Shuitt v Mylotte [2006] IEHC 89 80
Sidaway v Board of Governors of the Bethlem Royal Hospital
  [1985] 1 AC 871 116
SPUC v Grogan [1989] IR 753 ....223n, 225n
SR (a Minor and a Ward of Court): An Irish Hospital v RH and
  J McG [2012] 1 IR 305 ....254n, 259, 260n
State (C) v Frawley [1976] 1 IR 365 .... 266n

Tarasoff v Regents of the University of California 551 P 2d 334
  (Cal, 1976)..156
Tarrade v Northern Area Health Board [2002] IEHC 32 213
Teehan v Health Service Executive & Minister for Health
  [2013] IEHC 383...214
Thake v Maurice [1986] QB 644 177
The Medical Council v M.A.G.A. [2016] IEHC 779.............................65
The People (Attorney General) v Dunleavy [1948] IR 95...................68
The State (Harrington) v Wallace [1988] IR 290
Thomas Marshall (Exports) v Guinle (1979) 1 Ch 227 143
Tysiac v Poland (2007) 45 EHRR 42..118

United States of America v Karl Brandt et al, 21 November
  1946–20 August 1947 .... 298n

Van Gen den Loos v Nederlandse [1963] ECR 1...................................20

W v Egdell [1990] Ch 359; [1990] 1 All ER 835.......................159, 160
Walsh v Family Planning Services [1992] 1 IR 496 113
Walsh v South Tipperary County Council [2011] IEHC 503 .... 88, 89n
Wilsher v Essex Area Health Authority [1988] AC 1074 90
Winspear v City Hospitals Sunderland NHS Foundation Trust
  [2015] EWHC 3250 275

X v Denmark (1992) 15 EHRR 437.. 266n

Z v Finland (1997) 25 EHRR 371 150

Table of Legislation

Constitutional Provisions

Bunreacht na hÉireann 12
   8.1 13
   12 13
   12.3.1 27
   13 13
   13.7.2 13
   13.9 31
   14 13
   15.2.1 ....13, 17
   25.4.4 13
   26 ....27, 32
   28.2 13
   28.4.1 13
   29.4 13
   29.4.6 19
   29.6 21
   30 31
   31 13
   31.1 13
   31.2 14
   32 13
   33 26
   34 ....14, 24, 27, 30
   34.1 14
   34.2 24
   34.4.1 26
   34.3.4 ....14, 24n
   35 ....14, 24
   35.1 ....30, 31n
   35.2 24
   36 ....14, 24
   37 ....14, 24
   37.1 24
   38.3.1 28
   40 242
   40.1 ....14, 16n, 269
   40.3 ....15, 16
   40.3.1 ....15, 99
   40.3.3 ....222, 223, 225, 227, 228, 230, 236, 237, 238

| Table of Legislation

41	14, 15, 242
42	14, 242
43	14, 242
44	14, 242

Acts of the Oireachtas

Assisted Decision-Making (Capacity) Act 2015	3, 94, 105, 107, 121, 122, 123, 125, 135, 136, 138, 155, 254, 260
3(1)	110, 125
3(2)	110, 111n
3(3)	111
3(4)	111n
3(5)	111
3(6)	111
8	125, 260
8(2)	106
8(3)	111, 125
8(4)	126n
8(5)	126
8(6)	126
8(6)(c)	126n
8(6)(d)	126n
8(7)	126
8(7)(d)	126n
8(7)(e)	126n
8(7)(f)	126n
8(8)	127, 260
8(9)	104, 127
10(5)	128
11	128
13	128
14	128
15	129n
17(2)	129n
17(3)	129
18	129
19	129, 130n
19(5)	130
21	130n
21(3)	130
24(2)	130n
27	131n
28	131n
29	131n
30	131n

32	131n
33	131n
34	131n
38(2)	131n
38(3)	131
38(4)	132n
38(5)	132
38(6)	132
38(7)	132n
39	132
40	132, 252
43	132
44	132
44(1)	132n
44(2)	132n
44(3)	132n
44(5)	132n
46	133
46(7)	133n
46(8)	133n
47	133
59	133
60	133, 134
61	134n
62	134
62(5)	134
63	134
64	134n
65	134
66	134
68(1)	134n
68(3)	134n
69	133, 135n
69(5)	135
73	135n
75(3)	135
76	135n
78	135n
80	135n
82	135n
84	137
84(2)	137n
84(3)	137
84(3)(a)	121, 122n
84(3)(b)	122
84(5)	137

84(7) 137n
85(1) 138n
85(2) 138
85(3) 138n
85(4) 138n
85(5)(a) 139n
85(5)(b) 139n
85(6)(a) 139
85(6)(b) 139n
85(6)(c) 139n
86 139
86(2)(a) 139n
86(2)(b) 140
86(3) 140n
86(4) 140
86(5) 140
90 140
90(1) 140n
90(2) 140n
95 .... 123, 124n
96 124
96(2) 124
103 124
Part 7 135
Part 8 137

Child Care Act 1991 .... 25, 234
Children First Act 2015 236
Children's Act 2001 .... 44, 234
Civil Law (Miscellaneous Provisions) Act 2008 153
   27 153
   27(1) 153n
   27(3) 153n
Civil Liability Act 1961
   11 87
   11(1) 87, 88n
   11(2) 88n
   Part III 87
Civil Liability (Amendment) Act 2017 179
   7 .... 180n
   8 .... 179n
   10 180
   10(1)(a) 180n
   10(1)(b) 180n
   16 180
   16(4) 180

Part 4 179
Civil Registration Act 2004
   41 280
   42 279
   42A 280
Civil Registration (Amendment) Act 2014 280
Control of Clinical Trials Act 1987 187
Coroners Act 1962 281
   8 281
   8(1) 281n
   13(1) 281n
   14 281
   17 285
   18 285
   24 285
   26 285
   31 287
   35 281
   35(2)(a) 281n
   38 286
   39 286
   40 .... 286n
   41 .... 286n
   44 287
Coroners (Amendment) Act 2019 ....281, 282, 284, 285
   10 .... 285n
   10(1)(c) 285n
   19 287
   24 286
Courts and Court Officers Act 1995
   13(1) 31n
Criminal Justice Act 1964
   4 268
Criminal Justice Act 1967
Criminal Justice (Female Genital Mutilation) Act 2012
   2(1) 101
   2(3) 101
Criminal Justice (Withholding of Information on Offences
   against Children and Vulnerable Persons) Act 2012 249
Criminal Law (Sexual Offences) Act 2006 236
Criminal Law (Suicide) Act 1993 ....269, 270
   2(1) 268n
   2(2) 268, 269, 270
Criminal Law Amendment Act 1935 ....
   17 15

Data Protection Acts 1988 and 2003 ....4, 44, 142, 161
Data Protection Act 2018 ....161, 326
Disability Act 2005 44
Domestic Violence Act 1996 .... 25n

Eight Amendment of the Constitution Act 1983 ....222, 223,
....229, 230, 279
Equal Status Act 2000 2
Equal Status Acts 2000–2011 4
European Convention on Human Rights Act 2003 ....22, 149, 242
 3 ....22, 243

Family Law (Maintenance of Spouses and Children)
 Act 1976 .... 25n
Freedom of Information Act 1997 173
Freedom of Information Act 2014 ....38,142, 151, 161, 169, 312
 2 ....171n
 6(1) 170
 9 .... 170n
 10 .... 170n
 11(1) 170
 15 .... 171n
 21 .... 172n
 24 .... 172n
 28 .... 170n
 29 .... 170n
 32 .... 170n
 32 .... 170n
 32(1)(b) 171n
 35 .... 170n
 36 .... 170n
 37 .... 170n, 171
 37(1) 175, 176
 37(2) 171
 37(2)(e) 171
 37(4) 171
 37(8) 172, 175
 42 170
 Part 4 ....170, 171, 172

Guardianship of Infants Act 1964 .... 25n

Health Act 1947 ....154, 159
Health Act 1970 187
 62 ....212, 213, 214
Health Act 2007 ....245, 246

11 245
Health (Family Planning) Act 1979... 15n
Health (Fluoridation of Water Supplies) Act 1960 15
Health (Regulation of Termination of Pregnancy) Act 2018..........4,
....210, 222, 230, 231
   2 222
   9 ....230, 231, 232
   9(1)..231
   9(2)..231
   10 ....230, 231, 233
   10(1)..231
   11 ....230, 231, 232
   11(1)..231
   11(2)..232
   12 ....230, 232
   22 ....230, 232, 233
   22(1)..232
   22(2)...233n
   22(3)...233n
   23 ....230, 233, 234
   23(1)...233, 234
   23(2)...233, 234
   23(4)..234
   23(5)...234n

Industrial Relations Act 1946..28
Infectious Diseases Regulations 1981...154
Irish Medicines Board Act 1995...187
Irish Medicines Board (Miscellaneous Provisions) Act
   2006...186, 187

Legal Services Regulation Act 2015..30
Liability for Defective Products Act 1991 69
   2(1)..69

Medical Practitioners Act 1978
Medical Practitioners Act 2007...50
Medicinal Products (Prescription and Control of Supply)
   Regulations 2003, SI 540/2003............................... 187, 199, 204n
   5A..202
   5(1)..201
   7 201
   7(5)(b)...200
   8 201
   8(1)..201
Mental Capacity Act 2005 275

Mental Health Act 2001	44, 234
69	251
69(2)	251
Midwives (Ireland) Act 1918	33, 34
Midwives Act 1931	34
Midwives Act 1944	34
Misuse of Drugs Act 1977	187
Non-Fatal Offences Against the Person Act 1997	44, 152
23	151
23(1)	151n, 234
Nurses Act 1950	35
2	35
7	35
Nurses Act 1961	35
Nurses Act 1985	35, 36, 50
Nurses and Midwives Act 2011	3, 33, 35, 36, 40, 48, 50, 52, 53, 54, 190
2	50, 51, 55n
2(2)	36
8	37, 46
9	37, 43
9(2)(g)	41, 42n
11	43n
13	37, 46n
22	38n
24	39
24(5)	51
24(8)	39n
24(9)	39n
24(10)	39n
24(11)	58
27	39
29	44n
38	41
39	39, 49, 210, 211
40	211
40(1)	210
40(2)	211n
40(3)	211n
41	211
41(1)	211n
43	211
44	47, 211
44(1)	211
45(1)	211

51	51
52(4)	51
55	46, 57
55(1)	46, 47n
55(1)(f)	61
55(1)(i)	52
55(2)	47n
55(3)	54
55(6)	52
55(6)(b)	53
56	54
56(3)	54n
57(4)	55n
57(5)	55n
57(7)	56n
57(11)	56
58	57
58(1)	57n
58(2)	57n
58(3)	57, 58n
59	56
59(1)	56n
59(1)(b)	56
59(2)	56, 57n
59(2)(f)	57
61	57
61(2)	57n
62	59, 64n
62(1)	59n
62(2)(a)	60n
63(4)	60n
64	60
64(1)	60n
64(3)	60n
64(5)	153
64(5)(a)	61n
64(5)(b)	61n
64(5)(c)	61n
65	52, 61
65(1)	62
65(1)(b)	61
65(1)(d)	51
67	62n
69	63n
69(1)	53
69(1)(f)	53

71	63n
73	51
73(3)(a)	64n
73(3)(b)	64n
74	51, 65
74(3)	65n
76	65
77	41
79	66
79(3)	51, 66n
79(5)	66n
80	66
81(3)	51
85	40
85(1)	40
87(1)	40
87(2)	61
Part 1	36
Part 2	36
Part 3	36
Part 4	36
Part 5	36
Part 6	36, 210
Part 7	36, 43, 54
Part 8	36, 43, 58
Part 9	36, 62, 123
Part 10	37
Part 11	37
Part 12	37
Part 13	37
Nurses Registration (Ireland) Act 1919	34

Offences against the Person Act 1861
58	222
59	222
Offences Against the State Act 1939	28
Official Languages Act 2003	38
Ombudsman Act 2012	38

Powers of Attorney Act 1996	133
Prosecution of Offences Act 1974	31
Protected Disclosures Act 2014	44
Protection of Life During Pregnancy Act 2013	222, 228
7	228n
8	228n
9	228n

17 232

Regulation of Information (Services Outside the State for
 Termination of Pregnancies) Act 1995......................................225

Safety, Health and Welfare at Work Act 1989..............................286
Standards in Public Office Act 2001 38
Statutory Instruments Act 1947...17
 1(1).. 17, 18n
Succession Act 1965 .... 288n
Suicide Act 1961..117

Thirty-sixth Amendment of the Constitution Act 2018.......221, 236

Workplace Relations Act 2015..28

Statutory Instruments, Directives and Regulations

Commencement Order SI No 385 of 2012 36
Convention against Torture and Other Cruel, Inhuman or
 Degrading Treatment or Punishment 1984
Council Directive 89/595 EC of 10 October 1989
 amending Directive 77/452/EEC concerning the
 mutual recognition of diplomas, certificates and
 other evidence of the formal qualifications of nurses
 responsible for general care, including measures
 to facilitate the effective exercise of the right of
 establishment and freedom to provide services,
 and amending Directive 77/453/EEC concerning
 the coordination of provisions laid down by law,
 regulation or administrative action in respect of the
 activities of nurses responsible for general care [1989] L341/30
Council of Europe, European Social Charter (Revised),
 3 May 1996, ETS 163.. 76n

Data Protection Act 2018 (Section 36(2)) (Health Research)
 Regulations 2018, SI 314/2018
 3 326
 3(1)(c) 327n
 3(2)...327
 3(2)(b)... 327n
Directive 2001/20/EC of the European Parliament and of
 the Council of 4 April 2001 on the approximation of
 the laws, regulations and administrative provisions of
 the Member States relating to the implementation of
 good clinical practice in the conduct of clinical trials

on medicinal products for human use [2001]
OJ L121..303, 310n, 316n

European Communities (Clinical Trials on Medicinal
Products for Human Use) Regulations 2004,
SI 190/2004..303, 322
1(1)...309n
10..308, 309n
13...310n
13(6)...310, 311n
European Communities (Clinical Trials on Medicinal
Products for Human Use) (Amendment) Regulations
2004, SI 878 of 2004..303
European Communities (Clinical Trials on Medicinal
Products for Human Use) (Amendment No. 2)
Regulations 2006, SI 374 of 2006.......................................303

Freedom of Information Act 2014 (s 37(8)) Regulations
2016, SI 218/2016
5..172n
6..173n
7..175

General Data Protection Regulation (*see below Regulation
(EU) 2016/679*)

Health Act 2007 (Care and Support of Residents in
Designated Centres for Persons (Children and Adults
with Disabilities) Regulation 2013............................249, 250, 252
Health Act 2007 (Care and Welfare of Residents in
Designated Centres for Older People) Regulations 2009 249
Health Act 2007 (Care and Welfare of Residents in
Designated Centres for Older People) Regulations
2013..250, 252
2...250n

Infectious Diseases (Amendment) Regulations 2020,
SI 2020/53..154

Medicinal Products (Control of Placing on the Market)
Regulations 2007 202
Medicinal Products (Control of Placing on the Market)
(Amendment) Regulations 2018, SI 529/2018........................202
Medicinal Products (Prescription and Control of Supply)
Regulations 1996 204

Medicinal Products (Prescription and Control of Supply)
　　(Amendment) Regulations 2007, SI 201 of 2007 ....187, 199
　　5A 187
　　5A(1) 187n
　　5A(2) 188n
Misuse of Drugs (Amendment) Regulations 2007,
　　SI 200/2007 188
Misuse of Drugs (Amendment) Regulations 2020,
　　SI 99/2020 190
Misuse of Drugs Regulations 2017, SI 173/2017........ 187, 188, 188n
　　2 190
　　3 190
　　8 190
　　15(2) 190
　　Part 5 188

Nurses and Midwives Rules 2013, SI 2013/435 .... 40n
Nurses and Midwives (Candidate Register) Rules 2018, SI
　　2018/217 .... 38n
Nurses and Midwives (Education and Training) Rules
　　2018, SI 2018/218 .... 38n, 191n
Nurses and Midwives (Recognition of Professional
　　Qualifications) Rules 2018, SI 2018/220 .... 38n
Nurses and Midwives (Register of Nurses and Midwives)
　　Rules 2018, SI 2018/219 .... 38n
Nurses and Midwives (Registration) Rules 2018,
　　SI 2018/221 .... 38n

Protected Disclosures of Information (SI No 27 of 2009) 44

Regulation (EU) No 536/2014 of the European Parliament
　　and of the Council of 16 April 2014 on clinical trials
　　on medicinal products for human use, and repealing
　　Directive 2001/20/EC [2014] L 158/1 ...... 310n, 316 318, 320, 322
　　2(20) 324
　　2(21) 316n
　　29 .... 317, 318n
　　29(2) 321, 323
　　31 .... 323, 324n
　　31(3) 324
　　32 ....321, 322n
　　32(3) 322n
　　80 ....303n, 304n
　　81 .... 303n
Regulation (EU) 2016/679 of the European Parliament
　　and of the Council of 27 April 2016 on the protection

of natural persons with regard to the processing of personal data and on the free movement of such data, and repealing Directive 95/46/EC (**General Data Protection Regulation**) [2016] L119/1 ....4, 142, 161, 326
4... 161, 162, 166, 168n, 169n
4(1) 161n
4(2) 162n
4(15) 165n
5.. 162n
5(2) 162n
6...164
6(1) 167
6(1)(f) 164
7...166
9.. 161, 165, 166n
9(2) 167
9(2)(h) 167
9(2)(i) 167
12... 163n
13.. 163, 164n, 166
14...166
15.. 166n
16...166
17...167
17(1) 167n
18...167
20...168
21...168
21(1) 167
21(2) 167
21(6) 168n
22...168
25...168
33(3) 169
34.. 169n

Treaties and Conventions

Council of Europe Treaty
23 ....241, 242

EU Charter of Fundamental Rights
4 .... 266n
25 242
52 242
European Convention on Human Rights ...22, 28, 29, 242, 266, 270

1 .... 226n
2 .... 22n, 100, 117, 120, 243
3 .... 22, 100, 117, 120, 226n, 243, 252, 253, 266
3(1) 23n
5 243
6 ....22n
8 .... 22n, 100, 117, 120, 144, 149, 150, 215, 226n, 227, 243, 274
8(1) 100, 149
8(2) 100, 149, 275
9 .... 100, 117, 243
10 .... 223, 226n, 243
13 .... 226n
14 .... 100, 117, 226n, 243
European Social Charter
   23 242

International Covenant on Civil and Political Rights
   2(1) 229
   3 229
   7 229
   17 229
   19 229
   26 229
International Covenant on Economic, Social and Cultural
   Rights 242

Treaty of Lisbon 19
Treaty of Rome 19
Treaty on the European Union
   13 ....19, 20
Treaty on the Functioning of the European Union 19
   288 21

UN Convention on the Rights of Persons with Disabilities 122
Universal Declaration of Human Rights 1949 266

Abbreviations

ABA	An Bord Altranais
ADMC Act	Assisted Decision-Making (Capacity) Act
AG	Attorney General
ANH	Artificial nutrition and hydration
BMA	British Medical Association
CEU	Continuing Education Unit
CFA	Child and Family Agency
CIS	Clinical Indemnity Scheme
CJ	Chief Justice
CoA	Court of Appeal
CPA	Collaborative Practice Agreement
CPR	Cardiopulmonary resuscitation
DC	District Court
DNAR	Do Not Attempt Resuscitation
DNACPR	Do Not Attempt Cardio-Pulmonary Resuscitation
DPP	Director of Public Prosecutions
DSS	Decision Support Service
D&T	Drugs and Therapeutics
EAPC	European Association of Palliative Care
ECHR	European Convention on Human Rights
ECtHR	European Court of Human Rights
ECJ	European Court of Justice
EU	European Union
FGM	Female genital mutilation
FOI	Freedom of Information
FTPC	Fitness to Practise Committee
HC	High Court
HIQA	Health Information and Quality Authority
HPRA	Health Products Regulatory Authority
HPSC	Health Protection Surveillance Centre
HSE	Health Service Executive
GDPR	General Data Protection Regulation
GMC	General Medical Council
GP	General Practitioner
ICM	International Confederation of Midwives
ICSI	Intensive Care Society of Ireland
MCA	Mental Capacity Act
MCS	Minimally Conscious State
MR	Master of the Rolls

NREC	National Research Ethics Committee
NHS	National Health Service
NIMS	National Incident Management System
NMBI	Nursing and Midwifery Board of Ireland
PPC	Preliminary Proceedings Committee
PPPG	Policies, Procedures, Protocols and Guidelines
QUANGO	Quasi-Autonomous Non-Governmental Organisations
REC	Research Ethics Committee
RCN	Royal College of Nursing
SC	Supreme Court
SCA	State Claims Agency
SECM	Self-employed Community Midwife
SI	Statutory Instrument
SR	Special Rapporteur
TFEU	Treaty on the Functioning of the European Union
UN	United Nations
UNCRPD	UN Convention on the Rights of Persons with Disabilities
WHO	World Health Organization

Chapter 1
Introduction

Introduction 1
Chapter Structure 2

1.0 Introduction

This book outlines the law relevant to nursing and midwifery in Ireland. A recurring theme in this book is that the role of the nurse and midwife has expanded and evolved over the years. This change has been especially clear in the last 30 years during which time there have been changes in education, greater professional autonomy, increased competencies, and a broader scope of practice. Such developments are to be welcomed but they also raise a host of challenges, not least of which is the need to be informed and aware of the legal framework that shapes medical treatment and care. The legal framework is composed of legislation, the Irish Constitution, European Union directives and regulations, international human rights instruments, and professional standards and guidance documents. While the legal framework may seem like an abstract concept it is this framework that defines the duties, responsibilities, and rights that shape nursing and midwifery practice.

The legal framework has a substantial role in shaping the scope of practice for nurses and midwives in Ireland. The scope of practice is 'the range of roles, functions, responsibilities and activities which a registered nurse or registered midwife is educated, competent and has authority to perform'.[1] It therefore defines the parameters within which the nurse or midwife is permitted to practise. In addition to outlining the legal framework, this text will draw attention to developments that have reframed the scope of practice in recent years. Examples of this include changes in midwife-led care and the advent of nurse and midwife prescribing. These topics are addressed in chapter 8 and chapter 6 respectively.

---

[1] Nursing and Midwifery Board of Ireland, *Scope of Nursing and Midwifery Practice Framework* (NMBI 2015) 3.

Familiarity with the legal framework is a component of the Nursing and Midwifery Board of Ireland (NMBI) *Code of Professional Conduct and Ethics for Registered Nurses and Registered Midwives*.[2] Adherence to the Code requires the nurse or midwife to have an understanding of the legal framework in Ireland. For instance, principle one on the respect for the dignity of the person is drawn from the Universal Declaration of Human Rights. Moreover, the values and standards of conduct for this principle are informed by the European Convention for the Protection of Human Rights and Fundamental Freedoms, the Irish Constitution, and the Equal Status Acts. Principle 2 on professional responsibility and accountability includes the value: 'Nurses and midwives advocate for patients' rights'.[3] Under standards of conduct the NMBI set out the following:

> You must act within the law and follow the rules and regulations of the Nursing and Midwifery Board of Ireland.
>
> You should act as an advocate on behalf of patients who require you to do so to ensure their rights and interests are protected.[4]

References and links to the legal framework are also apparent in the subsequent principles on quality of practice, trust and confidentiality, and collaboration with others.

The objective of this text is to provide an introduction to some of the key legal concepts that a nurse or midwife will encounter in practice. The text also addresses some of the more legally challenging issues that can arise. This information should equip the nurse with a robust knowledge of fundamental legal principles that can be used across a range of divisions. Invariably, owing to the breadth of divisions in the Register of Nurses and Midwives there are some topics that could not be covered within the scope of this text.

1.1 Chapter Structure

This book is composed of 10 chapters. These chapters introduce and outline the legal framework for nursing and midwifery

---

[2] Nursing and Midwifery Board of Ireland, *Code of Professional Conduct and Ethics for Registered Nurses and Registered Midwives* (NMBI 2014).
[3] ibid 16.
[4] ibid 17.

practice in Ireland. This starts with an introduction to the Irish legal system in chapter 2. The legal system is explained over the course of four main sections, the first of which describes the concept of law along with distinctions between common law and civil law, private and public law, and criminal law and civil law. The sources of law are set out in the second section and this includes discussion of the Irish Constitution, legislation, common law, European Union law, and international law. The final two sections describe the structure of the courts system, and the role of the various legal professionals who contribute to the effective functioning of the legal system.

Chapter 3 is titled 'The Nursing and Midwifery Board of Ireland'. It serves to explore the evolution of nursing practice in Ireland through the lens of legislation and professional regulation. Part of this is a historic look at nursing and midwifery in Ireland before going on to discuss more recent developments such as the Nurses and Midwives Act 2011. The chapter also lays out the role and function of the NMBI. As part of this, the standard setting and professional oversight function of the NMBI will be specifically addressed.

Negligent practice is the subject of chapter 4. Central to this chapter is the law of torts. Torts are civil actions where an injured party is seeking compensation for a wrong, an example of which is negligence. Sections of this chapter address the duty of care, the standard of care, causation, harm, and the liability of a healthcare facility.

The importance of involving the patient in decisions and discussions about their healthcare is repeated at several points in this text. The patient is not the passive subject of healthcare but actively shapes the form of treatment and care by virtue of their will and preferences. This approach to healthcare is underpinned by a respect for patient autonomy. This ethical and legal concept is described in chapter 5 over the course of five sections, the first of which outlines the elevation, interpretation, and legal recognition of autonomy. The chapter proceeds to discuss informed consent including voluntariness, the role of capacity, the disclosure of appropriate information, and the use of therapeutic privilege. In the third and fourth sections, the right to refuse or demand medical treatment is set out. The final section discusses the Assisted Decision-Making (Capacity) Act 2015. The discussion of this legislation will include an outline of various decision-making supports, enduring power of attorney, and advance healthcare directives.

Chapter 6 is titled 'Confidentiality and Access to Personal Health Information'. Confidentiality is a well-accepted principle of medical practice and is an integral component in the patient–healthcare professional relationship. Chapter 6 describes the various elements that underpin the control of personal health information. The concept of confidentiality and the basis for its protection will be set out along with the exceptions that can arise. The chapter outlines the application of the Data Protection Acts and the influence of the General Data Protection Regulation. Furthermore, access to information under the Freedom of Information Act 2014 is clarified. The closing sections in chapter 6 define the practice of open disclosure for the nursing profession and briefly discuss the relationship of confidentiality and social media.

The advent of nurse and midwife prescribing is a relatively new development in Ireland. Nurse and midwife prescribing is underpinned by a patchwork of legislation, professional standards, and guidance documents. Chapter 7 commences by drawing out the background to nurse and midwife prescribing before going on to define its legal basis. As part of this the role of the Office of the Nursing and Midwifery Services Director, the clinical governance framework, and the *Practice Standards for Nurses and Midwives with Prescriptive Authority* are discussed. The second section in chapter 7 examines the prescribing and administration of medicines. This includes the clinical decision-making process, prescription practices and limitations, self-administration and the covert administration of medicines. The final section outlines the management of errors or incidents in the administration of medicines.

Chapter 8 explores the legal aspects of pregnancy. This is a broad and historically controversial topic in Ireland. The chapter deals with some of the more pressing matters in this area and should be read in conjunction with other chapters to ensure familiarity with the duty of care, record-keeping, and general principles of autonomy. The first section considers the regulation of midwifery, where the birth environment, accessing home birth services, and the legal status of a birth plan are discussed. The second section focuses on the legal framework for abortion in Ireland, specifically the Health (Regulation of Termination of Pregnancy) Act 2018. The third section addresses treatment refusal during pregnancy.

Chapter 9 is titled 'Legal Aspects of End-of-Life Treatment and Care'. The starting point for this chapter is care of the older person. It addresses human rights, elder abuse, and the use of restraint.

Further sections outline autonomy and medical treatment, the provision of palliative care, euthanasia and assisted suicide, do not attempt resuscitation orders, the definition of death, the role of the coroner, and the drafting of wills.

Chapter 10 concludes this text with an examination of clinical research ethics. Among the ways in which nursing and midwifery has changed in recent years is the increased focus on research. Nurses and midwives design and lead research projects, assist in research and clinical trials, and engage with published research as part of continuous professional education and the delivery of professional care. The first section in this chapter outlines the broad spectrum of ways in which nurses engage with research. As part of this, the emerging role of the clinical research nurse and clinical research midwife will be outlined. The chapter goes on to discuss the conduct of clinical trials, including randomised controlled trials and the use of placebos. The third section addresses international ethical codes, namely the Nuremberg Code and the Declaration of Helsinki. The fourth section in chapter 10 examines regulations on research, professional guidance, proposed legislation, and the function of research ethics committees. The ethics approval process requires close scrutiny of the proposed research, particularly issues relating to vulnerability of research participants, informed consent, and confidentiality surrounding research data. These points are addressed in the final sections of chapter 10.

Encountering these various issues in practice will of course be a different experience and multiple duties and responsibilities will arise at any given time. It is therefore hoped that this text allows the reader to develop an appreciation for the mosaic that is the legal framework for nursing and midwifery in Ireland. Taken together, each chapter serves to provide a practical and accessible outline of the relevant legal framework, comprised of case law, legislation, human rights, professional standards, and guidance documents.

Chapter 2
An Introduction to the Irish Legal System

Introduction 7
What Is Law? 8
Sources of Law 11
    Bunreacht na hÉireann 12
    Legislation 17
    Common Law 18
    European Union Law 19
    International Law 21
    Canon Law. 23
    Academic Commentary 23
Structure of the Courts System. 23
The Legal Profession 29

2.0 Introduction

Familiarity with the structure of the legal system can allow for a deeper appreciation of the rules and obligations that arise in nursing practice. This includes a knowledge of the various sources of law, the structure of the courts system, and awareness of the various professionals who contribute to the functioning of the legal system. As is evident in subsequent chapters, nursing is shaped by many sources of law and is a profession that interacts with a wide range of legal specialties. It follows that nurses have multiple domains of accountability, including criminal liability, civil liability, professional liability, and accountability to their employer. To fully understand developments in any of these areas the nurse must possess a good knowledge of the legal system. There is also accountability to oneself, namely moral accountability, although discussion of this is largely outside the scope of this work.

The purpose of this chapter is to provide an introduction to the Irish legal system. It does this over the course of four main sections. The first section addresses the question of what law is: law is not a globally uniform or homogenous concept but can be broken into distinct categories. The first section explains distinctions such as the difference between a common law and a civil law system, Ireland being a common law jurisdiction. Sources of law are outlined in the second section of this chapter. This includes discussion of the Irish Constitution, legislation, common law, European Union law, and international law. The third section turns to outline the structure of the courts system. While the primary focus is on the courts in Ireland, reference will also be made to the European Court of Justice (ECJ) and the European Court of Human Rights (ECtHR). The role of legal professionals is outlined in the fourth section. The combination of these four sections provides a rounded account of the legal system in Ireland.

2.1 What Is Law?

The concept of law can be explored through theory and philosophy as in jurisprudence. However, for the purposes of this work, it suffices to say that 'law' refers to the system of regulation that applies in a jurisdiction. It describes the way in which the legal system is structured, and rules enforced. There are two substantial legal systems to be aware of. These are the common law and civil law systems and these are discussed in detail below. Depending on state involvement, law may be further categorised as being private or public. Following on from this, nurses should also be aware of the distinction between civil law and criminal law.

Common Law and Civil Law Systems

The common law system has its origins in England following the Norman invasion of 1066. This legal system is built on thousands of court decisions in which legal principles are identified, refined, and applied in subsequent cases thereby promoting consistency and coherence in the law. Ireland is a common law jurisdiction along with former British colonies such as Australia, New Zealand, India, Kenya, 49 US States (Louisiana is the exception as it was colonised by the French), and the provinces of Canada (Quebec being the exception as it was a French colony).

Court decisions are fundamental to the workings of the common law system. The analysis of court decisions allows for the identification of legal principles that lie at the core of judicial reasoning. The legal principle(s) represents a necessary step in reaching the final judgment in a case. However, the identification of a legal principle alone is not sufficient for the development of an effective legal system. The common law system is therefore rooted in the doctrine of precedent. This doctrine provides that, where appropriate, these legal principles will be followed and applied in subsequent cases. The common law system requires an accurate recording of prior decisions, an acceptance of the binding nature of precedent, and a hierarchy of courts. Under the doctrine of precedent, lower courts must follow the decision of higher courts. A lower court, such as the District Court, must follow the legal principles approved by higher courts, such as the Supreme Court. This is known as vertical precedent. Courts are also required to follow the earlier decisions of courts of equal jurisdiction, known as horizontal precedent. Over the years there have been substantial changes in the legal system and it has developed to the point where more power is held by democratically elected institutions. Nonetheless, court decisions are still influential, particularly in areas such as constitutional and legislative interpretation.

The civil law system is the dominant legal system across European states and is applied in France, Italy, Spain, Germany, and Switzerland. The primary characteristic of the civil law system is that it is comprised of laws or codes that are created by the State. These laws are detailed and comprehensive in nature, the effect of which is to minimise the margin for judicial interpretation, further distinguishing it from the common law system. An example of the comprehensive nature of these laws can be found in the French Code de la Santé Publique (Code of Public Health). The Code is composed of more than 10,000 Articles relating to public health law. The comprehensive nature of the system does, however, result in a considerable burden as the legislation must be continuously reviewed and updated by the government to ensure accuracy.

Private Law and Public Law

The terms 'private law' and 'public law' reflect differing domains of legal practice and the involvement of different parties. Public law governs the relationship between the state and individuals. It is a form of law which, in some way, is concerned with the public interest. It includes sub-divisions such as criminal law, administrative law, and constitutional law. Laws relating to all three of these areas will be explored over the course of this work.

Law that focuses primarily on the relationship between individuals is known as private law. It is likely to involve a dispute between one or more parties who are acting in a private or personal capacity. Accordingly, a substantial public interest is absent in private law. Nonetheless, a public body may be subject to private law in circumstances where they acted in the same capacity as a private body. Private law disputes are generally led by an individual rather than the State. Examples of private law are family law, contract law, and torts. Subsequent chapters will highlight the relevance of both public and private law for nursing practice.

Criminal Law and Civil Law

Patients are often in a vulnerable position and may be exposed to harmful situations during medical treatment or care. Depending on the nature of the harm it may be that a criminal prosecution is warranted, or a patient may bring a civil claim against the relevant healthcare professional and their employer. Criminal and civil law are not mutually exclusive, and it is possible for one act to lead to both criminal charges and a civil action.

Criminal law encompasses statutory law and common law that centres on crime and the associated punishment. Criminal law has several functions, including the maintenance of public order, the promotion of public safety, and the establishment of transparent social norms in the community. A crime is not only harmful to an individual, but it can seriously undermine the confidence and trust in public institutions. An offence can have repercussions that extend well beyond the parties originally affected. The criminal law deals with crimes such as murder, manslaughter, sexual offences, assault, and theft.

A criminal prosecution is usually commenced by the Director of Public Prosecutions, although other entities also have the power to prosecute crime in this jurisdiction. An individual could initiate a private prosecution, but this very rarely occurs. Criminal proceedings can be initiated by way of a summons or the charge sheet procedure. A summons is an order to appear in court to respond to a complaint. The charge sheet procedure involves the arrest of the alleged offender and their transportation to the Garda station where they are presented with the particulars of the alleged offence; this is known as the charge sheet.[1] A copy of these details must be given to the alleged offender. The Garda formally charges a person by reading each charge to them and cautions them after each charge is read out. Any remarks or comments made by the accused are to be noted on the charge sheet by the Garda. The seriousness of the offence will determine which court will hear the case. The parties involved in a criminal case are referred to as the 'prosecution' and the 'defendant', the latter being the party accused of some form of wrongdoing.

---

[1] RDC Order 17.

A criminal prosecution can have serious personal and professional consequences for a nurse. Accordingly, the standard of proof is such cases is necessarily high and requires proof beyond a reasonable doubt. If the prosecution fails to discharge this burden of proof, then the court or jury will find the accused not guilty. This does not mean that the accused person was innocent. Instead, it means that guilt was not sufficiently proven.

Civil actions may be grounded in torts or breach of contract. Torts include negligence, trespass to property or person, breach of a statutory duty, or defamation. Negligence is a failure to deliver an appropriate standard of treatment or care in circumstances where a legal duty of care existed, and is outlined in chapter 4. The purpose of a civil action is usually to seek damages or a form of specific relief such as an injunction. A civil case is commenced by issuing and serving a written court document referred to as a writ or pleading. The parties involved in a civil action are known as the 'claimant' or 'plaintiff', and the 'defendant' or 'respondent'. The burden of proof departs from the criminal standard and is lower. Civil cases are decided on the balance of probabilities. This approach requires a weighing of the evidence presented by the claimant and the respondent to determine which version of events was most likely to have occurred.

2.2 Sources of Law

To understand the law underpinning a criminal or civil action the nurse should be aware of the various sources of law. This knowledge is equally important where the nurse is presented with a medico-legal dilemma in the workplace or wants to ensure compliance with a professional standard. The nurse must be aware of how the various sources of law fit together in the overarching legal framework and which source is to prevail in case of conflict. In this respect, a hierarchy exists across the sources of law that assists in determining which source is to prevail.

A source of law establishes the rules and principles that form the law. If a rule is not based on an identifiable source, then it is not to be considered a legal rule. There are both primary and secondary sources of law in Ireland. Primary sources of law include Bunreacht na hÉireann (Constitution of Ireland), legislation, case law, and European Union law. At the top of the domestic hierarchy is the Constitution of Ireland, followed by legislation and case law. As will be seen, these domestic sources must comply with the law of the European Union. Secondary sources of law include international law such as customs, treaties, and decisions of international courts and tribunals.

2.2.1 Bunreacht na hÉireann

Constitutions have both legal and symbolic functions. A constitution can define the geographical parameters of the State and can determine how legal power is distributed and exercised. It can establish checks and balances that prevent against the abuse of power and ensures that the executive, legislative, and judicial branches of the state have clearly defined roles – a concept known as the separation of powers. Constitutions may also include more aspirational elements, which reflect their symbolic function, such as the setting of goals and moral standards. These legal and symbolic functions are apparent in the Irish Constitution.

Bunreacht na hÉireann is the Constitution of Ireland and is a primary source of law. It is superior to all other domestic sources of law in Ireland. Legislation enacted in Ireland and other forms of domestic law must comply with the Constitution. A rule that stems from a lower source of law depends on the Constitution for validity. In circumstances where such a rule conflicts with a constitutional provision, the rule will be deemed invalid and lacking legal effect. Nonetheless, the supremacy of the Irish Constitution is somewhat lessened by the need to ensure that Ireland fulfils its obligations as a European Union Member State. The State must ensure that all domestic sources of law, including the Constitution, are in accordance with European Union law.

The Constitution came into effect on 27 December 1937. It is composed of 50 provisions, referred to as articles. Articles 1–37 establish state institutions such as the office of the President, the National Parliament, the Government, and the courts. Articles 38 and 40–44 protect fundamental rights. Article 45 addresses principles of social policy. The steps required for a constitutional amendment are detailed in Articles 46 and 47, while Articles 48–50 repeal the 1922 Constitution. Changes to the Constitution generally involve a protracted process. A first step is the passing of a bill by the Dáil and the Seanad. The bill is then put to the people in a referendum. A simple majority of the votes cast is required to carry an amendment. If accepted, the President is to then sign the bill into law. The process ensures that amendments to the Constitution are well reasoned and have been the subject of detailed consideration. Recent referendums in Ireland addressed issues such as children's rights, marriage equality, and abortion.

If you consult a hard copy or digital version of the Constitution you will notice that there is both an English and Irish language text.[2] Article 8.1 designates Irish as the national language and first official language in the jurisdiction. The English language is recognised as the second official language. The existence of two texts could give rise to conflicting interpretations and ambiguity. As a result, Article 25.4.4° provides that the national language is to prevail where there is a conflict between the texts.

Institutions of the State

The functioning of State institutions is set out in the Constitution and is underpinned by the separation of powers, which divides power and responsibility across the executive,[3] the legislature,[4] and the judiciary.[5] The Government has executive power over domestic affairs under Article 28.2 and has executive power with external relations under Article 29.4. There are checks in place on these powers as the Government is responsible to Dáil Éireann per Article 28.4.1°.

Article 15.2.1° provides that the 'sole and exclusive power of making laws for the State is hereby vested in the Oireachtas'.[6] The Oireachtas is composed of the Dáil, the Seanad, and the President of Ireland. The functions of the President are set out in Articles 12–14 of the Constitution. Article 12 outlines the election process, who is eligible to vote, the term of office, eligibility for election, and the nomination process. Article 13 outlines functions and responsibilities of the President such as the appointment of the Taoiseach on the nomination of the Dáil.

Articles 31–32 of the Constitution address the Council of State. The Council serves to 'aid and counsel' the President as certain powers and functions of the President are only exercisable after consultation with the Council.[7] For instance, the President may address a message to the nation only after he/she has consulted the Council of State.[8] Members of the Council include the Taoiseach, the Tánaiste, the Chief Justice, the President of the Court of Appeal, the President of the High Court, the Chairman of

---

[2] Constitution of Ireland <http://www.irishstatutebook.ie/eli/cons/en/html> accessed 30 June 2020.
[3] Bunreacht na hÉireann, Arts 28–29.
[4] ibid Arts 15–27.
[5] ibid Arts 34–37.
[6] ibid Art 15.2.1°.
[7] ibid Art 31.1.
[8] ibid Art 13.7.2°.

Dáil Éireann, the Chairman of Seanad Éireann, and the Attorney General.[9] The Council is also comprised of former Presidents, Taoisigh, and people who have held the office of Chief Justice. The sitting President may also appoint people to be members of the Council of State.

The courts are addressed by Articles 34–37 of the Irish Constitution. Article 34.1 provides that 'Justice shall be administered in courts established by law by judges appointed in a manner provided by this Constitution'.[10] The superior courts are specifically set out in the Constitution. These are the Supreme Court, the Court of Appeal, and the High Court. The lower courts are not mentioned by name but are provided for in Article 34.3.4°, which refers to courts of local and limited jurisdiction. The courts system is discussed at section 2.3 of this chapter.

Fundamental Rights

The Irish Constitution recognises a number of fundamental rights, several of which are directly relevant to nursing practice. Fundamental rights are found in Articles 40–44. The protection and recognition of human rights in the Constitution is significant as it underlines their status in society and protects them from political interference. Fundamental rights include equality before the law[11] and rights relating to family,[12] education,[13] property,[14] and religion.[15] These are examples of enumerated rights – rights expressly set out by the Constitution. Over the years the courts have recognised the existence of rights not expressly written in the Constitution. These are referred to as unenumerated rights. The foundation for such a right may be an existing enumerated right; it may flow from the 'Christian and democratic nature of the State', be grounded in natural law, or it may stem from another unenumerated right.

One of the first unenumerated rights to be recognised was the right to bodily integrity, which was identified in *Ryan v Attorney General*.[16] The plaintiff in *Ryan* challenged the fluoridation of the

---

[9] ibid Art 31.2.
[10] ibid Art 34.1.
[11] ibid Art 40.1.
[12] ibid Art 41.
[13] ibid Art 42.
[14] ibid Art 43.
[15] ibid Art 44.
[16] *Ryan v Attorney General* [1965] IR 294.

public water supply as provided for by the Health (Fluoridation of Water Supplies) Act 1960. The plaintiff argued that the addition of fluoride would be harmful to her health and that of her children. Accordingly, it was suggested that this would amount to a breach of their right to bodily integrity. Although not expressly set out in the Constitution, it was argued that it was among the 'personal rights' guaranteed under Article 40.3.1°. The plaintiff was unsuccessful in her challenge, but the case is notable for the courts willingness to recognise the unenumerated right to bodily integrity. Ó Dálaigh CJ (Chief Justice) in the Supreme Court made it clear that there were further unspecified rights protected by Article 40.3.1°. Courts in Ireland subsequently recognised unenumerated rights such as the right of access to the courts,[17] the right not to be treated inhumanely,[18] the right to die a natural death,[19] and the right to privacy.[20]

The right to privacy in marital affairs was recognised in *McGee v Attorney General*.[21] A majority of the Supreme Court held that s 17 of the Criminal Law Amendment Act 1935 was invalid. The 1935 Act prohibited the selling or importation of contraceptives into the State. Mrs McGee had attempted to import spermicidal jelly from England on foot of medical advice. The prohibition was judged to conflict with her right to marital privacy under Articles 40.3 and 41. The decision caused a degree of political consternation and it was not until 1979 that legislation was enacted to regularise the statutory position.[22] *McGee* is illustrative of many of the strengths and weaknesses associated with unenumerated rights. The recognition of an unenumerated right is an example of judicial activism. An activist court may advance the law in circumstances where the legislature has failed to do so. However, this stretches the constitutionally permissible role of the courts and may be viewed as judicial law-making. This usurps the role of the Oireachtas and means that law is being made by unelected individuals, thereby raising concerns about accountability. The period of judicial activism in Irish courts was relatively brief and more recent decisions reflect a greater degree of judicial restraint.

---

[17] *Byrne v Ireland* [1972] IR 241.
[18] *People (AG) v O'Brien* [1965] IR 142.
[19] *Re a Ward of Court* [1996] 2 IR 79.
[20] *Kennedy v Ireland* [1987] IR 587.
[21] *McGee v Attorney General* [1974] IR 284.
[22] Health (Family Planning) Act 1979.

Limits on Constitutional Rights

Regardless of whether a right is enumerated or unenumerated there is no absolute right contained in the Constitution. Many of the rights specifically identified in the Constitution have express limitations and include qualifying words. For instance, Article 40.1 on the right to equality provides that the State is entitled to 'have due regard to differences of capacity, physical and moral, and of social function'.[23] Rights stemming from Article 40.3 are guaranteed 'as far as practicable', and the State shall 'by its laws protect as best it may from unjust attack'.[24] The rights enjoyed by an individual may need to be weighed against those of other citizens. The infringement of a right may therefore be justified on the basis that it vindicates the superior personal rights of other citizens or it may be necessary for the common good or public order. Moreover, there are cases in which the courts have recognised a hierarchy of rights. There is no fixed list that grants certain rights priority, although the right to life has been described as the 'pre-eminent personal right'.[25] It follows that the court may be tasked with a delicate balancing exercise to determine which right takes precedence. The court's assessment may be informed in part by its approach to constitutional interpretation.

Constitutional Interpretation

There is no consistent approach to constitutional interpretation. Judges may draw on a range of methods such as the literal approach, the harmonious approach, the purposive approach, and the historical approach. The literal approach is whereby a word or phrase in the Constitution is given its ordinary, everyday meaning. The harmonious approach requires the court to look beyond the specific word or article and to interpret it with reference to other articles in the Constitution. The purposive approach attempts to interpret a Constitutional provision in line with the purpose it was intended to fulfil. This provides for more flexibility and a broader scope of interpretation. The historical approach attempts to reflect the original understanding of the Constitution. In effect, it seeks to interpret the Constitution in the manner consistent with the intention of the drafters of the 1937 Constitution. It is difficult to accurately determine what the relevant intention may have been and is a rarely used method of constitutional interpretation.

---

[23] Bunreacht na hÉireann, Art 40.1.
[24] ibid Art 40.3.
[25] *Re a Ward of Court* [1996] 2 IR 79, 160.

2.2.2 Legislation

Legislation is the second highest domestic source of law in Ireland.[26] It is composed of measures enacted or adopted by the legislature. The Oireachtas is accorded legislative authority by Article 15.2.1°. Legislation establishes rules in a written and fixed form, thereby promoting clarity and certainty in the law. This is an essential feature of legislation as people are entitled to have notice of the rules and standards that govern their life. This includes the rules and standards that govern the provision of healthcare.

Legislation can be divided into two categories, primary and secondary legislation. Primary legislation consists of Acts of the Oireachtas and are referred to as statutes. An Act of the Oireachtas may be one of three types, namely: Acts to amend the Constitution; public general Acts; or private Acts. In relation to an Act to amend the Constitution, it was noted in the previous section that the Constitution can only be amended by way of a referendum. The procedure for amending the Constitution requires that the proposed change be put to the people for a vote. If the amendment is accepted by a majority of the votes cast, only then is the legislation sent to the President for signature. Far more common is the enactment of a public general Act, which establishes law for the public at large. This represents the majority of legislation passed by the Oireachtas. The third form of primary legislation is the private Act. The private Act is addressed to a particular individual or group such as a local authority.

Secondary legislation is known as subordinate or delegated legislation. It consists of measures, usually in the form of a 'statutory instrument', enacted by a person/body to whom the Oireachtas has delegated legislative authority. The person to whom authority is assigned is often the Minister with responsibility for the area in question. However, such power may also be delegated to local authorities, State boards, or Quasi-Autonomous Non-Governmental Organisations (QUANGOs). This element of flexibility allows the Oireachtas to delegate authority to those with specific expertise pertaining to the area. Such expertise is essential as secondary legislation is focused on specific details rather than general principles. Consequently, secondary legislation is regularly used in the regulation and oversight of professions.

Secondary legislation, in the form of statutory instruments (SIs), is governed by the Statutory Instruments Act 1947. Section 1(1)

---

[26] Bunreacht na hÉireann, Article 15.4.2°.

of the 1947 Act defines a statutory instrument as an 'order, regulation, rule, scheme, or bye-law made in exercise of a power conferred by statute'.[27] An order is a statutory instrument that has a one-time effect such as a commencement order. The commencement order provides for legislation to be brought into force. Accordingly, not all legislation commences at the date of enactment. An interim period may be required in which various measures or appointments can be made, thereby facilitating the effective operation of the primary legislation. Once such measures are completed a commencement order may be issued. As for a 'regulation', this serves to develop and give effect to the principles and policies contained in the parent Act.

2.2.3 Common Law

Common law lies below the Constitution and legislation in the hierarchy of domestic sources of law. It previously held a much higher position, but the emergence and expansion of legislation diminished its status. Common law is composed of thousands of past court decisions, which have legal effect due to the doctrine of precedent. The accumulation of such decisions facilitated the development of the common law as an extensive body of law. The development of law in this manner can be challenging as it requires cases to be brought before the courts for a decision. This allows for the incremental development of the law but makes far-sweeping legal change less likely. Despite the Constitution and legislation being higher domestic sources of law, the common law still has a substantial role in shaping the legal framework. Court decisions are essential in framing the interpretation of constitutional and legislative provisions. These decisions are fundamental in understanding the scope of the Constitution and in resolving disputes about the interpretation of legislation. The resulting judgment shapes how the provision is interpreted in the future; it therefore becomes part of the legal framework. As such, there are many references to judicial decisions over the course of this book.

Court decisions can be located in law reports. Law reports are volumes of books in which judgments are published and a brief synopsis of the case set out. Examples of law reports include the Irish Reports, the Irish Law Reports Monthly, and the All England Law Reports. Judgments are increasingly made directly available

---

[27] Statutory Instruments Act 1947, s 1(1).

online through websites such as the British and Irish Legal Information Institute[28] and the Courts Service of Ireland.[29]

2.2.4 European Union Law

The fundamental laws and rules of the EU are set out in the Treaties. The first major treaty was the Treaty of Rome, which established the European Economic Community in 1957. In the intervening years there have been several treaties agreed and ratified by all EU Member States. Ireland joined the EEC in 1973. The original objective of the Community was to reduce barriers to trade in a common market for goods, services, capital, and labour. As the European Union expanded it also began to pursue other objectives such as public health and the adoption of health legislation.[30]

The supremacy of EU law is set out in the Treaties that established the European Union. Acceding to membership of the EU, therefore, meant a curtailment of national sovereignty as the law of the EU has primacy over all domestic sources of law in Ireland. In situations where there is a conflict between national law and EU law it is the EU law which is to be followed. Article 29.4.6° of the Irish Constitution provides that 'No provision of this Constitution invalidates laws enacted, acts done or measures adopted by the State, before, on or after the entry into force of the Treaty of Lisbon, that are necessitated by the obligations of membership of the European Union …'[31] This provision was inserted following the 28th Amendment, which allowed the State to ratify the Treaty of Lisbon. The Treaty of Lisbon amended core EU treaties, the Treaty on European Union, and the Treaty establishing the European Community now known as the Treaty on the Functioning of the European Union. Several Protocols and Declarations were also attached to the Treaty of Lisbon.

Article 13 of the Treaty on the European Union sets out that the EU is to have 'an institutional framework which shall aim to promote its values, advance its objectives, serve its interests, those of its citizens and those of the Member States, and ensure

---

[28] British and Irish Legal Information Institute <https://www.bailii.org/> accessed 6 July 2020.
[29] The Courts Service of Ireland <http://courts.ie/Courts.ie/Library3.nsf/PageCurrent/56F2259BE71F74E180257FB00055003D?opendocument&l=en> accessed 6 July 2020.
[30] John Lombard, 'The Implementation and Operation of the Cross-Border Healthcare Directive' (2016) 22(1) Medico-Legal Journal of Ireland 29.
[31] Bunreacht na hÉireann, Art 29.4.6°.

the consistency, effectiveness and continuity of its policies and actions.'[32] Article 13 provides that the Union's institutions are: the European Parliament; the European Council; the Council of the EU; the European Commission; the Court of Justice of the European Union; the European Central Bank; and the Court of Auditors.

The European Commission is the executive of the EU. It is comprised of a commissioner from each EU Member State. These Commissioners are not to act in the interests of their home territory but must instead act in the interests of the EU. Commissioners are each assigned a portfolio that is his/her area of responsibility. The European Commission has several essential functions including the proposal of new laws, acting as a guardian of EU treaties, and representing the EU internationally.

The Council of the European Union represents Member States within the EU and is the main forum in which issues are discussed and decisions taken. The Council is made up of one government minister from every Member State. Different ministers meet based on the topic to be discussed. For instance, if the meeting relates to a finance issue, the ministers for finance from each Member State will be in attendance. The Council of the European Union has three core functions. These functions are the power to legislate, the co-ordination of economic policies of Member States, and the power to approve the EU budget.

The European Parliament is the only directly elected institution in the EU, thereby representing the citizens of the Member States. The Parliament meets and deliberates at the Parliament buildings in Strasbourg, France. It forms part of a decision-making triangle along with the European Commission and the Council of the European Union. The legal system of the EU is overseen by the Court of Justice, which sits in Luxembourg.

EU law does not only apply to states but also applies to individuals. This was not clear until the ECJ decision in *Van Gen den Loos v Nederlandse*.[33] This decision established that provisions of the Treaty of Rome were capable of creating legal rights that could be enforced by individuals before domestic courts.

As noted above, the primary sources of EU law are the treaties. Community treaties are binding agreements between EU Member

---

[32] Treaty on European Union, Art 13.
[33] Case 26/62 *Van Gen den Loos v Nederlandse* [1963] ECR 1.

States and serve to define the EU's sphere of competence. On this basis, the EU does not have competence to act outside the specific terms of these treaties. Article 288 of the Treaty on the Functioning of the European Union sets out that in order to exercise the Union's competences, 'the institutions shall adopt regulations, directives, decisions, recommendations and opinions'.[34] Article 288 TFEU outlines the meaning of these secondary sources of EU law. A regulation is a law that is to have general application. It is binding in its entirety and is directly applicable in all Member States. Once a regulation is made it automatically becomes law in all EU Member States. Regulations are commonly used to address areas that do not overlap with the national laws of a Member State. A directive is to be binding as to the result to be achieved but national authorities have a choice in the form and methods used to achieve this. A directive will usually set a deadline for the implementation of legislation. A decision is binding in its entirety. It usually has a limited scope as a decision that specifies to whom it is addressed shall be binding only on them. In contrast, recommendations and opinions have no binding force and no legal consequences.

2.2.5 International Law

International law is the body of law that is binding in relations between states. This set of rules is made up of customary international law, treaties, and the decisions of judicial bodies. The application and effect of international law in domestic legal systems is influenced by whether the state is monist or dualist. In a monist system international law does not need to be translated into national law for it to take effect. Instead the ratification of an international treaty or agreement is sufficient to incorporate it into the domestic legal framework. The dualist framework requires an additional step to incorporate international law into national law. It is only when this additional step is taken that the law can be applied by the national courts. Ireland is a dualist legal system. Article 29.6 of the Irish Constitution sets out that 'No international agreement shall be part of the domestic law of the State save as may be determined by the Oireachtas.'[35] On this basis, the signing of an international agreement by Ireland does not mean it has legal effect in the jurisdiction. Nevertheless, a failure to complete domestic incorporation does not absolve the State from a failure to comply with international obligations.

---

[34] Treaty on the Functioning of the European Union, Art 288.
[35] Bunreacht na hÉireann, Art 29.6.

While there are many examples of international legal treaties, this section will focus on the European Convention on Human Rights (ECHR). This is an important source of human rights and will be referenced throughout this book. In this regard, nurses play an important role in the promotion and protection of human rights in healthcare. Nurses should be aware of the various rights they must seek to protect but should also be cognisant of their own personal rights.

The European Convention on Human Rights

The ECHR was drafted by the Council of Europe in 1950 and entered into force in 1953.[36] The ratification of the ECHR by a State results in a legal obligation 'to guarantee to individuals within their jurisdiction a select number of civil and political rights'.[37] The ECHR was incorporated into Irish domestic law by way of the European Convention on Human Rights Act 2003. The manner of incorporation was at a sub-constitutional level, thereby maintaining the supremacy of the Irish Constitution.

Individuals who feel that their rights under the Convention have been violated by the State can ultimately bring a case to the ECtHR. States are obliged to comply with the decision of the ECtHR in circumstances where the Court holds there to be a violation of the Convention. In this regard, the Committee of Ministers of the Council of Europe has responsibility for monitoring whether states have complied with the judgment of the ECtHR. Accordingly, there are two sources of rights stemming from the ECHR. There is the ECHR itself, which can be drawn on before the ECtHR, and the ECHR Act 2003, which is applicable in the domestic sphere. Rights protected by the ECHR include the right to life,[38] a right to be protected from torture and inhuman or degrading treatment,[39] right to a fair trial,[40] and right to respect for family and private life.[41]

Section 3 of the ECHR Act 2003 requires that 'every organ of the State shall perform its functions in a manner compatible with the

---

[36] Ed Bates, *The Evolution of the European Convention on Human Rights: From its Inception to the Creation of a Permanent Court of Human Rights* (Oxford University Press 2011) 1–2.
[37] ibid 2.
[38] European Convention on Human Rights, Art 2.
[39] ibid Art 3.
[40] ibid Art 6.
[41] ibid Art 8.

State's obligations under the Convention provisions'.[42] An organ of the State is a body established by law or a body 'through which any of the legislative, executive or judicial powers of the State are exercised'.[43] This would include bodies such as the Health Information and Quality Authority, the Irish Medical Council, the Nursing and Midwifery Board of Ireland, and the Health Service Executive. These bodies must carry out their functions in a way that is compatible with the obligations placed on the State.

2.2.6 Canon Law

Canon law is the law of the Christian Church. It consists of ordinances and regulations for the purposes of governing the Church and its members. Canon law is therefore largely separate to the secular law of the State and does not have the force of law. Despite this, the laws of the Christian Church have shaped and influenced a small number of legal rules, particularly in relation to the laws on marriage.

2.2.7 Academic Commentary

Academic commentary refers to research monographs, textbooks, journal articles, and reports written by academics. The use of such resources may provide a valuable opinion or a new argument that influences the courts or the Oireachtas in the drafting of legislation. The volume of academic commentary has grown substantially in recent years and was aided by the changes in legal education as well as a greater willingness from the courts to engage with the work of living academics. Traditionally, only the work of deceased authors was cited as it was felt that these works represented a definitive position as the author could no longer change their mind. Academic commentary can be recognised as a source of law in a relatively narrow sense as it may be drawn on in the formulation of law or the interpretation of a legal provision. It follows that academic commentary is merely persuasive and there is no requirement that it be considered or adopted.

2.3 Structure of the Courts System

The structure of the courts system in Ireland is based on a hierarchy of courts. The domestic courts system is comprised of a District Court, Circuit Court, Central Criminal Court, High Court, Court of Appeal, Supreme Court, and Special Criminal Court.

---

[42] European Convention on Human Rights Act 2003, s 3(1).
[43] ibid s 1.

There are also independent bodies that exercise a judicial function such as the Employment Appeals Tribunal. Moreover, there are international courts of relevance for the practice of nursing. These include the ECJ, and the European Court of Human Rights.

Articles 34–37 of the Irish Constitution address the structure and functioning of the courts system in Ireland. Article 34 provides that 'Justice shall be administered in courts established by law by judges appointed in the manner provided by this Constitution, and, save in such special and limited cases as may be prescribed by law, shall be administered in public.'[44] Justice must therefore be administered in public and in courts by judges. There are exceptions to the 'in public' requirement and in some instances a case may be heard 'in camera'. The effect of this is to exclude the media and the public from the court but this only occurs in cases where there is an urgent or extremely sensitive matter to be considered.

Article 34.2 sets out that the courts shall comprise: Courts of First Instance; a Court of Appeal; and a Court of Final Appeal. The Constitution names the High Court, the Court of Appeal, and the Supreme Court. The Courts of First Instance are to include 'Courts of local and limited jurisdiction with a right of appeal as determined by law.'[45] The courts of local and limited jurisdiction are not specifically named in the Constitution. Instead, the District and Circuit Courts are established by statute and, technically, could be abolished without the need for a referendum.

Article 35.2 establishes the independence of the judiciary: 'All judges shall be independent in the exercise of their judicial functions and subject only to this Constitution and the law.'[46] It is notable that Article 37.1 permits persons other than judges to exercise limited functions and powers of a judicial nature, in matters other than criminal matters. This reflects the powers held by some bodies at the time of the enactment of the Constitution and provides for the establishment of certain specialist statutory bodies such as the Labour Court.

District Court

The District Court is a court of local and limited jurisdiction organised on a local basis. It consists of 63 judges, including a

---

[44] Bunreacht na hÉireann, Article 34.
[45] ibid Art 34.3.4°.
[46] ibid Art 35.2.

President of the District Court. There are 23 districts and a Dublin Metropolitan District. The District Court is the lowest court in the hierarchy and handles a large number of cases.

The Court sits with a presiding judge and no jury. The district court hears cases relating to the areas of criminal, civil, family law, and licensing. The civil jurisdiction of the District Court is limited to cases where the claim or award does not exceed €15,000. The District Court largely deals with cases involving road traffic offences, possession of small quantities of drugs, minor thefts, minor assault, and criminal damage. The District Court has a broad jurisdiction in family law matters. It hears family law cases involving domestic violence,[47] the Guardianship of Children,[48] the award of maintenance,[49] and applications under the Child Care Act 1991.[50] The District Court does not hear tort cases such as defamation and cannot grant decrees of judicial separation or divorce. It also has no jurisdiction in equity where declarations or specific performance are sought. A decision of the District Court can be appealed to the Circuit Court. A case can also be stated to a higher court on a point of law.

Circuit Court

The Circuit Court is composed of 37 ordinary judges and six specialist judges along with a President of the Circuit Court. The country is divided into eight circuits (Cork, Dublin, Eastern, Midlands, North, South East, South West, and Western Circuits). A judge assigned to a circuit travels to different towns located in that circuit several times a year. A Circuit Court judge exercises jurisdiction in the circuit in which they are assigned. Permanent Circuit Courts are based in Dublin and Cork. Ten judges may be assigned to Dublin and there is provision for three judges in Cork.

The Circuit Court has four main areas of responsibility: civil, criminal, family law, and jury selection. In addition to hearing appeals from the District Court, it also serves as an appeal court for decisions issued by the Labour Court, Unfair Dismissals Tribunal and the Employment Appeals Tribunal. The civil jurisdiction of the Court is limited and this can only be lifted in circumstances where all parties to an action consent. The civil claim in the Circuit Court is not to exceed €75,000 and the market value does not exceed

---

[47] Domestic Violence Act 1996.
[48] Guardianship of Infants Act 1964.
[49] Family Law (Maintenance of Spouses and Children) Act 1976.
[50] Child Care Act 1991.

€3,000,000. The Circuit Court enjoys concurrent jurisdiction with the High Court in matters of family law. Proceedings on judicial separation, divorce, nullity and appeals from the District Court may be heard by the Circuit Court. It has the same jurisdiction as the Central Criminal Court in all indictable offences with the exception of murder, rape, and aggravated sexual assault among others. Decisions of the Circuit Court can be appealed to the High Court. In cases where a point of law is to be clarified then the Court of Appeal is to be consulted.

High Court

The High Court is composed of 37 ordinary judges and a President of the High Court (expanded by two judges in 2015). There are additional judges of the High Court, namely the Chief Justice, the President of the Court of Appeal, and the President of the Circuit Court. The High Court hears both civil and criminal matters and has 'full original jurisdiction' under Article 34.3.1. It therefore deals with civil and criminal matters and enjoys jurisdiction over questions of constitutional validity. The High Court also has exclusive jurisdiction over 'reserved offences'. In exercising the criminal jurisdiction of the High Court, it is referred to as the Central Criminal Court and sits with a judge and jury. It tries cases such as murder, rape, treason, and piracy. As noted in the discussion of the lower courts, the High Court has an appellate jurisdiction and can hear appeals on a point of law from these courts. As for civil matters, there is no limit to the damages that can be awarded by the High Court.

The High Court sits in the Four Courts in Dublin but visits other centres such as Limerick, Cork, Galway, Waterford, Sligo, Ennis, and Dundalk. This is known as the High Court on Circuit. While many of the cases before the High Court will be heard and decided by one judge, there are cases that require greater judicial scrutiny. In such cases, the High Court may sit as a divisional court and the case will be heard by a panel of three judges.

Court of Appeal

The Court of Appeal came into existence on 28 October 2014 and was provided for by the 33rd Amendment to the Irish Constitution. It hears appeals about decisions on civil matters from the High Court, including questions on the constitutionality of legislation. The Court also has an appellate jurisdiction over criminal matters, a function previously exercised by the Court of Criminal Appeal. The Court of Appeal occupies an appellate jurisdictional level in between the High Court and the Supreme Court in the hierarchy of courts. In addition to these roles, the Court of Appeal can also decide on questions of law stated to the Court. This function would previously have been exercised by the Supreme Court.

The Court of Appeal consists of 15 ordinary judges as well as a President of the Court of Appeal. In addition, the Chief Justice and the President of the High Court are ex officio judges of the Court. The Court may sit as a three-judge court although there are some interlocutory and procedural applications that can be heard by the President of the Court of Appeal alone or can be heard by another judge nominated by the President.

Supreme Court

The Supreme Court is at the top of the domestic court hierarchy in Ireland. The Supreme Court is the court of final appeal in Ireland as per Article 34 of the Constitution. The Supreme Court is based in Dublin, but it has sat outside the capital on occasion. The Supreme Court consists of the Chief Justice and nine ordinary judges. Ex officio members of the Supreme Court include the President of the Court of Appeal and the President of the High Court. It is primarily an appellate court and may sit as a seven-, five-, or three-judge court. When determining a case on the constitutional validity of an Act of the Oireachtas, the Constitution requires a minimum of five judges. Similarly, this quorum applies in cases of an Article 26 referral from the President of Ireland. For certain interlocutory and procedural applications, the Chief Justice or another Supreme Court judge may sit alone. The Supreme Court does not sit with a jury and the decisions of the Court are 'final and conclusive'.

The Supreme Court has an appellate and a relatively limited original jurisdiction. It can hear appeals from the High Court as well as the Court of Appeal. The Supreme Court has two instances of original jurisdiction, namely an Article 26 Reference or under Article 12.3.1°, which addresses the incapacity of the President. Article 26 provides for the referral of a Bill to the Supreme Court to determine whether the Bill or a provision contained therein is repugnant to the Constitution. There is also a limited original jurisdiction under Article 12.3.1°, which provides that 'only the Supreme Court, consisting of not less than five judges, can establish whether the President of Ireland has become permanently incapacitated'.[51]

---

[51] Bunreacht na hÉireann, Article 12.3.1°.

Special Criminal Court

The Special Criminal Court was established for the trial of offences in cases where the ordinary courts are inadequate to secure the effective administration of justice and the maintenance of social order.[52] The Offences Against the State Act 1939 provides for the appointment of judges to this Court. In total, 11 judges are appointed by the Government and this is comprised of four High Court judges, three Circuit Court judges, and four District Court judges. The Court sits with three judges and no jury. Appeals against conviction or a sentence can be brought before the Court of Appeal.

Labour Court

It must first be acknowledged that the Labour Court is not a court of law. It was established by the Industrial Relations Act 1946 and, in recent years, the functions have been altered and extended by the Workplace Relations Act 2015. Stemming from the 2015 Act, the Labour Court now enjoys appellate jurisdiction in all disputes under employment rights provisions. The Labour Court functions as 'an industrial relations tribunal'. Upon hearing from the parties to a dispute, the Court then issues a recommendation. This sets out the Court's opinion on the dispute and the manner in which it should be settled. The recommendations issued by the Court are not binding but the parties are to give it serious consideration.

European Court of Justice

The ECJ is the judicial institution of the European Union. The ECJ sits in Luxembourg and has one judge from each Member State. The work of the Court is supported by 11 Advocates General who deliver detailed opinions on cases to assist the ECJ in deciding a case. Both judges and Advocate Generals are appointed by joint agreement of the governments of EU Member States and have a renewable term of six years. The function of the ECJ is to uphold the Treaties and ensure that EU law is interpreted and applied in a consistent manner across EU Member States. This is achieved through preliminary rulings, proceedings for failure to fulfil an obligation, and proceedings for annulment.

European Court of Human Rights

The ECtHR is not a European Union institution. It is an institution of the Council of Europe and is designed to enforce the ECHR. An

---

[52] ibid Art 38.3.1°.

individual who feels that their rights have been violated by the State can bring a case to the ECtHR. The ECtHR has 47 judges, equal to the number of contracting states. The judges are elected by the Parliamentary Assembly of the Council of Europe for a nine-year term.

The ECtHR sits in Strasbourg, France. The ECtHR has responsibility for determining whether an ECHR Contracting State is in compliance with Convention obligations. States are obliged to comply with the decision of the ECtHR in circumstances where the Court holds there to be a violation of the ECHR. The Committee of Ministers of the Council of Europe has responsibility for monitoring whether states have complied with the judgment of the ECtHR. Superior courts are authorised to issue a declaration of incompatibility where a national law does not meet the standards required by the ECHR.

2.4 The Legal Profession

The effective functioning of a legal system requires many different legal personnel. Solicitors and barristers form the core of the legal profession in Ireland and will be discussed in this section. Other members of the legal profession include judges, the Director of Public Prosecutions, and the Attorney General.

Solicitors

The regulation and education of solicitors is overseen by the Law Society of Ireland. As of June 2019, there were 11,618 practising certificates issued for solicitors in Ireland. The solicitor is generally the first point of contact for a person seeking legal advice and their work involves a mix of contentious and non-contentious matters. Among the non-contentious tasks undertaken by a solicitor is the purchase of land and the drafting of wills. Contentious work involves dealing with legal disputes and litigation. In practice, solicitors will often specialise in a small number of areas, which allows them to develop their expertise and provide the most appropriate advice to a client. The day-to-day functions of a solicitor are also influenced by the place of employment. A solicitor may work as a sole-practitioner or may work for a medium-size firm, a boutique law firm, a large commercial firm, or 'in-house' for a large company. The legal issue arising will influence the type of solicitor you contact for assistance. For instance, a professional negligence action may be best handled by a boutique or small law firm instead of an international commercial firm.

In contentious matters involving litigation, it is the solicitor who completes most of the preparatory work in advance of a court hearing. This work involves research, the collection of evidence, and the compiling of documents for court. A solicitor can appear in court as an advocate, however, this role is usually performed by a barrister. The solicitor will 'brief' the barrister and the barrister will present the case in court.

Barristers

In June 2018 there were 2,149 practising barristers in Ireland. A barrister specialises in court advocacy and providing legal opinion.[53] Barristers appear in criminal and civil proceedings. The profession of barrister is divided into junior counsel and senior counsel. The majority of barristers in Ireland in June 2018 were Junior Counsel, 84 per cent, with only 16 per cent Senior Counsel.[54] Senior counsel are highly experienced legal advocates who represent clients in the High Court and the Supreme Court. Usually, a junior counsel will assist in cases where a senior counsel is involved.

The court dress for a barrister is widely known and easily identified. Barristers wear a dark robe and may choose to wear a horsehair wig. The wearing of a wig is no longer mandatory but is still a common sight in court. The barrister cannot be approached directly by a member of the public who is seeking legal representation. However, there is a limited direct professional access scheme whereby barristers can issue non-contentious advice. Moreover, the Legal Services Regulation Act 2015 sought to bring about substantial changes in the operation of the legal profession, including allowing barristers greater freedom in the provision of non-contentious legal services.

Judges

Despite the separation of powers, the Irish legal system is structured in such a way that the judiciary have a substantial and influential role. The decision of a judge can impact not only on the individual but may also have repercussions for broader society and the administration of the State. The appointment of judges is addressed by the Constitution of Ireland: Article 35.1 sets out that 'The judges of the Supreme Court, the Court of Appeal, the High Court and all other Courts established in pursuance of article 34

---

[53] The Bar of Ireland, *Annual Report 2017/2018* (Law Library 2018).
[54] ibid.

hereof shall be appointed by the President.'[55] Despite this, it is set out in Article 13.9 that 'The powers and functions conferred on the President by this Constitution shall be exercisable and performable by him only on the advice of the Government.'[56] It follows that the decision to appoint a judge is made by the Government. The process has been the subject of repeated criticism, particularly due to the perceived political influence. This resulted in the establishment of the Judicial Appointment Advisory Board, which provides input into the decision and has responsibility for 'identifying appropriate candidates for judicial office; and informing the Government of the suitability of those candidates for judicial office'.[57]

A key qualifying criterion for appointment to the judiciary is based on years in practice as either a solicitor or barrister. For the District and Circuit Court, a person must have been practising for at least 10 years. Appointment to the High Court, Court of Appeal and Supreme Court requires a minimum 12 years of practice but will normally be much more.

Director of Public Prosecutions (DPP)

The office of the DPP was established by the Prosecution of Offences Act 1974. The DPP does not investigate crimes but decides whether to prosecute people for committing a crime and determines the most appropriate charges. It is an independent office; neither the Government nor the gardaí can force the DPP to prosecute or not prosecute a specific case. The decision of the DPP is especially sensitive and has implications for the victim and the accused. If the DPP decides not to prosecute then they will inform the Garda Síochána, or other investigating agency, of the reasons for the decision. The reasons are to be kept confidential as a public comment may prejudice a person without trial and could be seen as being unjust.

Attorney General

Article 30 of the Constitution provides, 'There shall be an Attorney General who shall be the adviser of the Government in matters of law and legal opinion.'[58] The Attorney General is appointed by the President on the nomination of the Taoiseach. Moreover, the

---

[55] Bunreacht na hÉireann, Article 35.1.
[56] ibid Art 13.9.
[57] Courts and Court Officers Act 1995, s 13(1).
[58] Bunreacht na hÉireann, Art 30.

Attorney General is to retire from office upon the resignation of the Taoiseach. The person appointed to this role is usually a lawyer who has some political association with the party in government.

The Office of the Attorney General contains the Advisory Counsel to the Attorney General and the Office of Parliamentary Counsel to the Government as well as the Chief State Solicitor's Office. As legal adviser to the Government, the Attorney General attends Government meetings, despite not being a member of the Government. The functions of the Attorney General include advising the Government on constitutional and legal issues, including whether proposed legislation complies with the Constitution, EU law, the ECHR, and other international legal treaties to which Ireland has acceded. In addition, the Attorney General represents the State in legal proceedings and defends the constitutionality of Bills referred to the Supreme Court under the Article 26 procedure.

Chapter 3
The Nursing and Midwifery Board of Ireland

Introduction 33
The Legislative Development of Nursing and
Midwifery in Ireland 34
The Nursing and Midwifery Board of Ireland 37
Standards of Practice and Professional Guidance 41
    The Code of Professional Conduct and Ethics
        for Registered Nurses and Registered Midwives. . . . 42
        Practice Standards for Midwives 44
The Complaints Process 46
    Administrative and Procedural Concerns 53
    Preliminary Proceedings Committee 54
    Fitness to Practise Inquiries 58
    Measures Taken Following the Fitness to
    Practise Inquiry 62

3.0 Introduction

Increased competencies for the nursing and midwifery professions have led to the publication of more guidance and more detailed standards. These developments are accompanied by new challenges in professional regulation. This chapter explores the evolution of nursing practice in this jurisdiction and will explore these changes through the lens of legislation and professional regulation. The legislative history of nursing and midwifery practice in Ireland will be set out before going on to explore the modern-day regulation of the professions. This will range from the Midwives (Ireland) Act 1918 to the Nurses and Midwives Act 2011. Through this discussion, this chapter will also explore the role and function of the Nursing and Midwifery Board of Ireland (NMBI). In particular, the standard setting and the professional oversight function of the NMBI will be outlined. These functions are demonstrated and shaped in part by the Code of Professional Conduct and Ethics. The standards and guidance published by the NMBI forms a core part of subsequent chapters.

3.1 The Legislative Development of Nursing and Midwifery in Ireland

Legislation on nursing and midwifery in Ireland goes back to the early 20th century, prior to the founding of the Irish Free State. The path of nursing and midwifery legislation illustrates points of convergence and divergence between these professions over time. It can therefore provide an interesting historical perspective on many of the debates and challenges faced by nursing and midwifery.

The Midwives (Ireland) Act 1918 was the first legislation to address the practice of midwifery in the jurisdiction. It marked the culmination of a drawn-out process, which included many failed bills. The 1918 Act established the first Central Midwives Board. The Central Midwives Board set out rules for certification, training and examinations, supervisory functions, and the issuing of professional sanctions. This Act also provided for the establishment of a register for midwives in Ireland, known as the Roll of Midwives. The next legislative development for midwifery was the Midwives Act 1931. This Act provided for the issuance of midwives' badges, which were intended to denote the wearer as a midwife. Members of the public, or patients, could therefore identify a midwife who was qualified and registered. In addition, the 1931 Act established an offence of attending a woman in childbirth where the relevant person did not have appropriate medical qualifications or justification for attending the women. Persons found guilty of an offence were liable to a fine not exceeding £10. The 1931 Act was followed by the Midwives Act 1944, which expanded the professional disciplinary system, introduced the designation 'State Certified Midwife', and sought to make better provision for the enrolment, certification, control and training of midwives in Ireland.

The first legislation to address nursing in Ireland was the Nurses Registration (Ireland) Act 1919. This Act established the General Nursing Council for Ireland. It required the Council to maintain a register of nurses. The register distinguished between different specialties such as mental health nursing and paediatric nursing. It also contained a register of general nurses and a supplementary register for male nurses. This distinction between sexes underlined how nursing was primarily the preserve of women at the time. The corresponding English Act was influenced by the campaigning of Ethel Fenwick, the Matron of St Bartholomew's Hospital.[1] The importance of a clear legal framework for nursing practice was recognised by the Matron when stating:

> Had hospital managers and certificated nurses responded to a sense of public and professional duty thirty years ago, the profession of nursing would by now be a highly-skilled, well-disciplined, and well-remunerated body; as it is, abuses have multiplied, and although the Act lays sound foundations upon which to build, the whole superstructure of professional organisation must be built up.[2]

In Ireland, The General Nursing Council and the Central Midwives Board were subsequently dissolved by the Nurses Act 1950. These bodies were replaced by An Bord Altranais, as established by s 7 of the Nurses Act 1950. The 1950 Act provided for a register of nurses with a midwives division. Under this Act, midwifery was subsumed under the title 'nurse' as 'nurse' includes a midwife and 'nursing' includes 'midwifery'.[3] Developments such as this marked a decline in the perception of midwifery as a distinct profession. This was reflected in the dissolution of the independent Board and the associated diminution of professional autonomy in terms of control and organisation of the profession. Further amendments to the statutory framework for nursing and midwifery in Ireland occurred with the Nurses Act 1961 and the Nurses Act 1985.

The Nurses Act 1985 repealed all other nursing and midwifery acts. It provided an enhanced and expanded role for An Bord Altranais. In this respect, An Bord Altranais had responsibility for professional registration, oversight of education and training, and responsibility for promoting high standards of professional conduct.

The legal framework for nursing in Ireland has continued to develop in the intervening years. On 21 December 2011, the Nurses and Midwives Act 2011 was signed into law. The 2011 Act updated the provisions relating to the regulation of nurses and midwives. Moreover, it recognised midwifery as a distinct

---

[1] The Health Foundation, 'The Nurses Registration Act 1919' <https://navigator.health.org.uk/content/nurses-registration-act-1919> accessed 7 July 2020.
[2] ibid.
[3] Nurses Act 1950, s 2.

profession. This change was reflected in the title of the professional body. Following the signing of Commencement Order SI No 385 of 2012, An Bord Altranais was renamed the Nursing and Midwifery Board of Ireland. The change was underlined by s 2(2), which provides, 'For the avoidance of doubt, it is hereby declared and recognised that midwifery is a separate profession to nursing.'[4]

The purpose of the 2011 Act is encapsulated in the long title, which describes it as:

> An act for the purpose of the enhancement of the protection of the public in its dealings with nurses and midwives and, for that purpose, to provide for a board to be known as Bord Altranais agus Cnáimhseachais na hÉireann, or in the English language, the Nursing and Midwifery Board of Ireland, to recognise midwifery as a separate profession, to provide for the registration, regulation and control of nurses and midwives, to enhance the high standards of professional education, training and competence of nurses and midwives, to investigate complaints against nurses and midwives and to increase the public accountability of the board, to dissolve the national council for the professional development of nursing and midwifery, to repeal the nurses act 1985 and to provide for related matters.[5]

The 2011 Act is comprised of 13 sections. This represents a considerable expansion from the Nurses Act 1985, which contained six sections. Part 1 of the 2011 Act addresses preliminary and general matters such as the interpretation of various terms and the making of regulations relating to the Act. Part 2 is titled Bord Altranais agus Cnáimhseachais na hÉireann. This part defines the object and functions of the Board. It therefore has an important role in shaping the NMBI and is discussed in more detail in section 3.2 of this chapter. Part 3 deals with the statement of strategy, business plan, and annual report of the Board. Part 4 outlines members, committees, and employees of the NMBI and is also discussed in section 3.2. Part 5 addresses the accounts and finances of the Board. This includes the power to borrow, expenses, and fees. Part 6 of the 2011 Act deals with registration and practice: this includes requirements relating to issues such as designated titles, offences, registers, and conditions. Parts 7, 8, and 9 of the Act define the steps involved in responding to a complaint about a registered nurse or midwife. This includes the role of the Preliminary Proceedings

---

[4] Nurses and Midwives Act 2011, s 2(2).
[5] Nurses and Midwives Act 2011.

Committee (PPC), and the Fitness to Practise Committee (FTPC). This process is outlined in section 3.4 of this chapter. Parts 10 and 11 address education and training, and the maintenance of professional competence. Part 12 deals with the dissolution of the National Council for the Professional Development of Nursing and Midwifery. Miscellaneous provisions are covered by Part 13 of the Act.

3.2 The Nursing and Midwifery Board of Ireland

The NMBI is the independent regulatory body of the nursing and midwifery professions in Ireland. Section 8 of the Nurses and Midwives Act 2011 establishes the object of the Board as:

> the protection of the public in its dealing with nurses and midwives and the integrity of the practice of nursing and midwifery through the promotion of high standards of professional education, training and practice and professional conduct among nurses and midwives.[6]

The functions of the NMBI are set out under s 9 of the 2011 Act. Core functions of the Board include:

- establish and maintain the register of nurses and midwives;
- approve programmes of education and further education;
- evaluate applications from Irish and overseas applicants who want to practise as nurses and midwives in Ireland;
- specify standards of practice for registered nurses and midwives;
- establish committees to inquire into complaints; and
- advise the public on all matters of general interest relating to the functions of the Board, its area of expertise, and other matters of interest to the public relating to nurses and midwives and their practice.[7]

In addition to primary legislation, the functions of the NMBI are also shaped by secondary legislation in the form of nurses and midwives rules. Under s 13 of the Nurses and Midwives Act 2011, the NMBI is vested with the power to make rules in relation to the operation of its primary functions.[8] The Nurses Rules of 2010

---

[6] ibid s 8.
[7] ibid s 9.
[8] ibid s 13.

and 2013 established the framework for the implementation of legislation governing the nursing and midwifery professions. In 2018, secondary legislation was introduced to address registration,[9] qualification recognition,[10] the candidate register,[11] and the structure of registers.[12]

While the work of the NMBI is primarily framed by the Nurses and Midwives Act 2011, it is not the only piece of legislation the Board must take account of. The NMBI must satisfy legislative requirements provided for under the Ombudsman Act 2012, Freedom of Information Acts, the Official Languages Act 2003, Ethics in Public Office Acts and Standards in Public Office Act 2001. There are a range of additional codes and guidelines the NMBI must also adhere to. For instance, the *Code of Practice for the Governance of State Bodies* provides a framework for achieving the highest standards of corporate governance. This framework is based on principles of accountability, transparency, probity and a focus on sustainable success.[13] The NMBI must also follow the *National Public Procurement Policy Framework* and the *Public Procurement Guidelines – Competitive Process*.

Board of the NMBI

The Board of the NMBI is to consist of 23 persons.[14] These persons include academics, directors of nursing/midwifery, registered nurses/midwives, a nominee of the Medical Council, a nominee of the Minister for Education and Skills, two Health Service Executive nominees, a nominee of the Health and Social Care Professionals Council, a nominee of the Health Information and Quality Authority, a person with experience of health or personal social care in the volunteer sector, and five other persons who are not and never have been registered nurses/midwives but who have appropriate qualifications or experience to make a contribution. There is a lay majority of 12 on the Board. The remaining 11 members include eight registered nurses and midwives as elected by the professions. A further three nurses and midwives are appointed by the Minister for Health. No person is permitted to

---

[9] Nurses and Midwives (Registration) Rules 2018, SI 2018/221.
[10] Nurses and Midwives (Recognition of Professional Qualifications) Rules 2018, SI 2018/220; Nurses and Midwives (Education and Training) Rules 2018, SI 2018/218.
[11] Nurses and Midwives (Candidate Register) Rules 2018, SI 2018/217.
[12] Nurses and Midwives (Register of Nurses and Midwives) Rules 2018, SI 2018/219.
[13] Department of Public Expenditure and Reform, *Code of Practice for the Governance of State Bodies* (August 2016).
[14] Nurses and Midwives Act 2011, s 22.

hold office as a member of the Board for more than two terms of five years.[15] If a Board member is unable to carry out their duties, has committed stated misbehaviour, or has contravened an applicable provision of the Ethics in Public Office Acts, they may be removed from office. Additional grounds for removal from office are set out by s 27 of the 2011 Act.[16]

There are several committees and sub-committees that report to the Board and serve to support the Board's activities. These committees are provided for by s 24 of the Nurses and Midwives Act 2011.[17] Committees include: the Audit and Risk Committee; the Education and Training Committee; the Registration Committee; the Midwives Committee; the Governance and Finance Committee; the PPC; and the FTPC. A committee may include persons who are not members of the Board, however, there are specific requirements for the composition of the Midwives Committee, the PPC, and the FTPC. No person is permitted to be a member of the PPC and the FTPC at the same time.[18] Both the PPC and the FTPC require at least one-third of the members, including the chairperson, to be members of the Board, and the majority of the membership of that committee shall consist of persons who are not and never have been registered nurses or registered midwives in the State or nurses or midwives in another jurisdiction.[19] This ensures a lay majority, which supports the independence and legitimacy of these committees. For further discussion see section 3.4 of this chapter.

Registration and Practice

Among the functions of the NMBI is the establishment and maintenance of the Register of Nurses and Midwives in Ireland. This is a live register, which means that it is to be kept up to date on an ongoing basis. It can also be accessed by members of the public through the NMBI website. Section 39 of the Nurses and Midwives Act 2011 provides that unregistered nurses or midwifes are not to practise or advertise that he/she practices that profession.[20]

There are ten divisions under which a person may be registered: general, midwives, children's, psychiatric, intellectual disability,

---

[15] Nurses and Midwives Act 2011 Schedule, part 2.
[16] Nurses and Midwives Act 2011, s 27.
[17] ibid s 24.
[18] ibid s 24(8).
[19] ibid s 24(9) and 24(10).
[20] ibid s 39.

public health, nurse tutor, nurse prescriber, advanced nurse practitioner, and advanced midwife practitioner. The 2011 Act also provided for the establishment of a candidate register for the various divisions.[21] A nurse or midwife with more than one qualification can be registered in the corresponding divisions. For instance, at one point it was relatively common for nurses to also train as midwifes and this dual qualification would be reflected in the register.

Education and Training of Nurses and Midwives

The Board has certain duties in respect of the education and training of nurses and midwives. Section 85 of the Nurses and Midwives Act 2011 provides, 'The Board shall – (a) set and publish … the standards of nursing and midwifery education and training for first time registration and post-registration specialist nursing and midwifery qualifications' and will monitor adherence with such standards.[22] The Board does not itself educate or train nurses and midwives but instead approves programmes of education to be delivered by other bodies. As such, undergraduate and postgraduate nursing and midwifery programmes must adhere to the standards and requirements set out by the NMBI. A failure to meet these standards could result in the refusal or withdrawal of approval from the programme.

Bodies providing programmes of education and training are subject to inspection to ensure ongoing compliance with NMBI criteria. An inspection is to be carried out at least every five years at places in the State where training is provided to persons undertaking training for a nursing or midwifery qualification. Following the inspection, the NMBI is to issue recommendations to the management on any improvements in nursing or midwifery education and training standards that may be required or any other issues arising from the inspection.

Part 11 of the Nurses and Midwives Act 2011 addresses the maintenance of professional competence. Under this, s 87(1) provides, 'A registered nurse and a registered midwife shall maintain professional competence on an ongoing basis.'[23]

---

[21] Nurses and Midwives Rules 2013, SI 2013/435. 3.1 The following divisions of the Candidate Register are hereby established: (1) Nurse Candidate Division; (2) General Nurse Candidate Division; (3) Psychiatric Nurse Candidate Division; (4) Children's Nurse Candidate Division; (5) Intellectual Disability Nurse Candidate Division; (6) Midwives Candidate Division.
[22] Nurses and Midwives Act 2011, s 85(1).
[23] ibid s 87(1).

The NMBI also has an oversight role for forms of continued professional development. NMBI can approve short courses/conferences/seminars. These are increasingly provided online, and details can be obtained from NMBI's Education Department. The completion of such programmes of training ensures the continued professional competence of the nurse/midwife and they can earn Continuing Education Units (CEUs). In many professions, including legal practice, continued education is a condition of professional registration. This is not yet the case for nursing or midwifery as no minimum CEUs must be obtained to ensure continued registration.

Charging of Fees

Revenue to support the functioning of the NMBI can be generated through the charging of fees as provided for in s 38 of the Nurses and Midwives Act 2011. The legislation provides for the charging of fees for the registration of a person in the register of nurses and midwives, the annual retention of registration, and the restoration of the registration of the name of a person.[24] The NMBI may also charge fees for the annotation of registration with additional qualifications, entry to exams and assessments, and any other service the Board may provide.[25] There are serious consequences associated with a failure to pay the requisite registration fee. Section 77 of the 2011 Act provides that where a registered nurse or midwife fails to pay a required fee the Board may remove the nurse's or midwife's registration. This action is not to be taken earlier than 28 days after a reminder notice to pay the fee has been sent to the nurse or midwife. If removed from the register, the relevant person cannot practise nursing or midwifery until such time as their name is restored in the register. This requires the completion of a Restoration Form and the payment of the appropriate fee within a period of six months after the date on which the appropriate fee became due.

3.3 Standards of Practice and Professional Guidance

Section 9(2)(g) of the Nurses and Midwives Act 2011 provides that it is a function of the NMBI to:

> (g) specify standards of practice for registered nurses and registered midwives, including the establishment, publication, maintenance and review of—

---

[24] ibid s 38.
[25] ibid s 38.

> (i) appropriate guidance on all matters related to professional conduct and ethics for registered nurses and registered midwives,
>
> (ii) appropriate guidance on the maintenance of the professional competence of registered nurses and registered midwives, and
>
> (iii) a code of professional conduct for registered nurses and registered midwives[26]

In line with this, the NMBI have published numerous standards and guidance documents relevant to the practice of nursing and midwifery. For instance, increased professional competencies and responsibilities in prescribing practices are guided by the *Practice Standards and Guidelines for Nurses and Midwives with Prescriptive Authority.*[27] Standards and guidance have also been published on *Ethical Conduct in Research,*[28] *Working with Older People,*[29] *Quality Clinical Learning Environment,*[30] *Social Media and Social Networking,*[31] and *Recording Clinical Practice.*[32] However, it is the *Code of Professional Conduct and Ethics for Registered Nurses and Registered Midwives* that serves as the 'overarching structure' that shapes and underpins the NMBI's framework of professional guidance for registered nurses and midwives.[33]

3.3.1 The Code of Professional Conduct and Ethics for Registered Nurses and Registered Midwives

The current Code of Professional Conduct and Ethics has been effective from 10 December 2014. It replaced the Code of Professional Conduct for Each Nurse and Midwife (2000) and was the result of an extensive consultation process. The Code

---

[26] ibid s 9(2)(g).
[27] Nursing and Midwifery Board of Ireland, *Practice Standards and Guidelines for Nurses and Midwives with Prescriptive Authority* (3rd edition, NMBI 2018).
[28] Nursing and Midwifery Board of Ireland, *Ethical Conduct in Research* (NMBI 2015).
[29] Nursing and Midwifery Board of Ireland, *Working with Older People* (NMBI 2015).
[30] Nursing and Midwifery Board of Ireland, *Quality Clinical Learning Environment* (NMBI 2015).
[31] Nursing and Midwifery Board of Ireland, *Social Media and Social Networking* (NMBI 2013).
[32] Nursing and Midwifery Board of Ireland, *Recording Clinical Practice* (NMBI 2015).
[33] Nursing and Midwifery Board of Ireland, *Code of Professional Conduct and Ethics for Registered Nurses and Registered Midwives* (NMBI 2014) 7.

serves to support the nurse in making professional decisions, and in promoting high standards of professional conduct. Nurses practise in a variety of areas including clinical, research, education, and management roles. Regardless of the area of practice, the nurse is to adhere to the Code of Professional Conduct. Failure to comply with the Code may result in a complaint being made against the nurse. In such a case, the NMBI can investigate the nurse's or midwife's conduct as provided for under parts 7 and 8 of the Nurses and Midwives Act 2011.

The purpose of the Code is described as serving 'to guide nurses and midwives in their day-to-day practice and help them to understand their professional responsibilities in caring for patients in a safe, ethical and effective way'.[34]

The aims of the Code are to:

- support and guide nurses and midwives in their ethical and clinical decision-making, their on-going reflection and professional self-development;
- inform the general public about the professional care they can expect from nurses and midwives;
- emphasise the importance of the obligations of nurses and midwives to recognise and respond to the needs of patients and families; and
- set standards for the regulation, monitoring and enforcement of professional conduct.[35]

The Code is based on the principles of respect for the dignity of the person; professional responsibility and accountability; quality of practice; trust and confidentiality; and collaboration with others. The Code expands on these principles by outlining values and standards of conduct derived from each principle. The ethical values describe the primary goals and obligations of nurses and midwives. For example, values listed under principle 1, 'respect for the dignity of the person', include, 'Nurses and midwives respect each person as a unique individual', and 'Nurses and midwives respect and defend the dignity of every stage of human life.'[36] The standards of conduct are closely linked to the values and demonstrate 'the attitudes and behaviours that members of the public have the right to expect from nurses and midwives'.[37]

---

[34] ibid 8.
[35] ibid.
[36] ibid 11.
[37] ibid 9.

The Code describes the principles, values, and standards of conduct as being 'of equal importance and should be considered in association with each other'.[38]

Supporting guidance is also published under each principle. This provides additional information and background the nurse or midwife should also be aware of. The Code is informed and shaped by international human rights agreements as well as domestic law. Values and standards adhere to the European Convention for the Protection of Human Rights and Fundamental Freedoms, the United Nations Declaration of Human Rights, and the United Nations Convention on the Rights of the Child. The Code is also informed by the Irish Constitution, Children's Act 2001, Data Protection Acts 1988 and 2003, Disability Act 2005, Equal Status Acts 2000–2011, Non-Fatal Offences Against the Person Act 1997, Protected Disclosures Act 2014, Protected Disclosures of Information (SI No 27 of 2009), and the Mental Health Act 2001.[39] The values and standards of conduct set out in the Code, as well as associated legislation, will be discussed in more detail over the course of this work.

3.3.2 Practice Standards for Midwives

Midwifery raises complex legal, ethical, and clinical issues. It is therefore not surprising that standards specific to midwives have been published by the NMBI. *Practice Standards for Midwives* came into effect on 31 May 2015 and is aligned with the *Code of Professional Conduct and Ethics for Registered Nurses and Registered Midwives*, as is evidenced by the overlap in principles.

All registered midwives practising in Ireland are to comply with the Practice Standards, along with the broader legal framework for midwifery in Ireland. In addition to the five principles, the Practice Standards contain details on standards of conduct and midwifery values. The principles are: respect for the dignity of the person; professional responsibility and accountability; quality of practice; trust and confidentiality; and collaboration with others. The meaning of these principles in the context of midwifery is expressly outlined in the document and takes the form of Practice Standards. Each of these Practice Standards are expanded upon by standards of conduct, which are also outlined in the document.

---

[38] ibid.
[39] ibid 29.

Practice Standard 1: 'Midwifery practice is underpinned by a philosophy that protects and promotes the safety and autonomy of the woman and respects her experiences, choices, priorities, beliefs and values.'

Practice Standard 2: 'Midwives practise in line with legislation and professional guidance and are responsible and accountable within their scope of midwifery practice. This encompasses the full range of activities of the midwife as set out in EC Directive 2005/36/EC and the adapted Definition of the Midwife International Confederation of Midwives 2011 (ICM) as adopted by the NMBI.'

Practice Standard 3: 'Midwives use comprehensive professional knowledge and skills to provide safe, competent, kind, compassionate and respectful care. Midwives keep up to date with midwifery practice by undertaking relevant continuing professional development.'

Practice Standard 4: 'Midwives work in equal partnership with the woman and her family and establish a relationship of trust and confidentiality.'

Practice Standard 5: 'Midwives communicate and collaborate effectively with women, women's families and with the multidisciplinary healthcare team.'[40]

Eight values are listed in the *Practice Standards for Midwives*. These values are core to the Practice Standards and include points such as:

- Having a baby is a profound experience, which carries intense meaning to the woman, her baby, her family and the community.
- The woman is the primary decision-maker in her care and she has the right to information that helps her to make decisions.
- Birth is a normal physiological process.
- Midwives value empowerment of women to assume responsibility for their health and for the health of their families.
- Midwifery care combines art and science. Midwifery care is holistic, grounded in an understanding of the

---

[40] Nursing and Midwifery Board of Ireland, *Practice Standards for Midwives* (NMBI 2015) 7–8.

social, emotional, cultural, spiritual, psychological and physical experiences of women and based upon the best available evidence.
- Midwifery practice must always be based on principles of professional conduct as stated in the Code of Professional Conduct and Ethics for Registered Nurses and Registered Midwives and on the scope of midwifery practice as stated in the Scope of Nursing and Midwifery Practice.[41]

As noted previously, the midwife must also be cognisant of the broader legal and regulatory framework as shaped by guidance such as the *Guidance to Nurses and Midwives on Social Media and Social Networking Ethical Conduct in Research*[42]; *Practice Standards and Guidelines for Nurses and Midwives with Prescriptive Authority*[43]; and *Recording Clinical Practice*.[44]

3.4 The Complaints Process

The object of the NMBI is set out in s 8 of the Nurses and Midwives Act 2011 and includes the protection of the public and upholding the integrity of the practice of nursing and midwifery. One of the key functions of the NMBI in delivering on this object is the establishment of committees to inquire into complaints. A complaint may be submitted by members of the public, an employer, medical practitioners, and nurses or midwives. The Board can also make a complaint about a nurse or midwife.[45]

Possible grounds for complaint are set out by s 55(1) of the Nurses and Midwives Act 2011. A complaint may be based on one or more of the following grounds:

(a) professional misconduct;

(b) poor professional performance;

(c) non-compliance with a code of professional conduct;

---

[41] ibid 13.
[42] Nursing and Midwifery Board of Ireland, *Ethical Conduct in Research* (NMBI 2015).
[43] Nursing and Midwifery Board of Ireland, *Practice Standards and Guidelines for Nurses and Midwives with Prescriptive Authority* (3rd edn, NMBI 2018).
[44] Nursing and Midwifery Board of Ireland, *Recording Clinical Practice* (NMBI 2015).
[45] Nurses and Midwives Act 2011 s 55.

(d) a relevant medical disability;

(e) a failure to comply with a relevant condition;

(f) a failure to comply with an undertaking or to take any action specified in a consent given in response to a request under s 65(1);

(g) a contravention of a provision of this Act (including a provision of any regulations or rules made under this Act);

(h) an irregularity in relation to the custody, prescription or supply of a controlled drug under the Misuse of Drugs Acts 1977 and 1984 or another drug that is likely to be abused; or

(i) a conviction in the State for an offence triable on indictment or a conviction outside the State for an offence consisting of acts or omissions that, if done or made in the State, would constitute an offence triable on indictment. [46]

In relation to professional misconduct or poor professional performance, a complaint can be made notwithstanding that the matter to which the complaint relates occurred outside the State.[47] The complainant may specifically identify the ground(s) of complaint, but, a failure to do so will not prevent the complaint from being considered. The ground(s) of complaint may be subsequently modified by the PPC, as discussed below.

The Nurses and Midwives Act 2011 restructured the complaints process through the introduction of the PPC. The PPC is to consider whether there is a prima facie case arising from a complaint, and to determine whether the complaint should be referred to a fitness to practise inquiry. It follows that the function of the FTPC is to conduct such inquiries based on complaints referred by the PPC.

Section 44 of the 2011 Act provides that it is an offence for a person to practise as a nurse or midwife without being registered. However, the complaints function of the NMBI is limited to registered nurses and registered midwives. A search of the NMBI register should be conducted if there is any question about

---

[46] ibid s 55(1).
[47] ibid s 55(2).

registration status.[48] This search lists PIN, name, registration status, registration expiry date, division(s), and the fitness to practise conditions for registered nurses and registered midwives.

Professional Misconduct

The 2011 Act does not define 'professional misconduct'. Instead, it is necessary to draw on case law to gain an understanding of this ground for complaint. The meaning of 'professional misconduct' was considered in the context of a medical practitioner in *O'Laoire v Medical Council*.[49] Keane J set out several principles forming the test for professional misconduct and these can generally be grouped into two categories, namely infamous or disgraceful conduct or the 'moral turpitude test', and the 'expected standards test'. Principles (1) to (4) are under the former category, while principle (5) is the 'expected standards test'. The relevant principles are:

> (1) Conduct which is 'infamous' or 'disgraceful' in a professional respect is 'professional misconduct' …
>
> (2) Conduct which would not be 'infamous' or 'disgraceful' in any other person, if done by a medical practitioner in relation to his profession, that is, with regard either to his patients or to his colleagues, may be considered as 'infamous' or 'disgraceful' conduct in a professional respect.
>
> (3) 'Infamous' or 'disgraceful' conduct in turn is conduct involving some degree of moral turpitude, fraud or dishonesty.
>
> (4) The fact that a person wrongly but honestly forms a particular opinion cannot of itself amount to infamous or disgraceful conduct in a professional sense.
>
> (5) Conduct which could not properly be characterised as 'infamous' or 'disgraceful' and which does not involve any degree of moral turpitude, fraud or dishonesty may still constitute 'professional misconduct' if it is conduct connected with his profession in which the medical practitioner concerned has seriously fallen short, by omission

---

[48] Nursing and Midwifery Board of Ireland, 'Check the Register' <https://www.nmbi.ie/Check-the-Register> accessed 7 July 2020.
[49] *O'Laoire v Medical Council* (27 January 1995) HC.

or commission, of the standards of conduct expected among medical practitioners.[50]

The definition of professional misconduct was examined in the context of the nursing profession in *Perez v An Bord Altranais*.[51] The applicant was employed as a staff nurse at a nursing home. The general allegation against her was that she persistently failed to acquire adequate knowledge of her duties and had consistent difficulty with basic nursing skills. A finding of professional misconduct was made against her and a decision was made to erase her name from the register of nurses. The applicant applied to the High Court pursuant to s 39 of the Nurses Act 1985 for cancellation of this decision.

In considering the concept of professional misconduct, O'Donovan J stated:

> In my view, the principles declared by Mr. Justice Keane in *O'Laoire's* case with regard to medical practitioners and by the Privy Council in *Doughty's* case with regard to dentists are equally applicable to the nursing profession so that 'professional misconduct', so far as a nurse is concerned, is a serious falling short, whether by omission or commission, of the standards of conduct expected among nurses and it is irrelevant that such misconduct may be attributable to honest mistake. In that regard, I would adopt the statement by Lord Hoffmann in the course of a judgment which he delivered in a case of *David Noel McCandless v. The General Medical Council* (the Weekly Law Reports, 16th February, 1996) that 'there is a duty to protect the public against the genially incompetent as well as the deliberate wrongdoers'.[52]

O'Donovan J drew on the Code of Professional Conduct along with evidence from members of the nursing profession in determining whether the allegations against the applicant were established. On the standard of proof, O'Donovan J stated:

> I am satisfied that the onus is on the respondent to prove every relevant fact, save those facts which have been admitted by the applicant ... Moreover, it has been conceded on behalf

---
[50] ibid.
[51] *Perez v An Bord Altranais* [2005] IEHC 400.
[52] ibid; *Dowling v an Bord Altranais* [2017] IEHC 62, [67].

of the respondent that the standard of proof required of the respondent is beyond any reasonable doubt.[53]

The decision against the nurse was upheld by O'Donovan J.[54]

Poor Professional Performance

Section 2 of the 2011 Act defines 'poor professional performance' as 'a failure by the nurse or midwife to meet the standards of competence (whether in knowledge and skill or the application of knowledge and skill or both) that can reasonably be expected of a registered nurse or registered midwife, as the case may be, carrying out similar work'.[55] This ground of complaint did not exist under the Nurses Act 1985. As previously noted, poor professional performance may also relate to matters that occurred outside the jurisdiction.

The definition of poor professional performance contained in the 2011 Act closely resembles the definition under the Medical Practitioners Act 2007. The interpretation of this concept was at issue in *Corbally v The Medical Council and Ors*.[56] In this case, a consultant surgeon sought to quash a finding of poor professional performance and the sanction imposed by way of judicial review. A key consideration was the extent to which a once-off error in a handwritten description of a proposed surgical procedure could form the basis for a finding of poor professional performance under the Medical Practitioners Act 2007. The Supreme Court was satisfied that the 2007 Act was not intended to make non-serious failings by a medical practitioner sanctionable.[57] If this was intended, then the Oireachtas should have used explicit language to bring this about. The Court was of the opinion that a 'seriousness' threshold applies in respect of poor professional performance. Such a threshold was not reached in *Corbally* and, accordingly, the appeal was dismissed.

Hardiman J indicated that a medical practitioner would not be found guilty of poor professional performance simply because they fell below the expected standard. On this point, Hardiman J noted that there are 'many forms of shortcoming' and these do not necessarily 'amount to a serious falling short of the expected

---

[53] *Perez v An Bord Altranais* [2005] IEHC 400.
[54] See also *Kudelska v An Bord Altranais* [2009] IEHC 68.
[55] Nurses and Midwives Act 2011, s 2.
[56] *Corbally v The Medical Council* [2015] 2 IR 304.
[57] ibid 304, [20].

standards of the profession'.[58] The gravity of the act or omission is therefore a pertinent factor to be taken into account in determining the correct course of action.[59] It may also be possible to demonstrate a pattern of poor professional performance through 'persistent and repeated' events.[60] However, it is not essential that a pattern be established where a single serious incident has taken place.[61]

Non-Compliance with a Code of Professional Conduct

The timing of the alleged non-compliance under this ground of complaint is particularly important. The non-compliance with a code of professional conduct must relate to the code in effect at the time the alleged event occurred. It follows that a new edition of the code that is published after the period of alleged non-compliance will not be directly relevant to the proceedings.

A Medical Disability

The term 'relevant medical disability' is defined in s 2 of the Nurses and Midwives Act 2011 as 'a physical or mental disability of the nurse or midwife (including addiction to alcohol or drugs) which may impair his or her ability to practise nursing or midwifery or a particular aspect thereof'.[62] This ground for complaint needs to be supported by expert evidence that indicates that at the time of the inquiry the relevant medical disability impaired the nurse or midwife's ability to practise. Section 24(5) of the 2011 Act provides for the establishment of a Health Committee, which will perform functions in support of registered nurses and midwives with relevant medical disabilities, as well as nurses and midwives who have given consent under s 65(1)(d). At the time of writing (September 2020), the Health Committee has not yet been established. If introduced, the Health Committee is likely to alter how this ground for complaint is addressed and may provide new avenues for complaint resolution.

A Failure to Comply with a Condition

A condition can be attached to the registration of a nurse or midwife per the Nurses and Midwives Act 2011. The imposition of a condition is provided for in ss 51, 52(4), 73, 74, 79(3), 81(3) of the 2011 Act. Conditions may be attached when the nurse or

---

[58] ibid 304, [41].
[59] ibid 304, [51].
[60] ibid 304, [162].
[61] ibid 304, [162].
[62] Nurses and Midwives Act 2011, s 2.

midwife is included on the register, following a fitness to practise inquiry, or upon restoration to the register. Conditions may be attached by the NMBI or by the High Court.

A Failure to Comply with an Undertaking or to Take Any Action to which Consent Was Given

Section 65 of the Nurses and Midwives Act 2011 is titled, 'If registered nurse or registered midwife consents to censure or remedial action, etc.'[63] This agreement may occur as part of a fitness to practise inquiry. A subsequent failure to comply with the agreement could therefore result in a further complaint based on this ground.

A Breach of the Provisions of the Nurses and Midwives Act 2011 or Any Rules or Regulations Made under the Act

This ground for complaint is relatively self-explanatory. In short, a complaint may be made in circumstances where there is a breach of the Nurses and Midwives Act 2011, or any rule or regulation made under the Act.

An Irregularity in Relation to the Custody, Prescription or Supply of a Controlled Drug under the Misuse of Drugs Acts 1977 or 1984 or Another Drug that Is Likely to Be Abused

The control, prescription, and supply of drugs is framed by legislation, rules, regulations, and professional guidance. In this respect, Chapter Seven on the administration of medicines provides a detailed discussion of the legal framework for medicines and prescriptive authority in this jurisdiction.

A Conviction in the State for an Offence Triable on Indictment

An offence triable on indictment is a more serious offence. In practice, it is an offence that can or must be tried before a judge and jury. In circumstances where a complaint comes within s 55(1)(i) of the 2011 Act, the PPC is to immediately refer the complaint to the Board. The Board is to consider the complaint and next steps are set out by s 55(6). Where the Board is of the opinion that the nature of the specific offence or the circumstances in which the offence was committed render the nurse or midwife permanently unfit to continue to practise nursing or midwifery, and it is in the public interest that the Board take action immediately, the Board shall

---

[63] ibid s 65.

decide under s 69(1) to cancel the nurse's or midwife's registration under s 69(1)(f). Section 55(6)(b) of the 2011 Act provides that 'in any other case, the Board shall refer the complaint back to the Preliminary Proceedings Committee and direct the Committee to deal with the complaint as if the complaint had never been so referred'.[64]

3.4.1 Administrative and Procedural Concerns

Prior to discussing the workings of the PPC and the FTPC it is important to outline some of the key principles that shape the disciplinary function of the NMBI. The exercise of a disciplinary function is framed by administrative law and principles of natural justice that seek to ensure fairness in the proceedings. These principles are expressed by the Latin phrases *audi alteram partem* and *nemo judex in causa sua*.

Audi alteram partem means 'hear the other side'. In the context of disciplinary proceedings, it means that no person should be judged without the opportunity for a fair hearing. In practice this will involve giving the nurse/midwife notice of the allegation as well as information relating to the potential consequences of the proceedings. The principle requires that a person be given an opportunity to respond to evidence against them. This must be a real opportunity for the nurse/midwife to respond so they may explain and potentially refute or mitigate the claim. Moreover, this explanation should be considered without bias or pre-determination, and should not be influenced by extraneous considerations.

The second principle is *nemo judex in causa sua*, which means that no person is judge in their own cause. It is essentially a rule against bias and requires that the people on the PPC and FTPC must be sufficiently removed from the issue under consideration. In this respect, they should not be in a direct management role or have a close relationship with the nurse or midwife who is the subject of the complaint. This need for impartiality on the part of PPC/FTPC members also extends to other parties who may be involved in the hearing such as members of the public. As discussed in the next section, conflict of interest checks must be carried out to ensure fairness in the proceedings.

The functions of the PPC and the FTPC are shaped by the Nurses and Midwives Act 2011. Legislation therefore shapes the remit

---

[64] ibid s 55(6)(b).

of the disciplinary functions, and to go beyond this would be to act *ultra vires*, to act beyond their powers or authority. A failure to adhere to the statutory powers leaves any decision open to challenge through judicial review. This is a process through which the High Court reviews and ensures that administrative bodies have made their decisions properly and in accordance with the law. Accordingly, the PPC and FTPC must be careful in exercising their powers under the 2011 Act.

3.4.2 Preliminary Proceedings Committee

The PPC is the starting point in the complaints process. The work of this Committee is guided by Part 7 of the Nurses and Midwives Act 2011. Section 55(3) of the 2011 Act provides some general guidance on the functioning of the PPC. It is recommended that the complainant be kept informed of all relevant decisions, and the PPC should act expeditiously and process complaints in a timely manner.[65] To assist the work of the PPC a 'case worker' may be appointed under s 56 of the 2011 Act. A person appointed to this role is to carry out tasks such as:

> (a) interviewing persons for the purposes of assessing the relevance or evidential value of information or documents they wish to give to the Preliminary Proceedings Committee;
>
> (b) interviewing persons as to the evidence they propose to give to the Preliminary Proceedings Committee;
>
> (c) recording, in writing or otherwise, the statements given and answers made by persons whilst being so interviewed;
>
> (d) reporting to the Preliminary Proceedings Committee on the results of those interviews;
>
> (e) requesting persons to provide the Preliminary Proceedings Committee with statements in writing concerning any matter relevant to the Committee's functions and examining statements given in response to the requests; and
>
> (f) providing the Preliminary Proceedings Committee with any other advice or assistance required in relation to the preparation of its reports.[66]

---

[65] ibid s 55(3).
[66] ibid s 56(3).

Once a complaint is submitted to the NMBI it is then assigned to a case officer who will assist the NMBI. The case officer will notify the complainant that the NMBI has received the complaint and may require the submission of documents referenced in the written complaint. The case officer will also send details of the complaint to the registered nurse or registered midwife who is the subject of the complaint and will invite them to respond within a defined timeframe, usually a six-week period.[67] The documentation is compiled by the case officer and is passed on to the PPC for consideration.

Membership of the PPC was discussed at section 3.2 of this chapter. The PPC is comprised of Board and non-Board members and includes nurses, midwives, and lay members who are not and never have been nurses or midwives in Ireland or any other country. There are 10 members of the PPC and they undertake regular training for this role. The *Guide to Fitness to Practise* sets out that 'Conflict of interest checks are carried out before every case is considered and if a member of the PPC has a conflict of interest, they do not participate in the consideration of the case.'[68]

In considering the complaint, the PPC can do one or more of the following:

> (a) require the complainant to verify, by affidavit or otherwise, anything contained in the complaint;
>
> (b) request the complainant to supply to the Committee, within a reasonable period specified in the notice, more information relating to the matter the subject of the complaint;
>
> (c) require that information requested under paragraph (b) be supplied by the complainant by means of a statutory declaration.[69]

If the complainant, without reasonable excuse, does not comply with the above requirements then the PPC may refuse to consider or further consider the complaint.[70]

---

[67] Nursing and Midwifery Board of Ireland, *A Guide to Fitness to Practise* (NMBI 2017).
[68] ibid 2.
[69] Nurses and Midwives Act 2011, s 57(4).
[70] ibid s 57(5).

Information may be supplied to the PPC by the nurse or midwife who is the subject of the complaint.[71] Depending on the seriousness of the complaint, the PPC may commission an expert report. If such a step is taken, then the report is to be sent to the nurse or midwife for further response.[72] The consideration of a complaint by the PPC may be delayed in limited circumstances such as where there is an on-going criminal investigation.[73]

Section 57(11) of the 2011 Act provides that where a complaint is withdrawn while being considered by the PPC, the Committee may, with the Board's agreement, decide to take no further action or proceed as if the complaint had not been withdrawn.[74] Under s 59, the PPC is to inform the Board where it of the opinion that:

(a) there is not sufficient cause to warrant further action being taken in relation to the complaint;

(b) the complaint should be referred to another body or authority or to a professional competence scheme; or

(c) the complaint is one that could be resolved by mediation or other informal means.[75]

It should be noted that, at the time of writing (September 2020), s 59(1)(b) insofar as it relates to a professional competence scheme has not been commenced. The responses available to the Board are set out in s 59(2) of the Nurses and Midwives Act 2011. The Board may elect to do one or more of the following:

(a) decide that no further action is to be taken in relation to the complaint;

(b) direct the Preliminary Proceedings Committee to refer the complainant to another body or authority;

(c) refer information in relation to the complaint in accordance with a co-operation agreement entered into under section 15;

(d) refer the complaint to a professional competence scheme;

---

[71] ibid s 57(7).
[72] Nursing and Midwifery Board of Ireland, *A Guide to Fitness to Practise* (NMBI 2017) 3.
[73] ibid.
[74] Nurses and Midwives Act 2011, s 57(11).
[75] ibid s 59(1).

(e) refer the complaint for resolution by mediation or other informal means; or

(f) if it considers it necessary to do so, direct that further action be taken under section 61.[76]

Section 61 provides that the PPC shall refer a complaint to the FTPC where the PPC is of the opinion that there is a prima facie case that warrants further action, or where directed to do so by the Board under s 59(2)(f). As noted earlier in this chapter, the PPC may refer a complaint to the FTPC even if the ground(s) on which it arrived at the opinion that there is a prima facie case differ from those on which the original complaint was based.[77] The grounds for the complaint should still come within s 55 of the 2011 Act.

Immediate Suspension of Registration

Section 58 of the Nurses and Midwives Act 2011 provides for the immediate suspension of registration in circumstances where it is necessary for the protection of the public. On receipt of a complaint or further information relating to the complaint, it is reviewed for the purposes of determining whether there are any immediate public protection issues if the nurse or midwife is permitted to continue practising.[78] The Board is to be made aware of any public protection issues that are identified as a matter of urgency. A Board meeting is then to be held and the relevant nurse or midwife, along with their representative, is invited to attend.[79] This process is described in the NMBI's *A Guide to Fitness to Practise*.

The Board may determine that it is appropriate to make an ex parte application to the High Court for 'an order to suspend the registration of a registered nurse or registered midwife, whether or not the nurse or midwife is the subject of a complaint'.[80] This application is heard in private unless the Court considers otherwise.[81] Section 58(3) of the 2011 Act provides that the Court may determine an application by:

---

[76] ibid s 59(2).
[77] ibid s 61(2).
[78] Nursing and Midwifery Board of Ireland, *A Guide to Fitness to Practise* (NMBI 2017) 6.
[79] ibid.
[80] Nurses and Midwives Act 2011, s 58(1).
[81] ibid s 58(2).

(a) making any order it considers appropriate, including an order directing the Board to suspend the registration of the registered nurse or registered midwife the subject of the application for the period specified in the order, and

(b) giving to the Board any direction that the Court considers appropriate.[82]

The order will usually remain in effect until the fitness to practise process has been completed. Where an order is granted by the High Court, it will also permit the NMBI to notify the employer, and make necessary amendments to the online register in respect of the nurse's or midwife's registration status.[83]

3.4.3 Fitness to Practise Inquiries

Part 8 of the Nurses and Midwives Act 2011 addresses complaints referred to the FTPC. The procedures of the FTPC are framed by NMBI guidance, although this is not legally binding and merely serves as a guide.

The FTPC is composed of nurses, midwives, and lay members. It includes both Board and non-Board members. Section 24(11) of the 2011 Act provides that there be at least one nurse and one midwife on each FTPC and at least one-third of the membership of the FTPC shall consist of persons who are either registered nurses or registered midwives.[84] *A Guide to Fitness to Practise* sets out that five members of the FTPC normally convene to hear a case; one nurse, one midwife, and three lay members, thereby providing a lay majority.[85] At least two Board members will sit on the FTPC. FTPC members complete training for this role and checks are carried out for a potential conflict of interest prior to each case. The FTPC member is not to participate in instances where a conflict is identified. One member of the panel acts as chairperson for the running of the FTPC. A legal assessor also sits with and advises the Committee on relevant law and procedure.

The question of potential conflict or bias arose in *O'Ceallaigh v An Bord Altranais*.[86] O'Ceallaigh sought to quash a decision of

---

[82] ibid s 58(3).
[83] Nursing and Midwifery Board of Ireland, *A Guide to Fitness to Practise* (NMBI 2017) 6.
[84] Nurses and Midwives Act 2011, s 24(11).
[85] Nursing and Midwifery Board of Ireland, *A Guide to Fitness to Practise* (NMBI 2017) 5.
[86] *O'Ceallaigh v An Bord Altranais* [2009] IEHC 470.

the FTPC as the chairperson of the Committee worked in the same hospital as one of the witnesses who gave evidence against the nurse. O'Ceallaigh argued that the chairperson could not be objective and that the professional relationship established an apprehension of objective bias. The High Court did not find that an apprehension of bias existed. The mere fact that the chairperson and the witness were employed at the same hospital was not sufficient and it would be necessary to determine if there was some other element or factor that would establish 'a reasonable apprehension that the outcome of the Inquiry could be affected'.[87] The Court recognised that in a country such as Ireland there will often be a small pool of experts to draw upon and 'the likelihood of some degree of familiarity between expert witnesses and professional nurses sitting as members of an inquiry is very high, if not inevitable'.[88]

In determining the presence of objective bias, *O'Cealligh* set out that it would need to be shown that 'the circumstances of that relationship and its connection with the proceedings are such that it has the capacity to influence the mind of the decision-maker'.[89] It also set out that, for objective bias to arise, the impugned relationship must display a 'community of interest' directly related to the subject matter of the proceedings.[90] This link is to be 'cogent and rational'.[91] There is a higher threshold to establish objective bias in circumstances where the relationship is between the chairperson and witness or some other third party to the proceedings.

Section 62 of the Nurses and Midwives Act 2011 addresses the responsibility of the chief executive officer to provide notice of the referral to, and hearing by, the FTPC. After the complaint is referred to the Committee, the chief executive officer shall, as soon as practicable but not later than 30 days after receipt of complaint, give notice in writing to the nurse or midwife who is the subject of the complaint. The notice is to inform the relevant person of the referral of the complaint to the FTPC; the opportunity for the nurse or midwife, or their representative, to be present and to defend the nurse or midwife at the hearing; and the option of requesting that some or all of the hearing be held in private.[92] The chief executive is to provide the nurse or midwife with details of the subject

---

[87] ibid 470, [39].
[88] ibid 470, [41].
[89] ibid 470, [37].
[90] ibid.
[91] ibid.
[92] Nurses and Midwives Act 2011, s 62(1).

matter of the inquiry as well as details relating to supporting evidence.[93] The default position is that such inquiries are to be held in public and, accordingly, it is possible for members of the public to attend. Nonetheless, where the inquiry is to be heard in private, the complainant will be permitted to attend should they choose to do so. Experts called upon as part of the inquiry may also be permitted to attend the full proceedings despite an inquiry being heard in private.

At the hearing, the chief executive officer, or any other person with leave of the Committee, shall present the evidence in support of the complaint; witness testimony is to be given under oath; and there is a right to cross-examine witnesses and call evidence in defence and reply.[94] The allegations against the nurse or midwife must be proven beyond reasonable doubt. This establishes a high threshold for the proof of an allegation. After the CEO or their legal representative has presented the case, then the nurse or midwife, or their legal representative, may make submissions to the Committee and/or call witnesses to give evidence. These witnesses may be cross-examined and the FTPC can ask questions of these witnesses.[95]

Section 64 of the Nurses and Midwives Act 2011 sets out the powers and protections relating to witnesses and evidence:

> For the purposes of an inquiry, the Fitness to Practise Committee has all the powers, rights and privileges that are vested in the Court or a judge of the Court on the occasion of an action and that relate to –
>
> > (a) enforcing the attendance of witnesses,
> >
> > (b) examining witnesses on oath or otherwise, and
> >
> > (c) compelling the production (including discovery) of records.[96]

The Committee may receive evidence given orally, by affidavit, or by way of a live video link, video recording, sound recording or any other mode of transmission.[97] *A Guide to Fitness to Practise*

---

[93] ibid s 62(2)(a).
[94] ibid s 63(4).
[95] Nursing and Midwifery Board of Ireland, 'Fitness to Practise Inquiries' <https://www.nmbi.ie/Complaints/Inquiries> accessed 7 July 2020.
[96] Nurses and Midwives Act 2011, s 64(1).
[97] ibid s 64(3).

indicates that evidence may be given via video-link in situations where the witness is living outside of Ireland or where it is not feasible to travel back to Ireland for the purposes of the hearing.[98]

As the FTPC has the powers, rights, and privileges as vested in the court, it follows that a witness is entitled to the same immunities and privileges as a witness appearing in court. A witness may commit an offence where they fail to attend the FTPC after being duly summoned.[99] A refusal to take an oath, produce records, or answer questions where lawfully required to do so by the Committee may also constitute an offence.[100] While attending the FTPC, a witness may commit an offence if they do anything that would constitute contempt of court in a court of law.[101]

Section 65 of the Nurses and Midwives Act 2011 permits the FTPC to request, with the agreement of the Board, the registered nurse or registered midwife who is the subject of the complaint to do one or more than one of the following:

> (a) if appropriate, undertake to not repeat the conduct the subject of the complaint;
>
> (b) pursuant to section 87(2), demonstrate her or his relevant competencies to the satisfaction of the Board;
>
> (c) take such steps as may be specified by the Board, which may include taking a course of education or training or gaining clinical practice experience for the express purpose of updating her or his skills and knowledge;
>
> (d) consent to undergo medical treatment; or
>
> (e) consent to being censured by the Board.[102]

If the registered nurse or registered midwife gives such an undertaking, then the inquiry into the complaint will be considered complete. It should be noted that at the time of writing (September 2020), s 65(1)(b) was still to be commenced. A failure to comply with the undertaking is itself a ground for complaint under s 55(1)(f) of the 2011 Act.

---

[98] Nursing and Midwifery Board of Ireland, *A Guide to Fitness to Practise* (NMBI 2017) 4.
[99] Nurses and Midwives Act 2011, s 64(5)(a).
[100] ibid s 64(5)(b).
[101] ibid s 64(5)(c).
[102] ibid s 65.

On completion of an inquiry, the FTPC is to submit a written report to the Board that details their findings. This report is to specify the nature of the complaint, the evidence presented, Committee findings, whether there is an undertaking or consent under s 65(1), and any other matters relating to the registered nurse or registered midwife as the Committee considers appropriate.[103] There should be clarity and sufficient detail in the submitted report. In *Brennan v An Bord Altranais*, a midwife sought to challenge the decision of the Board on a number of grounds.[104] The first ground of challenge was that the FTPC 'failed to provide sufficient reasons for its findings against the applicant in its report'.[105] On this point, Dunne J held:

> In the first instance, it is necessary to provide reasons so that the party affected can consider those reasons and go on to make appropriate submissions to the Board or Council as the case may be in relation to the reasons for the findings. The Board itself must have the reasons for the findings in order to consider whether it should confirm the findings of the Fitness to Practice Committee. Thirdly it is necessary to have the reasons for a decision in order to enable an applicant to consider whether judicial review proceedings may be appropriate.[106]

3.4.4 Measures Taken Following the Fitness to Practise Inquiry

Part 9 of the Nurses and Midwives Act 2011 addresses the measures taken with regard to registered nurses and registered midwives following the FTPC report. The Board, after receiving and considering the report, may determine that one or more of the following sanctions be imposed on the nurse or midwife:

(a) an advice or admonishment, or a censure, in writing;

(b) a censure in writing and a fine not exceeding €2,000;

(c) the attachment of conditions to the nurse's or midwife's registration, including restrictions on the practice of nursing or midwifery that may be engaged in by the nurse or midwife;

---

[103] ibid s 67.
[104] *Brennan v An Bord Altranais* [2010] IEHC 193.
[105] ibid.
[106] ibid.

(d) the transfer of the nurse's or midwife's registration to another division;

(e) the suspension of the nurse's or midwife's registration for a specified period;

(f) the cancellation of the nurse's or midwife's registration from the register of nurses and midwives or a division of that register;

(g) a prohibition from applying for a specified period for the restoration of the nurse's or midwife's registration in the register of nurses and midwives or a division.[107]

These sanctions have a meaningful public facing role. They are not primarily intended as a punishment for the nurse or midwife but can instead be seen as a tool to protect the public and serve the public interest.[108] Rather than weakening any public perception, the imposition of appropriate sanctions can facilitate greater public confidence in the nursing and midwifery professions. The identification of an appropriate sanction can be challenging but should be guided by factors including proportionality; outcome; submissions and mitigating or aggravating factors; insight on the part of the registrant; evidence of observance of the Code of Professional Conduct; references and testimonials; and previous Committee findings and sanctions.[109]

The Board is required to notify the nurse or midwife after it has decided to impose a sanction. The notification should include the nature of the sanction, date on which the decision was made, and the reasons for the imposition of the sanction.[110] The NMBI's *Guidance on Sanctions* recommends that the reasons for the sanction(s) should also include reasons for the level of any fine imposed, conditions imposed, any period of suspension, and any period of prohibition from applying for restoration of registration.[111]

---

[107] Nurses and Midwives Act 2011, s 69.
[108] Nursing and Midwifery Board of Ireland, *Guidance on Sanctions* (NMBI 2018) 4.
[109] Nursing and Midwifery Board of Ireland, *Guidance on Sanctions* (NMBI 2018).
[110] Nurses and Midwives Act 2011, s 71.
[111] Nursing and Midwifery Board of Ireland, *Guidance on Sanctions* (NMBI 2018) 19.

The plaintiffs in *Dowling v An Bord Altranais* sought cancellation of the An Bord Altranais decision that their names be erased from the register of nurses.[112] It was argued that the Board failed to take account of a number of distinct mitigating factors when determining what sanction to impose. Mitigating factors included the lapse of time, that the incident was a once-off, that the hospital had a lack of stated policy for unexpected deaths, and the insight displayed by both nurses at the Inquiry as regards the inadequacy of the documentation drawn up in the aftermath of the person's death.[113] The Board's decision did not explicitly refer to these factors but included a line which stated: 'having considered submissions made on your behalf by [your legal representative] to include mitigating factors …'[114] This led Ní Raifeartaigh J to state that 'the generalised manner in which the mitigating factors were dealt with in its letter may be indicative of inadequate weight having been placed on these factors'.[115] Having further considered the treatment of the various factors, Ní Raifeartaigh J concluded that 'the Court cannot be satisfied that the Board properly approached the matter of sanction with adequate regard to the various mitigating factors'.[116] The Court quashed the decision and directed the Board to reconsider the sanction in light of the comments made in the judgment relating to sentencing, and, in particular, issues of mitigation.

A registered nurse or registered midwife may appeal the decision to impose a sanction to the Court. This should be done within 21 days of receiving notice of the Board's decision. An appeal may involve a full rehearing of the case in the High Court. Upon hearing the appeal, the Court may:

> i. confirm the decision the subject of the application, or
>
> ii. quash that decision and substitute such other decision as the Court considers appropriate.[117]

The Court may also 'give the Board such directions as the Court considers appropriate and direct how the costs of the appeal are to be borne'.[118]

---

[112] *Dowling v An Bord Altranais* [2017] IEHC 62.
[113] ibid 62, [26].
[114] ibid 62, [77].
[115] ibid 62, [78].
[116] ibid 62, [92].
[117] Nurses and Midwives Act 2011, s 73(3)(a).
[118] ibid s 73(3)(b).

Should a registered nurse or registered midwife decide not to appeal a sanction within the 21-day period then the decision must be confirmed by the High Court pursuant to s 74 of the Nurses and Midwives Act 2011. Such an application may be made on an ex parte basis, meaning that it is an application brought by one party absent any other parties. On hearing the application, the High Court shall confirm the decision unless it sees good reason not to do so.[119] The interpretation of 'good reason' was addressed by Kelly P in *The Medical Council v MAGA*[120] and *The Nursing and Midwifery Board of Ireland v OCM*.[121] These cases clarified the role of the High Court in dealing with applications by the IMC and the NMBI to confirm sanctions. These bodies have a defined statutory role and, in light of this, the jurisdiction of the High Court is limited in deciding whether to confirm a sanction. In *MAGA*, Kelly P stated:

> The fact that I might take a different view as to sanction does not at all enter into consideration. That is because I am not exercising an appellate jurisdiction on the merits. The questions I have to ask myself is has there been any procedural impropriety here and there clearly has not. Has there been any failure to adhere to the rules of natural and constitutional justice and clearly there has not. The third question, and this is the only pertinent one, is can it be said that the decision arrived at here is so unreasonable as to warrant the intervention of the court. If the court comes to the conclusion that the decision here is so unreasonable as to warrant its intervention then there is 'good reason' to depart from it.[122]

In short, the High Court will concentrate on the adherence to procedural norms, the requirements of natural and constitutional justice, and whether the Board's decision is such that no reasonable Board could have decided. Both *MAGA* and *OCM* illustrate that the High Court will not easily intervene or encroach on the jurisdiction of the IMC or the NMBI in the context of disciplinary proceedings and sanctions imposed. Once a decision is confirmed or given by the High Court, there is a duty on the Board to notify the registered nurse or registered midwife of compliance with such decisions pursuant to s 76 of the Nurses and Midwives Act 2011.

---

[119] ibid s 74(3).
[120] *The Medical Council v MAGA* [2016] IEHC 779.
[121] *Nursing and Midwifery Board of Ireland v OCM* [2016] IEHC 780.
[122] *The Medical Council v MAGA* [2016] IEHC 779, [31].

Section 79 of the Nurses and Midwives Act 2011 provides for the restoration of registration which has been cancelled. The Board may decide to restore registration if:

> (a) the nurse or midwife has requested the Board to make the decision and has paid the appropriate fee required at the time of the request for restoration,
>
> (b) the nurse or midwife is not prohibited under this Part from applying for restoration of the registration,
>
> (c) the nurse or midwife has been given an opportunity to make an oral or written submission to the Board,
>
> (d) the Board has considered any submission made under paragraph (c) and the criteria specified in the rules for the restoration of registration pursuant to this section, and
>
> (e) after considering all relevant facts, the Board considers it appropriate to make the decision.[123]

If a decision to restore registration is made, the Board may deem it appropriate to attach conditions to the nurse's or midwife's registration.[124] Notice of restoration and/or conditions should be given in writing as soon as is practicable by the Board. Similarly, where the Board refuses to restore a nurse's or midwife's registration, written notice should be provided as soon as is practicable. This notice should state the decision, the date on which the decision was made, and the reasons for the decision.[125] It is also open to the Board under s 80 of the 2011 Act to remove all or any conditions attached to the registration of a registered nurse or registered midwife.[126]

---

[123] Nurses and Midwives Act 2011, s 79(2).
[124] ibid s 79(3).
[125] ibid s 79(5).
[126] ibid s 80.

Chapter 4
Negligent Practice in Nursing

Introduction 67
Gross Negligence Manslaughter 68
The Law of Torts..69
The Tort of Negligence 70
The Duty of Care 71
The Standard of Care..73
    Dunne (an Infant) v National Maternity Hospital..............78
Causation..82
    Factual Causation 83
    Legal Causation...86
Harm 88
Liability of a Healthcare Facility 90
    Direct Liability 90
    Enterprise Liability 91
    Vicarious Liability 91

4.0 Introduction

Negligence is often the first topic that comes to mind when a person thinks about the relationship between law and medicine. For the nurse or midwife, a claim of negligence can be an extremely stressful experience. It has consequences for the personal and professional life of the healthcare professional, and places the actions of the healthcare professional under intense scrutiny. In addition to legal scrutiny, there may also be media coverage of the medical negligence claim. Such scrutiny and attention are understandable as the compensation paid out annually by the HSE for medical negligence is well in excess of €100 million.[1]

The legal action of negligence forms part of the 'law of torts'. This chapter will introduce and outline this area of law. In essence, torts are civil actions where an injured party is seeking compensation for a wrong. In addition to negligence, there are torts based on

---

[1] National Incident Management System, 'PQ 26517–19 – Hospital Groups Payments' <https://data.oireachtas.ie/ie/oireachtas/debates/questions/supportingDocumentation/2019-06-25_pq454-25-06-2019_en.pdf> accessed 3 July 2020.

trespass against a person, false imprisonment, and nuisance. Trespass against a person will be touched on again in chapter 5. The law on negligence is a substantial topic and is the subject of many textbooks and research monographs.[2] An exhaustive treatment of the subject is therefore beyond the scope of this work. This chapter will instead guide the reader through some of the key elements of negligence, thereby equipping the nurse with the requisite knowledge. Sections will address the duty of care, the standard of care, causation, and various forms of liability. Prior to this, the chapter will briefly discuss the concept of gross negligence manslaughter.

4.1 Gross Negligence Manslaughter

A healthcare professional may face a charge of gross negligence manslaughter where they have been negligent in their duties to the extent that it caused the death of a patient. In the United Kingdom there have been numerous prosecutions of healthcare professionals for gross negligence manslaughter.[3] Moreover, it would seem that the rate of prosecution and conviction has risen in recent years. This can be contrasted with the position in Ireland where a healthcare professional has never been convicted of gross negligence manslaughter.

The objective test for gross negligence manslaughter was set out in The *People (AG) v Dunleavy* where the accused, a taxi driver, drove his unlit car on the wrong side of the road, resulting in the death of a cyclist.[4] The Court of Criminal Appeal held that a conviction for gross negligence manslaughter will not arise unless it is proved that the negligence was of a very high degree and involved a high degree of risk or likelihood of substantial personal injury to others. This offence was the subject of review by the Law Reform Commission, which recommended retaining the existing test.[5]

---

[2] Bryan ME McMahon and William Binchy, *Law of Torts* (4th edn, Bloomsbury 2013); Rachel Mulheron, *Medical Negligence: Non-Patient and Third Party Claims* (Routledge 2010); Vivienne Harpwood, *Medicine, Malpractice and Misapprehensions* (Routledge-Cavendish 2007).
[3] Jo Samanta and Ash Samanta, 'Gross Negligence Manslaughter and the Delivery of Healthcare: A Time for Change?' (2019) 26(5) European Journal of Health Law 389.
[4] *The People (Attorney General) v Dunleavy* [1948] IR 95.
[5] Law Reform Commission, *Report on Homicide: Murder and Involuntary Manslaughter* (LRC 87–2008).

There is a sense that the offence of gross negligence manslaughter is somewhat vague and uncertain. It may appear unfair where the cause of the failure can be tied to institutional failures and weaknesses over which the individual has little control. While there has not yet been a conviction in Ireland, this does not mean that such a charge will not be brought in the future. Nevertheless, the reality is that the healthcare professional is far more likely to be the subject of or party to a civil claim for negligence rather than a criminal charge.

4.2 The Law of Torts

The law of torts is concerned with the private relationship and interaction between individuals. McMahon and Binchy define tort as 'a civil wrong (other than a breach of contract or a breach of trust) for which the normal remedy is an action for unliquidated damages'.[6] The wrong may result in a personal injury, damage to property, or financial detriment. A claim in torts is not brought by the State, but is instead brought by the injured party who may seek damages from the wrongdoer, known as the tortfeasor. This is monetary compensation for the wrong suffered. However, it is not the only remedy that may be available. An injured party may also seek a remedy in the form of an injunction that would prohibit the continuance of the wrongful behaviour.

Forms of tort include negligence; trespass to the person/to land/to goods; false imprisonment; breach of a statutory duty; nuisance; defamation; and malicious prosecution. There are three categories into which torts can be divided: intentional, negligent, and strict liability. An intentional tort occurs where the defendant knows, or should know, that his/her actions would bring about some form of interference with another party. Negligent torts arise where the defendant fails to exercise appropriate care or falls short of the standards that are expected of such a person. Strict liability torts arise where liability will attach regardless of whether we would consider the defendant to be blameworthy in a traditional sense. For instance, the Liability for Defective Products Act 1991 provides that a producer would be liable in damages in tort for damage caused wholly or partly by a defect in his product.[7] It is not necessary to prove any form of malevolent intent on the part of the defendant in such a case.

---

[6] McMahon and Binchy (n 2) [1.09].
[7] Liability for Defective Products Act 1991, s 2(1).

4.3 The Tort of Negligence

In *Blyth v The Company of Proprietors of the Birmingham Waterworks*, negligence was described as:

> the omission to do something which a reasonable man, guided upon those considerations which ordinarily regulate the conduct of human affairs, would do, or doing something which a prudent and reasonable man would not do.[8]

Negligence can arise through the acts or omissions of a nurse or midwife. It is a failure to deliver treatment or care of an expected standard such that it causes loss or damage to another person. To succeed in an action for negligence there are several elements that must be proven, namely:

1. a duty of care must be established;

2. there must be a breach of the required standard of care;

3. there must be actual loss or damage to the recognised interests of the plaintiff; and

4. there must be a sufficiently close causal connection between the conduct and the resulting injury to the plaintiff.[9]

The duty of care is an obligation on one party to take appropriate care so as to prevent harm or injury to another party. In general, it is the plaintiff who must prove that the defendant was negligent. The sole exception is where the negligence of the defendant is evident for all. In such a case the negligence is presumed and the defendant must rebut the presumption. This is the principle of *res ipsa loquitur* (the thing speaks for itself).

Familiarity with each element listed above is not simply about the tort of negligence but it allows the nurse to regulate his/her conduct in a wider setting. For instance, a nurse must be aware of when a duty of care arises and to whom such a duty is owed. The nurse must also be aware of the standard of care against which their conduct is to be judged.

---

[8] *Blyth v The Company of Proprietors of the Birmingham Waterworks* (1956) 11 Ex Ch 781, 784.
[9] McMahon and Binchy (n 2) [5.02].

4.4 The Duty of Care

Lord Esher in *Le Lievre v Gould* stated that:

> the question of liability for negligence cannot arise at all until it has been established that the man who has been negligent owed some duty to the person who seeks to make him liable for his negligence. A man is entitled to be as negligent as he pleases towards the whole world if he owes no duty to them.[10]

In short, there is no universal duty of care. In order to bring an action in negligence the plaintiff must first show that a duty of care was owed to them. Where no such duty exists an action will fail. It therefore has the effect of defining the boundaries of liability. Originally these boundaries were tightly circumscribed. The concept has, however, been developed by the courts over time and this has given way to a more expansive concept.

A foundational case in the development of the test for a duty of care was *Donoghue v Stevenson*.[11] This House of Lords decision involved a woman who suffered from shock and severe gastro-enteritis after consuming a bottle of ginger-beer. The woman had drunk a portion of the ginger-beer by the time her friend poured out the remaining contents of the bottle, which included a decomposed snail. The bottle was made of dark opaque glass and it had not been possible to see the snail before pouring out the contents. The question arose as to whether an action could be brought against the manufacturer of the ginger-beer. This was by no means a clear-cut decision, although the plaintiff was ultimately successful. The majority based their decision on the principle that a duty of care is owed to your 'neighbour'. This is not a geographical or location-based test as Lord Aiken explained:

> You must take reasonable care to avoid acts or omissions which you can reasonably foresee would be likely to injure your neighbour. Who then in law is my neighbour? The answer seems to be persons who are so closely and directly affected by my act that I ought reasonably to have them in contemplation as being so affected when I am directing my mind to the acts or omissions which are called in question.

---

[10] *Le Lievre v Gould* [1893] 1 QB 491, 497.
[11] *Donoghue v Stevenson* [1932] AC 562.

The interpretation of the neighbour principle and the test to be applied was refined by the courts over time. In Ireland, the test for imposing a duty of care was reassessed in *Glencar Explorations v Mayo County Council*.[12]

In *Glencar Explorations* Keane CJ advanced a four-step test for a duty of care. This test is to consider:

1. reasonable foreseeability;

2. proximity of the relationship;

3. countervailing public policy considerations; and

4. the justice and reasonableness of imposing a duty of care.

In some subsequent cases this has been treated as three steps by combining policy considerations with the requirement of justice and reasonableness.[13]

Foreseeability looks at whether the injury or damage was reasonably foreseeable. If a person can reasonably foresee that their conduct is likely to injure another person then this is a factor in favour of recognising a duty of care.

Proximity is viewed as something beyond foreseeability as it considers the nature of the relationship and connection between the parties. It is not a geographical assessment.

For a duty of care to be imposed it must be just and reasonable to do so. McMahon and Binchy suggest that the intent behind this is 'for courts to hesitate long and hard before imposing a duty of care, even where the facts can plausibly be characterized as involving foreseeability and proximity of relationship'.[14] This step tends to involve a broader assessment that ties in with concerns for public policy and public interest.

Nursing and the Duty of Care

In traditional healthcare settings there will be little question about whether a duty of care exists. The conduct of the nurse will clearly have an effect on the patient. It is therefore reasonably foreseeable

---

[12] *Glencar Explorations v Mayo County Council* [2002] 1 IR 84.
[13] McMahon and Binchy (n 2) [6.52].
[14] ibid [6.124].

that the nurse's conduct could potentially pose a risk of injury or harm. In effect, the nurse/patient relationship is such that a nurse owes a duty of care to the patient.

There are of course instances in which the clinical expertise of the nurse will be called on outside of a traditional healthcare setting. The nurse may be called on by friends and family for medical advice or may be present at the scene of an accident or emergency. The duty of care can arise regardless of whether the nurse is being paid or not. In providing medical advice or care, the nurse is acting in a manner that gives rise to a duty of care. However, absent a pre-existing relationship, there is no duty to stop at the scene of an emergency so as to provide first aid. If a nurse does stop and offer help then he/she must satisfy the requisite standard of care, as discussed in the next section.

4.5 The Standard of Care

Once it is established that a duty of care exists, we then turn to consider what standard of care is to be provided and how the defendant has conducted themselves according to this standard. In general, this standard is based on the idea of the 'reasonable person'. This is a hypothetical person to whom we ascribe a certain level of understanding, intelligence and foresight. This was discussed in *Kirby v Burke & Holloway*[15] where Gavan Duffy J stated:

> ... the foundation of liability at common law for tort is blameworthiness as determined by the average standards of the community; a man fails at his peril to conform to these standards. Therefore, while loss from an accident generally lies where it falls, a defendant cannot plead an accident if, treated as a man of ordinary intelligence and foresight, he ought to have foreseen the danger which caused injury to his plaintiff.[16]

The law does not require perfection on the part of the defendant. This would set a standard that would be all but impossible to satisfy. Instead, the person's conduct is to be judged against the standard expected of a reasonable person. It is the Court that determines whether or not this standard has been met.

---

[15] *Kirby v Burke & Holloway* [1944] IR 207.
[16] ibid 207, 214.

In the context of medical treatment and care, it would make little sense to compare the conduct of the healthcare professional against the objective standard of the reasonable person. Medical treatment and care involve training, knowledge and experience that is not possessed by the ordinary person. Accordingly, the expected standard of care is different and rules of professional negligence have been developed by the courts. The conduct of a professional is judged against the practice and standards of their profession. It follows that the professional person is compared against other individuals within that profession. The concept of a 'profession' and 'professional' negligence has resulted in the courts drawing a distinction between various healthcare practitioners. The status of the nursing profession was considered in *Kelly v St Laurence's Hospital*.[17]

The Supreme Court in *Kelly v St Laurence's Hospital* applied a general negligence test instead of that which applies to professionals. The plaintiff, Kelly, was admitted to the defendant hospital where he was taken off all medication, the purpose of which action was to accurately diagnose the source of his medical condition. No special instructions were issued as to particular nursing care for him, though the medical and nursing staff dealing with him were made aware of his history and the condition from which he suffered. At some point during the night, the plaintiff left the ward, crossed a corridor, and entered a ladies' toilet. He proceeded to climb through a window in the toilet, leading him to fall to the ground 20 feet below and sustaining extensive physical injuries. The hospital appealed a finding of negligence made in the High Court.

In the Supreme Court Finlay CJ stated that:

> I am satisfied, however, that as appears from the form of the question left to the jury, the propriety of which is not challenged, that this is more precisely a case where the issue is one of nursing care and attention than it is of one where the allegation of negligence is to be categorised as negligence in medical treatment. Undoubtedly, the extent and nature of the care and attention which a reasonably careful hospital would have afforded to the Plaintiff whilst he was an in-patient thereon the 15th July 1981 and in particular, of course, the question as to whether a reasonably careful hospital staff would have arranged for a person to attend him when he left the ward in the middle of the night to go to the toilet,

---

[17] *Kelly v St Laurence's Hospital* [1989] ILRM 437.

depends to a very large extent on the foreseeability from a medical point of view of the risk that the Plaintiff would, if allowed to go unattended to the toilet in the middle of the night, injure himself in some way.

That does not, however, seem to me to make this a case solely to be tested by the standards which have been accepted by the courts with regard to allegations of negligence in treatment afforded to their patients by professional medical people.[18]

Similarly, Walsh J noted:

> What was in issue in this case was not a question of medical negligence in the strict sense as arose in the case of *O'Donovan v The Cork County Council*. What was in issue was the adequacy of the system and of care for the plaintiff by the hospital authorities while he was in their hospital. There is no question of any allegation of negligence against the consultant who treated the plaintiff while he was in hospital. It is also clear from the evidence given by the consultant that he, in effect, was distancing himself from any responsibility for the way the nurses in question and the rest of the nursing staff carried out their duties, and, as he pointed out in his evidence, in effect, that it was up to them to know their patient and to give him the care appropriate to his condition and his case history and, above all, appropriate to the reason why he was in the ward in question.[19]

The approach in *Kelly* is not to suggest that the nurse's conduct will be assessed against an ordinary person without any particular skills or training. Instead, the standard of a reasonable skilled nurse will apply. The more deferential test for professional negligence would, however, not be applied to nurses in Ireland. Such an approach seems to strike at the reputation and standing of the nursing profession. In this regard, it is perhaps best to view this decision in light of nursing education and practice as it existed in the 1980s.

During the 1980s, the student nurse was a salaried service provider who had a dual role of student and employee. The three-year training programme consisted of 28 weeks of theory, which took

---

[18] ibid 437, 440.
[19] ibid 437, 444.

place in hospital-based Schools of Nursing.[20] The remaining time was spent in clinical practice. Research indicated that this training system produced nurses who were unquestioning and passive.[21] This created a lack of professional autonomy and resulted in deference to other healthcare professionals. McCarthy suggested the system:

> neither challenged the other health care professions nor made demands on administration. It could only have existed in a world where women were prepared to be so self-denying, hard working and so amenable to discipline.[22]

Subsequent changes in education and training were motivated by developments in EU law[23] as well as by steps taken by bodies such as An Bord Altranais.[24] In the mid 1990s a Diploma in General Nursing was established by Galway University Hospital School of Nursing in conjunction with NUIG.[25] This led to greater connections with third-level institutions and universities. A watershed moment occurred with the establishment of the Commission on Nursing in 1997. One of the key recommendations made by the Commission was that the Minister for Health and Children 'facilitate the transition of pre-registration nursing education into third-level institutes at degree level'.[26] The first degree pre-registration nurses commenced their studies in 2002. Since that time, nurse education has continued to expand with a range of undergraduate, postgraduate and PhD programmes on offer.

On the issue of professional negligence and nursing, McMahon and Binchy stated:

---

[20] Sarah L Condell, 'Changes in the Professional Role of Nurses in Ireland: 1980–1997' (The Stationery Office 1998) 18.
[21] ibid.
[22] Geraldine McCarthy, 'Nursing and the Health Services' in Joseph Robins (ed), *Reflections on Health* (Institute of Public Administration 1997) 178.
[23] Council Directive 89/595 EC of 10 October 1989 amending Directive 77/452/EEC concerning the mutual recognition of diplomas, certificates and other evidence of the formal qualifications of nurses responsible for general care, including measures to facilitate the effective exercise of the right of establishment and freedom to provide services, and amending Directive 77/453/EEC concerning the coordination of provisions laid down by law, regulation or administrative action in respect of the activities of nurses responsible for general care.
[24] An Bord Altranais, *The Future of Nurse Education and Training in Ireland* (ABA 1994).
[25] Condell (n 20) 19.
[26] The Commission on Nursing, *Report of the Commission on Nursing: A Blueprint for the Future* (The Stationery Office 1998) [5.19].

With changing social attitudes as well as the transformation of the education process and work responsibilities of nurses, there is a greater acceptance that nurses exercise true professional judgment and should be judged by the professional standard like their other medical colleagues.[27]

Mills and Mulligan also reflected on the continued application of *Kelly v St Laurence's Hospital* and offered the following comment:

> One possibility is that the decision that held that nurses were not professionals must now be regarded as anachronistic, rooted in an old-fashioned mind-set or predicated on the non-university-based education that previously characterised nursing training. It seems on balance that a course of study conferring a formal qualification in a particular skill that, first, the public regards as a 'special' skill not possessed by the majority of persons and which, secondly, is used to achieve specific outcomes (such as health gain) would make an individual a 'professional'.[28]

Kelly was subsequently considered in the High Court case of *Ava Kiernan v Health Service Executive*.[29] The plaintiff brought a case in negligence for failing to detect hydrocephalus before it caused significant neurological damage. The central issue was whether the public health nurse should have been alert to the plaintiff's developing situation and taken action. Cross J could not see any reason why the professional standards of a public health nurse should be assessed differently from the professional standards of doctors or solicitors. In line with the points noted earlier, Cross J underlined the changed standards of education and increased professional autonomy of the nursing profession:

> To apply a different and lesser obligations to a nurse than a doctor is to adopt what, in this day, seems to me to be to be an outdated view dating from a time nursing was a Vocational rather than a Professional qualification, and to revert to an age in which nurse had little, if any, professional autonomy and deferred entirely to the directions of doctors.
>
> There may be a significant number of instants in which a nurse is acting in accordance with a prescribed system in

---

[27] McMahon and Binchy (n 2) [14.212].
[28] Simon Mills and Andrea Mulligan, *Medical Law in Ireland* (3rd edn, Bloomsbury 2017) 219.
[29] *Ava Kiernan v Health Service Executive* [2015] IEHC 141.

which the alleged negligence is, in effect, the negligence of the system rather than of the individual, but in this case, I hold that the standard to be assessed is that standard appropriate to medical professional, as set out in *Dunne v. National Maternity Hospital*.

Public health nurse R. was acting as an autonomous public health nurse professional and she had professional standards to maintain and her obligations were to perform to the standard of a public health nurse. Any fault, in a legal sense, must be a fault within the *Dunne* principles.[30]

A robust argument can therefore be made that the decision in *Kelly* should not be applied in future decisions about the nursing profession and the rules of clinical negligence.

4.5.1 *Dunne (an Infant) v National Maternity Hospital*

Dunne (an Infant) v National Maternity Hospital is the leading case of medical negligence in Ireland. This case involved the delivery of twins and questions were raised about the management of the woman's labour and the plaintiff's birth. One of the twins was born dead while the other child suffered irreversible brain damage as a result of which, in the language of the judgment, he is 'a mentally handicapped spastic quadriplegic'.[31] In the High Court, the plaintiff was awarded damages of £1,039,334. The defendants appealed against the finding of liability and the assessment of damages. Finlay CJ in the Supreme Court set out a number of principles that can be drawn on to determine whether a practitioner has behaved reasonably:

1. The true test for establishing negligence in diagnosis or treatment on the part of a medical practitioner is whether he has been proved to be guilty of such failure as no medical practitioner of equal specialist or general status and skill would be guilty of if acting with ordinary care.

2. If the allegation of negligence against a medical practitioner is based on proof that he deviated from a general and approved practice, that will not establish negligence unless it is also proved that the course he did take was one which no medical practitioner of like specialisation and skill would

---

[30] ibid 141, [8.4]–[8.7].
[31] *Dunne (an Infant) v National Maternity Hospital* [1989] ILRM 735, 735.

have followed had he been taking the ordinary care required from a person of his qualifications.

3. If a medical practitioner charged with negligence defends his conduct by establishing that he followed a practice which was general, and which was approved of by his colleagues of similar specialisation and skill, he cannot escape liability if in reply the plaintiff establishes that such practice has inherent defects which ought to be obvious to any person giving the matter due consideration.

4. An honest difference of opinion between doctors as to which is the better of two ways of treating a patient does not provide any ground for leaving a question to the jury as to whether a person who has followed one course rather than the other has been negligent.

5. It is not for a jury (or for a judge) to decide which of two alternative courses of treatment is in their (or his) opinion preferable, but their (or his) function is merely to decide whether the course of treatment followed, on the evidence, complied with the careful conduct of a medical practitioner of like specialisation and skill to that professed by the defendant.

6. If there is an issue of fact, the determination of which is necessary for the decision as to whether a particular medical practice is or is not general and approved within the meaning of these principles, that issue must in a trial held with a jury be left to the determination of the jury.[32]

Finlay CJ went on to state:

> Fully to understand these principles and their application to any particular set of facts, it is, I believe, helpful to set out certain broad parameters which would appear to underline their establishment.
>
> The development of medical science and the supreme importance of that development to humanity makes it particularly undesirable and inconsistent with the common good that doctors should be obliged to carry out their professional duties under frequent threat of unsustainable legal claims.

---

[32] ibid 735, 745–746.

> The complete dependence of patients on the skill and care of their medical attendants and the gravity from their point of view of a failure in such care, makes it undesirable and unjustifiable to accept as a matter of law a lax or permissive standard of care for the purpose of assessing what is and is not medical negligence.
>
> In developing the legal principles outlined and in applying them to the facts of each individual case, the courts must constantly seek to give equal regard to both of these considerations.[33]

The principles set out in Dunne have been followed in subsequent cases such as *Collins v Mid-Western Health Board*[34] and *Shuitt v Mylotte*.[35] A clearer picture of these principles emerges through discussion of some of the key elements.

General and Approved Practice

Finlay CJ clarified this point by stating that general and approved practice need not be universal but must be approved of and adhered to by a substantial number of reputable practitioners holding the relevant specialist or general qualifications. The practice should be judged according to the standards in place at the time the negligent event occurred. Simply because medical practice progresses does not change what had been general and approved practice at the time.

Equal Specialisation

Principles 1 and 2 both refer to other medical practitioners of like specialisation and skill. The conduct of a healthcare professional is therefore compared with a comparable professional acting with ordinary care. The defendant is not absolved of liability simply by finding another healthcare professional who would have acted in a similar manner, as the test for ordinary care must still be satisfied.[36]

Changes in nurse education were noted earlier in this section. There are a wide range of post-registration courses that allow the nurse to augment their knowledge and skills. Such training

---

[33] ibid 735, 746.
[34] *Collins v Mid-Western Health Board* [2000] 2 IR 154.
[35] *Shuitt v Mylotte* [2006] IEHC 89.
[36] McMahon and Binchy (n 2) [14.11].

would need to be accounted for in examining alleged negligence. For instance, a nurse with an MSc in Gerontological Nursing should be compared with a nurse of equal specialist skill in this area of care.

Deviation from a General and Approved Practice

Deviation from accepted practice constitutes negligence if no healthcare professional of like specialisation and skill would have so deviated if taking appropriate ordinary care. This does not mean that there is a single correct course of action in each instance. Mills and Mulligan suggest that 'the test is not really one of general *and* approved practice, but rather one of general *or* approved practice'.[37] A practice may not be general in that only a small number of professionals apply a particular approach, nonetheless the practice may be supported by a reputable body of opinion and evidence such that it can be considered 'approved'. To depart from such a practice requires a reasonable justification.

General and approved practice may be set out in the likes of policies, procedures, guidelines, and standards. There may, however, be circumstances in which it would not be appropriate to follow such guidance. This is likely to be a very rare occurrence and would require detailed consideration. On this point, Diamond states:

> Clearly, advice from others would be required to ascertain whether rigid compliance with the procedure would be justified. The courts require a reasonable standard to be followed, a standard that would be supported by competent professional opinion and practice. Where the practitioner decides that circumstances justify a modification of the usual procedure, it is essential that they record exactly why the usual practice was not followed.[38]

If a policy or similar guidance document is not appropriate for clinical practice and patient care then it should be addressed as soon as possible. A revised document can then be produced, which takes account of scientific opinion and is in line with reasonable standards of care.

---

[37] Mills and Mulligan (n 28) 223.
[38] Richard Griffith and Iwan Dowie, *Dimond's Legal Aspects of Nursing: A Definitive Guide to Law for Nurses* (8th edn, Pearsons 2019) 49.

Honest Difference of Opinion between Healthcare Professionals

Under the fourth principle, a difference of opinion between healthcare professionals as to which is the better of two ways of treating a patient must be both honest and reasonable. There will be no exemption from liability where there is an honest but unreasonable belief as to the desirability for a particular form of treatment.[39]

Inherent Defects

Healthcare professionals must be alert to potential defects in practice. It is not sufficient to adhere to general and approved practice in circumstances where the inherent defects of a practice would be obvious to any person giving the matter due consideration and where steps could be taken to resolve the matter. The burden of proof is placed on the party asserting that there is an inherent defect.

4.6 Causation

To succeed in an action for negligence it must be proven that there is a sufficiently close causal connection between the conduct and the resulting injury to the plaintiff. This connection between the defendant's conduct and the plaintiff's alleged injury is referred to as causation. There are two tests for causation, namely the factual causation test and the legal causation test. To prove causation, it must be shown that the defendant was both the factual and legal cause of the injury or harm that occurred.

Factual causation focuses on whether the defendant caused the harm in a factual sense. It draws on evidence of fact and involves the application of tests such as the 'but for' test and the material contribution test. Factual causation is not, however, determinative of liability as the defendant's conduct may not have been the legal cause of the harm. Legal causation looks to whether there is an intervening act that breaks the chain of causation. This concept is known as the *novus actus interveniens*. As will be discussed, foreseeability is perhaps one of the most important elements in assessing legal causation.

The burden of proof is placed on the plaintiff and it must generally be shown on the balance of probabilities that the harm was caused by the defendant. In *Cosgrave v Ryan and the Electricity Supply Board*,

---

[39] McMahon and Binchy (n 2) [14.12].

Murphy J stated, 'Causation must be proved by the plaintiff. Any argument in relation to the shifting of the onus of proof in respect of breach of duty of care cannot extend to the fundamental issue of causation.'[40]

4.6.1 Factual Causation

Factual causation asks whether the defendant caused the plaintiff's injury. McMahon and Binchy describe it as 'a question of fact, in the scientific or physical sense of cause and effect'.[41] This could be viewed as a first step in determining liability. In determining factual causation, the courts have developed two tests, namely the 'but for' test and the material contribution test.

The 'But For' Test

The traditional way of determining responsibility is referred to as the 'but for' test. The question to be asked in applying this test is: 'but for' the conduct of the defendant, would the injury have arisen? If the injury or harm would not have occurred without the defendant then they may be considered a factual cause. Likewise, if the injury would have occurred regardless of the defendant's conduct then they will not be held to be the factual cause.

This approach is demonstrated by the English case of *Barnett v Chelsea and Kensington Hospital Management Committee*.[42] Three night-watchmen presented at a hospital casualty department. All three complained to a nurse on duty that they had been vomiting for three hours after drinking tea. The nurse reported their complaints by telephone to the duty medical casualty officer, who thereupon instructed her to tell the men to go home to bed and call in their own doctors. The three men left, and around five hours later one of them died from poisoning by arsenic, which had been introduced into the tea. He might have died from the poisoning even if he had been admitted to the hospital and treated with all due care. The man's widow brought an action claiming that the death resulted from the defendants' negligence in not diagnosing or treating his condition when he presented at the casualty department.

---

[40] *Cosgrave v Ryan and the Electricity Supply Board* [2003] 1 ILRM 544, 558; see also *Quinn v Mid Western Health Board and Donal O'Sullivan* [2005] IESC 19.
[41] McMahon and Binchy (n 2) [2.09].
[42] *Barnett v Chelsea and Kensington Hospital Management Committee* [1969] 1 QB 428.

The action was dismissed by the Court. It noted that the medical casualty officer was negligent *but* the man would have died of the poisoning even if he had been admitted to the ward and treated with all care five hours before his death. The plaintiff had failed to establish on the balance of probabilities that the defendants' negligence had caused the death; therefore, the claim failed.

A relatively straightforward application of this test was seen in the Supreme Court decision of *Kenny v O'Rourke*.[43] The plaintiff was a housepainter who was injured when he fell from a ladder while painting the upper storey of a house. The ladder was provided by the general contractors and, although it was defective, the contractors were not held to be liable. The plaintiff's fall was due to his having leaned over too far and thus overbalanced. His fall was not brought about by the defect in the ladder.

The application of the 'but for' test appears relatively straightforward in circumstances where there is one defendant and the cause of the harm is readily identifiable. The reality is often far more complicated, particularly in the context of a medical negligence action. The patient may receive care from a range of healthcare professionals and the exact cause of a harm may be difficult to determine. The Court could possibly turn to the material contribution test as an aid in determining causation.

It should be noted that while a nurse may not be liable under the strict rules of negligence there may still be a question of professional misconduct or poor professional performance to be addressed.

Material Contribution Test

The material contribution test can be viewed as a more flexible approach to causation. The test provides that a defendant's conduct can be viewed as a causative factor if it materially contributed to the plaintiff's injury. There has, however, been some reluctance in applying this test in Ireland.

The application of the test can be seen in the English case of *Fairchild v Glenhaven Funeral Services*.[44] The plaintiffs developed mesothelioma caused by exposure at work to asbestos dust. This exposure had taken place during periods of employment with more than one employer. The House of Lords recognised a need to

---

[43] *Kenny v O'Rourke* [1972] IR 339.
[44] *Fairchild v Glenhaven Funeral Services* [2002] 3 All ER 305.

adopt a modified approach to proof of causation. The wrongdoing of each of the defendants had materially increased the risk of contracting the disease and this was sufficient to satisfy the causal requirements for liability. Accordingly, the appeal was allowed and the defendants were held liable for the harm suffered. The approach taken by the Court allows for a move away from the rigid 'but for' test in cases where it is impossible for the plaintiff to show anything more substantial than a material increase in risk.

Quinn v Mid Western Health Board demonstrates a hesitancy in moving from the 'but for' test.[45] The plaintiff in this case was born with severe brain damage. The defendants ultimately did not dispute that there had been negligence in the management of the pregnancy and that the plaintiff should have been delivered earlier than she was. However, the defendants contended that the plaintiff's brain damage was sustained as a result of an acute episode that occurred between 28–30 weeks of the pregnancy and that the outcome would not have been any different had she been delivered at an earlier time than she was.[46] The plaintiff sought a modified approach to proof of causation. In advancing this argument, counsel for the plaintiff cited the House of Lords decision in *Fairchild v Glenhaven Funeral Services*.

Kearns J described the House of Lords as taking an 'exceptional course' in the case of *Fairchild*. It is therefore not surprising that the Court adhered to the 'but for' test. Kearns J set out:

> Any approach which had the effect of reversing the onus of proof, or transferring the onus of proof to the defendant, would be one of such importance, even in the few exceptional cases where it might be appropriate, that it would require a full court – or perhaps even legislation – before a change of such magnitude to existing law could take place. Nor do special circumstances arise or exist in this case to bring it within the more relaxed requirements for establishing causation which were found to exist in *McGhee v. National Coal Board* and *Fairchild v. Glenhaven Funeral Services*.[47]

Quinn demonstrates a reluctance in moving away from the 'but for' test in all but exceptional cases. However, this does suggest that there are circumstances in which the material contribution test can be applied in determining causation.

---

[45] *Quinn v Mid Western Health Board* [2005] IESC 19.
[46] ibid 19, [4].
[47] ibid 19, [60].

4.6.2 Legal Causation

Factual causation does not serve to allocate legal responsibility, and can be viewed as a preliminary step in the process. A further step is therefore required in order to determine whether the defendant's conduct was the legal cause of the injury suffered by the plaintiff. McMahon and Binchy describe the process as follows: 'When the field is narrowed by the elimination of the factually irrelevant causes the inquiry must continue among those causes considered to be factually relevant, to establish whether they are legally relevant to the court's inquiry.'[48] As part of this process it will be necessary to consider whether there is an intervening act that breaks the chain of causation. Moreover, foreseeability is of fundamental importance in determining legal causation.

Novus Actus Interveniens

Some form of intervention in the course of affairs leading to a harm may result in breaking the chain of causation. In effect, the causal link between the defendant's conduct and the harm suffered can be broken by such an event. This is referred to as a *novus actus interveniens* and it can relieve the defendant of liability. Not every intervening act will provide such absolution, as McMahon J noted in *Murray v Miller and Brady*: 'It is only some intervening acts that possess the disruptive quality.'[49] Moreover, the initial wrongdoer may still share some element of liability. The *novus actus* may stem from the conduct of a third party, the conduct of the plaintiff, or some form of force majeure.

Foreseeability

In considering the effect of the intervening act on the liability of the original wrongdoer it is necessary to have regard to the issue of 'foreseeability'. The courts are concerned with whether the course of events put in train by the original wrongdoer were foreseeable. If the *novus actus* was a 'predictable and inevitable'[50] consequence then liability will continue to attach to the original wrongdoer.

In *Crowley v Allied Irish Banks and O'Flynn*[51] the plaintiff was a minor who fell from a flat roof on premises owned by AIB. The

---

[48] McMahon and Binchy (n 2) [2.37].
[49] *Murray v Miller and Brady* (14 November 2001) CC (Roscommon); see McMahon and Binchy (n 2) [2.46].
[50] McMahon and Binchy (n 2) [2.50].
[51] *Crowley v Allied Irish Banks and O'Flynn* [1988] ILRM 225.

roof was part of an extension designed by a firm of architects and did not have a guard rail around it. The plaintiff, along with friends, regularly played on the roof and the bank was aware of this behaviour. The architecture firm had judgment given against them in the High Court. Their appeal was allowed by the Supreme Court. There was no evidence that the appellants could reasonably have foreseen that children would be permitted to play on the roof. There was no sufficient nexus or connection between any negligence on the part of the architecture firm and the occurrence of the accident.

Recklessness

The intervening act may constitute a *novus actus* where it is considered to be unreasonable or reckless. The defendants in *Conole v Redbank Oyster Co*[52] were aware that a boat was unseaworthy and unsafe. Despite recognising that there were defects in the construction of the boat, the captain proceeded to bring 50 children out on the boat. The boat capsized, resulting in the death of several children. The defendants sought to recover contribution from the manufacturer of the vessel. The Supreme Court refused to award contribution as the sole cause of the accident was the negligence of the defendants, by way of the reckless behaviour of the captain. Bringing the boat out to sea constituted a *novus actus*, which relieved the manufacturers of liability.

Division of Liability

The cases discussed to this point illustrate that harm or injury may be caused by one or multiple parties. If different forms of damage are inflicted by distinct parties then this would give rise to separate actions for the damage caused. However, if multiple parties act so as to cause the same damage then they are referred to as concurrent wrongdoers. Concurrent wrongdoers can be held jointly liable or severally liable for the resulting harm. The division of liability for concurrent wrongdoers is addressed by Part III of the Civil Liability Act 1961.

Section 11 of the Civil Liability Act 1961 addresses persons who are concurrent wrongdoers. Section 11(1) of the 1961 Act provides that 'two or more persons are concurrent wrongdoers when both or all are wrongdoers and are responsible to a third person (in this Part called the injured person or the plaintiff) for the same damage, whether or not judgment has been recovered against

---

[52] *Conole v Redbank Oyster Co* [1976] IR 191.

some or all of them'.[53] The Act defines the circumstances in which a person might become a concurrent wrongdoer. This can arise from 'vicarious liability of one for another, breach of joint duty, conspiracy, concerted action to a common end or independent acts causing the same damage'.[54]

4.7 Harm

A further step in succeeding in an action for negligence is that it must be proven that there was actual loss or damage to the interests of the plaintiff. Accordingly, where loss or damage cannot be shown then no compensation will be payable. Furthermore, not all types of harm can be compensated for in a civil action. The harm suffered should be a reasonably foreseeable consequence of the breach of duty. Moreover, the harm suffered should not be too remote. Remoteness defines the parameters of liability for harm suffered and is perhaps more a question of policy rather than clear legal principles.

The leading case for the foreseeability of harm is known as *Wagon Mound (No 1)*.[55] The defendant's vessel leaked furnace oil into Sydney Harbour. Several hours later the oil flowed to a nearby wharf where ship repair was being carried out. The oil was subsequently ignited when molten metal from welding work came into contact with a cotton rag floating on the surface of the water. Viscount Simonds set out that 'the essential factor in determining liability is whether the damage is of such a kind as the reasonable man should have foreseen'.[56] Liability was not imposed as the injury to the plaintiff's property was an unforeseeable consequence.

Eggshell Skull Rule

In some cases, the harm suffered by a plaintiff may be far greater than would ordinarily be expected. This increased harm may be linked to some inherent frailty or predisposition on the part of the plaintiff. This does not provide an escape from liability for the defendant. Instead, the defendant is expected to take the plaintiff as he is found. This is referred to as the 'eggshell skull rule'. In *Walsh v South Tipperary County Council* Clark J set out:

---

[53] Civil Liability Act 1961, s 11(1).
[54] ibid s 11(2).
[55] *Overseas Tankship (UK) Ltd v Morts Dock & Engineering* [1961] AC 388.
[56] ibid 388, 426.

in the oft quoted case of the injured party with the so-called 'eggshell skull' it can, on occasion, turn out that, due to some weakness or predisposition, a particular injured party suffers much more severe consequences from a relatively innocuous incident than might be expected. However, it again remains the case that, if personal injury is a foreseeable consequence of whatever wrongdoing is concerned (say the negligent driving of a motor vehicle), then the fact that those injuries may, in the peculiar circumstances of the case, be much more severe than might have been expected, does not deprive the injured party from an entitlement to recover whatever may be appropriate for those injuries.[57]

The principle of the eggshell skull was applied in *Burke v John Paul & Co Ltd*.[58] The plaintiff spent a period of time cutting steel bars required for building purposes. The tool supplied for this purpose was blunt, thereby making the job more difficult and physically demanding. The efforts of the plaintiff resulted in a hernia developing near the top of his groin. The defendants argued that for a hernia to develop there must be 'some congenital weakness –some predisposition to getting a hernia, and that, since this could not be discovered on any ordinary examination, it was impossible for the defendants to know of any predisposition of the plaintiff to develop a hernia, and that consequently they could not foresee that the use of extra exertion and pressure by the plaintiff in cutting the bars would result in a hernia developing'.[59] In response, the Court set out the following:

> It was clearly implicit in the medical evidence that unwonted bodily exertion may cause straining or tearing of the muscles. It cannot, I think, be suggested that it is necessary to have the statement of a medical expert that an employer should know that if one of his employees is forced to use great exertion in the course of his work that may cause a straining, or even a tearing, of muscles, as that is a matter of common knowledge; but the point taken is that it could not be reasonably anticipated that a hernia would result without knowledge that the plaintiff had a predisposition to hernia. The answer to this, I think, is what is generally referred to as 'the egg-shell skull rule' and I do not think that that rule has been impugned in any way by the *Wagon Mound* decision.[60]

---

[57] *Walsh v South Tipperary County Council* [2011] IEHC 503, [5.6].
[58] *Burke v John Paul & Co Ltd* [1967] IR 277.
[59] ibid 277, 282–83.
[60] ibid 277, 283.

Burke was subsequently applied in *McCarthy v Murphy* where McCracken J stated:

> Of course the Defendant could not have anticipated that [the plaintiff] was a person with a pre-disposition to depression, but he could have reasonably foreseen a soft tissue injury and, that being so, he is liable for damage which flows from that injury, as he has to take the plaintiff as he finds her.[61]

In the healthcare setting considerable caution must be advised. The nurse should be conscious of the patient's medical history and factors that could exacerbate any harm suffered.

4.8 Liability of a Healthcare Facility

There will often be more than one defendant named in an action for clinical negligence. In addition to the healthcare professional, a claim may be brought against the HSE, a private hospital or company. The plaintiff will often look beyond the healthcare professional for pragmatic reasons. The compensation sought by the plaintiff may include medical supports and resources which a body such as the HSE are best placed to provide. In any case, the healthcare institution will generally be subject to some form of liability, such as direct liability, enterprise liability, or vicarious liability.

4.8.1 Direct Liability

The healthcare facility will be subject to direct liability where the act of negligence stems from some form of institutional failure. This may be a systemic weakness or deficiency over which the individual healthcare professional has little say or control. The issue may relate to a failure in systems of accountability, a failure to support continuing professional education, poor dissemination of policy and protocols within the institution, or a failure to ensure suitably qualified staff are employed. The issue of direct liability arose in the English case of *Wilsher v Essex Area Health Authority*.[62] It was held that there was no reason why, in specific circumstances, that a health authority would not be directly liable where it had failed to provide sufficient or appropriately qualified and competent healthcare professionals for the unit. There is a distinction to be drawn between the responsibility of the healthcare facility and the conduct of the employees. A

---

[61] *McCarthy v Murphy* [1998] IEHC 23, [11].
[62] *Wilsher v Essex Area Health Authority* [1988] AC 1074.

failure by the healthcare facility will go to direct liability, whereas the conduct of the employee may result in a claim of vicarious liability.[63]

4.8.2 Enterprise Liability

The State Claims Agency has a statutory remit to manage personal injury claims, including claims in respect of clinical negligence, on behalf of Delegated State Authorities such as the Health Service Executive. The Clinical Indemnity Scheme (CIS) was established in July 2002 for the purpose of rationalising the existing indemnity arrangements. This involved transferring the responsibility for managing clinical negligence claims and associated risks to the State, via the HSE, hospitals and other health agencies. Under the CIS, the State assumes full responsibility for the indemnification and management of all clinical negligence claims against healthcare enterprises and practitioners covered by the scheme.

The clinical indemnity is provided on the basis of enterprise liability. This means that the healthcare enterprise assumes liability, on a vicarious basis, for all its employees' alleged clinical negligence. This was intended to allow for the management of claims in a timely and cost-effective manner. For claimants, they do not need to sue the individual healthcare professional(s) and instead the action is brought against the healthcare enterprise. The action is handled by a single legal team that represents the healthcare enterprise. This provides a ready pool of expertise and is closely linked with the risk management function of the State Claims Agency. The combination of risk and claims management can promote a proactive response to potential claims and facilitates the development and adoption of effective clinical risk management policies, which should reduce the potential for negligence claims in the future.

4.8.3 Vicarious Liability

There will be circumstances where enterprise liability is not applicable and instead it will be necessary to establish vicarious liability. The concept of vicarious liability means that a person or body will be held liable for the actions of another. For such liability to arise, the conduct of the first person must have been negligent and the defendant must have had some element of control over the person. The rationale for vicarious liability has traditionally been linked to the promotion of staff discipline, as

---

[63] Mills and Mulligan (n 28) 208–12.

well as the fact that the employer is more likely to have sufficient financial resources to cover damages arising from litigation.

The test for establishing vicarious liability has been the subject of debate and review in recent years. The current approach is described as the 'close connection' test. O'Donnell J in the Supreme Court decision of *Hickey v McGowan* stated that '... the close connection test must be taken to represent the law in Ireland'.[64] The manner in which this test has been interpreted and applied by the courts is especially important as it serves to define the potential scope of liability for the employer. A 'two-stage' test is applied in determining whether an employer will be held vicariously liable.

> 1. Is there a relationship between the defendant and the wrongdoer?
>
> 2. Is the connection between that relationship and the wrongdoer's conduct such as to make it just that the defendant should be held responsible for the alleged negligence?

In short, where a Court is asked to determine whether or not an employer should be held liable, it will ask whether a sufficiently 'close connection' existed between the conduct of the employee and the work they were engaged to perform. It is generally accepted that nurses in full-time service of hospitals are employees for the purposes of vicarious liability.[65] However, it can be more challenging to determine whether the wrongdoer was acting in connection with her employment at the time of the alleged negligent incident. If such a connection is not proven, then vicarious liability will not be established.

---

[64] *Hickey v McGowan* [2017] IESC 6, [26].
[65] McMahon and Binchy (n 2) [43.32]; *Mooney v Terrett* [1939] Ir Jur Rep 56; *Keane (an infant) v HSE & Ors* [2011] IEHC 213.

CHAPTER 5
Patient Autonomy and Decision-Making

Introduction 93
Patient Autonomy 94
    The Elevation of Autonomy 95
    Legal Recognition of Autonomy 98
    Autonomy in Professional Guidelines 100
Informed Consent 101
    Civil and Criminal Liability 101
    Voluntary Consent 104
    The Role of Capacity 105
    Disclosure of Appropriate Information 111
    Therapeutic Privilege 116
The Right to Refuse Treatment 117
A Demand for Medical Treatment 120
The Assisted Decision-Making (Capacity) Act 2015 122
    Director of the Decision Support Service 123
    Functional Assessment of Capacity 125
    Guiding Principles 125
    Decision-Making Supports 127
    Enduring Power of Attorney 133
    Advance Healthcare Directives 135

5.0 Introduction

A defining feature of modern medicine in Ireland is the patient-centred nature of care. This is reflected in the shift from medical paternalism to a system that recognises and emphasises the ethical and legal concept of autonomy. The patient has much greater involvement in their healthcare and this has changed the responsibilities and duties of the healthcare professional. Nurses, doctors, and allied health professionals must take care to communicate with patients in a manner that ensures the patient is sufficiently informed about their care and any treatment options available to them. In this way patients can consent or refuse treatment for their own personal reasons or for no reason at all. A failure to seek consent or a failure to provide sufficient information can leave the healthcare professional open to a charge of battery, assault, or negligence. Nursing practice in this area is framed by a broad legal framework of common law, constitutional law, professional guidelines, and the European Convention on Human Rights (ECHR). It is further complicated by the need to be aware of the various power dynamics that can arise in a healthcare setting.

The nurse has regular close contact with the patient. In such situations, there is often an imbalance in power relations. The nurse is the qualified expert and must take care to support the patient. This may be achieved through the fostering of trust and confidence, which can flourish where there is open communication and a respect for the patient's autonomy. The expansion in nursing duties and roles means that there are situations where the nurse will have primary responsibility for obtaining the patient's consent. As nursing practice continues to evolve it is likely that this primary role will similarly expand. A further power dynamic arises where the nurse occupies an intermediate role between doctor and patient. This can give rise to an ethically and legally complex situation. For instance, a situation may arise where the doctor obtains the patient's consent, but the patient subsequently requests further information from the nurse. Such requests will be relatively innocuous for the most part but can be complicated where therapeutic privilege has been applied. All of this serves to underline the role of the nurse in navigating, supporting, and delivering on patient autonomy.

The chapter sets out the relevant law on patient autonomy and decision-making over the course of five sections. Section 5.1 outlines the elevation, interpretation, and legal recognition of autonomy. The concept of informed consent is addressed in section 5.2. This includes discussion of voluntariness, capacity, the disclosure of information, and therapeutic privilege. The right to refuse or demand medical treatment is addressed in sections 5.3 and 5.4. The law on capacity and decision-making supports will undergo substantial changes with the commencement of the Assisted Decision-Making (Capacity) Act 2015 (ADMC Act 2015). The discussion of this legislation will include an outline of various decision-making supports, enduring powers of attorney, and advance healthcare directives.

5.1 Patient Autonomy

The concept of autonomy is central to many of the clinical, legal, and ethical challenges that arise in nursing practice. It is therefore not surprising that this ethical concept is recognised in law and is expressed as a right to autonomy or self-determination. This section provides a brief overview of the ethical concept of autonomy and key points in its development. It also outlines the legal basis for the right of autonomy, which is commonly reflected in the practice of securing consent to medical treatment. A failure to obtain informed consent can potentially lead to a civil action or a criminal charge against the relevant healthcare professional.

Respect for autonomy can instil a sense of responsibility in the patient and can promote greater ownership and engagement with their medical care. There are, of course, instances where the views of the patient and the healthcare professional do not align. It is a recurring theme that autonomy is most at issue where the patient's decision conflicts with the opinion of the healthcare professional(s). Nevertheless, the patient's decision is to be respected provided they have the requisite capacity. This illustrates the strength of the patient's autonomous decision.

5.1.1 The Elevation of Autonomy

The term autonomy is derived from the Greek words *autos* and *nomos*, meaning self-rule or law. Autonomy was not originally connected to the individual but instead described the self-government of Greek city-states. The Enlightenment marked a period of change whereby autonomy became linked to individual moral agency. As the concept evolved over time, it has come to be most closely associated with the will and preferences of an individual.[1]

The practice of medicine was not traditionally defined by patient autonomy but was grounded in concepts such as beneficence and the sanctity of life. The doctor determined what was meant by doing good and this was decisive in the treatment of the patient. This is best described by the concept of paternalism, which '… centres on the notion that the physician … has better insight into the best interests of the patient than does the patient, or that the physician's obligations are such that he is impelled to do what is medically good, even if it is not "good" in terms of the patient's own value system'.[2] The culture of paternalism began to be displaced from the 1960s. This change was signalled by the emergence of

---

[1] Mary Donnelly, *Healthcare Decision-Making and the Law: Autonomy, Capacity and the Limits of Liberalism* (Cambridge University Press 2014); John Lombard, 'Autonomy' in N Emmerich et al (eds), *Contemporary European Perspectives on the Ethics of End of Life Care* (Springer 2020).
[2] Edmund Pellegrino, and David Thomasma, *For the Patient's Good* (Oxford University Press 1988) 7.

bioethics,[3] medical research scandals,[4] and societal changes that reflected people's desire for greater self-determination and self-realisation.[5]

The Belmont Report of 1978[6] and the publication of the first edition of *Principles of Biomedical Ethics* the following year were pivotal points in the development of autonomy as it applies to healthcare. *Principles of Biomedical Ethics* is a seminal text in which Beauchamp and Childress outline four principles of biomedical ethics: nonmaleficence, beneficence, justice, and autonomy.[7] There is no hierarchy among these principles, but autonomy has been accorded a dominant position by many commentators and this has translated into practice, where it often holds sway. This is not to suggest that there is a single correct interpretation of autonomy. Rather there are differing conceptions of autonomy, which frame the concept in different ways. The principle of autonomy as outlined by Beauchamp and Childress draws on both Kantian deontology and Millian liberalism. More recent formulations tend to lean towards the Millian model.

Conceptions of Autonomy

Autonomy is not given a homogenous interpretation across jurisdictions. Nonetheless, western interpretations of autonomy are principally based on the work of Immanuel Kant and JS Mill. The Kantian understanding of autonomy is based on a moral framework and closely linked to the 'categorical imperative'. The 'categorical imperative' requires individuals to act 'only according to that maxim whereby you can at the same time will that it should become a universal law'.[8] A person can only be bound by a moral law in circumstances where they have a choice of whether or not to accept it.[9] The Kantian view of autonomy is therefore underpinned by a desire for 'appropriate or moral action'.[10]

---

[3] Tom L Beauchamp and James F Childress, *Principles of Biomedical Ethics* (1st edn, Oxford University Press 1979).
[4] Allan M Brandt, 'Racism and Research: The Case of the Tuskegee Syphilis Study' (1978) 8(6) The Hastings Center Report 21.
[5] Donnelly (n 1).
[6] The National Commission for the Protection of Human Subjects of Biomedical and Behavioral Research, *The Belmont Report: Ethical Principles and Guidelines for the Protection of Human Subjects of Research* (US Government Printing Office 1978).
[7] Beauchamp and Childress (n 3).
[8] Immanuel Kant, *Ethical Philosophy* (Hackett Publishing Company 1994) 30.
[9] Raanan Gillon (ed), *Principles of Healthcare Ethics* (John Wiley & Sons 1995) 64.
[10] Donnelly (n 1) 19.

The work of JS Mill is most closely associated with the liberal conception of autonomy. In short, an individual's autonomy should be respected due to the gains it can bring about for both the individual and society.[11] It follows that a person should be allowed to act in accordance with their own beliefs and values, regardless of how they might be viewed by other people. The liberal interpretation of autonomy is based on negative and positive rights. A negative right is a right not to do something or a right to be free from something. In the healthcare context, a patient's refusal of medical treatment is an example of a negative right. By contrast, a right to receive a form of care or treatment is a positive right and has come to be reflected in the principle of informed consent. Yet, the principal focus in this interpretation of autonomy is largely on non-interference and, presuming the patient does not lack capacity, they are generally understood as being able to refuse any or all treatment should they so decide.

An individual's autonomy is not, however, unrestricted under this Millian interpretation. An interference with a person's autonomy can be justified in circumstances where harm could be caused to another individual. In relation to this 'harm principle', Mill stated:

> the only purpose for which power can be rightfully exercised over any member of a civilized community, against his will, is to prevent harm to others. His own good, either physical or moral, is not sufficient warrant. He cannot rightfully be compelled to do or forbear because it will be better for him to do so, because it will make him happier, because, in the opinions of others, to do so would be wise, or even right. These are good reasons for remonstrating with him, or persuading him, or entreating him, but not for compelling him, or visiting him with any evil in case he does otherwise.[12]

In applying this to healthcare, Dworkin suggested, 'We allow someone to choose death over radical amputation or a blood transfusion, if that is his informed wish, because we acknowledge his right to a life structured by his own values.'[13] The liberal perspective of autonomy would therefore appear to be most pervasive in Western healthcare ethics. Yet, the move from a theoretical discussion to clinical application can be challenging and is often problematic for healthcare professionals. The

---

[11] JS Mill, *On Liberty* (JW Parker and Son 1859) 207.
[12] ibid 223–24.
[13] Ronald Dworkin, *Life's Dominion: An Argument about Abortion, Euthanasia, and Individual Freedom* (Alfred A Knopf 1993) 224.

difference between jurisdictions should be kept in mind, as nurses who have trained in Ireland have often gone on to practice in other countries and it is necessary to recognise and adapt to local interpretations of autonomy that frame the patient–healthcare professional relationship.

5.1.2 Legal Recognition of Autonomy

The ethical concept of autonomy has been recognised and protected in common law, constitutional provisions, the ECHR, and the Charter of Fundamental Rights. The legal endorsement of autonomy allows for reliance on and enforcement of ethical principles in individual situations.[14] As noted earlier, autonomy has come to be reflected in non-interference and the right to refuse treatment. It is well captured by Justice Cardozo's statement in *Schloendoff v Society of New York Hospital*:

> Every human being of adult years and sound mind has a right to determine what shall be done with his own body; and a surgeon who performs an operation without his patient's consent, commits an assault, for which he is liable in damages.[15]

This statement not only reflects the importance of obtaining consent but also underlines the right of a person to determine what shall be done with or to his or her body.

The common law origins of autonomy are demonstrated by the English case of *Re T (Adult: Refusal of Medical Treatment)*.[16] Miss T had been raised by her mother, a Jehovah's Witness, but was not practising her religion at the time of this case. While in hospital, Miss T indicated that she would not consent to a blood transfusion. The right to refuse treatment was unanimously recognised by the Court of Appeal in England and Wales. Lord Donaldson stated:

> An adult patient who, like Miss T, suffers from no mental incapacity has an absolute right to choose whether to consent to medical treatment, to refuse it or to choose one rather than another of the treatments being offered. This right of choice is not limited to decisions which others might regard as sensible. It exists notwithstanding that the reasons for

---

[14] Mary Donnelly, 'The Right of Autonomy in Irish Law' (2008) 14 Medico-Legal Journal of Ireland 34, 34.
[15] *Schloendoff v Society of New York Hospital* 105 NE 92 (NY 1914) 92–93.
[16] *Re T (Adult: Refusal of Medical Treatment)* [1992] 4 All ER 649.

making the choice are rational, irrational, unknown or even non-existent.[17]

Nonetheless, the Court was of the opinion that Miss T lacked sufficient capacity and the decision could therefore be made by the medical practitioners in accordance with the best interests of the patient.

The right of autonomy is also recognised and protected by Article 40.3.1° of the Irish Constitution. The right of autonomy formed an element of the Supreme Court decision in *Re a Ward of Court*.[18] The facts of this case are set out in section 5.3, 'The Right to Refuse Treatment'. It will also be discussed in subsequent chapters as it has shaped medical practice in Ireland in a variety of ways. Hamilton CJ considered the right of autonomy to be an aspect of the right to privacy. In contrast to this, Denham J viewed autonomy as a separate constitutional right. The Court did not provide a detailed analysis of the concept but it was expanded on by subsequent cases.

The case of *JM v Board of Management of St Vincent's Hospital* was described by Donnelly as the 'first significant judicial engagement with the right'.[19] The woman in *JM* refused a blood transfusion due to her religious beliefs as a Jehovah's Witness. Finnegan P stated that she had not made 'a clear final decision as the notice party was pre-occupied with her husband and his religious beliefs rather than her own welfare and whether or not to have treatment'.[20] On this basis the Court held that the woman's decision was not a 'real' or 'true' decision. Therefore, her decision was not autonomous, and the refusal was not upheld. Laffoy J in *Fitzpatrick v FK* provided further support for the recognition of a right of autonomy.[21] This right provides a clear basis for treatment refusal and such a decision is to be respected provided the individual has the requisite capacity. In what might appear to be a recurring theme, the right of autonomy was recognised but the Court held that it did not apply in the circumstances. We will return to these cases when setting out the law on capacity and the refusal of treatment.

---

[17] ibid 649, 652–53.
[18] *Re a Ward of Court* [1996] 2 IR 79.
[19] *JM v Board of Management of St Vincent's Hospital* [2003] 1 IR 321; Donnelly (n 14) 35.
[20] *JM v Board of Management of St Vincent's Hospital* [2003] 1 IR 321, 321.
[21] *Fitzpatrick v FK* [2008] IEHC 104, [2009] 2 IR 7.

The right of autonomy is not limited to the domestic sphere but has also been recognised by the European Court of Human Rights (ECtHR) as a part of the ECHR. Article 8(1) ECHR provides: 'Everyone has the right to respect for his private and family life, his home and his correspondence.' This is not an unlimited right of autonomy but can be restricted by the State in certain situations. Any restriction must be in accordance with Article 8(2) ECHR, which states:

> There shall be no interference by a public authority with the exercise of this right except such as is in accordance with the law and is necessary in a democratic society in the interests of national security, public safety or the economic well-being of the country, for the prevention of disorder or crime, for the protection of health or morals, or for the protection of the rights and freedoms of others.[22]

The recognition and interpretation of autonomy was the subject of discussion by the ECtHR in *Pretty v United Kingdom*.[23] Mrs Pretty suffered from motor neurone disease and had sought an assurance from the Director of Public Prosecutions (DPP) that if her husband assisted her in committing suicide that he would be immune from prosecution. This assurance was not forthcoming, and she ultimately brought a case before the ECtHR alleging the infringement of her rights under Articles 2, 3, 8, 9 and 14 of the Convention. The Court recognised that a person has a right of autonomy protected under Article 8 ECHR. However, the interference with this right could be justified in the circumstances.

5.1.3 Autonomy in Professional Guidelines

Autonomy has come to be reflected in professional guidelines and standards of conduct. It is seen in guidelines published by the Irish Medical Council and the Nursing and Midwifery Board of Ireland. The Irish Medical Council *Guide to Professional Conduct and Ethics*[24] illustrates the close relationship between consent and respect for patient autonomy. In section 9.2 of the *Guide to Professional Conduct and Ethics* it is set out that 'Consent is required by law and is an essential part of respect for patients' autonomy.'[25]

---

[22] European Convention on Human Rights, Art 8(2).
[23] *Pretty v United Kingdom* [2002] ECHR 423, (2002) 35 EHRR 1.
[24] Irish Medical Council, *Guide to Professional Conduct and Ethics for Registered Medical Practitioners* (8th edn, IMC 2016).
[25] ibid 15.

The principle of autonomy is also acknowledged by the Nursing and Midwifery Board of Ireland in the *Code of Professional Conduct and Ethics for Registered Nurses and Registered Midwives*. Under the standards of conduct for Principle 1: Respect for the dignity of the person, it is set out, 'You should protect and promote the autonomy of patients: respect their choices, priorities, beliefs and values.'[26] There are additional values and standards in the *Code of Professional Conduct and Ethics* that underline this commitment to autonomy and self-determination. These will be drawn out in discussion of the elements required for valid consent.

5.2 Informed Consent

The patient's consent must be obtained prior to the provision of medical treatment. Several elements are required for valid consent, namely: voluntariness, capacity, and the disclosure of appropriate information. The absence of consent may result in trespass against the person, battery, or a breach of a patient's rights. It follows that informed consent is a fundamental part of treatment and should not be neglected simply because the patient is in a vulnerable condition. The following sub-sections will outline the potential for civil and criminal liability, the requisite elements for informed consent, and will address the topic of therapeutic privilege.

5.2.1 Civil and Criminal Liability

A failure in the consent process can result in civil and/or criminal liability. In general, if consent is obtained for medical treatment then no criminal liability will arise. Consent does not, however, absolve a healthcare professional of liability in circumstances where they provide or administer a prohibited medical procedure. For instance, female genital mutilation is considered an offence under s 2(1) of Criminal Justice (Female Genital Mutilation) Act 2012. The issue of consent is directly addressed by s 2(3) of the 2012 Act as it provides that '… it is hereby declared that it shall not be a defence to proceedings for an offence under this section for the accused person to show that he or she believed that the act concerned was consented to by the girl concerned or her parents or guardian, or the woman concerned'.[27]

If a nurse or other healthcare professional carries out a medical or surgical procedure without the patient's consent, they could be

---

[26] Nursing and Midwifery Board of Ireland, *Code of Professional Conduct and Ethics for Registered Nurses and Registered Midwives* (NMBI 2014) 13.
[27] Criminal Justice (Female Genital Mutilation) Act 2012, s 2(1).

charged with assault. The decision would rest with the DPP, but it is very rare that such a charge would be brought. Instead, there is a greater likelihood that the healthcare professional would be charged with battery. Battery is a form of trespass to the person, which arises from the non-consensual touching or contact with a person.[28] It is not necessary to prove that the non-consensual touching caused damage. The fact that touching took place is itself enough to justify an action. Despite this, the nurse will not be liable for every act of touching that could arise. As Tingle commented, 'an action is unlikely to result from the nurse accidentally brushing a patient's shoulder as she passes in a corridor'.[29]

In other cases, consent may have been obtained but there may be some deficiency in the process. The courts have held that an action in battery would not be appropriate in these circumstances and instead a claim of negligence may be brought. In *Chatterton v Gerson*, Bristow J stated:

> Once the patient is informed in broad terms of the nature of the procedure which is intended ... the consent is real, and the cause of the action on which to base a claim for failure to go into risks and implications is negligence, not trespass.[30]

If a nurse becomes aware that a patient does not adequately understand the treatment to which they have purported to consent to, it is advisable that the nurse contact the relevant healthcare professional and ensure appropriate information is provided. Similarly, if the nurse is responsible for seeking consent then it will be their responsibility to ensure additional information is provided to the patient.

Consent can be given in a variety of ways and may be categorised as express or implied. Express consent, whether verbal or in writing, occurs where there is a clear indication from the patient that they accept the offer of medical treatment. Written consent may be favoured for more serious healthcare interventions. The process of signing to indicate consent emphasises and highlights the consent process for the patient. Furthermore, written consent can provide valuable evidence of consent should a dispute arise at some point in the future. Nonetheless, the signing of a consent form

---

[28] See *Malette v Shulman* (1990) 67(4) DLR 321.
[29] John Tingle and Alan Cribb (eds), *Nursing Law and Ethics* (4th edn, Wiley-Blackwell 2013) 133.
[30] *Chatterton v Gerson* [1981] QB 432, 443.

is not a guarantee that the consent is valid. As noted previously, there could be a deficiency at some stage in the process.

In practice, consent will often be implied as it is indicated by the actions of the patient. For instance, a patient may hold out their arm when told that a blood sample is to be taken.[31] The actions of the patient could be interpreted as compliance with the request or could be viewed as implicit consent to the procedure. Nurses must therefore be vigilant to ensure that appropriate consent is given by the patient and that the patient does not feel that their consent is simply a formality. This is best achieved through clear communication with the patient and seeking verbal consent for the procedure.

The need to align consent with the gravity of the procedure or treatment is reflected in the NMBI's *Code of Professional Conduct and Ethics*:

> The verbal or implied (for example, by a gesture) consent of patients to normally risk-free nursing or midwifery care is a sufficient indication that the consent is valid. As with medical interventions, the consent of patients to more serious and riskier procedures should be informed, written consent. There must be no doubt that informed consent was given and it is documented in the nursing or midwifery notes and the patient consent form.[32]

In recent years there has been a move towards person-centred care in healthcare. Key elements of this are service user involvement and health literacy, which necessitates clear communication, informed consent, and respect for an individual's autonomy. In adhering to these elements, the nurse can promote and encourage greater patient involvement.

Treating in an Emergency

Situations may arise where the individual is unable to provide valid consent and where treatment must urgently be provided if the patient's life is to be sustained. If there is no relevant or applicable advance healthcare directive, then the healthcare professional may provide medical treatment without the patient's

---

[31] *O'Brien v Cunard SS Co*, 28 NE 266 (1891).
[32] Nursing and Midwifery Board of Ireland, *Code of Professional Conduct and Ethics for Registered Nurses and Registered Midwives* (NMBI 2014) 15.

consent. Treatment can be given based on necessity. The NMBI's *Code of Professional Conduct and Ethics* provides:

> In exceptional circumstances – such as emergencies where a patient lacks capacity – consent to treatment or care is not necessary. A nurse or midwife may treat the person when it is immediately necessary to save their life or to prevent a serious deterioration in their condition and there is no advance refusal of treatment.[33]

The nurse should reflect on whether the procedure is immediately necessary or whether it could possibly be delayed until some point at which the patient would have the requisite capacity to make their own decision. This is reflected in s 8(9) of the Assisted Decision-Making (Capacity) Act 2015 (ADMC Act 2015), which provides:

> In the case of an intervention in respect of a person who lacks capacity, regard shall be had to –
>
> (a) the likelihood of the recovery of the relevant person's capacity in respect of the matter concerned, and
>
> (b) the urgency of making the intervention prior to such recovery.[34]

At the time of writing (September 2020), this section, along with the majority of the Act, remains to be commenced.

5.2.2 Voluntary Consent

The decision to consent to a healthcare intervention must be voluntary. The patient must be afforded sufficient freedom and space that they can make a decision. The patient should not be subjected to duress or undue influence as this will negate consent. The HSE's *National Consent Policy* sets out, 'For consent to be valid the service user must not be acting under duress and their agreement should be given freely, in other words they must understand that they have a choice.'[35] The requirement of voluntariness also applies in circumstances where the patient wishes to refuse treatment.

---

[33] ibid 14.
[34] Assisted Decision-Making (Capacity) Act 2015, s 8(9).
[35] Health Service Executive, *National Consent Policy* (HSE 2019) 29.

Duress and undue influence are distinct concepts. Duress may involve threats, violence, or any related action that has the aim of forcing someone to do something against their will. Undue influence is most closely associated with the exertion of psychological pressure on the patient to the extent that this distorts the decision-making process.

No amount of information will remedy a situation where the patient has been subjected to duress or undue influence. In such situations, the patient's decision will not be viewed as real and will be vitiated by the absence of voluntariness. Consent should be informed by a person's own thoughts, desires, and goals for care. This is not to suggest that the patient must decide in a vacuum. Patients will regularly consult with family and friends, but such input should not dominate the decision-making process to the detriment of the person's subjective wishes and judgement. In short, the patient should not be coerced into making a particular decision based on input from friends or family. The nurse should also consider the potential influence of drugs or pathological conditions. The influence of either may severely constrain the patient's ability to make a decision in a manner that could be considered truly voluntary.

5.2.3 The Role of Capacity

The validity of a patient's consent or refusal of treatment is dependent on the patient having the requisite capacity. The HSE's *National Consent Policy* describes capacity as the 'ability to understand the nature and consequences of a decision in the context of available choices at the time the decision is to be made'.[36] This topic is framed by case law, professional guidelines and, upon commencement, the ADMC Act 2015.

Capacity can be a stumbling block for the exercise of autonomy. It is a complex concept that requires many factors be considered and appropriately balanced. An assessment of capacity can be challenging due to the effects of an illness as well the impact sedative or pain-killing drugs may have on the patient. The task of assessing capacity is normally undertaken by the healthcare professional providing medical treatment or care to the patient. As discussed later, this is not a once-off assessment but is a continual process of close engagement with the person to ensure their views and desires effectively shape their healthcare.

---

[36] ibid 12.

Presumption of Capacity

The starting point is a presumption that the patient has decision-making capacity. This presumption applies where the person is over the age of 18, as there are distinct considerations for younger persons. The presumption of capacity is illustrated by *Re C (Adult: Refusal of Treatment)*[37] and was recognised by the Irish High Court in *Fitzpatrick and Another v K and Another*.[38] There is, therefore, no compulsory test that must first be satisfied before a patient may consent or refuse treatment. This presumption will continue under the ADMC Act 2015. Section 8(2) of the 2015 Act provides: 'It shall be presumed that a relevant person … has capacity in respect of the matter concerned unless the contrary is shown in accordance with the provisions of this Act.'[39] The presumption of capacity may therefore be challenged in circumstances where an adequate 'trigger' exists.

The HSE's *National Consent Policy* sets out the following on when to consider incapacity:

> The possibility of incapacity and the need to assess capacity formally should only be considered, if, having been given all appropriate help and support, a service user:
>
> - is unable to communicate a clear and consistent choice or
> - is obviously unable to understand and use the information and choices provided.[40]

Models of Capacity

Different models for the assessment of capacity have been advanced. These include the status approach, outcome approach, and the functional approach. The status approach establishes the patient's medical condition as the defining and overarching factor. The outcome approach to capacity places the focus on the consequences associated with the decision. The effect of a decision is perceived as being an indicator of the person's capacity. It is the functional model of capacity that has come to be favoured and applied in this jurisdiction. It is not a general or once-off assessment of cognitive ability – it can be described as issue- and time-specific. Under the functional model, a person

---

[37] *Re C (Adult: Refusal of Treatment)* [1994] 1 All ER 819.
[38] *Fitzpatrick and Another v K and Another* [2008] IEHC 104.
[39] Assisted Decision-Making (Capacity) Act 2015, s 8(2).
[40] Health Service Executive, *National Consent Policy* (HSE 2019) 32.

may have sufficient capacity to make certain decisions about their healthcare but there may be more complex decisions beyond their level of capacity at that time. There is a clear link between the level of capacity required and the seriousness or complexity of the decision to be made. This approach has come to be reflected in case law, the HSE's *National Consent Policy*, and is a prominent element of the ADMC Act 2015.

Assessment of Capacity

The cases of *Re C (Adult: Refusal of Treatment)* and *Fitzpatrick and Another v K and Another* are relevant in framing the assessment of capacity and, consequently, merit careful consideration. *Re C (Adult: Refusal of Treatment)* came before the Family Division of the High Court in England. The applicant, Mr C, was a 68-year-old man who had paranoid schizophrenia. Mr C developed gangrene of the foot and a consultant surgeon recommended an amputation from below the knee. The prognosis was that Mr C would have a 15% chance of survival without the amputation. However, the patient refused to countenance the procedure. The provision of antibiotics and conservative surgery averted the threat of imminent death. Nonetheless, the hospital did not rule out the potential for the amputation to be carried out at some point in the future were Mr C to develop gangrene once more. Mr C's legal representative applied to the Court for an injunction restraining the hospital from carrying out an amputation without Mr C's express written consent. The hospital argued that Mr C lacked the requisite capacity due to his mental illness and that he had not appreciated the risk of death were the operation not to be performed.

In his judgment Thorpe J stated:

> Although his general capacity is impaired by schizophrenia, it has not been established that he does not sufficiently understand the nature, purpose and effects of the treatment he refuses. Indeed, I am satisfied that he has understood and retained the relevant treatment information, that in his own way he believes it, and that in the same fashion he has arrived at a clear choice.[41]

This statement demonstrates an analysis of the decision-making process as divided into three stages. The first being the comprehending and retaining of treatment information. The

---

[41] *Re C (Adult: Refusal of Treatment)* [1994] 1 All ER 819, 824.

second is that the person should believe the relevant information. The third element is that the person must weigh the information in the balance to arrive at a choice. These elements were satisfied by Mr C and, accordingly, the Court indicated that the presumption in favour of his right to self-determination had not been displaced. To an objective third party the decision of Mr C may appear unwise or even highly questionable. The focus, however, is to be placed on the decision-making process and not the final decision. To focus solely on the final decision has overtones of medical paternalism.

The principles informing the determination of capacity in Ireland were outlined in *Fitzpatrick and Another v K and Another*. This decision drew in part on the reasoning set out in *Re C (Adult: Refusal of Treatment)*. At the centre of *Fitzpatrick* was a young woman, Ms K, who had given birth to a child. Ms K subsequently suffered a massive post-partum haemorrhage resulting in cardiovascular collapse. As blood was being prepared for immediate transfusion, the medical team were informed that she would not accept blood for religious reasons. The team were concerned that she would die without a blood transfusion and contacted the Master of the Hospital. The Master had doubts about the quality of her refusal and an application was made to the Court for authority to transfuse Ms K Abbott J granted the ex parte order authorising the transfusion. The hospital subsequently sought declaratory relief that it was and is entitled to apply for such an injunction and that the Court was and is entitled to grant such relief. A defence and counterclaim were advanced on behalf of Ms K. It was argued that the ex parte order should not have been granted; her ECHR rights were infringed; and she was entitled to refuse all or any medical treatment. She therefore sought damages for assault, trespass to the person and breach of constitutional rights, as well as damages for breach of her Convention rights.

There is a clear order in which these various questions are to be considered. The starting point must necessarily be a determination of capacity. It is only then that the balancing of rights may need to be considered. This is illustrative of capacity acting as a gatekeeper for the exercise of patient autonomy. In the absence of capacity then there could be no valid refusal of medical treatment. Laffoy J drew on an analysis of legal authorities from other jurisdictions and had regard to the constitutional framework that defined the parameters of capacity. On this basis, Laffoy J identified and set out six principles applicable to the determination of capacity:

1. There is a presumption that an adult patient has the capacity, that is to say, the cognitive ability, to make a decision to refuse medical treatment, but that presumption can be rebutted.

2. In determining whether a patient is deprived of capacity to make a decision to refuse medical treatment whether –

> (a) by reason of permanent cognitive impairment, or
>
> (b) temporary factors, for example, factors of the type referred to by Lord Donaldson in In re T,
>
>> the test is whether the patient's cognitive ability has been impaired to the extent that he or she does not sufficiently understand the nature, purpose and effect of the proffered treatment and the consequences of accepting or rejecting it in the context of the choices available (including any alternative treatment) at the time the decision is made.

3. The three-stage approach to the patient's decision-making process adopted in the C case is a helpful tool in applying that test. The patient's cognitive ability will have been impaired to the extent that he or she is incapable of making the decision to refuse the proffered treatment if the patient –

> (a) has not comprehended and retained the treatment information and, in particular, has not assimilated the information as to the consequences likely to ensue from not accepting the treatment,
>
> (b) has not believed the treatment information and, in particular, if it is the case that not accepting the treatment is likely to result in the patient's death, has not believed that outcome is likely, and
>
> (c) has not weighed the treatment information, in particular, the alternative choices and the likely outcomes, in the balance in arriving at the decision.

4. The treatment information by reference to which the patient's capacity is to be assessed is the information which the clinician is under a duty to impart – information as to what

is the appropriate treatment, that is to say, what treatment is medically indicated, at the time of the decision and the risks and consequences likely to flow from the choices available to the patient in making the decision.

5. In assessing capacity it is necessary to distinguish between misunderstanding or misperception of the treatment information in the decision-making process (which may sometimes be referred to colloquially as irrationality), on the one hand, and an irrational decision or a decision made for irrational reasons, on the other hand. The former may be evidence of lack of capacity. The latter is irrelevant to the assessment.

6. In assessing capacity, whether at the bedside in a high dependency unit or in court, the assessment must have regard to the gravity of the decision, in terms of the consequences which are likely to ensue from the acceptance or rejection of the proffered treatment. In the private law context this means that, in applying the civil law standard of proof, the weight to be attached to the evidence should have regard to the gravity of the decision, whether that is characterised as the necessity for 'clear and convincing proof' or an enjoinder that the court 'should not draw its conclusions lightly'.[42]

Laffoy J also drew on expert evidence and considered the necessity of the blood transfusion. In applying the law to the relevant facts, it was noted that 'the plaintiffs were objectively justified in doubting Ms K's capacity to refuse a blood transfusion'.[43] The Court concluded that Ms K did not have the requisite capacity to make a valid refusal. No balancing of rights was required in the circumstances.

The functional model of capacity is provided for in the ADMC Act 2015. Under s 3(1), 'a person's capacity shall be assessed on the basis of his or her ability to understand, at the time that a decision is to be made, the nature and consequences of the decision to be made by him or her in the context of the available choices at that time'.[44] Section 3(2) provides that a person lacks the capacity to make a decision if he or she is unable –

---

[42] *Fitzpatrick and Another v K and Another* [2008] IEHC 104, [120]–[131].
[43] ibid 104, [291].
[44] Assisted Decision-Making (Capacity) Act 2015, s 3(1).

(a) to understand the information relevant to the decision;

(b) to retain that information long enough to make a voluntary choice;

(c) to use or weigh that information as part of the process of making the decision; or

(d) to communicate his or her decision (whether by talking, writing, using sign language, assistive technology, or any other means) or, if the implementation of the decision requires the act of a third party, to communicate by any means with that third party.[45]

Section 3(3) of the 2015 Act sets out that a 'person is not to be regarded as unable to understand the information relevant to a decision if he or she is able to understand an explanation of it given to him or her in a way that is appropriate to his or her circumstances'.[46] This is linked to s 8(3) of the 2015 Act, which requires 'all practicable steps' to be taken to help the patient in making a decision. There will of course be cases where such steps are not effective, and a treatment decision must be made. This will be discussed later in this chapter and will involve consideration of the guiding principles contained in the ADMC Act 2015. A person does not need to retain information relevant to the decision for an indefinite period. Instead, a person need only retain the information for as long as it takes to weigh and consider the information, thereby allowing the person to decide.[47] Sections 3(5) and (6) of the 2015 Act provide that the assessment of capacity is time- and issue-specific. This reflects the fact that capacity may fluctuate over time and that more complex decisions require a greater level of capacity.

5.2.4 Disclosure of Appropriate Information

The relevance of an appropriate disclosure of information was highlighted in section 5.2.1. A broad understanding of the medical treatment may be sufficient to avoid liability in battery but, in practice, more detailed information is usually needed to safeguard against an action in negligence. The information may relate to the risks associated with the treatment or alternative procedures that may be available. Of course, for every medical treatment there are

---

[45] ibid s 3(2).
[46] ibid s 3(3).
[47] ibid s 3(4).

a multitude of risks and harms that could potentially arise. It may not be feasible to outline every possible minute risk of harm. A decision must therefore be made as to what risks should be drawn to the patient's attention and which risks need not be highlighted. There is a balance to be achieved, which McCarthy described as follows, 'On the one hand, giving someone too little information about the treatment might seem patronising and pointless. On the other hand, giving someone too much information might prove unnecessary and counterproductive.'[48] There is clearly a subjective element in determining what constitutes a sufficient disclosure of information. This subjectivity has posed challenges as it is to be questioned whether the level of information should be determined from the perspective of the healthcare professional or whether the views and concerns of the patient should dominate. The preferred approach has shifted over time and is now more reflective of values such as patient autonomy and self-determination. This is encapsulated in the reasonable patient standard, which dislodged the reasonable doctor approach.

The reasonable doctor approach to informed consent requires the healthcare professional to inform the patient of the risks that a responsible body of medical opinion thinks a patient should be told of. This is grounded in the idea that the healthcare professional is best placed to know what risks should be communicated to the patient. It is a paternalistic approach to the disclosure of information and does not necessarily equip the patient to make a fully informed decision.

The reasonable patient standard allows the patient to set the agenda. The healthcare professional must pay close attention to risks the patient would consider particularly significant and should disclose risks that are important or material to the decision. This standard was applied in *Canterbury v Spence*.[49] In this US case, the Court stated, 'Respect for the patient's right of self-determination ... demands a standard set by law for physicians rather than one which physicians may or may not impose upon themselves.'[50]

Adherence to the reasonable patient standard can be challenging. It demands greater dialogue and engagement with the patient. The nurse, therefore, has an important role in supporting this

---

[48] Dolores Dooley and Joan McCarthy, *Nursing Ethics: Irish Cases and Concerns* (2nd edn, Gill & Macmillan 2012) 34.
[49] *Canterbury v Spence* 464 F 2d 772 (1972).
[50] ibid 784.

process. The nurse has regular close contact with the patient and may develop an understanding of and insight into the patient's values and priorities for care. This experience can shape and improve the overall standard of information provided to the patient, regardless of whether it is the nurse or another healthcare professional who has responsibility for seeking consent.

Risk Disclosure in Irish Law

Geoghegan v Harris

In the case of *Geoghegan v Harris*, the plaintiff, Mr Geoghegan, sued Dr Harris for alleged negligence in the carrying out of a dental implant procedure.[51] As part of the procedure, a bone graft was taken from Mr Geoghegan's chin and he suffered damage to the incisive nerve at the front of his chin. This resulted in severe pain at the mid-line of his chin, referred to as chronic neuropathic pain. The plaintiff also sued Dr Harris for failing to disclose to him in advance of the operation the risk that chronic neuropathic pain might occur as a consequence of the procedure. Dr Harris cautioned the plaintiff about the potential for pain and numbness but accepted that he did not discuss or disclose any possibility or risk of chronic neuropathic pain or prolonged pain that could occur. In cross-examination, Dr Harris stated, 'if you knew that a complication could occur, then you must tell the patient about it'.[52] He applied a standard whereby he considered what it is that he would want to know if he was in a similar situation and he suggested that he would give as much information as he could in the context of the specific procedure. In this instance, it did not occur to Dr Harris that chronic neuropathic pain was an associated risk. Mr Geoghegan attached considerable weight to this risk and was clear that he would not have undergone the procedure had he been aware of it, even if the risk was one in a thousand.

Kearns J analysed in detail the legal principles outlined in a previous case of *Walsh v Family Planning Services*.[53] He ultimately favoured the reasonable patient standard and described it as 'more logical in respect of disclosure'.[54] Kearns J went on to state:

> as a general principle, the patient has the right to know and the practitioner a duty to advise of all material risks associated

---

[51] *Geoghegan v Harris* [2000] IEHC 129, [2000] 3 IR 536.
[52] ibid 129, [60].
[53] *Walsh v Irish Family Planning Services* [1992] 1 IR 496.
[54] *Geoghegan v Harris* [2000] IEHC 129, [140].

with a proposed form of treatment. The Court must ultimately decide what is material. 'Materiality' includes consideration of both (a) the severity of the consequences and (b) statistical frequency of the risk. That both are critical is obvious because a risk may have serious consequences and yet historically or predictably be so rare as not to be regarded as significant by many people.[55]

A material risk is not defined in a rigid or inflexible manner but is instead shaped by the specific circumstances. On this point, Kearns J set out: 'Each case it seems to me should be considered in the light of its own particular facts, evidence and circumstances to see if the reasonable patient in the Plaintiff's position would have required a warning of the particular risk.'[56]

Kearns J also applied the reasonable patient standard to causation. The patient therefore needed to demonstrate that, had he been warned of the risk, he would not then have gone ahead with the procedure. The evidence in *Geoghegan* did not suggest that, prior to the procedure, the plaintiff was 'hypersensitive, or unusually cautious or the kind of man who would back away at the mention of a remote risk'.[57] Instead, the plaintiff appeared keen to undergo the procedure and was aware of the benefits to be gained. Taking account of his actions and behaviour in advance of the procedure, Kearns J held that Mr Geoghegan was 'not going to be put off having his operation because of some very remote risk when balanced against what he saw or perceived as the benefits the procedure would bring'.[58] As such, the plaintiff was unsuccessful in his claim. *Geoghegan v Harris* demonstrated judicial support for the reasonable patient standard. Further clarity was brought to this area with the case of *Fitzpatrick v White*.

Fitzpatrick v White

The plaintiff in *Fitzpatrick v White* underwent a procedure to correct a squint in his left eye. Thirty minutes before surgery and prior to being sedated, the plaintiff had spoken with the surgeon. The plaintiff suggested that there was no mention of 'complications, side-effects or adverse consequences that might ensue'.[59] He subsequently signed a standard consent form and this document did not 'specify any risks associated with the proposed

---

[55] ibid.
[56] ibid 129, [146].
[57] ibid 129, [199].
[58] ibid 129, [201].
[59] *Fitzpatrick v White* [2007] IESC 51, [5].

procedure'.[60] In cross-examination, the plaintiff stated that he had not been told of the risk of muscle loss or slippage resulting in double vision and suggested that if he had been told he would not have proceeded with the operation. In any case, the operation was carried out and, subsequently, the plaintiff experienced double vision and headaches.

In considering the obligation to warn, Kearns P outlined the changing attitudes in the English courts and drew on relevant Australian authorities such as *Rosenberg v Percival*.[61] This led Kearns J to comment:

> The analysis undertaken by both Kirby J and the other members of the High Court of Australia in *Rosenberg v Percival* supports the argument that the giving of an adequate warning, far from being a source of nuisance for doctors, should be seen as an opportunity to ensure they are protected from subsequent litigation at the suit of disappointed patients. I am thus fortified to express in rather more vigorous terms than I did in *Geoghegan v. Harris* my view that the patient centred test is preferable, and ultimately more satisfactory from the point of view of both doctor and patient alike, than any 'doctor centred' approach favoured by part of this Court in *Walsh v. Family Planning Services*.[62]

The Court held that the disclosure was adequate, and the plaintiff failed in his claim. Nonetheless, a final point to note is the issue of timing and whether a warning delivered a short period before an operation is sufficient to discharge the healthcare professional's duty of care.

The plaintiff was seen on three occasions prior to the operation. There was therefore ample time in which relevant information could have been disclosed and explained. While experts indicated that there are advantages of warning day patients on the day of the operation, Kearns J suggested that the disadvantages may be far greater:

> There are obvious reasons why, in the context of elective surgery, a warning given only shortly before an operation is undesirable. A patient may be stressed, medicated or in pain in this period and may be less likely for one or more of

---

[60] ibid 51, [5].
[61] *Rosenberg v Percival* [2001] HCA 18.
[62] *Fitzpatrick v White* [2007] IESC 51, [46].

these reasons to make a calm and reasoned decision in such circumstances.[63]

There was no evidence that the patient in this case was unduly stressed, anxious, in pain, or sedated at the time. He appeared to be in a clear and lucid mental state and was capable of making a decision. In the absence of clear evidence that the plaintiff was actually disadvantaged in some material way by the lateness of the warning, the judge would not find the warning to be invalid due to the timing. The judge went on to state: 'I would make the point strongly however that in other cases where a warning is given late in the day, particularly where the surgery is elective surgery, the outcome might well be different.'[64]

The cases of *Geoghegan* and *Fitzpatrick* were subsequently cited by the Court of Appeal in *Healy v Buckley*.[65] As it stands, the reasonable patient standard for the disclosure of information is favoured in this jurisdiction.

5.2.5 Therapeutic Privilege

In *Sidaway v Board of Governors of the Bethlem Royal Hospital*, Lord Templeman stated that 'some information may confuse, other information may alarm a particular patient ... the doctor must decide in the light of his training and experience and in the light of knowledge of the patient what should be said and how it should be said'.[66] This statement suggests that the doctor may decide that there is some information that should not be disclosed. This is referred to as therapeutic privilege and is, in many ways, an ethically and legally problematic concept.

Therapeutic privilege may be seen as the antithesis of patient autonomy as it involves secrecy and limits the scope of information disclosure. It involves the healthcare professional withholding information from the patient in circumstances where it is thought that a full disclosure may cause serious harm to the patient. In effect, the potential for psychological harm may require that information about diagnosis, prognosis, or available treatments be limited. The threshold at which therapeutic privilege could be relied on is necessarily high. It can never be used to justify the non-disclosure of information where the sole concern is that the

---

[63] ibid 51, [51].
[64] ibid 51, [52].
[65] *Healy v Buckley* [2015] IECA 251.
[66] *Sidaway v Board of Governors of the Bethlem Royal Hospital* [1985] 1 AC 871, 904.

information may lead to the patient's refusal of treatment. This would negate any informed consent given for the procedure. Moreover, the anticipated harm should not be trivial and should involve more than a temporary upset. It follows that any use of therapeutic privilege should be as limited as necessary and should involve considerable caution on the part of the healthcare professionals involved.

5.3 The Right to Refuse Treatment

The refusal of treatment can be challenging for healthcare professionals. It can bring values such as autonomy and beneficence into conflict and this may prove ethically challenging for the healthcare professionals involved in the provision of care and treatment. A person's autonomous decision must be respected even if it is not necessarily in their best interests from a purely medical perspective. Although the patient's refusal is to be respected it may be limited based on factors such as their level of capacity. The patient's decision is also likely to be questioned in circumstances where it conflicts with the sanctity of life or with the advice of healthcare professionals. Many of the cases that have come before the courts reflect this contentious dimension of treatment refusal. The cases discussed in this section were touched on in section 5.1.2 as they have served to define the concept and parameters of autonomy. This is not an exhaustive discussion of treatment refusal: the topic will also be addressed in Chapter Eight as it relates to treatment refusal during pregnancy and the refusal of caesarean sections.

The right of autonomy as protected by Article 8 ECHR was discussed in *Pretty v United Kingdom*.[67] The applicant alleged that her rights as protected by Articles 2, 3, 8, 9 and 14 of the ECHR were infringed due to the prohibition on assisted suicide under the Suicide Act 1961 and the refusal of the DPP to grant immunity to her husband for assisting in her suicide. The House of Lords did not consider that Article 8 ECHR had any relevance for the ending of life. This point is demonstrated by the view that although Article 8 'offered protection to autonomy during life, it did not say anything about the right of individuals to autonomy over their deaths'.[68] In contrast to this, the European Court of Human Rights (ECtHR) found that Article 8 allowed for the refusal of medical treatment even if it would result in the death of

---

[67] *Pretty v United Kingdom* (2002) 35 EHRR 1.
[68] Dan Morris, 'Assisted Suicide under the European Convention on Human Rights: A Critique' (2003) European Human Rights Law Review 65, 78.

the patient. The position of the ECtHR was subsequently affirmed in *Tysiac v Poland*.[69]

In Ireland, the right to refuse treatment has been acknowledged and accepted by the courts in cases such as *Re a Ward of Court*,[70] *JM v The Board of Management of St Vincent's Hospital*,[71] and *Fitzpatrick v FK*.[72]

The person at the centre of *Re a Ward of Court* was a middle-aged woman who was described as being in a near persistent vegetative state. In the first five to six months after the incident there were minimal signs of recovery, but these did not continue and there was no prospect of recovery. The woman had been made a ward of court and an application was made by the family for the withdrawal of life support. The life support at the time consisted of medication as well as artificial nutrition and hydration. Initially, Lynch J in the High Court held that artificial nutrition and hydration could be withdrawn from the ward. This decision was appealed to the Supreme Court, which upheld the High Court's decision by a 4:1 majority.

The patient's lack of capacity does not result in the diminution of personal rights as recognised and protected by the Irish Constitution. O'Flaherty J recognised that as a corollary of the right to consent, 'there is an absolute right in a competent person to refuse medical treatment even if it leads to death'.[73] On the issue of consent, Denham J commented:

> The consent which is given by an adult of full capacity is a matter of choice. It is not necessarily a decision based on medical considerations. Thus, medical treatment may be refused for other than medical reasons, or reasons most citizens would regard as rational, but the person of full age and capacity may make the decision for their own reasons.[74]

The refusal of treatment and the legal support for doing so can be problematic for healthcare professionals. Nonetheless, a refusal of treatment is specific and other forms of care may be provided to the patient. For instance, artificial nutrition and hydration was withdrawn in *Re a Ward of Court* but it was recognised that

---

[69] *Tysiac v Poland* (2007) 45 EHRR 42.
[70] *Re a Ward of Court* [1996] 2 IR 79.
[71] *JM v The Board of Management of St Vincent's Hospital* [2003] 1 IR 321.
[72] *Fitzpatrick v FK* [2008] IEHC 104.
[73] *Re a Ward of Court* [1996] 2 IR 79, 129.
[74] ibid 79, 156.

palliative care and medication would continue to be provided. A refusal may oblige the healthcare professional to adopt a more passive role than they envisaged, and this may challenge how they interpret or view their professional duty of care. The practice of medicine is not about adopting a vitalist position to the care of the patient; life need not be preserved at all costs. This is reflected in the comments of Hamilton CJ:

> As the process of dying is part, and an ultimate, inevitable consequence, of life, the right to life necessarily implies the right to have nature take its course and to die a natural death and, unless the individual concerned so wishes, not to have life artificially maintained by the provision of nourishment by abnormal artificial means, which have no curative effect and which is intended merely to prolong life.[75]

In *JM v The Board of Management of St Vincent's Hospital*, a woman was critically ill and required an immediate blood transfusion and liver transplant. She appeared to accept the carrying out of a blood transfusion but when a member of the liver transplant team returned ten minutes later with the consent form, the woman had changed her mind. The Court placed considerable emphasis on the woman's religious beliefs and cultural values. Her husband was a Jehovah's Witness, and she adopted her husband's religion upon their marriage. The application was brought by her husband for the purposes of having the blood transfusion administered. Finnegan P accepted that a right to refuse medical treatment exists but noted that this applies to the extent that a person is competent to make such a decision.[76] In considering the evidence, Finnegan P stated:

> I take the view because of her cultural background and her desire to please her husband and not offend his sensibilities, the notice party elected to refuse treatment. I am of the view that the notice party did not make a clear final decision to have, or not to have the treatment. She was pre-occupied with her husband and his religion as a Jehovah's Witness rather than with whether to have the treatment and her own welfare.[77]

Accordingly, the blood transfusion could be administered. The correctness of this decision can be questioned as the woman

---

[75] ibid 79, 124.
[76] *JM v The Board of Management of St Vincent's Hospital* [2003] 1 IR 321, 324.
[77] ibid 321, 325.

appeared to have made her decision without undue influence. Nevertheless, other factors prevailed in the Court's assessment. This is a common trend when these types of cases have come before the courts. This was also seen in *Fitzpatrick and Another v K and Another*, which was discussed in section 5.2.3. In *Fitzpatrick*, Laffoy J determined that a refusal of treatment was not valid as Ms K did not have the requisite capacity. These types of cases do not mean that the right to refuse treatment is illusory but are illustrative of the high threshold that must be achieved for such a refusal to be considered valid.

5.4 A Demand for Medical Treatment

Patient autonomy is often confined to discussions about consent and refusal of treatment. However, this is a somewhat limited conception of autonomy. The language of healthcare increasingly speaks of clients and customers. It follows that customers are active rather than passive and may demand forms of medical treatment. The extent to which a person could shape their medical treatment arose in the English Court of Appeal decision of *R(Burke) v General Medical Council*.[78]

Mr Burke had a condition known as spinocerebellar ataxia. This would eventually result in him becoming fully dependent on other people for his care. It would limit his ability to communicate but he would retain his cognitive abilities. As the condition worsened, Mr Burke would experience pain, discomfort, and choking episodes. Mr Burke became aware of General Medical Council (GMC) guidance, which suggested that artificial nutrition and hydration would be withdrawn in certain circumstances. Mr Burke's preference was to be fed and to receive appropriate hydration until he died of natural causes. He therefore sought judicial review of the GMC guidance to ensure his treatment would be continued even if he could not express his wishes in the future.

At first instance, the case was heard by Munby J, who held that the patient had a right to have the treatment continued and the GMC guidance was incompatible with Articles 2, 3, and 8 of the Human Rights Act.[79] It is not surprising that this decision was appealed by the GMC. Munby J went on to advance propositions of law and suggested that the competent patient 'decides what is in his best

---

[78] *R(Burke) v General Medical Council* [2006] QB 273, [2005] EWCA Civ 1003.
[79] Art 2 Right to life; Art 3 Prohibition of torture; Art 8 Right to respect for private and family life.

interests and what treatment he should or should not have'.[80] This gives the patient considerable control and the GMC feared that this might establish an obligation for doctors to provide treatment requested by the patient although it may not be in the patient's best interests.

The Court of Appeal allowed the appeal and held the guidance to be lawful. In relation to the autonomous request, Lord Phillips MR stated:

> the right to refuse a proposed treatment gives the patient what appears to be a positive option to choose an alternative. In truth the right to choose is no more than a reflection of the fact that it is the doctor's duty to provide a treatment that he considers to be in the interests of the patient and that the patient is prepared to accept.[81]

The Court did, however, indicate that in circumstances where a competent patient has made it clear that they wish to be kept alive through the provision of artificial nutrition and hydration then the deliberate withdrawal of such treatment would be a breach of duty and could potentially lead to a charge of murder.[82] The Court went on to consider the possibility that in some situations ANH might not be clinically indicated. On this point, the Court was of the opinion that 'a patient cannot demand that a doctor administer a treatment which the doctor considers is adverse to the patient's clinical needs'.[83]

It is likely that a similar position would be adopted in this jurisdiction. The healthcare professional will be guided by the clinical interests of the patient rather than acceding to all requests from the patient. Of course, the request may be considered where it would be relevant to the situation at hand. This is reflected in the provisions on advance healthcare directives as contained in the ADMC Act 2015. Section 84(3)(a) of the 2015 Act provides:

> A request for a specific treatment set out in an advance healthcare directive is not legally binding but shall be taken into consideration during any decision-making process which relates to treatment for the directive-maker if that

---

[80] *R(Burke) v General Medical Council* [2005] QB 424, [99].
[81] *R(Burke) v General Medical Council* [2006] QB 273, [51].
[82] ibid 273, [53].
[83] ibid 273, [55].

specific treatment is relevant to the medical condition for which the directive-maker may require treatment.[84]

Section 84(3)(b) of the 2015 Act sets out that where a request is not complied with then the reasons for not complying with the request are to be recorded and a copy of these reasons should be given, as soon as practicable, to the person's designated healthcare representative if one has been appointed.[85]

5.5 The Assisted Decision-Making (Capacity) Act 2015

The ADMC Act 2015 has been cited in relation to the assessment of capacity as well as requests for treatment that arise in the context of advance healthcare directives. The Act is extensive, detailed and, once fully commenced, will formalise and reshape many elements of healthcare decision-making in this jurisdiction.

The legislation was signed into law by President Michael D Higgins on 30 December 2015, however, much of the Act is still to be commenced. The enactment of the legislation took a considerable length of time from when it was first mooted. The origins of the Act can be traced back to the 2006 Law Reform Commission *Report on Vulnerable Adults and the Law*.[86] This Report followed on from the Law Reform Commission *Consultation Paper on Law and the Elderly*[87] and *Consultation Paper on Vulnerable Adults and the Law: Capacity*.[88] The Report recommended that a new capacity law be enacted and recommended that the ward of court system be replaced. The Government at the time indicated that it would respond to the recommendations set out by the Law Reform Commission. A further motivating factor underpinning the introduction of the ADMC Act 2015 was the UN Convention on the Rights of Persons with Disabilities (UNCRPD). The 2015 Act was necessary to ensure Ireland's compliance with the obligations established under the UNCRPD, specifically Article 12 'Equal recognition before the law'.

---

[84] Assisted Decision-Making (Capacity) Act 2015, s 84(3)(a).
[85] ibid s 84(3)(b).
[86] Law Reform Commission, *Report on Vulnerable Adults and the Law* (LRC 83 – 2006).
[87] Law Reform Commission, *Consultation Paper on Law and the Elderly* (LRC CP 23 – 2003).
[88] Law Reform Commission, *Consultation Paper on Vulnerable Adults and the Law: Capacity* (LRC CP 37 – 2005).

The ADMC Act 2015 applies to persons whose decision-making capacity is called into question or may shortly be called into question. Key elements of the legislation include the statutory recognition of the functional approach to capacity, the use of guiding principles in place of best interests, the establishment of the Decision Support Service, the formalisation of decision-making supports, the abolition of the wardship system, changes to enduring powers of attorney, and the creation of a statutory framework for advance healthcare directives. It is the Director of the Decision Support Service who has responsibility for the implementation of many of the substantial changes introduced by the 2015 Act.

5.5.1 Director of the Decision Support Service

Part 9 of the Act provides for the appointment of a Director of the Decision Support Service. The Director is appointed by the Mental Health Commission. Section 95 of the 2015 Act sets out the functions of the Director as follows:

> (a) to promote public awareness of this Act and matters (including the United Nations Convention on the Rights of Persons with Disabilities, done at New York on 13 December 2006) relating to the exercise of their capacity by persons who require or may shortly require assistance in exercising their capacity;
>
> (b) to promote public confidence in the process of dealing with matters which affect persons who require or may shortly require assistance in exercising their capacity;
>
> (c) to provide information to relevant persons in relation to their options under this Act for exercising their capacity;
>
> (d) to provide information to decision-making assistants, co-decision-makers, decision-making representatives, designated healthcare representatives and attorneys in relation to the performance of their functions under this Act;
>
> (e) to supervise, in accordance with the provisions of this Act, compliance by decision-making assistants, co-decision-makers, decision-making representatives and attorneys in the performance of their functions under this Act;
>
> (f) to provide information in relation to the management of property and financial affairs to relevant persons and to

decision-making assistants, co-decision-makers, decision-making representatives and attorneys;

(g) to provide information and guidance to organisations and bodies in the State in relation to their interaction with relevant persons;

(h) to provide information and guidance to organisations and bodies in the State in relation to their interaction with decision-making assistants, co-decision-makers, decision-making representatives, attorneys and designated healthcare representatives;

(i) to identify and make recommendations for change of practices in organisations and bodies in which the practices may prevent a relevant person from exercising his or her capacity under this Act;

(j) to establish a website on the internet or provide, or arrange for the provision of, other electronic means by which to disseminate information to members of the public relevant to the performance of the Director's functions and which will, in the opinion of the Director, assist members of the public to understand the operation of this Act and the Director's role in relation thereto;

(k) to make recommendations to the Minister on any matter relating to the operation of this Act.[89]

Section 103 of the Act sets out that the Director may 'prepare and publish a code of practice', 'request another body to prepare a code of practice' or 'approve of a code of practice prepared by another body'. Such codes are intended to assist persons engaging with various aspects of the legislation.

The Director has specific regulatory functions under the ADMC Act 2015. Section 96 of the Act allows the Director to initiate an investigation either on his or her own initiative or in response to a complaint made to him or her by any person, in relation to the conduct of a decision-making assistant, co-decision-maker, decision-making representative, designated healthcare representative or attorney for a relevant person. Section 96(2) sets out a range of powers to enable the Director to undertake the complaints function. This includes powers to summon witnesses,

---

[89] Assisted Decision-Making (Capacity) Act 2015, s 95.

to examine witnesses under oath, to require the production of documents in the power or control of the witness and, by notice in writing, require any person to provide the Director with such written information as the Director considers necessary.[90] The Director of the Decision Support Service will also carry out regulatory functions relating to the appointment and supervision of panels of special and general visitors and court friends.

5.5.2 Functional Assessment of Capacity

The functional assessment of capacity was seen in Laffoy J's decision in *Fitzpatrick v FK*. The 2015 Act places this approach on a statutory footing. While recognising that there is a rebuttable presumption of capacity, s 3(1) of the 2015 Act sets out that 'a person's capacity shall be assessed on the basis of his or her ability to understand, at the time that a decision is to be made, the nature and consequences of the decision to be made by him or her in the context of the available choices at that time'.[91] The assessment is time- and issue-specific. The functional assessment of capacity was discussed earlier in this chapter and an outline of the relevant provisions in the 2015 Act can be found at section 5.2.3, 'The Role of Capacity'.

5.5.3 Guiding Principles

The term 'best interests' is not used in the ADMC Act 2015. Instead, 'guiding principles' are set out under s 8 of the 2015 Act, which are intended to apply before and during an intervention in respect of a relevant person. Although the section provides structure, the 'intervener' still has considerable discretion in applying these principles. The combination of codes of practice and judicial guidance is likely to shape the application and interpretation of these principles in the future.

Section 8(3) provides that a person will not be considered as unable to make a decision, 'unless all practicable steps have been taken, without success, to help him or her to do so'.[92] The intervener must therefore be careful to ensure appropriate supports are provided to allow the person to make their voice heard. If the person has made or is likely to make an unwise decision, then this does not

---

[90] ibid s 96(2).
[91] ibid s 3(1).
[92] ibid s 8(3).

automatically render them unable to make a decision in respect of the matter concerned.[93]

Section 8(5) of the 2015 Act provides: 'There shall be no intervention in respect of a relevant person unless it is necessary to do so having regard to the individual circumstances of the relevant person.'[94] Section 8(6) sets out that any intervention should minimise the restriction of the relevant person's rights and freedom of action.[95] In addition, due regard should be had for the person's rights including dignity, bodily integrity, privacy, autonomy, and control over his or her financial affairs and property.[96] The intervention should be 'proportionate to the significance and urgency of the matter', and should be 'as limited in duration in so far as is practicable'.[97] The overall effect is that the least restrictive option should be pursued when making a decision for a person lacking capacity.

Section 8(7) of the Act focuses on the intervener's responsibilities. An intervener is required to permit, encourage and facilitate the participation of the relevant person as much as possible. Notably, the intervener is to 'give effect, in so far as is practicable, to the past and present will and preferences of the relevant person',[98] and the intervener should take account of the beliefs and values of the relevant person as well as any other factors the person would be likely to consider. The emphasis on the patient's will and preferences underlines the need to respect a person's autonomous desires. The intervener shall also consider the views of 'any person named by the relevant person as a person to be consulted', and 'any decision-making assistant, co-decision maker, decision-making representative or attorney for the relevant person'.[99] The intervener must 'act at all times in good faith and for the benefit of the relevant person, and consider all other circumstances of which he or she is aware and which it would be reasonable to regard as relevant'.[100] Much of this section is open to interpretation and elements could easily be neglected in the application. A careful and mindful approach to implementation is therefore required. In particular, given the close relationship to the requirements of the

---

[93] ibid s 8(4).
[94] ibid s 8(5).
[95] ibid s 8(6).
[96] ibid s 8(6).
[97] ibid s 8(6)(c) and (d).
[98] ibid s 8(7).
[99] ibid s 8(7)(d).
[100] ibid ss 8(7)(e) and (f).

UNCRPD, it is essential that the 'will and preferences' component be firmly incorporated in any intervention.

Section 8(8) of the Act outlines the persons whom the intervener may consult when making an intervention. The intervener may consider the views of 'any person engaged in caring for the relevant person', 'any person who has a bona fide interest in the welfare of the relevant person', or 'healthcare professionals'.[101] To say that the intervener 'may' consider these views is to indicate that it is not mandatory but is instead facilitative. This allows a degree of discretion for the intervener in considering the views and opinions of family members.

Section 8(9) was discussed earlier in this chapter and it was noted that the nurse should reflect on whether a procedure is immediately necessary or whether it could possibly be delayed until some point at which the patient would have the requisite capacity to make their own decision. In this respect, it provides that regard should be had to 'the likelihood of the recovery of the relevant person's capacity in respect of the matter concerned, and the urgency of making the intervention prior to such recovery'.[102]

5.5.4 Decision-Making Supports

The Act provides for a range of decision-making supports. These are intended to promote a person's autonomy to the greatest extent and assist the person in making healthcare decisions that reflect their own personal will and preferences. The Act also extends to decisions relating to a person's welfare, property and affairs. The types of decision-making support available reflect a hierarchy of assistance and capacity.

Assisted Decision-Making

Where a person considers that his or her capacity is in question or may shortly be in question, he or she may appoint a decision-making assistant to assist him or her in making one or more decisions about his or her personal welfare, and/or property and affairs. This appointment is to be made in a decision-making assistance agreement, which should adhere to the regulations set out by the Minister. There is no requirement to formally register a decision-making assistance agreement.

---

[101] ibid s 8(8).
[102] ibid s 8(9).

Under s 10(5) of the 2015 Act, a person may appoint more than one person as a decision-making assistant and may specify that the decision-making assistants are to act jointly, jointly and severally, or jointly in respect of some matters and jointly and severally in respect of other matters. In appointing a decision-making assistant, regard should be had to s 11, which outlines the persons who are not eligible for appointment. This includes persons who have been convicted of an offence in relation to the person or property of the appointer, have been the subject of a safety or barring order in relation to the appointer, or is an undischarged bankrupt or is currently in a debt settlement arrangement or personal insolvency arrangement or has been convicted of an offence involving fraud or dishonesty.[103] Disqualification as a decision-making assistant is addressed by s 13 of the Act.

A decision-making assistance agreement may be rendered null and void if the agreement relates to a matter that is covered by: a decision-making order, a decision-making representation order, or a co-decision-making agreement in relation to the appointer; an advance healthcare directive; or an enduring power of attorney.[104]

Section 14 of the 2015 Act provides that in exercising his or her functions as specified in the decision-making assistance agreement, the decision-making assistant shall:

(a) assist the appointer to obtain the appointer's relevant information;

(b) advise the appointer by explaining relevant information and considerations relating to a relevant decision;

(c) ascertain the will and preferences of the appointer on a matter the subject or to be the subject, of a relevant decision and assist the appointer to communicate them;

(d) assist the appointer to make and express a relevant decision; and

(e) endeavour to ensure that the appointer's relevant decisions are implemented.[105]

---

[103] ibid s 11.
[104] ibid s 12.
[105] ibid s 14.

The decision-making assistant is not to make the decision on behalf of the appointer. Any decision that is made will be deemed as having been made by the appointer only. The decision-making assistant is not to substitute their own decision for that of the appointer and should act to ensure that the appointer's decisions are effectively implemented. If there are concerns about the validity of the decision-making assistance agreement or the actions of the decision-making assistant, then a complaint may be made to the Director of the Decision Support Service.[106]

Co-Decision-Making

Co-decision-making represents a step up in the level of support required and involves a more formal process for appointment. Where a person considers that his or her capacity is in question or may shortly be in question, they may appoint a suitable person to jointly make with them one or more decisions about their personal welfare or property and affairs.

A person is considered suitable for appointment as a co-decision-maker if they are a relative or friend of the appointer such that a relationship of trust exists and they would be able to perform the functions under the co-decision-making agreement.[107] Under s 17(3) an appointment of a co-decision-maker shall be made in writing in a co-decision-making agreement that is in compliance with the regulations set out by the Minister. Persons not eligible to be appointed as a co-decision-maker are outlined by s 18 of the 2015 Act.

Section 19 provides that in exercising his or her functions as specified in the co-decision-making agreement, the co-decision-maker shall:

> (a) advise the appointer by explaining relevant information and considerations relating to a relevant decision;
>
> (b) ascertain the will and preferences of the appointer on a matter the subject of, or to be the subject of, a relevant decision and assist the appointer with communicating the appointer's will and preferences;
>
> (c) assist the appointer to obtain the appointer's relevant information;

---

[106] ibid s 15.
[107] ibid s 17(2).

(d) discuss with the appointer the known alternatives and likely outcomes of a relevant decision;

(e) make a relevant decision jointly with the appointer; and

(f) make reasonable efforts to ensure that a relevant decision is implemented as far as practicable.[108]

The co-decision-maker therefore has an important support role in assisting the appointer and should be careful not to dominate the decision-making process. This is illustrated by s 19(5), under which:

a reference to a relevant decision being made jointly means that a co-decision-maker –

(a) shall acquiesce with the wishes of the appointer in respect of the relevant decision, and

(b) shall not refuse to sign a document …

unless it is reasonably foreseeable that such acquiescence or signature, as the case may be, will result in serious harm to the appointer or to another person.[109]

A significant difference between a decision-making assistance agreement and a co-decision-making agreement is the need for registration. A co-decision-making agreement will not enter into force until it has been registered and registration should occur within five weeks of it being signed.[110] At the time an application is made to register a co-decision-making agreement, the appointer and co-decision-maker are to give notice and a copy of the agreement to persons specified under s 21(3) such as the spouse or civil partner (if any) of the appointer, any cohabitant of the appointer, and any children of the appointer who have attained the age of 18.[111] Such persons may, within five weeks of receiving notice, object to the proposed registration.[112] The Director will review the objection, consult with the appointer and co-decision-maker and give them a reasonable opportunity to respond to the objection. The Director will also consult with such other persons

---

[108] ibid s 19.
[109] ibid s 19(5).
[110] ibid s 21.
[111] ibid s 21(3).
[112] ibid s 24(2).

as she considers relevant before determining whether or not to register the agreement.

Each agreement is to be reviewed after one year and then at intervals of three years. The co-decision-maker is required to file a report with the Director every year. The report is to outline their performance in the role and should include details of all relevant transactions relating to the appointer's finances.[113] It should also contain details of all costs and expenses paid to and claimed by the co-decision-maker in the relevant period.

The terms of a registered co-decision-making agreement may be changed with the consent of the appointer and co-decision-maker.[114] Furthermore, a co-decision-making agreement, whether registered or not, may be revoked in whole or in part, by either party. The Director must be notified of any revocation and must update the Register accordingly.[115] Other provisions in this Part address complaints in relation to co-decision-makers,[116] applications to Court,[117] the role of the Director where nullity occurs,[118] and offences in relation to co-decision-making agreements.[119]

Decision-Making Representatives

While the ADMC Act 2015 includes measures intended to involve the patient in healthcare decision-making as fully as possible, there will be circumstances in which the patient will lack capacity and decisions will be made on their behalf by another person. In defined circumstances, the Court may intervene for the purposes of appointing a decision-making representative and/or may make the decision(s) on behalf of the relevant person where it is satisfied that the matter is urgent or that it is otherwise expedient for it to do so.[120] The will and preferences of the patient may still influence and inform the functions of the decision-making representative. Section 38(3) of the ADMC Act 2015 provides that the court is to have regard to the terms of any advance healthcare directive and is to ensure that the decision-making representative's functions are not inconsistent with the directive. The approach taken will

---

[113] ibid s 27.
[114] Additional formalities set out by ibid s 28.
[115] ibid s 29.
[116] ibid s 30.
[117] ibid s 32.
[118] ibid s 33.
[119] ibid s 34.
[120] ibid s 38(2).

also be shaped by any enduring power of attorney made by the relevant person.[121]

In considering the suitability of a person to be a decision-making representative, the court will consider a range of factors as outlined by s 38(5). Among the points to be considered are the known will and preferences of the relevant person, the desirability of preserving existing relationships within the family of the relevant person, and the relationship (if any) between the relevant person and the proposed representative.[122] There are additional points for the court to consider under s 38(6) where the court appoints a decision-making representative to make decisions on the relevant person's property and affairs.

If no suitable person is willing to act as a decision-making representative, then the court is to request that the Director of the Decision Support Service nominate two or more persons from an established panel for consideration by the court.[123] The eligibility of persons to act as a decision-making representative is addressed by s 39, and the disqualification of a decision-making representative is set out in s 40 of the ADMC Act 2015.

In exercising his or her functions, the decision-making representative will, insofar as this is possible, ascertain the will and preferences of the relevant person. The scope of decision-making or decision-making representation order relating to property and affairs is covered by s 43. Under s 44 the ADMC Act 2015 prohibits the decision-making representative from doing any of the following: prohibiting a particular person from having contact with the relevant person,[124] making decisions on behalf of the relevant person that are beyond the scope of the decision-making representation order,[125] settling any part of the property of the relevant person without the court's approval,[126] and doing any act that is intended to restrain the relevant person unless there are exceptional emergency circumstances and it would be proportionate to do so.[127] The issue of treatment withdrawal has arisen earlier in this chapter and is touched on again in s 44(4), which provides that – subject to the terms of a relevant advance healthcare directive, and subject to the relevant powers exercisable

---

[121] ibid s 38(4).
[122] ibid s 38(5).
[123] ibid s 38(7).
[124] ibid s 44(1).
[125] ibid s 44(2).
[126] ibid s 44(3).
[127] ibid s 44(5).

by a designated healthcare representative appointed under the directive – a decision-making representative for a relevant person shall not refuse consent to the carrying out or continuation of life-sustaining treatment or consent to the withdrawal of life-sustaining treatment for the relevant person.

Under s 46 ADMC Act 2015, each decision-making representative must prepare and submit a report on the performance of his or her functions to the Director of the Decision Support Service on an annual basis. The report should be in line with regulations made by the Minister and should include details of all relevant transactions, costs, expenses, and remuneration claimed by or to the decision-making representative. Failure to file a report may result in the decision-making representative being removed from the position.[128] Complaints in relation to decision-making representatives may be brought under s 47 of the ADMC Act 2015. Complaints may arise where the decision-making representative has acted, is acting, or proposing to act, outside the scope of the decision-making representation order or where it is felt that a person is not suitable to act in this role.

5.5.5 Enduring Power of Attorney

Section 59 of the ADMC Act 2015 Act describes an enduring power of attorney as an arrangement whereby a donor may appoint another person on whom he or she confers general authority to act on the donor's behalf in relation to all or a specified part of the donor's property and affairs, and/or authority to do specified things on the donor's behalf in relation to the donor's personal welfare or property and affairs. The enduring power of attorney does not enter into force until such time as the donor lacks capacity in relation to one or more of the relevant decisions that are the subject of the power, and the instrument creating the enduring power of attorney has been registered in accordance with s 69 of the Act.

The law on enduring powers of attorney was previously set out under the Powers of Attorney Act 1996. The powers provided under the 1996 Act did not extend to healthcare decisions and this has been addressed under the 2015 Act.

The instrument creating the enduring power of attorney must adhere to the requirements under s 60 of the 2015 Act, including the requirement for specific statements from the donor, legal

---

[128] ibid ss 46(7) and (8).

practitioner, medical practitioner, healthcare professional, and attorney. Section 60 also addresses the signing and witnessing of the instrument. Once the instrument has been executed, the donor is to give notice of the enduring power of attorney to his or her spouse or civil partner, cohabitant (if any), children over the age of 18, persons with a decision support role, any other attorney appointed, and any person specific to the instrument.[129]

The scope of authority as it relates to personal welfare decisions and property and affairs is addressed in ss 62 and 63 of the Act. Under s 62(5) an enduring power of attorney cannot contain a decision relating to the refusal of life-sustaining treatment, or a decision that is the subject of an advance healthcare directive made by him or her.

A donor is not restricted to the appointment of one attorney. More than one attorney may be appointed and the donor can specify that the attorneys shall act jointly, jointly and severally, or jointly in respect of some matters and jointly and severally in respect of other matters. If not specified, the attorneys shall be deemed to have authority to act jointly.[130] There are eligibility requirements for attorneys and these are specified under s 65. For instance, a person is not eligible for appointment as an attorney if they have been 'convicted of an offence in relation to the person or property of the person who intends to appoint an attorney' or have been the 'subject of a safety or barring order in relation to the person who intends to appoint an attorney'.[131] A broader list of exceptions is provided for under s 65. Circumstances in which an attorney may be disqualified from acting as such are addressed by s 66.

In circumstances where an attorney has reason to believe that the donor lacks capacity in respect of one or more decisions specified in the enduring power of attorney, the attorney shall apply to the Director of the Decision Support Service to register the instrument creating the enduring power of attorney and give the relevant notice.[132] On receipt of an application to register an enduring power of attorney, the Director shall review the application and any objections received, and shall make all enquiries necessary before registering the enduring power of attorney. If the Director refuses to register the enduring power of attorney, the attorney and donor are to be notified of the decision and be given an

---

[129] ibid s 61.
[130] ibid s 64.
[131] ibid s 65.
[132] ibid ss 68(1) and (3).

opportunity to respond within a reasonable timeframe. Section 69(5) provides that an attorney may appeal a refusal within 21 days after the date of the notification of refusal.

An attorney is subject to a degree of supervision under the ADMC Act 2015. An attorney with responsibility for a person's property and affairs is required to submit a schedule of the donor's assets and liabilities and a projected statement of the donor's income and expenditure to the Director within three months of the instrument being registered. Annual reports as to the performance of the attorney's functions must be submitted as per s 75(3). Other provisions under Part 7 address issues including the registration of enduring powers,[133] the revocation and variation of enduring powers,[134] complaints in relation to attorneys,[135] the removal of the instrument from the register,[136] and offences in relation to enduring powers of attorney.[137]

5.5.6 Advance Healthcare Directives

The ADMC Act 2015 describes an advance healthcare directive as 'an advance expression made by the person, ... of his or her will and preferences concerning treatment decisions that may arise in respect of him or her if he or she subsequently lacks capacity'.[138] It is a way of recognising a person's wishes in circumstances where they can no longer make a contemporaneous decision relating to their medical treatment. The concept of an advance healthcare directive was first introduced by Luis Kutner in 1969.[139] However, the legal recognition of advance care directives was to occur significantly later in this jurisdiction.

Pre-Assisted Decision-Making (Capacity) Act 2015

A tenuous recognition of advance healthcare directives was seen in the comments of O'Flaherty J in *Re a Ward of Court*. The case recognised the right to refuse treatment and this right of refusal could potentially apply to future treatments. O'Flaherty J stated:

---

[133] ibid s 69.
[134] ibid s 73.
[135] ibid s 76.
[136] ibid s 78.
[137] ibid s 80.
[138] ibid s 82.
[139] Luis Kutner, 'Due Process of Euthanasia: The Living Will, A Proposal' (1969) 44(4) Indiana Law Journal 539.

> I find it impossible to adapt the idea of the 'substituted judgment' to the circumstances of this case and, it may be, that it is only appropriate where the person has had the foresight to provide for future eventualities. That must be unusual (if it ever happens) at the present time: with increased publicity in regard to these types of cases it may get more common.[140]

This indirect reference established a foundation for the recognition of advance healthcare directives in the jurisdiction. This position was further supported by the *obiter* comments of Laffoy J in *Fitzpatrick v FK* in which she cited the decisions of the Ontario Court of Appeal in *Malette v Schulman*, and the English Court of Appeal in *Re T (Adult Refusal of Medical Treatment)*. Fortunately, the case of *Governor of X Prison v PMcD*[141] brought greater legal clarity on the issue.

Mr McD was a prisoner who conducted a hunger strike at X prison for the purposes of protesting against his prison conditions. An application was brought by the Governor of X Prison for declaratory relief in respect of Mr McD. Several declarations were sought, including a declaration as to the 'defendant's capacity to make a decision to refuse all forms of medical assistance should the necessity of such assistance arise'[142] and a declaration that the defendant's decision 'to refuse such medical assistance is valid and should remain operative in the event that the defendant becomes incapable of making a decision or whether to accept such treatment.'[143] Baker J was of the opinion that Mr McD had capacity to make the decision to refuse food, and that he fully understood the consequences of the decision. On the issue of the advance directive, Baker J stated: 'I consider that as a matter of law ... that a person may make a freely stated wish in regard to their future care and that this ought to be, and can in an appropriate case be, respected by those with care of that person.'[144] The judicial recognition of advance care directives brought welcome clarity to the legal status of such decisions. Yet, many of the procedural elements remained to be addressed by the ADMC Act 2015.

---

[140] *Re a Ward of Court* [1996] 2 IR 79, 133.
[141] *Governor of X Prison v PMcD* [2015] IEHC 259.
[142] ibid 259, [27].
[143] ibid 259, [27].
[144] ibid 259, [126].

Advance Directives under the Assisted Decision-Making (Capacity) Act 2015

Part 8 of the ADMC Act 2015 addresses the making of advance healthcare directives, issues of validity and applicability, the role of a designated healthcare representative, and the role of courts among other issues.

Section 84 of the ADMC Act 2015 Act establishes the requirements for making a valid advance healthcare directive and sets out conditions in which a refusal of treatment would be complied with.[145] A person should have attained the age of 18 years and should have the requisite capacity. A refusal of treatment will be complied with in circumstances where the directive-maker lacks capacity to give consent to the treatment, the treatment to be refused is clearly identified in the directive, and the circumstances in which the refusal of treatment is intended to apply are clearly identified in the directive.[146] Advance decisions are, for the most part, associated with treatment refusal. Section 84(3) is therefore notable as it provides that a 'request for a specific treatment set out in an advance healthcare directive is not legally binding but shall be taken into consideration'.[147] If the request is not adhered to, then it will be necessary to record the reasons for not complying with it and to provide this information to the person's designated healthcare representative within a specified period of time.[148]

Section 84 goes on to provide that an advance healthcare directive must be in writing and should contain the names and details required by s 84(5). The directive must also be signed and witnessed in accordance with the requirements set down by this section. An advance healthcare directive can subsequently be revoked should the directive-maker so decide.[149] The directive may also be altered but these changes would only have effect if it is appropriately signed and witnessed.[150]

Issues of validity and applicability are addressed by s 85 of the 2015 Act. A directive will not be valid if the directive-maker did not make the directive voluntarily or, while he or she had capacity to do so, has done anything clearly inconsistent with the relevant

---

[145] Assisted Decision-Making (Capacity) Act 2015, s 84(2).
[146] ibid s 84(2).
[147] ibid s 84(3).
[148] ibid s 84(3).
[149] ibid s 84(7).
[150] ibid s 84(7).

decisions outlined in the directive.[151] To describe behaviour as inconsistent will be challenging but the case of *HE v A Hospital NHS Trust* can provide some guidance on this point.[152] In *HE*, a practising Jehovah's Witness signed an advance healthcare directive refusing any blood transfusion. She subsequently reverted to her Muslim faith and was engaged to a fellow Muslim. There was doubt as to the validity of the advance decision owing to the change in her religious faith. Munby J was of the opinion that the burden of proof was to be placed on those who sought to uphold the validity of the advance decision. A change of faith or a substantial change of opinion on a social issue could potentially be interpreted as behaviour inconsistent with previously expressed wishes.

Section 85(2) set out that an advance healthcare directive is not applicable if:

> (a) at the time in question the directive-maker still has capacity to give or refuse consent to the treatment in question;
>
> (b) the treatment in question is not materially the same as the specific treatment set out in the directive that is requested or refused; or
>
> (c) at the time in question the circumstances set out in the directive as to when the specific treatment is to be requested or refused, as the case may be, are absent or not materially the same.[153]

If a refusal of treatment relates to life-sustaining treatment then it will only apply if it is supported by a statement indicating that it is to apply even where the individual's life is at risk.[154] The proceeding sub-section of the ADMC Act 2015 specifies, 'An advance healthcare directive is not applicable to the administration of basic care to the directive-maker.'[155] Basic care includes 'warmth, shelter, oral nutrition, oral hydration and hygiene measures but does not include artificial nutrition or artificial hydration'.[156] A person can therefore refuse treatment but the provision of basic care will be continued as this care is closely associated with upholding the patient's dignity.

---

[151] ibid s 85(1).
[152] *HE v A Hospital NHS Trust* [2003] EWHC 1017.
[153] Assisted Decision-Making (Capacity) Act 2015, s 85(2).
[154] ibid s 85(3).
[155] ibid s 85(4).
[156] ibid s 85(4).

An advance healthcare directive will not always be drafted in the clearest terms. There may be uncertainty surrounding the terminology used or the wishes of the person may not be sufficiently clear. In order to resolve this ambiguity, the healthcare professional shall 'consult with the directive-maker's designated healthcare representative (if any) or, if there is no designated healthcare representative, the directive-maker's family and friends, and seek the opinion of a second healthcare professional'.[157] If ambiguity remains after these consultations then the healthcare professional shall resolve the ambiguity in favour of the preservation of the directive-maker's life.[158]

As will be seen in Chapter Eight, a treatment refusal during pregnancy can be especially complex. Section 85(6)(a) sets out that where a person lacks capacity and is pregnant but their advance healthcare directive does not specifically address whether the refusal is to apply in such circumstances, and the healthcare professional considers that compliance with the directive would have a deleterious effect on the unborn, there shall be a presumption that treatment shall be provided or continued. The following sub-section addresses the circumstances in which the directive-maker has specifically taken account of their pregnancy and stipulates that a specific refusal of treatment is to apply in such a case. However, this is no guarantee that the directive would ultimately be complied with. If the healthcare professional is of the view that the refusal of treatment would have a deleterious effect on the unborn then an application shall be made to the High Court to determine whether or not the refusal of treatment should apply.[159] In considering the application, the High Court shall have regard to the potential impact of the treatment refusal on the unborn, the invasiveness and duration of the treatment and the risk of harm to the directive-maker if the treatment were administered, and any other matter the Court considers relevant to the application.[160]

The effect of an advance healthcare directive is set out by s 86 of the 2015 Act. This section addresses the possible imposition of civil and criminal liability on healthcare professionals. The Act does not impose civil or criminal liability on a healthcare professional who complies with an advance healthcare directive where they had reasonable grounds to believe, and did believe, that the advance healthcare directive was valid and applicable.[161]

---

[157] ibid s 85(5)(a).
[158] ibid s 85(5)(b).
[159] ibid s 85(6)(b).
[160] ibid s 85(6)(c).
[161] ibid s 86(2)(a).

In addition, s 86(2)(b) provides that the Act does not impose any civil or criminal liability on a healthcare professional where they have not complied with an advance refusal of treatment where they had reasonable grounds to believe, and did believe, that the advance healthcare directive was not valid or applicable, or both.[162] Healthcare professionals will not face civil or criminal liability where they were not aware a directive existed, or where they could not access the contents of the directive in sufficient time taking account of the urgency of the medical condition.[163] The Act, of course, does not provide a blanket immunity from civil and criminal liability and this may arise in other circumstances as indicated by s 86(4) and (5). Furthermore, s 90 addresses the broader range of offences that may arise in relation to advance healthcare directives. An offence is committed where a person uses fraud, coercion or undue influence to force another person to make, alter, or revoke an advance healthcare directive.[164] In addition, an offence is committed when a person knowingly creates, falsifies or alters, or purports to revoke, an advance healthcare directive on behalf of another person without that other person's consent in writing when the other person has the capacity.[165]

---

[162] ibid s 86(2)(b).
[163] ibid s 86(3).
[164] ibid s 90(1).
[165] ibid s 90(2).

Chapter 6
Confidentiality and Access to Personal Health Information

Introduction 141
Confidentiality 142
    Confidentiality in Professional Codes of Conduct. . 144
    Contractual Obligation for Confidentiality 147
    Equitable Basis for Confidentiality 148
    Constitutional Rights 148
    European Convention on Human Rights 149
Exceptions to the Duty of Confidentiality 150
    Consent to Disclosure 151
    Disclosure Required by Law 152
    Patient's Best Interests 154
    Risk of Harm to Another Person 156
    The Interests of Society 159
Data Protection 161
    Transparency 162
    Processing of Personal Data 164
    Rights of the Data Subject. 166
    Breach of the GDPR 169
Freedom of Information Act 2014 169
    Records Pertaining to Children 172
    Posthumous Protection of Information 175
Open Disclosure 177
Use of Social Media 181

6.0 Introduction

The engagement of an individual with the health services tends to generate a substantial volume of personal health information. The manner in which this information is protected, controlled, accessed, and made available is of considerable importance. The information generated may be of a deeply personal nature and it is therefore understandable that an individual would expect rigorous controls to be in place. The control over information is reflected in the obligation on the healthcare professional to maintain confidentiality. Confidentiality is a well-accepted principle of medical practice and is an integral component in the patient–healthcare professional relationship. This includes the patient–nurse relationship and applies to the information that arises and is shared in this context. The ethical principle of confidentiality is further supported by legislative and constitutional provisions, which frame the access and protection of personal health information.

This chapter will address the myriad of elements that underpin the control of personal health information. The concept of confidentiality and the basis for its protection will be outlined in the first section. However, the protection of confidentiality is subject to certain limitations and these will be defined in the second section. This chapter outlines the application of the Data Protection Acts and the influence of the General Data Protection Regulation (GDPR). Moreover, access to information under the Freedom of Information Act 2014 will be explored. The practice of open disclosure for nursing staff will be set out in section 6.5. The final point to discuss in this chapter will be the use of social media. While social media has closely connected the world it also provides a medium for the breach of confidentiality. As will be seen across this chapter, once information has been disclosed it can prove extremely difficult to prevent its broader dissemination, thereby underlining the need for appropriate controls.

6.1 Confidentiality

Confidentiality is central to the maintenance of trust and confidence in the nurse–patient relationship. Respect for confidentiality applies to all patients regardless of age or level of capacity. It is a pillar of open communication that contributes to the preservation of patient dignity. The concept of confidentiality involves the receipt and protection of personal information that has the qualities of secrecy and confidence. This information will regularly arise in the nurse–patient relationship. The information may be held in the mind of the nurse, it may be in writing, or it may be recorded as an audio or video file. It may also be stored electronically either on a hard drive, thumb drive, or in cloud storage. Regardless of the medium in which it is recorded it is essential that confidentiality be maintained, and steps taken to ensure the security of that information. The British Medical Association set out that confidentiality is to cover:

- any clinical information about an individual's diagnosis or treatment;

- a picture, photograph, video, audiotape or other images of the patient;
- who the patient's doctor is and what clinics patients attend and when; and
- anything else that may be used to identify patients directly or indirectly so that any of the information above, combined with the patient's name or address or full postcode or the patient's date of birth, can identify them.[1]

The combination of information can therefore potentially expose the identity of an individual. This is particularly true where there is a small patient population receiving treatment for a rare illness or a trial drug treatment. Demographic information should be protected and should not be disclosed to third parties without the consent of the patient.

The meaning of confidential information has arisen in cases such as *Coco v AN Clark (Engineers)*[2] and *Thomas Marshall (Exports) v Guinle*.[3] In *Thomas Marshall*, Sir Robert Megarry VC identified four relevant principles in identifying confidential information a court may protect:

> First, I think that the information must be information the release of which the owner believes would be injurious to him or of advantage to his rivals or others. Second, I think the owner must believe that the information is confidential or secret ... Third, I think that the owner's belief under the two previous heads must be reasonable. Fourth, I think that the information must be judged in the light of the usage and practices of the particular industry or trade concerned.[4]

There is a mix of subjective and objective tests in this assessment. The information may still be deemed worthy of protection even if all elements are not satisfied. Although this case relates to information in a trade context, information arising in healthcare is especially likely to be viewed as confidential and should be treated as such.

---

[1] British Medical Association, *Confidentiality and Disclosure of Health Information Tool Kit* (BMA 2020) 8.
[2] *Coco v AN Clark (Engineers)* [1968] FSR 415.
[3] *Thomas Marshall (Exports) v Guinle* (1979) 1 Ch 227.
[4] ibid 248.

The maintenance of patient confidentiality can protect autonomy and may also serve a utilitarian purpose. The security provided by confidentiality promotes an environment in which there can be open communication between the parties. This allows for honest discussion of symptoms and allows patients with an infectious disease to seek treatment without fear of private details being broadly disclosed. The provision of treatment can therefore limit the further spread of the disease and the dignity of the patient is not lessened. Furthermore, a healthcare professional is more likely to make an accurate diagnosis and provide appropriate treatment when the patient has communicated all salient facts relating to their condition. Confidentiality can therefore promote trust and can strengthen the patient–healthcare professional relationship.[5]

Confidentiality stems from a range of sources. The ethical obligation of confidentiality goes back to the Hippocratic Oath and can be seen in more recent formulations of codes of professional conduct. There is a basis for confidentiality in equity and in contract law. In addition, confidentiality can also be grounded in the right to privacy, which has been recognised in the Irish Constitution and is protected by Article 8 of the European Convention on Human Rights. The various foundations for confidentiality will be set out in the proceeding sub-sections.

6.1.1 Confidentiality in Professional Codes of Conduct

The starting point for a discussion of ethical obligations in medicine invariably leads to the Hippocratic Oath. It is one of the best-known Greek medical texts and it requires the physician to swear by Apollo, Asclepius, Hygieia, Panacea, and all other gods and goddesses that he will uphold certain ethical standards. Among these standards is the ethical obligation of confidentiality: 'Whatever I see or hear in the lives of my patients, whether in connection with my professional practice or not, which ought not to be spoken of outside, I will keep secret, as considering all such things to be private.'[6] The Hippocratic Oath is no longer sworn by physicians and instead has been replaced by modern formulations. Nonetheless, the need to guard patient information remains. While the Oath was traditionally sworn by physicians, confidentiality is not limited to one healthcare profession. This is illustrated by the writings of Florence Nightingale, who practised

---

[5] Onora O'Neill, *Autonomy and Trust in Bioethics* (Cambridge University Press 2002).
[6] 'The Hippocratic Oath' (National Library of Medicine 2002) <https://www.nlm.nih.gov/hmd/greek/greek_oath.html> accessed 14 June 2020.

and trained nurses during the Crimean War, and has come to be recognised as the founder of modern nursing.[7] Florence Nightingale wrote:

> And remember every nurse should be one who is to be depended upon, in other words, capable of being a 'confidential' nurse. She does not know how soon she may find herself placed in such a situation; she must be no gossip, no vain talker, she should never answer questions about her sick except to those who have a right to ask them.[8]

Confidentiality has also been recognised as an essential component in the patient–healthcare professional relationship by *The Declaration of Geneva*[9] along with *The International Code of Medical Ethics*.[10] Furthermore, the obligation of confidentiality is recognised and defined by the professional codes of conduct for doctors and nurses in Ireland.

Section 29 of the Irish Medical Council *Guide to Professional Conduct and Ethics for Registered Medical Practitioners* addresses confidentiality. Section 29.1 provides that:

> Confidentiality is central to the trust between you and your patients and is a core element of the doctor/patient relationship. However, sharing information, in appropriate circumstances, is also important, both for patient care and for the safety of the patient and others.[11]

This demonstrates that confidentiality is not absolute and the sharing of information may be necessary at times.

The Nursing and Midwifery Board of Ireland (NMBI) provide guidance on confidentiality under Principle 4 of the *Code of*

---

[7] Mark Bostridge, *Florence Nightingale: The Woman and Her Legend* (Viking 2008).
[8] Florence Nightingale, *Notes on Nursing: What It Is, and What It Is Not* (Appleton and Company 1898) 91.
[9] World Medical Association, *The Declaration of Geneva* (WMA 2017). This was intended to be a revision of the Hippocratic Oath. It was adopted by the 2nd General Assembly of the World Medical Association in 1948. Subsequent amendments were made in 1968, 1983, 1994, and 2017. Editorial revisions were made in 2005 and 2006.
[10] World Medical Association, *The International Code of Medical Ethics* (WMA 2006). This is based on the Declaration of Geneva and was adopted by the General Assembly of the World Medical Association in 1949.
[11] Irish Medical Council, *Guide to Professional Conduct and Ethics for Registered Medical Practitioners* (8th edn, IMC 2019) section 29.1.

Professional Conduct and Ethics for Registered Nurses and Registered Midwives.[12] Principle 4, 'Trust and Confidentiality', is divided into values, standards of conduct, and supporting documentation. There are three values identified for trust and confidentiality:

> 1. Trust is a core professional value in nurses' and midwives' relationships with patients and colleagues.
>
> 2. Confidentiality and honesty form the basis of a trusting relationship between the nurse or midwife and the patient. Patients have a right to expect that their personal information remains private.
>
> 3. Nurses and midwives exercise professional judgment and responsibility in circumstances where a patient's confidential information must be shared.[13]

The seven standards of conduct refer to trust, honesty, and confidence – concepts that underpin the relationship between the nurse and patient. Significantly, the standards also identify situations where it may be necessary to share confidential information. These are exceptional situations, which we will return to later in this chapter. The NMBI standards of conduct for trust and confidentiality are as follows:

> 1. You must try to develop relationships of trust with patients.
>
> 2. Honesty, integrity and trustworthiness must underpin your dealings with patients and colleagues.
>
> 3. You should give honest, truthful, balanced information and advice to patients. Information and advice should be based on best evidence or best available practice standards.
>
> 4. You must behave in a way that strengthens the public's trust and confidence in nurses and midwives. You should respect and uphold a patient's expectation that their personal information will remain private. You should use your professional judgment and act responsibly when you have to disclose and share information. There may be exceptional circumstances where you might need to share confidential

---

[12] Nursing and Midwifery Board of Ireland, *Code of Professional Conduct and Ethics for Registered Nurses and Registered Midwives* (NMBI 2014).
[13] ibid 23.

information. You might have to share confidential information if it is:

- required by law to do so,
- to protect the patient's interests,
- to protect the interests of society, or
- to protect the interests of other people. In these circumstances, you must only disclose the minimum amount of information necessary to the appropriate person.

5. You should tell patients (unless this could cause them serious harm) if you intend to share confidential information about them with others who are outside the immediate care team.

6. If the patient is considered to be incapable of giving or withholding consent to the disclosure of confidential information about them, you should consider whether disclosing the information to those close to the patient is what the patient would want or if it is in their best interests.

7. Your role in safeguarding confidentiality extends to all forms of record management including appropriate use of information technology and social media.[14]

As noted in chapter 4, a failure to adhere to these values and standards of conduct could result in a complaint being made against the nurse and the subsequent imposition of sanctions.

6.1.2 Contractual Obligation for Confidentiality

Respect for confidentiality may also have a contractual basis. This may be linked to an express or an implied agreement between the parties. The existence of a contract is a way in which the ethical concept of confidentiality can become part of the healthcare professional's legal obligations. The requirement of confidentiality as a contractual term would determine the control of information and, accordingly, would bind the healthcare professional. In the absence of an express agreement, there may be an implied understanding that confidentiality would be recognised and agreed upon between the parties. It is rare that such a contract would exist between the patient and the nurse

---

[14] Nursing and Midwifery Board of Ireland, *Code of Professional Conduct and Ethics for Registered Nurses and Registered Midwives* (NMBI 2014), 24–25.

and this may be limited to instances of private nursing care. In other situations, the nurse's employment contract may require an adherence to policy, professional standards, and obligations for confidentiality.

6.1.3 Equitable Basis for Confidentiality

Privacy protection can be grounded in equity by way of breach of confidence. There are several points that must be established for a breach of confidence action as set out by Costello J in *House of Spring Gardens v Point Blank Ltd*.[15] The principles set out by the trial judge were subsequently cited at length by O'Higgins CJ in the Supreme Court.[16] The equitable doctrine seeks to protect confidential information where there is an obligation of confidence between the parties, the information should be properly regarded as confidential, and the information must be used for unauthorised purposes to the detriment of the patient. There are therefore three elements which are to be established for an action in breach of confidence. A considerable drawback is that the main equitable remedy is an injunction, which may be of limited use. An injunction is of greatest utility if the person is aware that confidential information is likely to be released or revealed at some point in the future but less effective once the information has been disclosed.

6.1.4 Constitutional Rights

Courts in Ireland have recognised the existence of a right to privacy in various forms. In *McGee v Attorney General* the Supreme Court recognised a right to marital privacy.[17] The case of *Kennedy v Ireland* provided for a broader recognition of the right. The first and second plaintiffs were journalists with the *Irish Times*. Their private telephones were tapped, without justification, following an order of the Minister for Justice. The plaintiffs claimed damages for breach of constitutional rights to privacy under Article 40 of the Irish Constitution. Hamilton P stated:

> Though not specifically guaranteed by the Constitution, the right of privacy is one of the fundamental personal rights of the citizen which flow from the Christian and democratic nature of the State ...

---

[15] *House of Spring Gardens v Point Blank Ltd* [1984] IR 611.
[16] ibid 611, 696.
[17] *McGee v Attorney General* [1974] IR 284.

The nature of the right to privacy must be such as to ensure the dignity and freedom of an individual in the type of society envisaged by the Constitution, namely, a sovereign, independent and democratic society.[18]

The right is qualified and can be limited based on considerations such as the constitutional rights of others, the concept of the common good, and concerns for public order and morality. Although courts in Ireland have not yet expressly dealt with the constitutional basis for medical confidentiality, it appears to be generally assumed that a right to medical confidentiality can be made out.[19]

6.1.5 European Convention on Human Rights

Article 8 of the European Convention on Human Rights (ECHR) provides for the right to respect for private and family life. The scope of Article 8 is such that it extends to the concept of medical confidentiality. Article 8.1 states, 'Everyone has the right to respect for his private and family life, his home and his correspondence.'[20] This can be subject to limitations, as is evident from Article 8(2) ECHR:

There shall be no interference by a public authority with the exercise of this right except such as is in accordance with the law and is necessary in a democratic society in the interests of national security, public safety or the economic well-being of the country, for the prevention of disorder or crime, for the protection of health or morals, or for the protection of the rights and freedoms of others.[21]

Article 8(2) therefore represents a potential hurdle in bringing a successful claim for breach of confidentiality. A balance must be achieved that recognises the right of an individual to privacy while also taking account of countervailing interests such as the protection of the rights and freedoms of others. The ECHR has been ratified in Ireland at a sub-constitutional level through the European Convention on Human Rights Act 2003.

---

[18] *Kennedy v Ireland* [1987] IR 587, 592–93.
[19] See *Rotunda Hospital v Information Commissioner* [2011] IESC 26; *McGrory v Electricity Supply Board* [2004] 3 IR 407, 414: 'The plaintiff who sues for damages for personal injuries by implication necessarily waives the right of privacy which he would otherwise enjoy in relation to his medical condition.'
[20] European Convention on Human Rights, Art 8(1).
[21] ibid Art 8(2).

The protection of personal medical information under the ECHR is illustrated by *Z v Finland*.[22] Z was married to a person who was charged with several sexual offences. The person was HIV positive and it was necessary to determine when he became aware of his medical condition. The police sought access to Z's medical records and her condition as HIV-positive was subsequently disclosed in the text of the Court of Appeals judgment, which was made available to the press. The European Court of Human Rights (ECtHR) held this to be a violation of Article 8.

In determining whether the impugned measures were 'necessary in a democratic society', the Court stated:

> ... the protection of personal data, not least medical data, is of fundamental importance to a person's enjoyment of his or her right to respect for private and family life as guaranteed by Article 8 of the Convention. Respecting the confidentiality of health data is a vital principle in the legal system of all the Contracting Parties to the Convention. It is crucial not only to respect the sense of privacy of a patient but also to preserve his or her confidence in the medical profession and in the health services in general.[23]

The Court also recognised that some forms of medical information are more sensitive than other forms. For instance, information about HIV was especially sensitive.[24] It follows that the more intimate/sensitive the medical information, the stronger the countervailing interest to justify revealing it.

6.2 Exceptions to the Duty of Confidentiality

The obligation of confidentiality can be limited in certain circumstances. There are defined exceptions that permit the disclosure of patient information to a third party. This does not permit a disclosure to the entire world but should be as limited in scope as is necessary. For instance, it is appropriate for a nurse to disclose information relevant to patient care among a healthcare team, but this should not involve a disclosure to a hospital/ healthcare facility at large.

---

[22] *Z v Finland* (1997) 25 EHRR 371.
[23] ibid 371, [95].
[24] ibid 371, [96].

Information may be disclosed where the patient has provided appropriate consent. In other cases, consent may not be given but disclosure still required if it is:

- required by law to do so;
- to protect the patient's interests;
- to protect the interests of society; or
- to protect the interests of other people.

6.2.1 Consent to Disclosure

A patient with sufficient capacity can authorise the disclosure of personal information. This makes it one of the least controversial aspects of disclosure. Consent does not remove or eliminate the obligation of confidentiality but signals a voluntary suspension within the confines of the consent granted. The consent must be fully informed and should be free of undue influence or duress. Once valid consent is provided then any subsequent disclosure should not exceed or diverge from the terms of consent. The consent given does not need to be in writing. In practice, the nurse will often rely on implied consent. This might occur when sharing information within a healthcare team, medical emergency, or as part of a clinical audit. Nonetheless, express consent should be provided for disclosure to third parties such as employers, insurance companies, and benefits agencies. In general, healthcare professionals should seek the consent of the patient before any disclosure is made.

Consent Given by Children

Section 23 of the Non-Fatal Offences Against the Person Act 1997 provides: 'The consent of a minor who has attained the age of 16 years to any surgical, medical or dental treatment which, in the absence of consent, would constitute a trespass to his or her person, shall be as effective as it would be if he or she were of full age.'[25] A person over the age of 16 can consent to the disclosure of medical information. However, this does not dislodge the presumption that parents/legal guardians are entitled to access such information. A parent or legal guardian may be granted access to a child's medical records under the Freedom of Information Act 2014. It is assumed that such a disclosure would be in the best interests of the child. The Supreme Court in *McK v Information Commissioner* acknowledged the constitutional rights and duties a parent has in relation to their child. The Court held

---

[25] Non-Fatal Offences Against the Person Act 1997, s 23(1).

that there is a rebuttable presumption that a parent is entitled to access information about the medical care their child is receiving and the release of such information is in the best interests of the child.[26]

Children under the age of 16 are not addressed by the Non-Fatal Offences Against the Person Act. Moreover, the courts in Ireland have not endorsed the concept of Gillick competence, which reflects the greater understanding and emotional intelligence of the mature minor. Despite this, there is a recognition of the need to afford greater status to the increasing maturity of the child and this may imply an obligation of confidentiality in limited cases.[27] The child may consent to disclosure in circumstances where they understand the nature of secrecy and the consequences associated with the disclosure of personal information.

Fluctuating Capacity

The healthcare professional should exercise caution in disclosing information in relation to a person whose capacity may fluctuate. If the disclosure is not urgent then it may be possible to wait until the individual has sufficient capacity so a decision can then be made. Patients should have the capacity to understand the nature and implications of consenting to a disclosure of information. Undue influence or duress, as in other circumstances, would negate the consent given.

Next of Kin

As set out in chapter 5, the next of kin cannot provide consent on behalf of another person. There is no justification or basis in law for seeking the consent of a person's next of kin. Seeking to involve another person in a healthcare decision may only be appropriate where a decision-making assistant/representative etc has been formally appointed.

6.2.2 Disclosure Required by Law

Court Orders

The healthcare professional may be required to reveal confidential information in the context of legal proceedings. This can arise in

---

[26] *McK v Information Commissioner* [2006] IESC 2.
[27] Health Service Executive, *National Consent Policy* (HSE 2019); R Bensted and others, 'Comparison of Healthcare Priorities in Childhood and Early/Late Adolescence' (2015) 41(1) Child: Care, Health and Development 160.

criminal investigations, road traffic offences, or personal injury litigation. The disclosure may be compelled by a court order of discovery. Such an order requires medical records to be made available in the context of court proceedings and can be an onerous process for the persons involved.

A disclosure of information may also involve the nurse giving evidence in a court or tribunal. If unsure about the extent of the disclosure required then it would be advisable to seek guidance from the judge or FTPC chairperson. The question of patient confidentiality arose in *Hunter v Mann*.[28] It confirmed that a doctor is obliged to breach confidentiality when required by law or court order. The court noted: 'I accept that the doctor, in accordance with the first proposition, has no right to refuse to disclose confidential information in the course of judicial or quasi-judicial proceedings; but I also accept that the judge in certain circumstances, and in the exercise of his, the judge's, judicial discretion, may refuse to compel him to do so.'[29] The court therefore has discretion in determining whether it is necessary to compel the disclosure of confidential information. This requires a balancing of the public interest in maintaining confidentiality with other factors mitigating against such protection in the specific case.

Nurses should be aware of requirements stemming from the Nurses and Midwives Act 2011. Section 64(5) of the 2011 Act provides that a person is guilty of an offence where they refuse to produce any record in their power or control, or answer any question as lawfully required by the Fitness to Practise Committee.[30]

In the context of civil proceedings, the Civil Law (Miscellaneous Provisions) Act 2008 provides for an application to be made to the court that would prohibit 'the publication or broadcast of any matter relating to the proceedings which would, or would be likely to, identify the relevant person as a person having that condition'.[31] This statutory exception to the waiver of confidentiality may apply where there court is satisfied that: (a) the relevant person concerned has a medical condition; (b) his or her identification as a person with that condition would be likely to cause undue stress to him or her; and (c) the order would not be prejudicial to the interests of justice.[32] It is an offence to publish or broadcast any matter in contravention of an order under s 27 of the Act.

---

[28] *Hunter v Mann* [1974] QB 767.
[29] ibid 767, 773.
[30] Nurses and Midwives Act 2011, s 64(5).
[31] Civil Law (Miscellaneous Provisions) Act 2008, s 27(1).
[32] ibid s 27(3).

Infectious Diseases

The Health Act 1947 permits the Minister for Health to specify infectious diseases and require notification to appropriate authorities.[33] The principal regulations are the Infectious Diseases Regulations 1981. These have been updated on multiple occasions. At the time of writing (September 2020), the most recent amendment is the Infectious Diseases (Amendment) Regulations 2020.[34] Under the Infectious Diseases Regulations, the Health Protection Surveillance Centre (HPSC) was assigned responsibility for the surveillance of communicable diseases in the State.

The HPSC is authorised by law to collect information from doctors and laboratories, via Medical Officers of Health, about diagnoses of specified infectious diseases in Ireland. These infectious diseases are listed in the Infectious Disease (Amendment) Regulations and includes anthrax, bacterial meningitis, brucellosis, chlamydia, cholera, COVID-19, gonorrhoea, influenza, leprosy, measles, mumps, syphilis, and tuberculosis. Notifications may be made electronically through the Computerised Infectious Disease Reporting System. Access to this information is controlled so that personally identifiable information is only visible to persons involved in managing an individual case. Identifying information may be made available to a limited number of people where public health action is needed for international contact-tracing or if HPSC doctors are leading a national or international outbreak investigation. In general, the health information collected by the HPSC is used in a number of ways. It is used to evaluate the effectiveness of control and preventive health measures, to detect outbreaks, to monitor changes in infectious diseases, to educate health professionals, to support health planning and the allocation of appropriate resources within the healthcare system, to identify high-risk populations or areas to target interventions, and to inform research and audit practices.[35]

6.2.3 Patient's Best Interests

The disclosure of information is defined by patient autonomy. The patient must be consulted where a disclosure is contemplated, even if this disclosure is considered to be in the patient's best interests. A refusal is to be respected and should be complied

---

[33] Health Act 1947.
[34] Infectious Diseases (Amendment) Regulations 2020, SI 2020/53.
[35] Health Protection Surveillance Centre, 'HPSC: What Do We Do' <https://www.hpsc.ie/abouthpsc/hpscwhatdowedo/> accessed 14 June 2020.

with. This may well bring about a conflict between concepts of paternalism, beneficence, and autonomy. The nurse may wish to maintain a relationship of trust with the patient but must also take account of the professional duty to protect the patient from harm. Information will generally be shared with the immediate care team and this can be justified on the basis that if appropriate information was not disclosed to an appropriate healthcare professional, it could result in harm to the patient. The NMBI's *Code of Professional Conduct and Ethics* acknowledges that in exceptional circumstances it may be necessary to share confidential information so as to protect the patient's interests.[36] Any such disclosure should involve the minimum amount of information and should not be widely communicated. The person to whom the information is disclosed would also be subject to a duty of confidentiality.

A relatively common issue arises where family members enquire about the condition of the patient. Again, the extent of any disclosure is to be shaped by the consent provided by the patient. In a situation where consent is not given but the patient is to be cared for by family members on discharge, then it may be necessary to disclose information that will inform the care provided. In accordance with the *Code of Professional Conduct and Ethics*, the nurse should inform the patient of the intention to share confidential information.

Consent may not be possible where the patient lacks the requisite capacity. In such cases, confidential information can be disclosed where it is in the patient's best interests. A person who lacks capacity may be made a ward of court. The welfare and affairs of a ward are overseen by a 'committee', which may include one or more persons. While serious healthcare decisions are to come before the court, the committee may be involved in more general matters of personal welfare. On this basis, it would be permissible for information to be disclosed to the committee. Once commenced, the Assisted Decision-Making (Capacity) Act 2015 will provide for an expanded range of persons to whom information can legitimately be disclosed. This includes co-decision makers, decision-making assistants, decision-making representatives, and persons appointed under an enduring power of attorney.

---

[36] Nursing and Midwifery Board of Ireland, *Code of Professional Conduct and Ethics for Registered Nurses and Registered Midwives* (NMBI 2014), 24.

6.2.4 Risk of Harm to Another Person

The *Code of Professional Conduct and Ethics* acknowledges that there are exceptional circumstances where the disclosure of confidential information is necessary to protect the interests of other people.[37] The threshold for applying this exception is especially high and will only be applicable where a third party is exposed to a significant risk of death or very serious harm. The harm posed to a third party may stem from a threat of physical violence. Alternatively, a question might arise about the appropriateness of disclosure where the third party could potentially contract a transmissible disease.

The first case to be considered is *Tarasoff v the Regents of the University of California*.[38] This was decided by the California Supreme Court in 1976. Prosenjit Poddar was a graduate student at the University of California. He had a brief relationship with a fellow student named Tatiana Tarasoff. Ms Tarasoff did not view the relationship as serious and did not pursue a more intimate relationship. Mr Poddar subsequently became depressed and attended a psychologist, Dr Moore, at the University Health Service. It was alleged that Mr Poddar had confided an intention to kill Ms Tarasoff to Dr Moore. At Dr Moore's request, the campus police briefly detained Poddar, but released him when he appeared rational. Mr Poddar went on to kill Ms Tarasoff two months later. Ms Tarasoff's parents sued the campus police, Health Service employees, and the Regents of the University of California for a failure to warn of the impending danger to their daughter.

Ms Tarasoff was not a patient of Dr Moore. Nonetheless, the Supreme Court of California recognised that a duty was not only owed to patients, but also to individuals who are specifically threatened by a patient. This is best described as a duty to protect, as indicated by the following quote:

> When a therapist determines, or pursuant to the standards of his profession should determine, that his patient presents a serious danger of violence to another, he incurs an obligation to use reasonable care to protect the intended victim against such danger. The discharge of this duty may require the therapist to take one or more of various steps. Thus, it may call for him to warn the intended victim, to notify the police,

---
[37] ibid.
[38] *Tarasoff v Regents of the University of California* 551 P 2d 334 (Cal 1976).

or to take whatever steps are reasonably necessary under the circumstances.[39]

Tobriner J went on to state, 'The protective privilege ends where the public peril begins.'[40] Yet, the potential harm associated with a breach of confidentiality was recognised by Clark J in a dissenting opinion. Clark J was concerned that people may be deterred from seeking assistance without the guarantee of confidentiality. He viewed confidentiality as being essential in encouraging the full disclosure necessary for effective treatment, and considered confidentiality to be a key element in maintaining trust in the clinical relationship. The case law on disclosure continued to develop over time in the US but has often been inconsistent. However, it appears that a case is more likely to succeed where the third party is readily identifiable.

The question of disclosure to a third party arose in the Irish case of *Child and Family Agency v A*.[41] An application was brought by the Child and Family Agency (CFA) seeking an order to breach confidentiality for the benefit of a third party. The CFA sought the disclosure of a person's HIV status (A), without the consent and against the will of A, to a third party (B) who they believed to be having unprotected sex with A and was therefore at risk of contracting HIV. In making the application, the CFA relied on the medical opinion of a consultant paediatrician and infectious disease specialist, D. D described it as 'an extremely difficult situation', and suggested that 'this is one of the rare situations where disclosure of patient information without their consent is justifiable to prevent harm to another identifiable person who is potentially at risk'.[42] The Court provided that the appropriate test to apply to determine whether patient confidentiality should be breached is whether 'on the balance of probabilities, the failure to breach patient confidentiality creates a significant risk of death or very serious harm to an innocent third party'.[43] In determining whether this threshold is crossed, the Court indicated that the interests of A and B would be considered, as well as the public interest in ensuring public confidence in the disclosure of personal information to healthcare professionals.

---

[39] ibid 431.
[40] ibid 442.
[41] *Child and Family Agency v A* [2018] IEHC 112, [2018] 3 IR 531.
[42] ibid 112, [14].
[43] ibid 112, [4].

A was a 17-year-old male who had HIV since birth. B was described as one of A's closest friends, but A denied that B was his girlfriend or that they ever had sex. The CFA did not believe this, and were concerned that A and B were having unprotected sex. The CFA advanced a range of evidence that was suggestive of a sexual relationship. The Court acknowledged the possibility that A was engaging in sexual intercourse with B, but concluded that the CFA did not prove, on the balance of probabilities, that such a relationship existed. Based on this, the Court was of the opinion that there was no risk to B of her contracting HIV and, accordingly, no basis for the breach of patient confidentiality.

The Court was supported in reaching this decision by the medical evidence presented in the case. The medical evidence indicated that HIV is no longer a terminal condition but is instead a chronic and lifelong condition that can be managed. It was not viewed as a 'very serious harm' and the taking of appropriate steps meant there wasn't a 'significant risk' of the harm occurring. The risk of contracting HIV through sexual intercourse was put in the region of 0.04 per cent. The use of condoms could reduce the risk by up to 99.9 per cent, or by around 80 per cent if A did not consistently take antiretroviral drugs. B did not know of these proceedings and so did not become aware of A's HIV status. The Court also suggested that if A and B were having unprotected sex, then B would not be considered an 'innocent third party' in a legal sense as she would be undertaking an activity that she knows, or should know, to carry a risk of contracting sexually transmitted diseases.

The Court concluded that there was no basis for breaching A's patient confidentiality, even if he was engaging in unprotected sex with B. In reaching this decision, the Court was clearly cognisant of the public-interest factors that mitigated against the disclosure of confidential information. For instance, Twomey J examined the interest in ensuring people take responsibility for their care, the public interest in patients remaining open and frank with their doctors, and the public interest in not requiring doctors to monitor a patient's sex life. In effect, Twomey J was aware of and concerned by the broader consequences that would flow from an approval of the CFA's application. It would have established a responsibility for medical professionals to decide, in cases of sexually transmissible diseases, whether a patient's sexual partner(s) need to be notified of the harm. As a consequence, this could result in liability for healthcare professionals who fail to breach confidentiality, where that failure results in harm to a third party.

Although the decision concerned an application by the CFA, the principles set out in this case are of general applicability. The test demonstrates that confidentiality can be breached where it is shown that there is a significant risk of death or a significant risk of very serious harm to a member or members of the public. While the test was not satisfied in the case of A and B, there are likely to be cases in the future in which the disclosure of confidential information can be justified under this test.

6.2.5 The Interests of Society

A person's right to privacy must be balanced against broader societal interests. A well-recognised exception to confidentiality is that healthcare professionals may be entitled to breach personal privacy rights in cases of serious public health risks, as recognised by the Health Act 1947. A disclosure of information may also be made in the public interest where there is concern that a violent act may subsequently take place and that the disclosure may mitigate the likelihood of it occurring. This arose in *W v Egdell*,[44] and was recently considered by the High Court in *Child and Family Agency v A*.

In *W v Egdell*, the plaintiff had previously shot and killed five people. He pleaded diminished responsibility as he had been diagnosed with paranoid schizophrenia. This plea was accepted at trial and W was sentenced to be detained without limit of time in a secure hospital. Mr W subsequently sought a transfer to a lower security unit. To support his application, Mr W engaged Mr Egdell, an independent consultant psychiatrist. Mr Egdell concluded in a report that Mr W had a continued interest in home-made bomb-making and represented a danger to the public. This caused Mr W to withdraw his application and Mr W refused to allow the disclosure of the report to the medical officer of the secure hospital. Nevertheless, Mr Egdell made the report available to the medical officer as well as the Secretary of State in the United Kingdom. In turn, the Secretary for State forwarded the report to the tribunal dealing with applications for transfer. W brought an action against the independent psychiatrist, the health authority, the mental health review tribunal and the Secretary of State for breach of confidentiality.

Despite setting a high threshold for the breach of patient confidentiality, the Court of Appeal held that the breach was justified in the public interest, on grounds of protection of the

---

[44] *W v Egdell* [1990] Ch 359; [1990] 1 All ER 835.

public from dangerous criminal acts. The duty of the psychiatrist was not to W alone but a duty was also owed to the public. Bingham J stated:

> Where a man has committed multiple killings under the disability of serious mental illness, decisions which may lead directly or indirectly to his release from hospital should not be made unless a responsible authority is properly able to make an informed judgment that the risk of repetition is so small as to be acceptable. A consultant psychiatrist who becomes aware, even in the course of a confidential relationship, of information which leads him, in the exercise of what the court considers a sound professional judgment, to fear that such decisions may be made on the basis of inadequate information and with a real risk of consequent danger to the public is entitled to take such steps as are reasonable in all the circumstances to communicate the grounds of his concern to the responsible authorities.[45]

The risk should involve a real and serious risk of danger to the public and it should be an on-going risk.

The decision in *Egdell* was cited by Twomey J in *Child and Family Agency v A*. Twomey J went on to state that:

> this Court is in little doubt that if the factual circumstances that arose in the *Edgell* [sic] case were to arise before this Court, namely a significant risk of death to a member or members of the public from a known killer, a doctor would be entitled to breach patient confidentiality in order to seek to prevent the death of an innocent third party.[46]

Twomey J went beyond recognising an entitlement to breach confidentiality and suggested that it seems clear that a doctor 'would have a duty to act to seek to prevent innocent deaths'.[47] This responsibility may also apply to nurses where the relevant information has been disclosed to them. Any subsequent disclosure should not be made to the world at large, but instead should be limited to relevant persons, professional bodies or authorities.

---

[45] *W v Egdell* [1990] Ch 359, 424.
[46] *Child and Family Agency v A* [2018] IEHC 112, [63].
[47] ibid 112, [64].

6.3 Data Protection

There are two main laws that regulate personal data and access to information, namely the GDPR and the Freedom of Information Act 2014. The GDPR defines principles for the collection, processing, and storing of personal information, while the freedom of information legislation allows persons to seek access to data held by government departments, agencies, and other designated bodies in receipt of State funding in Ireland. The NMBI and Health Service Executive (HSE) are subject to both sets of legislation.

Concerns over data protection have been especially prevalent in the last few years owing to the introduction of the GDPR, which applied from 25 May 2018. It has general application to the processing of personal data, set more extensive obligations on data controllers and processors, and established stronger protections for data subjects. The GDPR is transposed and supplemented by the Data Protection Act 2018. However, there are limited circumstances in which the GDPR will not be applicable. For instance, where a complaint or possible infringement occurred prior to the GDPR taking effect, then the Data Protection Acts 1988–2003 are to apply. Similarly, if the processing of personal data is carried out for the purpose of law enforcement, then the Law Enforcement Directive, as transposed by the Data Protection Act 2018, is to apply.

Personal data is defined by Article 4 GDPR as 'any information relating to an identified or identifiable natural person' known as the data subject.[48] An identifiable natural person is a person who can either directly or indirectly be identified by: name; an identification number; location data; an online identifier; or one or more factors specific to the physical, physiological, genetic, mental, economic, cultural or social identity.[49]

Special categories of personal data are also defined by the GDPR. The processing of personal data will generally be prohibited if it reveals racial or ethnic origin; political opinions; religious or philosophical beliefs; trade union membership; genetic data; biometric data for the purposes of uniquely identifying an individual; data concerning health; or personal data concerning an individual's sex life or sexual orientation.[50]

---

[48] General Data Protection Regulation, Art 4.
[49] ibid Art 4(1).
[50] ibid Art 9.

The data protection law governs instances where personal data are processed. Article 4 defines processing as:

> any operation or set of operations which is performed on personal data, whether or not by automated means, such as collection, recording, organisation, structuring, storage, adaptation or alteration, retrieval, consultation, use, disclosure by transmission, dissemination or otherwise making available, alignment or combination, restriction, erasure or destruction.[51]

It follows that nurses will regularly engage in data processing relating to patient information. This information will often be a special category of personal data as it may relate to a patient's health, religion, genetic data, or even sexual history.

The GDPR is underpinned by six principles. These provide that personal data must be:

(a) processed lawfully, fairly and in a transparent manner in relation to the data subject

(b) collected for specified, explicit and legitimate purposes

(c) adequate, relevant and limited to what is necessary

(d) accurate and, where necessary, kept up to date

(e) kept in a form which permits identification of data subjects for no longer than is necessary

(f) processed in a manner that ensures integrity and confidentiality[52]

The data controller has responsibility for ensuring compliance with these principles, but must also be able to demonstrate compliance. This represents a further principle of 'accountability'.[53]

6.3.1 Transparency

The data controller is required to inform patients, as data subjects, why data is being collected. This should be done in a manner that

---
[51] ibid Art 4(2).
[52] ibid Art 5.
[53] ibid Art 5(2).

is in a 'concise, transparent, intelligible and easily accessible form, using clear and plain language, in particular for any information addressed specifically to a child'.[54] A privacy notice should be available to patients for when personal data are obtained. This serves to comply with Article 13 GDPR and should include the following information:

Information relating to the organisation

- Identity and contact details of the controller
- Details of the data controller's representative, where applicable
- Contact details of the data protection officer

Reasons for collecting data

- The purposes of the processing for which the personal data are intended, and whether it will be used for automated decision-making
- The legal basis for the processing, including any legitimate interests relied on
- The recipients or categories of recipients of the personal data, if any

Data subject rights

- The right to request from the controller access to and rectification or erasure of personal data or restriction of processing concerning the data subject or to object to processing as well as the right to data portability
- The right to withdraw consent for processing, where consent is the basis for the processing
- The right to lodge a complaint with a supervisory authority

Additional information

- Where applicable, the fact that the controller intends to transfer personal data to a third country or international organisation and the existence or absence of an adequacy decision by the Commission
- The period for which personal data will be stored or the criteria used to determine that period

---

[54] ibid Art 12.

- Whether the provision of personal data is a statutory or contractual requirement, or a requirement necessary to enter into a contract, as well as whether the data subject is obliged to provide the personal data and of the possible consequences of failure to provide such data[55]

6.3.2 Processing of Personal Data

Article 6 GDPR provides that processing shall only be lawful if and to the extent that at least one of the following reasons applies:

(a) the data subject has given consent to the processing;

(b) processing is necessary for the performance of a contract to which the data subject is party or in order to take steps at the request of the data subject prior to entering into a contract;

(c) processing is necessary for compliance with a legal obligation;

(d) processing is necessary in order to protect the vital interests of the data subject or of another natural person;

(e) processing is necessary … in the public interest or in the exercise of official authority;

(f) processing is necessary for legitimate interests …, except where such interests are overridden by the interests or fundamental rights and freedoms of the data subject.

Article 6(1)(f) does not, however, apply to the processing of data carried out by public authorities in the performance of their tasks. On this basis, public authorities such as the HSE cannot rely on the legitimate interests clause to justify processing. Instead, reliance must be placed on one of the other reasons as set out above.

The data that nurses engage with will often concern the health of the individual. This is defined as 'personal data related to the physical or mental health of a natural person, including the provision of health care services, which reveal information about

---

[55] ibid Art 13.

his or her health status'.[56] As previously noted, much of the data encountered in a healthcare setting will be of a special category. The conditions associated with the processing of special categories of personal data are set out by Article 9 GDPR. Processing of this data is generally prohibited unless:

(a) the data subject has given explicit consent;

(b) processing is necessary for the purposes of carrying out the obligations and exercising specific rights of the controller or of the data subject in the field of employment and social security and social protection law;

(c) processing is necessary to protect the vital interests of the data subject or of another natural person where the data subject is physically or legally incapable of giving consent;

(d) processing is carried out in the course of the legitimate activities of a church or not-for-profit body;

(e) processing relates to personal data which are manifestly made public by the data subject;

(f) processing is necessary for the establishment, exercise or defence of legal claims or whenever courts are acting in their judicial capacity;

(g) processing is necessary for reasons of substantial public interest;

(h) processing is necessary for the purposes of preventive or occupational medicine, for the assessment of the working capacity of the employee, medical diagnosis, the provision of health or social care or treatment or the management of health or social care systems and services on the basis of Union or Member State law or pursuant to contract with a health professional …;

(i) processing is necessary for reasons of public interest in the area of public health, such as protecting against serious cross-border threats to health or ensuring high standards of quality and safety of health care and of medicinal products or medical devices, on the basis of Union or Member State law which provides for suitable and specific measures to

---

[56] ibid Art 4(15).

safeguard the rights and freedoms of the data subject, in particular professional secrecy;

(j) processing is necessary for archiving purposes in the public interest, scientific or historical research purposes or statistical purposes in accordance with Article 89(1) based on Union or Member State law ...[57]

As noted above, appropriate consent can permit the lawful processing of personal data and special categories of personal data under the GDPR. Article 4 GDPR defines consent as 'any freely given specific, informed and unambiguous indication of the data subject's wishes by which he or she, by a statement or by a clear affirmative action, signifies agreement to the processing of personal data relating to him or her'.[58] Conditions for consent are also addressed by Article 7 GDPR.

6.3.3 Rights of the Data Subject

Chapter 3 GDPR sets out the rights of the data subject. These include the right to be informed, the right of access, the right to rectification, the right to erasure, the right to restriction of processing, the right to data portability, the right to object to processing, and the right not to be subject to a decision based on automated processing, including profiling.

Right to be informed: The provision of information is linked to the need for transparency. Articles 13 and 14 of the GDPR outline the types of information a controller is to provide to a data subject.

Right of access: Under Irish legislation and the GDPR, patients have a right to access personal data held about them.[59] If a person's data is being processed, they may request that a copy of that data be sent to them.

Right to rectification: Article 16 GDPR provides for a right to rectification. Data controllers such as the HSE and NMBI must ensure that the information they hold is accurate. The data subject is entitled to have inaccurate personal data concerning him or her rectified without undue delay. In addition, the data subject has the right to have incomplete personal data completed, including by means of providing a supplementary statement.

---

[57] ibid Art 9.
[58] ibid Art 4.
[59] ibid Art 15.

Right to erasure: The right to erasure, or right to be forgotten, is provided for by Article 17 of the GDPR. A data subject can request the erasure of personal data if one of the following grounds applies:

> (a) the personal data are no longer necessary in relation to the purposes for which they were collected or otherwise processed;
>
> (b) the data subject withdraws consent on which the processing is based according to point (a) of Article 6(1), or point (a) of Article 9(2), and where there is no other legal ground for the processing;
>
> (c) the data subject objects to the processing pursuant to Article 21(1) and there are no overriding legitimate grounds for the processing, or the data subject objects to the processing pursuant to Article 21(2);
>
> (d) the personal data have been unlawfully processed;
>
> (e) the personal data have to be erased for compliance with a legal obligation in Union or Member State law to which the controller is subject;
>
> (f) the personal data have been collected in relation to the offer of information society services referred to in Article 8(1).[60]

The right of erasure is not an absolute right and requests for erasure will be determined on a case-by-case basis. For instance, the right does not apply where processing is necessary for exercising the right of freedom of expression and information, or for a legal or public interest. Furthermore, it does not apply where the processing is necessary for reasons of public interest in the area of public health in accordance with Article 9(2)(h) or (i).

Right to restriction of processing: The right to restriction of processing is provided for by Article 18 GDPR. A data subject has a right to restrict a controller from processing personal data where the accuracy of the personal data is contested; the processing is unlawful and the data subject opposes the erasure of the personal data; the data controller no longer needs the personal data, but the subject requires it to be kept for legal claims; or the data

---
[60] ibid Art 17(1).

subject has objected to the processing pending the verification of legitimate grounds.

Right to data portability: Article 20 GDPR provides for a right to data portability, under which data subjects have the right to receive personal data concerning them in a commonly used and machine-readable format. This only applies where the processing is based on consent and the processing is carried out by automated means. The right to data portability also allows the data subject to request the transfer of personal data from one controller to another, where technically feasible.

Right to object: The right to object is set out by Article 21 GDPR. In a healthcare context, this will apply where the lawful basis for processing was the performance of a task carried out in the public interest or in the exercise of official authority. The data controller is not permitted to continue processing the personal data unless it can demonstrate compelling legitimate grounds for the processing that override the interests, rights and freedoms of the data subject or for the establishment, exercise or defence of legal claims. The right to object is limited where the data processing is for research or statistical purposes in the public interest.[61]

Right not to be subject to a decision based on automated processing, including profiling: Article 22 of the GDPR provides that the data subject has the right not to be subject to a decision based solely on automated processing, including profiling, which produces legal effects concerning him or her or similarly significantly affects him or her.

The data controller has a fundamental role in ensuring the rights of the data subject are upheld and protected. This is also reflected in Article 25 of the GDPR, which addresses data protection by design and by default. This requires the data controller to implement appropriate technical and organisational measures so as to minimise the risk to the data subjects' rights. The concept of data minimisation requires that only personal data necessary for each specific purpose of the processing are processed. Pseudonymisation may also be applied as a technical and organisational measure intended to protect the data subjects' rights.[62]

---

[61] ibid Art 21(6).
[62] ibid Art 4. Pseudonymisation is defined as: the processing of personal data in such a manner that the personal data can no longer be attributed to a specific data subject without the use of additional information, provided that such additional information is kept separately and is subject to technical and

6.3.4 Breach of the GDPR

A personal data breach is a 'breach of security leading to the accidental or unlawful destruction, loss, alteration, unauthorised disclosure of, or access to, personal data transmitted, stored or otherwise processed'.[63] Once a data controller becomes aware of a personal data breach, the controller shall without undue delay and, where feasible, not later than 72 hours after having become aware of it, notify the Office of the Data Protection Commissioner. In circumstances where the personal data breach is likely to result in a high risk to the rights and freedoms of natural persons, the controller shall communicate the personal data breach to the data subject without undue delay.[64] Such a notification allows the individuals affected to take any necessary steps to protect themselves from the potential consequences of the breach.

Article 33(3) provides that a breach notification should at least include the following:

> (a) describe the nature of the personal data breach including, where possible, the categories and approximate number of data subjects concerned and the categories and approximate number of personal data records concerned;
>
> (b) communicate the name and contact details of the data protection officer or other contact point where more information can be obtained;
>
> (c) describe the likely consequences of the personal data breach;
>
> (d) describe the measures taken or proposed to be taken by the controller to address the personal data breach, including, where appropriate, measures to mitigate its possible adverse effects.[65]

6.4 Freedom of Information Act 2014

The Freedom of Information (FOI) Act 2014 is intended to promote the transparency and accountability of public bodies. The Act applies to all public bodies that conform to the definition of public

---

organisational measures to ensure that the personal data are not attributed to an identified or identifiable natural person.
[63] ibid Art 4.
[64] ibid Art 34.
[65] ibid Art 33(3).

body under s 6(1) of the Act (unless they are specifically exempt or partially exempt under the provisions of s 42 or Schedule 1 of the Act). It includes Government departments, higher education institutions, the HSE, voluntary hospitals, and other bodies in receipt of State funding. These bodies are obliged to respond to requests from the public for records they hold. This can be a challenging and time-consuming process. In 2018, 29 per cent of FOI requests to public bodies were made to the HSE, while 15 per cent were submitted to voluntary hospitals, mental health services and related agencies.[66]

The FOI Act 2014 sets out certain rights that people have in relation to the information stored by public bodies. People have a right to access official records held by public bodies; a right to have personal information held on them corrected or updated where the information is incomplete, incorrect, or misleading; and a right to be given reasons for decisions taken by public bodies where those decisions expressly affect them.[67]

The FOI Act provides for a broad entitlement to access records. This is illustrated by s 11(1) of the FOI Act 2014:

> Subject to this Act, every person has a right to and shall, on request therefor, be offered access to any record held by an FOI body and the right so conferred is referred to in this Act as the right of access.[68]

There are, however, restrictions to the type of information that can be accessed. Key exemptions are set out by Part 4 of the FOI Act 2014 and include records relating to meetings of the Government,[69] deliberations of FOI bodies,[70] records which may prejudice or impair law enforcement and public safety,[71] information obtained in confidence,[72] commercially sensitive information,[73] and personal information other than information relating to the person making the request.[74] Access to a record may be refused where it could reasonably be expected to endanger the life or safety of

---

[66] Information Commissioner, *Annual Report 2018: Supporting the Right to Information* (Government of Ireland 2019) 18.
[67] Freedom of Information Act 2014, ss 9–10.
[68] ibid s 11(1).
[69] ibid s 28.
[70] ibid s 29.
[71] ibid s 32.
[72] ibid s 35.
[73] ibid s 36.
[74] ibid s 37.

any person.[75] A request may also be refused on administrative grounds where it is unclear, voluminous, or the information is already in the public domain.[76] Many of the exemptions set out under Pt 4 of the 2014 Act contain a public-interest override. In effect, while the records are exempt under the FOI Act, a decision may be made that the overall public interest justifies its release.

Personal information under the Act is defined as:

> information about an identifiable individual that, either –
>
>> (a) would, in the ordinary course of events, be known only to the individual or members of the family, or friends, of the individual, or
>>
>> (b) is held by an FOI body on the understanding that it would be treated by that body as confidential[77]

Access to a record that contains personal information will generally be refused. However, access may be granted where the information concerned relates to the requester. Section 37(2) provides that a record may be made available where an individual to whom the information relates consents to the disclosure, information of the same kind is available to the general public, or the individual to whom it relates was aware that it would or might be made available to the general public.[78] Section 37(2)(e) provides for disclosure where the information is necessary to avoid a serious and imminent danger to the life or health of an individual.[79]

A further exemption under s 37 arises in circumstances where an FOI request relates to a medical or psychiatric record relating to the requester, or was kept or obtained in the context of social work in relation to the requester. Disclosure of such a record may be refused where disclosure 'might be prejudicial to his or her physical or mental health, well-being or emotional condition'. Nonetheless, where the FOI request is refused, s 37(4) provides that the record may be made available to a health professional who has expertise in relation to the subject matter of the record.[80]

---

[75] ibid s 32(1)(b).
[76] ibid s 15.
[77] ibid s 2.
[78] ibid s 37(2).
[79] ibid s 37(2)(e).
[80] ibid s 37(4).

This underlines the sensitive nature of these records but also hints at a paternalistic approach to the disclosure of such records.

If a requester is not satisfied with a decision, then an 'internal review' can be requested.[81] The review is to be carried out by a more senior member of staff and a decision should be communicated to the relevant person no later than three weeks after the request for review was received. A further appeal is provided for under Chapter 4 of the FOI Act 2014. This allows the matter to be reviewed by the Information Commissioner. In turn, the decision of the Information Commissioner may be appealed to the High Court on '(a) a point of law from the decision, or (b) where the party or person concerned contends that the release of a record concerned would contravene a requirement imposed by European Union law, on a finding of fact set out or inherent in the decision.'[82]

6.4.1 Records Pertaining to Children

Section 37(8) of the FOI Act 2014 addresses access to personal information relating to children. It provides that a request may be granted where the requester is a parent or guardian of the individual to whom the record relates and that individual belongs to one of the following classes:

> (a) individuals who, on the date of the request, have not attained full age, or
>
> (b) individuals who have attained full age, being individuals who –
>
>> (i) at the time of the request have, or are subject to, a psychiatric condition, mental incapacity or severe physical disability, the incidence and nature of which are certified by a registered medical practitioner, and
>>
>> (ii) by reason of that condition, incapacity or disability, are incapable of exercising their rights under the Act.[83]

On this basis, a parent or guardian may access a record where it relates to a minor or an incapacitated individual provided that

---

[81] ibid s 21.
[82] ibid s 24.
[83] Freedom of Information Act 2014 (Section 37(8)) Regulations 2016, SI 218/2016, reg 5.

such access would, having regard to all the circumstances, be in the individual's best interests.[84]

The Supreme Court in *McK v Information Commission*[85] held that there is a rebuttable presumption that a parent is entitled to access information about the medical care their child is receiving and the release of such information is in the best interests of the child. It follows that evidence may be produced, including reference to the views of the minor if appropriate, that it would not serve her interests, and in considering the circumstances, her welfare. At issue in *McK* was whether a father, a widower who had been separated from his late wife, and who was a joint guardian of his children, was entitled under the FOI Act 1997 to information in the form of hospital notes about his daughter's medical condition.

The requester was advised that his daughter had been admitted to a Dublin hospital for an unspecified viral infection. As he was unable to obtain any further information, the girl's father submitted a request seeking access to the personal medical records of his daughter. The request was refused and this decision was subsequently affirmed. The refusal was then appealed to the High Court, which found in favour of the requester. The Commissioner appealed against that finding, bringing the case before the Supreme Court where Denham J stated:

> The [FOI] Act of 1997 and the Regulations fall to be interpreted in accordance with the Constitution. A parent, the requester, has rights and duties in relation to a child. It is presumed that his or her actions are in accordance with the best interests of the child. This presumption while not absolute is fundamental. The Commissioner took an incorrect approach in requiring tangible evidence of the parent rather than applying the presumption that a parent was acting in the child's interests. ...
>
> A parent's rights and duties include the care of a child who is ill. As a consequence a parent is entitled to information about the medical care a child is receiving so that he or she may make appropriate decisions for the child, as his or her guardian. ... The presumption is that the release of such medical information would best serve the interests of the minor. However, evidence may be produced that it would not serve

---

[84] ibid reg 6.
[85] *McK v Information Commission* [2006] IESC 2.

her interests, and, in considering the circumstances, her welfare is paramount.[86]

The presumption in favour of a parent or guardian will not be easily displaced. The Department of Public Expenditure and Reform published guidance on these type of requests and asks: (i) would the minor consent to release of the material, (ii) would release of the material damage the minor in some way, and (iii) are the records held in the minor's own right? On the question of consent, it is suggested that consultation with the minor is not compulsory. Instead, the amount of consultation and the weight to be given to a minor's views is at the discretion of the decision-maker and may be determined on a case-by-case basis.[87] When undertaking a consultation, a decision-maker is advised to take account of (a) the capacity of the person to understand the issues involved, (b) the presence of a parent or guardian, (c) the nature of the record, (d) the nature of the consultation, (e) guardianship and custody issues, and (f) proof of consent.[88]

The guidance document indicates that a minor's objection to the release of information will not always be sufficient to justify refusal. However, if the records are held in the minor's own right, the general position is that such records would not be released unless it was in the minor's best interest: for instance, '[c]ertain medical records which may not be appropriate for automatic release to parents/guardians, such as records a GP might have on prescribing contraceptives to a minor'.[89]

Although the records at issue in *McK v Information Commissioner* related to medical treatment, the Commissioner takes the view that the judgment is likely to apply to any personal information of a minor that is relevant to his or her welfare. This interpretation is linked to the comments of McMahon J in *HSE v Information Commissioner*.[90] McMahon J noted that the Supreme Court in *McK* did not place undue emphasis on the nature or content of the records in question. On this basis, McMahon J adopted the 'court's reasoning as being applicable also to the records involved

---

[86] ibid 2, [15].
[87] Department of Public Expenditure and Reform, *Freedom of Information: Access to Records by Parents/Guardians. Access to Records Relating to Deceased Persons Prepared Under Section 37(8) of the Freedom Of Information Act 2014* (FOI Central Policy Unit 2017).
[88] ibid.
[89] ibid 5.
[90] *HSE v Information Commissioner* [2008] IEHC 298.

in this case which were concerned with allegations of physical abuse of the child'.[91]

6.4.2 Posthumous Protection of Information

Section 37(1) of the FOI Act 2014 exempts records containing personal information, including personal information of a deceased person, from disclosure, subject to specific exceptions. Section 37(8) provides that the Minister may make regulations for access by specific classes of requester, and these are set out in SI 218 of 2016:

> (a) the requester concerned belongs to one or other of the following classes:
>
> > (i) a personal representative of the individual acting in due course of administration of the individual's estate or any person acting with the consent of a personal representative so acting,
> >
> > (ii) a person on whom a function is conferred by law in relation to the individual or his or her estate acting in the course of the performance of the function, or
>
> (b) the requester is the spouse or the next of kin of the individual and, in the opinion of the head, having regard to all the circumstances, the public interest, including the public interest in the confidentiality of personal information, would on balance be better served by granting than by refusing to grant the request.[92]

The first category only covers a personal representative who has taken out a grant of probate in cases of testacy or letters of administration in cases of intestacy of the deceased person and any agent acting for the personal representative. The second category covers cases where the estate and subsequent affairs of the deceased are taken over by a court or State agency. The third category permits, in appropriate circumstances, access to certain records to be given to the different individuals who enjoyed a particular relationship with the deceased. An applicant under this class is required to produce evidence of their relationship to the deceased.

---

[91] ibid 298, [46].
[92] Freedom of Information Act 2014 (s 37(8)) Regulations 2016, SI 218/2016, reg 7.

The burden of establishing the death of an individual lies with the person requesting the record. The requester must submit an affidavit or other appropriate proof to the public body identifying the deceased and exhibiting the necessary death certificate. These proofs are not required if the public body already has sufficient proof of the death of the person whose records are being sought.

The persons set out at (i) and (ii) above have the same right of access to records as the deceased person enjoyed when living. In relation to the spouse or next of kin, the release of records is subject to a public-interest test, which is to be carried out having regard to the circumstances of the request and in accordance with the guidelines. Each case is to be determined based on its own merit. The decision-maker will be required to balance the public interest in confidentiality of personal information against the public interest in the right of the requester to access the records. In reach a decision on an individual case, the guidance document provides that the decision-maker should take the following factors into consideration:

- The confidentiality of personal information as set out in s 37(1) of the Act
- Would the deceased have consented to the release of the records to the requester when living?
- Has the person outlined arrangements in his or her will or other instrument in writing consenting to release of personal records?
- Would the release damage the good name and character of the deceased?
- The nature of the relationship of the requester to the deceased and the circumstances of the relationship prior to the death of the deceased.
- The nature of the records to be released
- Can the requester obtain the information they seek without accessing the records of the deceased, for example from another family source?
- Any other circumstances relevant to the request as set out by the requester.[93]

A case may arise where a request is received for records of a deceased person from an individual not part of the classes set

---

[93] Department of Public Expenditure and Reform, *Access to Records by Parents/Guardians. Access to Records Relating to Deceased Persons Prepared Under Section 37(8) of the Freedom Of Information Act 2014* (FOI Central Policy Unit 2017) 12–13.

out above. The FOI Act does not prohibit access to records being granted to such persons. These requests are to be assessed on their merits outside the parameters of the FOI Act, with decisions on access expected to follow such enquiries and consultations as the public body deems necessary depending on the particular case.

6.5 Open Disclosure

Neil LJ in *Thake v Maurice* stated, 'Medicine, though a highly skilled profession, is not, and is not generally regarded as being, an exact science.'[94] Mistakes and errors are an inevitable part of healthcare and can have a serious impact on the lives of all parties. There may be fears of a negligence action or a charge of poor professional performance for the healthcare professional. It is therefore understandable that healthcare professionals may respond with silence or secrecy. Such a response would exclude the patient and results in further stress and uncertainty. In response, a policy of open disclosure has emerged through professional standards and legislation.

Open disclosure has been defined by the Australian Commission on Safety and Quality as:

> An open discussion with a patient about an incident(s) that resulted in harm to that patient while they were receiving health care. The elements of open disclosure are an apology or expression of regret ..., a factual explanation of what happened, an opportunity for the patient to relate their experience, and an explanation of the steps being taken to manage the event and prevent recurrence.[95]

The move towards open disclosure is marked by the need for transparency and changes in healthcare culture. Greater transparency has been associated with improved patient outcomes, reduced litigation costs, and increased trust and confidence with the healthcare system. There are prospective benefits for both the patient and the healthcare professional. Yet, a policy of open disclosure can be challenging to implement. As Lazare commented, 'Far and away the biggest stumbling block to apologizing is our belief that apologizing is a sign of weakness and an admission of guilt. We have the misguided notion we are

---

[94] *Thake v Maurice* [1986] QB 644, 685.
[95] Australian Commission on Safety and Quality in Health Care, *Australian Open Disclosure Framework: Better Communication, a Better Way to Care* (ACSQHC 2013) 4.

better off ignoring or denying our offenses and hope that no one notices.'[96]

The legal system has not traditionally facilitated disclosure as is evident from the comments of Peart J in *O'Connor and Tormey v Lenihan*:

> I have little doubt that no award of damages would be even half as useful in easing their feelings of anger and distress as a forthright and sincere and appropriately tendered apology for the anger, hurt and distress caused ... But the problem is that our legal system is not conducive to such steps being taken by defendants exposed to a claim for damages once fault might be seen to be acknowledged by such an apology, and are inhibited from taking a step which perhaps in other circumstances they would wish to take in order to assist those who have suffered distress and hurt.[97]

Due to the legal lacunae which existed, the ethical basis for disclosure therefore took on greater significance. Section 67.1 of the Irish Medical Council's *Guide to Professional Conduct and Ethics* sets out, 'Open disclosure is supported within a culture of candour. You have a duty to promote and support this culture and to support colleagues whose actions are investigated following an adverse event.'[98] Section 67.2 outlines the steps to be followed when discussing events with patients and families. These steps require the medical practitioner to 'acknowledge that the event happened; explain how it happened; apologise, if appropriate; and assure patients and their families that the cause of the event will be investigated and efforts made to reduce the chance of it happening again'.[99]

Slightly less information is contained in the NMBI's *Code of Professional Conduct and Ethics*. Under the Quality of Practice principle, it is set out: 'Safe, quality practice is promoted by nurses and midwives actively participating in incident reporting, adverse event reviews and open disclosure.'[100] Open disclosure is also supported by a national policy, which was prepared by the HSE in 2019. The policy applies to all staff working in the HSE

---

[96] Aaron Lazare, 'Go Ahead, Say You're Sorry' (1995) Psychology Today 40.
[97] *O'Connor and Tormey v Lenihan* [2005] IEHC 176, [131].
[98] Irish Medical Council, *Guide to Professional Conduct and Ethics for Registered Medical Practitioners* (8th edn, IMC 2019) section 67.1.
[99] ibid section 67.2.
[100] Nursing and Midwifery Board of Ireland, *Code of Professional Conduct and Ethics for Registered Nurses and Registered Midwives* (NMBI 2014) 22.

health- and social-care services and in any services funded by the HSE.[101] It is to be used in conjunction with a range of other guidelines and documents, such as the HSE *Incident Management Framework*.

Although the ethical duty is relatively clear, the absence of a statutory framework to provide protection and certainty in relation to disclosure was problematic. The ethical duty alone does not address concerns healthcare professionals may have about the potential exposure to civil proceedings or professional reputation. The absence of a statutory basis for open disclosure has now been addressed by the enactment of the Civil Liability (Amendment) Act 2017 and the Civil Liability (Open Disclosure) (Prescribed Statements) Regulations 2018.

Part 4 of the Civil Liability (Amendment) Act 2017 addresses 'Open Disclosure of Patient Safety Incidents'. The Act does not impose a mandatory obligation but instead provides for a voluntary open disclosure to be made in instances where a patient safety incident has occurred. The Act defines a patient safety incident as:

> (a) an incident which has caused an unintended or unanticipated injury, or harm, to the patient and which occurred in the course of the provision of a health service to that patient,
>
> (b) an incident (i) which has occurred in the course of the provision of a health service to the patient and did not result in actual injury or harm, and (ii) in respect of which the health services provider has reasonable grounds to believe placed the patient at risk of unintended or unanticipated injury or harm, or
>
> (c) the prevention, whether by timely intervention or by chance, of an unintended or unanticipated injury, or harm, to the patient in the course of the provision, to him or her, of a health service, and in respect of which the health services provider has reasonable grounds for believing that, in the absence of such prevention, could have resulted in such injury, or harm, to the patient.[102]

---

[101] Health Service Executive, *Open Disclosure: A Brief Guide for Health and Social Care Staff* (HSE 2019).
[102] Civil Liability (Amendment) Act 2017, s 8.

The Civil Liability (Amendment) Act 2017 provides considerable detail on the preparations for and the making of an open disclosure. The open disclosure meeting is specifically addressed by s 16 of the 2017 Act. This addresses the method of communication, the provision of information related to the patient safety incident, and the type of information to be provided such as the date on which the patient safety incident occurred and the date it was identified. A description of the patient safety incident is also to be provided along with details of the physical or psychological consequences. Section 16(4) of the Act provides for the issuance of an apology at the meeting if the health service provider has deemed it appropriate.

The disclosure is to be made to the patient and/or a relevant person. The relevant person may be a parent, guardian, son or daughter, spouse, or civil partner of the patient. Moreover, the relevant person should be cohabiting with the patient or be specifically nominated in writing by the patient as a person to whom clinical information may be disclosed.[103]

As noted above, the issuance of an apology may raise concerns about potential liability. Section 10 of the 2017 Act establishes important protective elements that underpin the open disclosure process. This section provides that an apology issued at an open disclosure meeting shall not constitute an express or implied admission of fault or liability[104]; it shall not be admissible as evidence of fault or liability[105]; it shall not, subject to other considerations, invalidate or otherwise affect the cover provided by an insurance contract; and it shall not constitute an express or implied admission of fault, professional misconduct, poor professional performance, or unfitness to practise a health service.

Despite the protections the Act put in place, it did not go so far as to make disclosure mandatory. There were moves in this direction during the legislative process, but the proposed amendment was rejected. The cervical check scandal in Ireland subsequently highlighted the importance of transparency and disclosure in healthcare. The Minister for Health brought forward measures that would require mandatory open disclosure where a serious patient safety incident has occurred. Head 5 of the General Scheme of the Patient Safety Bill 2018 provides a wide-ranging non-exhaustive definition of a serious patient safety incident. There is therefore a

---

[103] ibid s 7.
[104] ibid s 10(1)(a).
[105] ibid s 10(1)(b).

distinction between a patient safety incident as defined in the Act and a serious patient safety incident as described in the Bill. On 12 December 2019, the Bill lapsed with the dissolution of the Dáil.[106]

6.6 Use of Social Media

Since the mid 2000s the use of social media has become ubiquitous. Social media platforms include the likes of Facebook, Twitter, Snapchat, and Instagram. These sites present enormous potential for the healthcare professional. They provide an easy and effective tool to connect with professional networks, access research, and contribute to national and international discussion on aspects of nursing and midwifery. Yet, social media also poses a very real risk to patient confidentiality. Information can be quickly disseminated online, leaving the original poster with little control over who accesses, shares, or even modifies the content.

The NMBI has published guidance on social media use.[107] It suggests that when using social media, nurses and midwives should adhere to the 6 Ps, namely: be professional; positive; posts should be patient or person-free; protect your professionalism; maintain privacy; and, pause before you post. Patient confidentiality should be maintained at all times as legal and ethical obligations do not cease on the internet. In this regard, the succinct advice of the NMBI is 'Post appropriately.'[108]

---

[106] Patient Safety Bill 2018.
[107] NMBI, *Guidance to Nurses and Midwives on Social Media and Social Networking* (NMBI 2013).
[108] ibid 10.

CHAPTER 7
The Administration of Medicines

Introduction 183
The Registered Nurse/Midwife Prescriber.............. 184
    The Legal Framework for Prescriptive
    Authority 185
    The Department of Health and the Health
    Service Executive................................ 191
    Registration as a Nurse or Midwife Prescriber..... 192
    Clinical Governance 194
    Practice Standards and Guidelines for Nurses
    and Midwives with Prescriptive Authority 196
The Prescribing and Administration of Medicines 197
    The Clinical Decision-Making Process............. 197
    Prescription Practices and Limitations............ 199
    Self-Administration of Medicines 205
    Covert Administration of Medicines 205
Responding to Errors and Incidents in Medication
Management... 206
    Professional Accountability 207

7.0 Introduction

The responsibility and professional competencies of the nurse have expanded considerably in recent years and this is particularly clear in the control and prescription of medicines. The advent of nurse prescribing is a relatively new development for the nursing profession in Ireland but nurses have traditionally played an important role in the control and administration of medicines. This chapter will address both the concept of the registered nurse/midwife prescriber and the role of the nurse/midwife in administering medicines prescribed by other healthcare professionals.

This chapter is composed of three main sections. The first section outlines the legal framework for the registered nurse/midwife prescriber: the oversight role of the Nursing and Midwifery Board of Ireland (NMBI), clinical governance, and the registered nurse/midwife prescriber register is outlined. The second section examines the prescribing and administration of medicines.

This includes discussion of clinical decision-making, as well as prescription practices and limitations such as prescribing for family members and exempt medicinal product prescribing. Many of these topics also require consideration of the ethical concerns surrounding the management of medicines. The third section addresses the management of errors or incidents in the administration of medicines. On this point, professional accountability and clinical indemnity is considered. These sections serve to underline the necessity of a good knowledge and awareness of the law in this area. As will be seen over the course of this chapter, the legal framework is composed of professional standards, rules, and legislation. The framework has, in part, emerged through the work and collaboration of groups such as the NMBI, the Health Service Executive (HSE), the Office of the Nursing and Midwifery Services Director, higher education bodies, and health service providers. This is illustrative of the collaborative component that lies at the heart of effective and appropriate prescribing practices.

7.1 The Registered Nurse/Midwife Prescriber

The prescribing of medicines by nurses and midwives was provided for in Ireland in 2007. This system of prescribing has also been introduced in the United Kingdom, the United States, Sweden, Australia, and New Zealand. It is an important feature of the healthcare system and it has been suggested that there are many advantages in expanding the nurse's and midwife's scope of practice in this regard. Nurse prescribing has been linked to increased professional autonomy, especially in neo-natal and palliative care.[1] It has been linked to longer consultation periods,[2] clearer communication with patients,[3] and improved

---

[1] An Bord Altranais and National Council for the Professional Development of Nursing and Midwifery, *Review of Nurses and Midwives in the Prescribing and Administration of Medicinal Products* (June 2005) 19–20. Benefits include safer patient care, influence of nursing, professional development, and more timely treatment for patients.

[2] P Venning and others, 'Randomised Controlled Trial Comparing Cost Effectiveness of General Practitioners and Nurse Practitioners in Primary Care' (2000) 320 British Medical Journal 1048.

[3] Jonathan Drennan and others, *National Independent Evaluation of the Nurse and Midwife Prescribing Initiative* (HSE 2009) 13–14; Dianne Berry, 'Attitudes Towards, and Information Needs in Relation To, Supplementary Nurse Prescribing in the UK: An Empirical Study' (2006) 15 Journal of Clinical Nursing 22.

documentation and record-keeping.[4] Moreover, nurse prescribing can contribute to the safe and timely access to appropriate medicines, thereby alleviating the prescribing burden on medical practitioners.[5] The achievement of these outcomes can be linked to the legal framework that establishes and defines the remit of nurse prescribing. This section will outline the legal basis for prescriptive authority including legislation and Nurses Rules. Second, registration as a nurse prescriber will be set out, as will the oversight role of the NMBI.

7.1.1 The Legal Framework for Prescriptive Authority

The origins of nurse prescribing in Ireland can be traced back to two reports. The first was the *Report of the Commission on Nursing: A Blueprint for the Future*.[6] The Commission on Nursing was established by the Minister for Health, Michael Noonan, in March 1997. This followed a recommendation issued by the Labour Court, which drew attention to the substantial changes across the nursing profession, including changes in training and service delivery.[7] During the consultation process for the Report it was suggested that An Bord Altranais should 'empower nurses and midwives to a much greater extent to make professional decisions, rather than have narrowly focused prescriptive guidelines in certain areas'.[8] The Commission on Nursing went on to examine the provision of non-prescribed drugs, also known as over-the-counter drugs. On this point, it was suggested that greater flexibility was needed for nurses and midwives in the administration of non-prescribed drugs according to agreed protocols with medical practitioners.[9] This led the Commission to recommend that An Bord Altranais needed to urgently review the guidelines on the administration and application of non-prescribed drugs by nurses and midwives.

---

[4] Drennan (n 3) 14; Nicola Carey and others, 'An Evaluation of a Diabetes Specialist Nurse Prescriber on the System of Delivering Medicines to Patients with Diabetes' (2008) 17(12) Journal of Clinical Nursing 1635.
[5] Corina Naughton and others, 'An Evaluation of the Appropriateness and Safety of Nurse and Midwife Prescribing in Ireland' (2013) 69(7) Journal of Advanced Nursing 1478; Greg Weeks and others, 'Non-Medical Prescribing versus Medical Prescribing for Acute and Chronic Disease Management in Primary and Secondary Care' (22 November 2016) Cochrane Database Systematic Reviews.
[6] *Report of the Commission on Nursing: A Blueprint for the Future* (Government of Ireland 1998).
[7] ibid 1.1; Labour Court (Recommendation No LCR15450).
[8] ibid 4.10.
[9] ibid 4.15.

The second key document was the *Review of Scope of Practice for Nursing and Midwifery*.[10] Among the issues examined in this review was the prescribing and administration of medicines by nurses and midwives, and international developments in nurse prescribing. A detailed consultative process was completed as part of the review and participants highlighted the need for greater flexibility in prescribing practices. It was suggested that the existing structure resulted in fragmentation of care, delays, and wasted time in situations where the nurse had sufficient expertise to prescribe appropriate medicines. An Bord Altranais ultimately recommended that a review of the relevant legislation be conducted with the possibility of permitting nurse and midwife prescribing of 'prescription-only' medicines in appropriate circumstances.[11]

The two preceding reports led to a joint review by An Bord Altranais and the National Council for the Professional Development of Nursing and Midwifery. The review was titled *Review of Nurses and Midwives in the Prescribing and Administration of Medicinal Products*.[12] The main objective of this review was to examine the possible role of nurses and midwives in the prescribing of medicines. The conclusion stated, 'Prescriptive authority, the utilisation of medication protocols and over-the-counter medication supply/administration by nurses and midwives can have a significant impact on addressing current and future challenges in meeting the health needs of the individual patient and client.'[13] The Steering Committee recommended that, subject to appropriate regulation, prescriptive authority should be extended to nurses and midwives.[14] It was also recommended that a clear legislative basis should be established for the supply and administration of medicines using medication protocols by nurses and midwives.[15] After the publication of this review, the then Minister for Health Mary Harney enacted the Irish Medicines Board (Miscellaneous Provisions) Act 2006. This Act provided for the establishment of nurse and midwife prescribing. The 2006 Act forms part of a broader statutory and professional regulatory framework for nurse and midwife prescribing. Other

---

[10] An Bord Altranais, *Review of Scope of Practice for Nursing and Midwifery: Final Report* (ABA 2000).
[11] ibid 37.
[12] An Bord Altranais and National Council for the Professional Development of Nursing and Midwifery, *Review of Nurses and Midwives in the Prescribing and Administration of Medicinal Products* (June 2005).
[13] ibid 29.
[14] ibid Recommendation 4.
[15] ibid Recommendation 2.

components in the framework include the Medicinal Products (Prescription and Control of Supply) (Amendment) Regulations 2007, the Misuse of Drugs Regulations, and the Nurses Rules.

Irish Medicines Board (Miscellaneous Provisions) Act 2006

The 2006 Act is the primary legislation that provides for nurse and midwife prescribing in this jurisdiction. It amended a wide range of legislation and regulations including the Irish Medicines Board Act 1995, Control of Clinical Trials Act 1987, Health Act 1970, the Medicinal Products (Prescription and Control of Supply) Regulations 2003, and the Misuse of Drugs Act 1977. The Irish Medicines Board (Miscellaneous Provisions) Act 2006 was commenced by way of the Irish Medicines Board (Miscellaneous Provisions) Act 2006 (Commencement) Order 2007.

Medicinal Products (Prescription and Control of Supply) (Amendment) Regulations 2007

The 2007 Regulations established the conditions to be satisfied when issuing a prescription for a medicinal product. These are set out under regulation 5A:

> (a) the nurse is employed by a health service provider in a hospital, nursing home, clinic or other health service setting (including any case where the health service is provided in a private home);
>
> (b) the medicinal product is a medicinal product which would be given in the usual course of the provision of the health service provided in the health service setting in which the nurse is employed; and
>
> (c) the prescription is in fact issued in the usual course of the provision of that health service.[16]

The prescription should also include the NMBI Personal Identification Number assigned to the nurse. The Regulations carefully define the process of nurse prescribing but stipulate that additional conditions may be imposed by the health service provider:

---

[16] Medicinal Products (Prescription and Control of Supply) (Amendment) Regulations 2007, SI 201/2007, Reg 5A(1).

Nothing in this Regulation shall be construed as restricting -

(a) a health service provider from -

(i) prohibiting a registered nurse employed by the provider from issuing, in the course of that employment, a prescription for any medicinal product, or any class of medicinal product, for which the nurse may otherwise issue a prescription pursuant to these Regulations; or

(ii) imposing conditions, in addition to those referred to in paragraph (1), which must be satisfied before a registered nurse employed by the provider may issue a prescription pursuant to these Regulations[17]

A situation may therefore arise in which a nurse has satisfied the relevant legal requirements for prescribing but is limited by restrictions placed on him/her by the health service provider. This may amount to a prohibition on prescribing or it may involve the imposition of additional conditions that must be satisfied before a valid prescription can be issued.

Misuse of Drugs Regulations 2017

The prescribing of controlled drugs is detailed in the Misuse of Drugs Regulations 2017.[18] The conditions for prescription of a controlled drug are broadly similar to those set out under the 2007 Regulations.

The form of the prescription for a controlled drug is addressed in Part 5 of the 2017 Regulations and includes elements intended to aid identification and promote accuracy. The requirements are as follows:

(a) the prescription shall be in ink or otherwise so as to be indelible, or shall be transferred via the national electronic prescription transfer system;

(b) the prescription shall clearly indicate the full name (including the first name) of the practitioner issuing it and

---

[17] Medicinal Products (Prescription and Control of Supply) (Amendment) Regulations 2007, SI 201/2007, Reg 5A(2).
[18] Misuse of Drugs Regulations 2017, SI 173/2017.

state whether he or she is a registered medical practitioner, registered dentist, registered veterinary practitioner, registered nurse or registered midwife and state his or her registration number;

(c) the prescription shall be signed by the practitioner issuing it with his or her usual signature and be dated by him or her, or, in the case of a prescription transferred via the national electronic prescription transfer system, clearly indicate the date of issuance and be traceable electronically back to the practitioner issuing it

(d) except in the case of a health prescription, the prescription shall specify the address of the practitioner issuing it;

(e) subject to paragraph (3), the prescription shall specify the telephone number at which the practitioner issuing it may be contacted;

(f) subject to paragraph (3), the prescription shall specify the name (including the first name), and address of the person for whose treatment it is issued ...;

(g) subject to paragraphs (4) and (5), the prescription shall specify in the practitioner's handwriting –

(i) the name of the controlled drug to be prescribed,

(ii) the dose of the controlled drug to be taken by the person ... for whose treatment the prescription is issued,

(iii) in the case of a prescription for a controlled drug which is a preparation –

(I) the form and, where appropriate, the strength of the controlled drug to be supplied, and

(II) either the total quantity (in both words and figures) of the preparation or the number (in both words and figures) of dosage units, as appropriate, to be supplied, and

(iv) in the case of a prescription for a controlled drug which is not a preparation, the total quantity (in both words and figures) of the controlled drug to be supplied;

(h) in the case of a prescription for a total quantity intended to be dispensed in instalments, the number of instalments and the intervals at which the instalments may be dispensed.[19]

In paragraph 2(e) and (f) there is a reference to paragraph 3. This stipulates that where the prescription is issued for the treatment of a patient in a hospital or a nursing home, it will be sufficient if the prescription is written on the patient's bed card or medication record.

Schedule 8 of the Misuse of Drugs Regulations 2017 governs the drugs nurse or midwife prescribers may prescribe within Schedules 2 and 3. It also outlines the route of administration for each drug listed, e.g. transdermal, oral, intramuscular, or subcutaneous administration. Schedule 8 of the Regulations is divided into five parts and addresses drugs for pain relief, palliative care, midwifery, neonatal care, and drugs used in mental health or intellectual disability.

Nurses Rules

As noted in earlier chapters, the Nurses and Midwives Act 2011 establishes the legislative framework for the nursing and midwifery professions in Ireland. As part of this, the 2011 Act requires the NMBI to make rules in relation to the operation of its main functions. This is achieved by way of the Nurses Rules. The Rules have been updated multiple times and serve to provide the professional regulatory framework for nurse and midwife prescribing. It was the Nurses Rules 2007 that first established the separate division of the Register of Nurses, thereby providing for the role of the Registered Nurse Prescriber. This has since been amended by the Nurses Rules 2010 and Nurses and Midwives Rules 2013, which provided for the creation of a division of the Register for Nurse and Midwife Prescribers. Rule 3.11 of the Nurses Rules 2010 stipulates: 'Only those persons whose name is entered in the Nurse Prescribers Division of the Register may issue a prescription pursuant to the prevailing legislation at the time.'[20] The Nurses and Midwives (Education and Training) Rules 2018 addresses the criteria for admission to post-registration specialist programmes, including nurse and midwife prescribing. The candidate is to be registered in the nurses or midwives division of the register and should have such clinical experience

---

[19] Misuse of Drugs Regulations 2017, SI 173/2017, Reg 15(2). Amended by the Misuse of Drugs (Amendment) Regulations 2020, SI 99/2020.
[20] Nurses Rules 2010, 3(11).

as is prescribed by the Board in the entry requirements set out in the standards and requirements.[21] Nurse prescribing programmes and associated learning outcomes are discussed later in this chapter under section 7.1.3.

7.1.2 The Department of Health and the Health Service Executive

The Department of Health and the HSE have published guidelines and information leaflets intended to provide additional guidance on nurse and midwife prescribing. A majority of the publications have been overseen by the Office of the Nursing and Midwifery Services Director. One example is the *Guiding Framework for the Implementation of Nurse and Midwife Prescribing in Ireland*,[22] which was published in November 2008 and provided detailed guidance on the initiation and continued development of the prescribing initiative. Additional documents include *Information and Guidance on the Introduction of Nurse and Midwife Medicinal Product Prescribing in General Practice*,[23] the *National Nurse and Midwife Medicinal Product Prescribing Guideline*,[24] *Guidance on Governance for the Registered Nurse and Midwife Prescriber Working in an Integrated Role*,[25] and *Nurse and Midwife Medicinal Product Prescribing Toolkit – Authorised Medicinal Products, Off-Label Prescription and Exempt Medicinal Products*.[26]

The HSE Office of the Nursing and Midwifery Services Director oversees the Nurse and Midwife Prescribing Data Collection System. This is a web-based system that was implemented to record and monitor prescribing activity across the country. The system can be accessed at www.nurseprescribing.ie. Access to

---

[21] Nurses and Midwives (Education and Training) Rules 2018, SI 218/2018.
[22] Office of the Nursing Services Director, *Guiding Framework for the Implementation of Nurse and Midwife Prescribing in Ireland* (HSE 2008).
[23] Office of the Nursing and Midwifery Services Director, *Information and Guidance on the Introduction of Nurse and Midwife Medicinal Product Prescribing in General Practice* (HSE 2011); Office of the Nursing Services Director, *Patient and Service User Information Leaflet* (HSE 2008); Office of the Nursing and Midwifery Services Director, *Medicinal Product Authorisation Information and Frequently Asked Questions for Registered Nurse Prescribers* (HSE 2011); Office of the Nursing and Midwifery Services Director, *Nurse and Midwife Medicinal Product Prescribing: Toolkit for Implementation* (HSE 2014).
[24] Office of the Nursing and Midwifery Services Director, *National Nurse and Midwife Medicinal Product Prescribing Guideline* (HSE 2020).
[25] Office of the Nursing and Midwifery Services Director, *Nurse and Midwife Medicinal Product Prescribing: Guidance on Governance for the Registered Nurse and Midwife Prescriber Working in an Integrated Role* (HSE 2020).
[26] Office of the Nursing and Midwifery Services Director, *Authorised Medicinal Products, Off-Label Prescription and Exempt Medicinal Products Information Sheet* (HSE 2020).

the dataset requires use of the NMBI PIN and a password that accompanies the username. The Nurse and Midwife Prescribing Data Collection System can only be accessed by directors of nursing/midwifery/public health, prescribing site coordinators and nurse/midwife prescribers.

The nurse or midwife prescriber is to enter the details of each prescription they write. All information is entered retrospectively and is not linked to individual patients. Patient or clinical information is not recorded in the system. The collection of this data allows for patterns of prescribing to be identified and it can also be used to support auditing requirements. The identification of patterns of prescribing allows for national and international comparisons to be made, can better inform hospital budgeting and human resource planning, and can be used to inform the development of nursing education programmes. Nonetheless, the input of data into the system can be time-consuming and this has been recognised as a weakness in ensuring that it operates effectively.[27]

7.1.3 Registration as a Nurse or Midwife Prescriber

The NMBI has three primary functions in this area. These are the professional regulation of prescribers, the setting of minimum standards of education, and a clinical governance role. Several of these elements have been touched on already and will be discussed in more detail later in this chapter. The professional regulation function is linked to the maintenance of the register for nurse and midwife prescribers. As for the minimum standards of education, these are outlined in *Prescriptive Authority for Nurses and Midwives: Standards and Requirements*.[28] This document was reviewed and re-issued in October 2015. It addresses minimum entry requirements, learning outcomes, competencies for prescriptive authority, and syllabus/indicative content.

The minimum entry requirements established by the NMBI are:

- The name of the nurse/midwife must already be entered on the General, Psychiatric, Children's, Intellectual Disability, Midwife or Public Health Nurse Divisions of the Register.

---

[27] Office of the Nursing and Midwifery Services Director, *Review of Nurse Midwife Prescribing Data Collection System* (HSE 2013).
[28] Nursing and Midwifery Board of Ireland, *Prescriptive Authority for Nurses and Midwives: Standards and Requirements* (NMBI 2015).

- A minimum of three years recent (within past five years) post registration clinical experience in nursing/midwifery with the equivalent of one year full time experience in the specific practice area.
- Nurse/midwife must be in possession of competencies recognised at Level 8 of the National Qualifications Authority of Ireland framework.
- Demonstrable evidence of further education.
- Nurse/midwife should possess a competent level of information technology literacy.[29]

Clinical governance to augment the medicines legislation previously took the form of a Collaborative Practice Agreement. However, the Board of the NMBI approved the removal of the Collaborative Practice Agreement in April 2018. The clinical governance for the prescribing of medicinal products is now determined by the local health service provider's medicinal product prescribing policy, procedures, protocols or guidelines.

In October 2015 there were 851 nurses and midwives registered with the NMBI as nurse/midwife prescribers. These represented 112 clinical specialties and 180 health service providers; 41 nurse/midwife prescribers were working for private health service providers.[30] The public can search the register of nurses and midwives through the NMBI website. This provides information on the nurse's pin, full name, and the divisions in which the nurse is registered. The availability of this information is beneficial as it can also be consulted by healthcare professionals such as pharmacists who may need to confirm nurse registration prior to dispensing drugs. Nurses and midwives included on the register must pay the annual retention fee to maintain registration with the NMBI. Failure to pay the annual retention fee can result in the removal of the nurse/midwife from the register.

Nurse Prescribing Programmes

The nurse prescribing programme is offered in many higher education institutions, including the Royal College of Surgeons, NUI Galway, the University of Limerick, Trinity College Dublin, and University College Cork. The Certificate in Nursing (Nurse/Midwife Prescribing) is a six-month course that combines theory

---
[29] ibid 4.
[30] Office of the Nursing and Midwifery Services Director, *Report on Nurse and Midwife Medicinal Product Prescribing Review Existing Systems and Processes* (HSE 2016) 12.

and clinical practice. The clinical component is specific to the clinical practice area of the nurse/midwife. Instruction and supervision are provided by a dedicated medical practitioner who acts as a mentor to the nurse/midwife.

In undertaking the certificate, candidates complete modules on systematic assessment and evaluation in patient care, pharmacology and prescribing science, and professional accountability in nurse/midwife prescribing. Although there will be some differences in the programme structure across higher education institutions, there are key learning outcomes identified by the NMBI. The NMBI also set out indicative content, which should be included in the designing of a detailed curriculum. As such, professional accountability and responsibility, legal and ethical aspects, pharmacology and pharmacotherapeutics, and principles of the prescribing process must be taken into account in designing an appropriate programme. Moreover, there are five domains of competence that must be reached by the nurse/midwife on completion of the education programme. These domains are professional/ethical practice, holistic approaches to care and the integration of knowledge, interpersonal relationships, organisation and management of care, personal and professional development. The objective of the competency framework is to ensure that candidates are equipped with sufficient skills for this expanded role. The NMBI therefore provides a comprehensive outline of the key components for a recognised nurse prescribing programme.

After successfully completing the programme, the nurse or midwife can apply for entry to the prescribers' register. The NMBI also maintains a candidate register. Candidates must be on the candidate register while completing the training programme.

7.1.4 Clinical Governance

The Collaborative Practice Agreement (CPA) provided a clinical governance structure that defined the scope of nurse prescribing and established a communication structure between the nurse/midwife prescriber and a collaborating medical practitioner(s).[31] This communication structure was intended to support the appropriate care of patients/service users. Information on the purpose and criteria for completing the CPA along with other

---

[31] Nursing and Midwifery Board of Ireland, *Collaborative Practice Agreement Guidance for Nurses and Midwives with Prescriptive Authority* (4th edn, NMBI 2016).

important elements relating to the CPA were set out in the *Collaborative Practice Agreement Guidance for Nurses and Midwives with Prescriptive Authority*.

In 2015, the NMBI and the Office of the Nursing and Midwifery Services Director undertook a review of the nurse and midwife medicinal product prescribing systems and processes. Included in the terms of reference was the CPA and its relationship to the registration and clinical governance processes for nurse and midwife prescribing. The CPA was associated with time delays; it was perceived as a barrier for nurses and midwives to expand their scope of practice; and the CPA's application was weakened by administrative burdens. As previously mentioned, in April 2018 the Board of the NMBI approved the removal of the CPA as a requirement for nurses and midwives registration and authority to prescribe. Instead, the clinical governance for the prescribing of medicinal products is now determined by the local health service provider's medicinal product prescribing policy, procedures, protocols or guidelines (PPPGs).

The Office of the Nursing and Midwifery Services' *National Nurse and Midwife Medicinal Product Prescribing Guideline* provides guidance on the development of a clinical governance framework for health service providers.[32] Local health service providers can adopt the *National Nurse and Midwife Medicinal Product Prescribing Guideline* for local governance requirements or can opt to develop their own PPPGs that incorporate regulatory and legal requirements applicable to nurse/midwife prescribing. Regardless of the option selected by the local health service provider, the Office of the Nursing and Midwifery Services sets out that PPPGs are to be 'comprehensive, appropriate, robust and up-to-date'.[33] Furthermore, it is recommended, 'Health service providers should continuously review PPPGs to ensure that they are in line with evidence based practice, legislation, regulation and that they continue to meet service user's needs and expectations.'[34]

The Office of the Nursing and Midwifery Services also identifies several points that should be incorporated in local PPPGs:

- The RN/MP refers to the Health Products Regulatory Authority (HPRA) website to access the Summary

---

[32] Office of the Nursing and Midwifery Services Director, *National Nurse and Midwife Medicinal Product Prescribing Guideline* (HSE 2020).
[33] ibid 8.
[34] ibid 8.

of Product Characteristics (SmPC) for all medicinal products they prescribe
- The RN/MP can refer and liaise with the National Medicines Information Centre (NMIC), which provides advice on the therapeutic use of medicinal products by way of publications (bulletins and newsletters) to all healthcare professionals and by their clinical enquiry answering service
- The RN/MP can refer to the British National Formulary for medicinal product information and the local health service provider's formulary where ones exist
- Liaise with members of the multidisciplinary team as appropriate regarding medicinal product prescribing
- Liaise with Director of Nursing/Midwifery/Service Manager/Designate, Practice Development/Prescribing Site Coordinator, regarding support for prescribing within the local health service provider
- Discuss and agree the process for audit of prescribing practice as per the Practice Standards and Guidelines for Prescriptive Authority (NMBI 2019).[35]

7.1.5 Practice Standards and Guidelines for Nurses and Midwives with Prescriptive Authority

A further element in the framework for nurse/midwife prescribing is the *Practice Standards and Guidelines for Nurses and Midwives with Prescriptive Authority*.[36] It is described as 'the overarching mechanism with which a nurse or midwife is expected to practice'.[37] These standards are intended to guide best practice and are to be drawn on in conjunction with the nurse/midwife's professional judgment. There are 11 practice standards listed in the document:

Practice Standard 1. Clinical decision-making process

Practice Standard 2. Communication and history talking

Practice Standard 3. Documentation

Practice Standard 4. Prescription writing

---

[35] ibid 8–9.
[36] Nursing and Midwifery Board of Ireland, *Practice Standards and Guidelines for Nurses and Midwives with Prescriptive Authority* (4th edn, NMBI 2019).
[37] ibid 8.

Practice Standard 5. Prescribing for self, family and significant others

Practice Standard 6. Repeat prescribing

Practice Standard 7. Prescribing of off-label and exempt medicinal products

Practice Standard 8. Prescribing by means of other than an original prescription

Practice Standard 9. Separation of responsibilities in the medication management cycle

Practice Standard 10. Influence of outside interests (relationships with pharmaceutical representation or similar organisations)

Practice Standard 11. Continuing professional development and competency

The document establishes the rationale for each practice standard, and addresses associated competencies and guidance for practice. Several of these standards are discussed in detail later in this chapter.

7.2 The Prescribing and Administration of Medicines

This section addresses the prescribing and administration of medicines. This will draw out the legal framework surrounding the practical aspects of nurse/midwife prescribing. The first sub-section outlines the clinical decision-making process, which includes appropriate patient consultation and communication. The second sub-section considers prescription practices and limitations. Among the practices and limitations are repeat prescribing, emergency prescribing, off-label prescribing, and the separation of responsibilities.

7.2.1 The Clinical Decision-Making Process

The NMBI published the *Decision-Making Framework for Nurse and Midwife Prescribing*,[38] which sets out the decision-making pathway that nurses and midwives are to follow when prescribing

---
[38] ibid 42.

medicines. The framework poses questions with yes/no responses that guide the nurse/midwife prescriber through the process. This framework forms a large part of Practice Standard 1, Clinical Decision-Making Process, under the NMBI's *Practice Standards and Guidelines for Nurses and Midwives with Prescriptive Authority*. Key elements of the framework are described in Practice Standard 1 as follows:

- Ensure that prescribing is within the registered nurse or midwife prescriber's scope of practice and competency.
- Prescribing is undertaken following an assessment of the person/service user.
- The registered nurse or midwife prescriber has gathered evidence to determine a treatment plan for the person/service user.
- The registered nurse or midwife prescriber has determined the required pharmacological/non-pharmacological treatment option(s) for the person/service user.
- The registered nurse or midwife prescriber initiates the treatment decision in discussion with and agreement with the person/service user (and/or carer, if applicable), providing a comprehensive description of the treatment prescribed, including expectations of treatment and side-effects, if any.
- The registered nurse or midwife prescriber ensures that record-keeping is accurate and up-to-date.
- The registered nurse or midwife prescriber documents the treatment plan including the prescribed medication monitoring, evaluation and follow-up care.
- The registered nurse or midwife prescriber refers the person/service user to the appropriate healthcare professional if required.[39]

Communication and history-taking have been described as 'fundamental principles of safe and effective prescribing practice'.[40] Practice Standard 2 identifies areas that should normally be considered as part of the consultation. These include assessing and clarifying the patient's clinical condition, conducting an appropriate physical examination, assessing the current and past medication history, awareness of precautions and potential drug interactions, social circumstances, and the patient's overall care plan, amongst other factors. Principles to be considered during

---
[39] ibid 11.
[40] ibid 12.

the prescribing consultation process include the presence of a valid clinical relationship with the patient, clear communication, active involvement of the patient, and monitoring of the patient's response to the medicinal product.

The prescribing consultation should be clearly documented by the nurse or midwife prescriber.[41] Accurate documentation allows for clear communication with other healthcare professionals and promotes the safety of the patient/service user. An error in completing the documentation should be bracketed and a single line should be drawn through it so the original entry is legible. Subsequent changes must be signed, dated, and provide an explanation for the change. Correction fluids should not be used on the documentation. If the nurse/midwife is not clear as to the drug to be prescribed, he/she should not administer it until he/she has consulted with the relevant prescriber. Administering the incorrect drug(s) to a patient is a serious error.

7.2.2 Prescription Practices and Limitations

The writing of a prescription is not only addressed by practice standards but is also framed by the Medicinal Products (Prescription and Control of Supply) Regulations 2003 and the Medicinal Products (Prescription and Control of Supply) (Amendment) Regulations 2007.

Requirements such as legibility, prescriber details, and necessary signatures were set out earlier in this chapter, as were many of the requirements for the prescribing of controlled drugs under the Misuse of Drugs Regulations 2017.

Practice Standard 4 specifically addresses prescription writing. Generic names or non-proprietary names for medicinal products should be used where possible. The strength/dosage of a medicinal product should be recorded in internationally and nationally accepted abbreviations only. The nurse/midwife prescriber should identify the maximum daily dose of the medicinal product. The standard also suggests, 'It is good practice to identify when the medication should be discontinued or if long-term medication is prescribed a review date must be indicated.'[42]

---

[41] ibid 16.
[42] ibid 21.

Prescribing for Self, Family and Significant Others

A nurse/midwife prescriber is prohibited from prescribing drugs for themselves, their family, and significant others. This prohibition protects from a conflict of interest arising that could place the nurse/midwife prescriber in a difficult ethical, legal and clinical position. Instead, an individual requiring a prescribed drug should be referred or directed to a healthcare professional who can provide appropriate care and can issue a prescription if necessary.[43]

Repeat Prescribing

Repeat prescribing occurs in situations where an original prescription was issued and the patient/service user subsequently requests and/or requires a continued course of medication.[44] The need for repeat prescribing will often occur as part of the treatment of chronic health conditions. The issuing of a repeat prescription requires an appropriate assessment to be conducted, careful documentation, and should involve discussion with the patient about the 'perceived effectiveness and adherence to the treatment plan'.[45] The nurse or midwife prescriber must be aware of their scope of practice as well as the limits of their professional competence. Accordingly, the nurse/midwife prescriber should refer the patient/service user to an appropriate healthcare professional for assessment and evaluation concerning the repeat prescription if required. In addition, it is recommended in Practice Standard 6 that there be 'regular review and appropriate clinical assessment of the patient/service user condition for continuing a specific medication in accordance with the overall treatment plan'.[46]

Note that schedule 2 and schedule 3 (schedule 8) controlled drugs cannot be repeated, but schedule 4 (part 1 and part 2) and schedule 5 controlled drugs may be repeated if specified by the prescriber.

Emergency Prescribing

Regulation 7(5)(b) of the Medicinal Products (Prescription and Control of Supply) Regulations 2003 (as amended) requires that a prescription be an original. There may be instances where the original prescription cannot be provided immediately. These

---

[43] ibid 22.
[44] ibid 23.
[45] ibid.
[46] ibid.

emergency situations, along with possible exemptions, are addressed by Regulation 8 of the 2003 Regulations, which state:

> 8(1) It shall not be a contravention of regulation 5(1) or regulation 7 for a person keeping open shop for the dispensing or compounding of medical prescriptions in accordance with the Pharmacy Acts, 1875 to 1977 to supply a medicinal product otherwise than in accordance with a prescription where –
>
>> (a) the authorised person by whom or under whose supervision the product is to be supplied has been requested to supply the product for a particular patient by a registered medical practitioner, registered dentist or registered nurse who by reason of an emergency is unable to furnish a prescription immediately,
>>
>> (b) the practitioner or nurse concerned has undertaken to furnish a prescription within 72 hours,
>>
>> (c) the product is supplied in accordance with the directions of the practitioner or nurse requesting it, and
>>
>> (d) subject to paragraph (3), the product is not a controlled drug specified in Schedule 1, 2, 3 or 4 to the Misuse of Drugs Regulations 1988 or any amendment thereof.[47]

Accordingly, a nurse or midwife prescriber can prescribe by other means in emergency situations. The use of communications technology such as fax or email is favoured as it provides an accurate form of documentation. This could then be attached to the patient/service user's medical records. Regardless of the medium used to communicate the prescription, a note should be made in the patient/service's records and a written prescription should be sent to the pharmacist within a period of 72 hours.

Off-Label Use and Exempt Medicinal Products

Off-label prescribing is the prescribing of a drug outside the terms of its licensed indications. The relevant legislation and regulations for nurse/midwife prescribing does not prohibit this form of prescribing. The prescription for an off-label indication

---

[47] Medicinal Products (Prescription and Control of Supply) Regulations 2003, SI 540/2003, Reg 8(1).

is to be in accordance with Regulation 5A of the Medicinal Products (Prescription and Control of Supply) Regulations 2003 as amended.

An exempt medicinal product is a medication that has not been approved for licensing or authorisation by a body such as the Health Products Regulatory Authority or by the European Medicines Agency. However, the Medicinal Products (Control of Placing on the Market) Regulations 2007, as amended, provides statutory authority for a registered medical practitioner or registered dentist to treat a patient under his/her care using exempt medicinal products. This authority did not extend to the registered nurse or midwife prescriber until the enactment of the Medicinal Products (Control of Placing on the Market) (Amendment) Regulations 2018.[48]

The limitation on nurse prescribing in this area was a significant lacuna and had not gone unnoticed. It had been highlighted in the *Report on Nurse and Midwife Medicinal Product Prescribing Review of Existing Systems and Processes*[49] and by the *National Independent Evaluation of the Nurse and Midwife Prescribing Initiative*.[50] Both reports recommended change in this area. The report on prescribing recommended: 'For the purposes of quality and patient safety the prescribing of exempt (unauthorised) medicines should be consistent for all prescribers, regardless of profession. The same set of principles should apply to all.'[51] The National Independent Evaluation recommended: 'Nurses and midwives should be enabled to prescribe unlicensed medications once they come within their scope of practice and nurse/midwife prescribers are cognisant of best practice in the prescribing of unlicensed medications.'[52]

Practice Standard 7 sets out guidance on the prescribing of off-label and exempt medicinal products. On this, it is recommended that the nurse/midwife prescriber be 'knowledgeable about the

---

[48] Medicinal Products (Control of Placing on the Market) (Amendment) Regulations 2018, SI 529/2018.
[49] Office of the Nursing and Midwifery Services Director, *Report on Nurse and Midwife Medicinal Product Prescribing Review of Existing Systems and Processes* (HSE 2016) 29: 'This anomaly prevents the provision of optimum patient care to patients/clients by RNPs.'
[50] Drennan (n 3) 101.
[51] Office of the Nursing and Midwifery Services Director, *Report on Nurse and Midwife Medicinal Product Prescribing Review of Existing Systems and Processes* (HSE 2016) 29.
[52] Drennan (n 3) 101.

best practice' for the prescribing of such products.[53] This requires the prescriber to ascertain the following:

- if there is an alternative, authorised medicinal product that could be prescribed;
- if the medicinal product is regularly used to treat person/service user in the registered nurse or midwife prescriber's area of clinical practice;
- if the specific medicinal product is listed within the health service provider's prescribing formulary (where such formulary exist).[54]

The prescribing of medicinal products for off-label use and exempt medicinal products must come within the nurse/midwife prescriber's scope of practice. Consequently, these forms of prescribing should be outlined in the local health service provider's PPPGs for nurse or midwife medicinal product prescribing. For further information, the nurse or midwife should consult the *Nurse and Midwife Medicinal Product Prescribing: Authorised Medicinal Products, Off-label Prescription and Exempt Medicinal Products Information Sheet.*[55]

Separation of Responsibilities

There are a range of responsibilities associated with the role of nurse/midwife prescriber and it is important that these responsibilities be clearly demarcated. Responsibilities include the prescribing and administering of drugs. The separation of responsibilities is addressed by Practice Standard 9 of the *Practice Standards and Guidelines for Nurses and Midwives with Prescriptive Authority*. In this standard it is recommended that there be a separation between the prescribing of a medicinal product and the act of administering the product. The administration element should be undertaken by another individual to ensure appropriate safety checks are completed in the medication management cycle. In a similar manner, the Practice Standard recommends that the actions of prescribing and supplying the medicinal product be separated. Situations may arise in which the nurse/midwife prescriber may be required to supply a medicinal product and, in

---

[53] Nursing and Midwifery Board of Ireland, *Practice Standards and Guidelines for Nurses and Midwives with Prescriptive Authority* (4th edn, NMBI 2019) 25.
[54] ibid.
[55] Office of the Nursing and Midwifery Services Director, *Authorised Medicinal Products, Off-Label Prescription and Exempt Medicinal Products Information Sheet* (HSE 2020).

these circumstances, the prescriber must take account of his/her responsibilities in the overall context of medication management.[56]

In practice, the distinction between these responsibilities is not always easily maintained and a 'crossover and merging of these activities' may occur.[57] The crossover should be addressed in the local health service provider's PPPGs. Moreover, the PPPGs are to outline the auditing of such practices. In sum, the separation of responsibilities reflects best practice and can contribute to the delivery of safer patient/service user care.

Medication Protocols

Medication protocols are often referred to as patient group directives or group protocols. It is not a form of traditional prescribing but instead is a written direction that allows healthcare professionals to supply and administer medicines to a group of patients that satisfy the criteria set out by the medication protocol. An individual named prescription is not necessary for the supply and administration of a medication in circumstances where a medication protocol is in effect. Benefits associated with such a system include efficiency in the delivery of healthcare and making the most effective use of a healthcare professional's skills and expertise. Medication protocols are especially useful in a clinical setting where a group of patients require the administration of certain medicines, for instance, childhood and travel vaccinations.

The legislative basis for medication protocols is the Medicinal Products (Prescription and Control of Supply) Regulations 1996, and the subsequent 2003 Regulations.[58] This provides authority for the use of medication protocols in the care and treatment of a patient/service user. However, the medication protocol should be limited to situations where it offers a clear benefit to the patient/service user and is in accordance with the patient–healthcare professional relationship.

The An Bord Altranais *Guidance to Nurses and Midwives on Medication Management* addresses the development and use of medication protocols. In this document, it is set out that medication protocols should be 'developed based on evidence of

---

[56] Nursing and Midwifery Board of Ireland, *Practice Standards and Guidelines for Nurses and Midwives with Prescriptive Authority* (4th edn, NMBI 2019) 27.
[57] ibid.
[58] Medicinal Products (Prescription and Control of Supply) Regulations 2003, SI 540/2003.

best practice and supported locally by a multidisciplinary team'.[59] Furthermore, it is set out that the protocol should identify 'who is responsible and competent to implement the protocol; specific exclusion, and inclusion criteria should be stated and should include a review date for evaluation of the protocol'.[60] Ultimately, it is the health service provider that has the duty to develop the medication protocol. The protocol should be supported by local policy that supports education, training, the dissemination of relevant information, and establishes appropriate review and audit processes to assess the use of medication protocols. It is essential that these key elements be in place to facilitate and support nurses and midwives in the safe and effective use of a medication protocol.

7.2.3 Self-Administration of Medicines

The self-administration of medicines is the independent use of medicines by a patient/service-user. In residential care, a resident may self-administer their medicines in accordance with their personal preferences and once an individual risk assessment has been completed. Details on the factors to be considered as part of the risk assessment were set out by the Health Information and Quality Authority (HIQA) in *Medicines Management Guidance*.[61] Factors include the resident's dexterity and ability to open containers, the ability to understand the process, the resident's knowledge of their medicines and treatment plan, and the responsibilities of residential care staff. The resident's care plan must be updated to record the level of support and responsibility of the staff. In addition, details on the monitoring, supervision, and review of self-administration should be clearly documented. These are continuous activities and form part of the person's care.[62]

7.2.4 Covert Administration of Medicines

Covert administration is an ethically challenging practice. It closely resembles medical paternalism and must not occur where an individual has sufficient capacity to consent to or refuse medical treatment. The term 'covert' is used where medicines are administered in a disguised form absent the consent or knowledge

---

[59] An Bord Altranais, *Guidance to Nurses and Midwives on Medication Management* (ABA 2007) 35.
[60] ibid.
[61] Health Information and Quality Authority, *Medicines Management Guidance* (HIQA 2015) 23.
[62] ibid 23–24.

of the person receiving them. The medicines may be disguised in food or drink. This practice also raises clinical concerns – the nurse or midwife must confirm that the administration of medicines in a covert manner does not alter the chemical nature of the medicines.[63]

HIQA recommend that a full written assessment of a resident should be conducted prior to the covert administration of medication. A decision to use covert administration requires multidisciplinary agreement that it is in the resident's best interests. The decision to use covert administration should be carefully documented and reviewed as appropriate. Nurses and midwives should be vigilant in the use of covert administration and steps should be taken to reduce and eliminate side effects.

7.3 Responding to Errors and Incidents in Medication Management

Medication errors are not a rare occurrence in healthcare facilities. The occurrence of such errors impacts on the availability of healthcare resources and can lead to waste and inefficiency.[64] This underlines the need to effectively respond to errors and incidents that arise in practice.

Errors can occur at all stages of the medication management cycle. This is reflected in the process categories listed in the National Incident Management System (NIMS). These categories include: prescribing; administration; preparation/dispensing; documentation/records; monitoring; supply/ordering/transport; communication/consent; equipment; storage; and presentation/packaging. NIMS is used by acute public hospitals covered by the Clinical Indemnity Scheme (CIS) to report incidents, including those relating to medication. In 2016, a total of 5,505 medication incidents were reported across 50 acute hospitals.[65] Yet, a report by the State Claims Agency suggested that this figure 'represents a significant under-reporting of medication incidents on the national system'.[66]

An Bord Altranais define medication errors as 'preventable events that may cause or lead to inappropriate medication use or

---

[63] ibid 22.
[64] State Claims Agency, *Review of Medication Incidents Reported in Irish Hospitals* (SCA 2016).
[65] ibid 1.
[66] ibid.

patient/service-user harm while the medication is in the control of the health care professional or patient/service-user'.[67] These errors therefore include near misses and incidents that do not necessarily result in harm. Examples of medication errors include the omission of medication, errors relating to a wrong medication or the wrong dose or strength for a medication. HIQA recommend that any medication incident be 'identified, recorded and the cause investigated'.[68] This can support improved competencies and prevent a similar error occurring in the future. However, the first step when a medication error is identified is to monitor the health of the patient. Medical and nursing interventions should be implemented as needed for the safety of the patient/service-user.[69]

Open disclosure is discussed in chapter 4 and is relevant in responding to medication errors. HIQA recommend that when a medication error or incident has been identified, it is necessary to inform the individual affected or their representative where appropriate. This is in line with Principle 3 on the quality of practice as set out by the NMBI *Code of Professional Conduct and Ethics*. The supporting guidance for this sets out, 'Safe, quality practice is promoted by nurses and midwives actively participating in incident reporting, adverse event reviews and open disclosure.'[70] Local policy should be in place to ensure a clear framework for nurses and midwives in responding to adverse events.

7.3.1 Professional Accountability

Nurse and midwife prescribers are accountable for their actions in the prescribing of medicines. A failure to meet required standards could result in a complaint to the NMBI resulting in fitness to practise proceedings.[71] It could also result in a clinical negligence claim. As was outlined in chapter 4, the State Claims Agency manages the CIS, under which the State assumes responsibility for the indemnification and management of all clinical negligence claims. It does not, however, provide representation for nurse or

---

[67] An Bord Altranais, *Guidance to Nurses and Midwives on Medication Management* (ABA 2007) 27.
[68] Health Information and Quality Authority, *Medicines Management Guidance* (HIQA 2015) 34.
[69] Office of the Nursing and Midwifery Services Director, *National Nurse and Midwife Medicinal Product Prescribing Guideline* (HSE 2020) 25.
[70] Nursing and Midwifery Board of Ireland, *Code of Professional Conduct and Ethics for Registered Nurses and Registered Midwives* (NMBI 2014) 22.
[71] See chapter 4 for discussion of the fitness to practise process.

midwife prescribers in relation to fitness to practise issues, nor does it provide cover for criminal matters.

The CIS provides vicarious indemnity cover to all healthcare professionals providing professional services for and on behalf of the health service provider. It therefore provides coverage for nurse and midwife medicinal product prescribing. In a statement issued in January 2018, the State Claims Agency clarified that 'general practitioners, private nursing homes or other private practice settings and/or their indemnity/insurance providers are not required to extend indemnity cover to registered nurse prescribers authorised to practise in their services'.[72] The CIS indemnifies the nurse/midwife prescriber practising in these settings.

---

[72] State Claims Agency, *Nurse and Midwife Medicinal Product Prescribing* (January 2018).

CHAPTER 8
Legal Aspects of Pregnancy

Introduction 209
The Regulation of Midwifery 210
    The Birth Environment 212
    A Right to Home Birth Services? 212
    The Memorandum of Understanding/
    Agreement for Home Birth Services 215
    Accessing Home-Birth Services 218
    Use of a Birthing Pool 219
    The Legal Status of a Birth Plan 220
Abortion Law in Ireland 221
    The Development of the Law on Abortion 222
    Health (Regulation of Termination of
    Pregnancy) Act 2018 230
    Abortion and the Young Person 234
Treatment Refusal During Pregnancy 236

8.0 Introduction

This chapter focuses on the issues of abortion, the birth environment, and autonomy during pregnancy.[1] These are historically divisive areas and present legal and ethical challenges for the nurse and midwife in obstetrics and gynaecology. This chapter will deal with some of the more pressing matters in these areas and should be read in conjunction with other chapters in this work to ensure familiarity with the duty of care, record-keeping, and general principles of autonomy, which will inform the broader aspects of nursing practice.

The *National Maternity Strategy – Creating a Better Future Together 2016–2026* provides: 'Women should be offered choice regarding their preferred pathway of care in line with safety, their clinical needs and best practice.'[2] The question of birth environment is considered in section 8.1 and includes discussion of home-birth

---

[1] For discussion of surrogacy see Lydia Bracken, *Same-Sex Parenting and the Best Interests Principle* (Cambridge University Press 2020).
[2] Department of Health, *National Maternity Strategy – Creating a Better Future Together 2016–2026* (Dept of Health 2016).

services, use of a birthing pool, and the legal status of a birth plan.

Over the past 40 years in Ireland, there has been public debate about the regulation of abortion. This has included the role of the Constitution, foetal rights, maternal rights, and debates about the ethics and morality of abortion. This chapter will concentrate solely on the legal framework. The healthcare system in Ireland now provides for abortion and healthcare professionals have a duty to provide appropriate care and support for women who have had a termination of pregnancy. The Health (Regulation of Termination of Pregnancy) Act 2018 does, however, provide for conscientious objection. This chapter will outline the 2018 Act and will consider issues relating to abortion and the young person.

8.1 The Regulation of Midwifery

Part 6 of the Nurses and Midwives Act 2011 addresses registration and practice. Section 39 of the 2011 Act provides that a person who does not hold a current registration in a division of the register of nurses and midwives shall not (a) practise the profession to which the division relates, or (b) advertise that he or she practices that profession.[3] Divisions include 'Midwives' and 'Advanced Midwife Practitioners'.

Section 40(1) of the Nurses and Midwives Act 2011 states:

> No person shall, for reward, attend a woman in childbirth unless the person is –
>
>> (a) a registered midwife who maintains adequate clinical indemnity insurance in accordance with the rules,
>>
>> (b) a registered medical practitioner,
>>
>> (c) a person undergoing training to be a registered medical practitioner or a registered midwife who gives such attention as part of a course of professional training, or

---

[3] Nurses and Midwives Act 2011, s 39.

> (d) a person undergoing experience and training in obstetrics who gives such attention as part of a course of professional training.[4]

An exception is recognised in a case of sudden or urgent necessity where neither a registered midwife nor a registered medical practitioner is immediately available.[5] There would also be no contravention of s 39 if the person's practice is only in the course of rendering first aid to a person[6]; or if the person is a foreign qualified midwife who is in the State for a humanitarian purpose and for a period not longer than 30 days and who is practising midwifery in accordance with the terms and conditions of a permit issued by the Board.[7]

For persons that contravene s 40 they are liable on summary conviction to a class A fine or imprisonment for a term not exceeding six months or both. Those convicted on indictment for a first offence are liable to a fine not exceeding €65,000 and/or to imprisonment for a term not exceeding five years, and in the case of a subsequent conviction to a fine not exceeding €160,000 and/or to imprisonment for a term not exceeding 10 years.[8]

Offences and penalties are also established by s 44 of the Nurses and Midwives Act 2011. This section focuses on misrepresentation, false declarations, and intent to deceive. For instance, under s 44(1) a person is guilty of an offence if the person (a) contravenes section 39 or 43 (use of designated titles); (b) falsely represents to be a registered nurse or registered midwife; or (c) being a registered nurse or registered midwife, falsely represents to be registered in a division of nurses and midwives other than the division in which the person is registered.[9]

Further to the potential criminal sanctions, s 45(1) of the 2011 Act provides that an unregistered midwife shall not be entitled to charge or recover fees or outlays for professional services provided in the course of practising midwifery. Subsection 1 does not apply where the midwife was registered at the time of providing professional services or such services were provided in any of the circumstances specified in s 41.

---

[4] ibid s 40(1).
[5] ibid s 40(2).
[6] ibid s 41(1).
[7] ibid s 40(2).
[8] ibid s 40(3).
[9] ibid s 44(1).

For a discussion of the NMBI *Practice Standards for Midwives* see chapter 3 at 3.3.2.

8.1.1 The Birth Environment

In 2017 there were 61,824 live births comprising of 31,779 males and 30,045 females in Ireland.[10] Of these, 61,538 births took place in hospital. There were 286 domiciliary births in 2017, 37 less than the 323 recorded in 2016. Domiciliary births include home births and other births that take place in a location other than a hospital. Data from the CSO indicates that such births have dropped from one in three births in the early 1950s to 4.6 per thousand live births in 2017.[11] Despite the drop in numbers over time, there is a demand for home birth, and it has been included in the Department of Health *National Maternity Strategy*. The strategy has recommended that 'homebirth services will be integrated with the community midwifery and the wider maternity service as part of the maternity network. Care will be provided in line with agreed national standards, with clear pathways identified for any change in the woman's risk profile.'[12] A key element in this strategy was the need to facilitate and promote choice, including choice of birth setting where it is safe to do so. Naturally, this can result in a degree of conflict between the various parties involved. These challenges are reflected in the legal framework governing home births in Ireland.

8.1.2 A Right to Home Birth Services?

There are a range of human rights that arise in maternity care. The Global Respectful Maternity Care Council highlighted these rights in the 'Respectful Maternity Care Charter: Universal Rights of Mothers and Newborns'.[13] Nonetheless, there is no statutory right to a home birth in Ireland. The HSE is obliged to provide free maternity services to woman, and this may include a home-birth service. Section 62 of the Health Act 1970 states:

---

[10] Central Statistics Office, 'Vital Statistics Annual Report 2017' <https://www.cso.ie/en/releasesandpublications/ep/p-vsar/vitalstatisticsannualreport2017/births2017/> accessed 23 June 2020.
[11] ibid.
[12] Department of Health, *National Maternity Strategy – Creating a Better Future Together 2016–2026* (Dept of Health 2016) 94.
[13] The White Ribbon Alliance, 'Respectful Maternity Care' <https://www.whiteribbonalliance.org/respectful-maternity-care-charter/> accessed 23 June 2020.

(1) A health board shall make available medical, surgical and midwifery services for attendance to the health of women in respect of motherhood.

> (1A) The services referred to in subsection (1) shall be provided otherwise than as in-patient services.
>
> (1B) A health board shall not charge for the services provided under subsection (1).

(2) A woman entitled to receive medical services under this section may choose to receive them from any registered medical practitioner who has entered into an agreement with the health board for the provision of those services and who is willing to accept her as a patient.

(3) When a woman avails herself of services under this section for a confinement taking place otherwise than in a hospital or maternity home, the health board shall provide without charge obstetrical requisites to such extent as may be specified by regulations made by the Minister.[14]

The provision of domiciliary midwife services has been the subject of legal challenge on a number of occasions. The four applicants in *Tarrade v Northern Area Health Board* sought an order of mandamus to compel the respondent to provide domiciliary midwife services.[15] It was argued that where no such service was made available the Health Board should compensate the applicants for the expense in hiring an independent midwife. The applicants based their claim largely upon s 62 of the Health Act 1970.

The first three applicants had contacted midwife Philomena Canning, who determined that each of the applicants was a suitable candidate for home birth, and the midwife was willing to take each of them on as a client. The fourth applicant, Mrs Redmond, had engaged the services of midwife Ann O'Ceallaigh, who considered Mrs Redmond to be a suitable candidate for home birth. The children were, in fact, born before the hearings took place, thereby giving rise to the issue of mootness. The only issue that was alive before the Court was the issue of damages. The Court noted that this raises two issues: whether a right to damages could exist in the absence of a positive determination of

---

[14] Health Act 1970, s 62.
[15] *Tarrade v Northern Area Health Board* [2002] IEHC 32.

a substantive claim and whether damages could be awarded for an alleged breach of public law.[16]

Under s 62 of the Health Act 1970, the health board was obliged to provide services by a medical practitioner. On this point, the Court set out:

> Midwives are not medical practitioners even though they may be more experienced in midwifery particularly where medical practitioners no longer hold themselves out as obstetricians. This is clearly a policy matter for the Health Boards and for the medical profession. It is not for the Court to second guess.[17]

The applicants in *Tarrade* could not therefore rely on s 62 of the 1970 Act. Murphy J dismissed all four applications.

In *O'Brien v South Western Area Health Board*, the applicants contended that s 62 of the Health Act 1970 created legally enforceable rights in their favour and sought orders to compel the health boards to provide home-birth services. A domiciliary home-birth service was available subject to certain criteria, including the possibility of transferring the woman to a consultant staffed maternity hospital within a specific period of time. None of the applicants satisfied this criterion. The application was rejected by Ó Caoimh J in the High Court, resulting in an appeal to the Supreme Court.

The Supreme Court dismissed the appeal. Geoghegan J stated that it was possible that midwifery services that were to be provided by a health board might include home midwifery services. Nevertheless, there was nothing in s 62 of the 1970 Act which would compel a health board to provide home midwifery services. The obligations of a health board would be complied with provided such services were provided within the confines of a hospital.[18]

The case of *O'Brien v South Western Area Health Board* was subsequently referred to in *Teehan v Health Service Executive & Minister for Health*.[19] The applicant was a woman who was pregnant for the second time and had applied to the HSE to

---

[16] ibid 32 [33].
[17] ibid 32 [36].
[18] *O'Brien v South Western Area Health Board* [2003] IESC 56 [14].
[19] *Teehan v Health Service Executive & Minister for Health* [2013] IEHC 383.

facilitate a vaginal birth at home following her experience of delivering her first child by caesarean section in a hospital setting. The Memorandum of Understanding (MoU) between the HSE and the self-employed midwife outlined how midwives were not clinically indemnified by the HSE for such a procedure. This was based on the belief that a vaginal birth after a caesarean section was not safe in a home setting. The applicant brought judicial review proceedings claiming that the medical risks were minimal and that the HSE's policy did not leave room for discretion where suitability was established. The reliefs sought were an order of certiorari quashing the HSE's decision; a declaration to the effect that the HSE's policy on this issue was unlawful because it did not leave an option of discretion in appropriate circumstances; a declaration that the policy violated the applicant's rights under Article 8 of the European Convention on Human Rights and Fundamental Freedoms (ECHR); and an order of mandamus directing the HSE to consider the applicant's request in accordance with law.

The reliefs sought were refused in the High Court, which cited *O'Brien v South Western Area Health Board* as the starting point for the decision.[20] Further, the HSE is entitled to adopt policy guidelines as it sees fit provided they are not 'wholly unreasonable'. The applicant in this instance was not able to sufficiently demonstrate that the HSE's policy on vaginal birth after a caesarean section was wholly unreasonable for a variety of reasons. For O'Malley J the heart of the problem was the issue of insurance as the applicant was effectively asking the HSE to assume the burden of liability for a risk they thought best avoided. Insurance has had a central role in shaping the practice of self-employed midwives as illustrated by the development of the MoU.

8.1.3 The Memorandum of Understanding/ Agreement for Home Birth Services

The system of governance for home-birth services provided by a self-employed community midwife (SECM) is framed by the MoU and the Agreement, prepared by the HSE, and agreed by the HSE and the SECM.[21]

In July 2002 the State-backed Clinical Indemnity Scheme (CIS) was introduced. The CIS was established as commercial insurers

---

[20] *O'Brien v South Western Area Health Board* [2003] IESC 56.
[21] Marie O'Shea, 'The Legal Aspects of the HSE National Home Birth Service: A Review of Legislation and Case Law' (HSE 2016).

either withdrew from offering insurance cover to obstetricians/gynaecologists and to obstetric units or were not in a position to provide cover at affordable rates. The CIS applied to all public hospital employees but did not extend to self-employed midwives. These were, however, covered by professional indemnity insurance offered through the Irish Nurses Organisation. This coverage continued until 2008. Coverage by the CIS was extended to self-employed midwives at that point, provided they agreed to the terms of a MoU, which provided a framework for their relationship with the HSE.

The purpose of the MoU is 'to provide a framework for the HSE and self-employed community midwives to facilitate choice for women in relation to home birth whilst addressing the overarching concern for safety of both mother and child'.[22] The MoU outlines the responsibilities of the HSE/SECM, and the governance arrangements for home-birth services. Schedule 1 of the MoU defines the qualifications, experience and continuing education and training/professional development of the SECM. Schedule 2 addresses the clinical circumstances regarding a woman's eligibility for home-birth services and the indications requiring intrapartum and postpartum transfer.

Under Schedule 2, tables 1 and 2 outline the medical and other factors requiring planned birth at an obstetric unit. Other factors are grouped into four categories: previous pregnancy complications, current pregnancy, fetal indications, and previous gynaecological history. Non-clinical factors to be considered include the level of family/peer support available, the adequacy of home facilities, and the distance from the midwife or nearest hospital maternity unit. Tables 3 and 4 outline medical and other conditions requiring referral to consultant obstetrician by the midwife for final assessment when planning place of birth. Table 5 lays out indications requiring intrapartum transfer. Table 6 sets out indications requiring postpartum transfer.

A contractual agreement between the HSE and the SECM was introduced in 2014. The purpose of the agreement is to provide for a contractual framework between the HSE and the SECM, which meets the service needs of the expectant woman; is in line with the HSE's policy, standards and criteria in relation to best clinical practice for low-risk expectant woman; and accounts for the payment to the SECM. The agreement lists the responsibilities of the HSE along with those of the SECM. It also provides for a

---

[22] See Memorandum of Understanding.

governance framework to underpin the commitment of the HSE to the successful implementation of the agreement.

Under the terms of the agreement, the SECM is to provide the HSE with evidence of their current registration; a signed statement confirming compliance with the NMBI's *Code of Professional Conduct and Ethics*; evidence of continuing professional development; their agreement to comply with the requirements under Schedule 3 for the assessment of eligibility and indications for intrapartum and postpartum care; to notify the HSE's designated Midwifery Officer in whose functional area the SECM is practising or intends/proposes to practice[23]; and to enter into a contract with the HSE in respect of the provision of a home-birth service. The signing of the agreement indicates an acceptance on the part of the SECM that they will form part of an organisation that provides the home-birth service.[24] As part of this, there is an acceptance of supervision and control by the HSE.

In addition to the MoU and the Agreement, the HSE established a Clinical Governance Group for the Home Birth Service, the purpose of which was to design, develop and deliver a home-birth clinical governance system and structures that would meet best international standards for home-birth services in Ireland. A set of policies, procedures and guidelines were developed to support SECMs to comply with their professional code of practice while delivering safe, quality services to women who choose a home birth. These policy and guidance documents include:

- HB001 *Policy for Governing Safety and Quality for the HSE Home Birth Service 2018*
- HB002 *Policy for Approval of SECM for HSE Home Birth Service 2018*
- HB003 *Policy to Support the SECM to Assess the Eligibility and Suitability for the HSE Home Birth Service*
- HB004 *Midwifery Practice Guidelines HSE Home Birth Service 2018*
- HB005 *VIT K Administration Policy HSE Home Birth Service 2018*
- HB006 *Policy and Procedure for Newborn Bloodspot Screening for the HSE Home Birth Service 2018*
- HB007 *Notification Newborn Hearing Screening HSE Home Birth Service 2018*

---

[23] Self Employed Community Midwife Agreement (March 2014) 2.
[24] See O'Shea (n 21).

- HB008 Transfer Policy HSE Home Birth Service 2018
- HB009 Perineal Repair Guidelines HSE Home Birth Service 2018
- HB010 PPH Guideline HSE Home Birth Service 2018
- HB011 Shoulder Dystocia Guideline HSE Home Birth Service 2018
- HB012 Mal Presentation Guideline HSE Home Birth Service 2018
- HB013 Water Birth Guideline HSE Home Birth Services 2018
- HB014 Record Keeping HSE Home Birth Service 2018
- HB015 CPD Guideline for SECM Providing HSE Home Birth Service 2018
- HB016 Guideline for Feedback Survey HSE Home Birth Service 2018
- HB017 Guideline to References HSE Home Birth Service 2018
- HB018 List of Stakeholders HSE Home Birth Service 2018

8.1.4 Accessing Home-Birth Services

The National Maternity Hospital and University Hospital Waterford offer a limited home-birth service to woman considered to be in a low-risk category. As noted in the previous section, the HSE also facilitate a home-birth service through SECMs. The SECM is to have regard to the risk factors identified in tables one to five of the MoU, and consider whether the expectant mother is a suitable candidate for a home birth. If satisfied, the parties can then proceed with the application/consent for home birth. In the application/consent form, the applicant is to acknowledge that the service provided by the SECM is under the terms of the HSE's Home Birth Service. The SECM has responsibility for ensuring that the applicant provides informed consent. On the matter of consent, Schedule 8 provides:

> The consent should not be given by the expectant woman or accepted by the Self-employed Community Midwife unless the expectant woman has received, read and understands the contents of the following HSE documents:
>
> - Information for Expectant Mothers Choosing a Home Birth
> - Risk Factors that Identify Women Who May Be at Risk for a Home Delivery
> - The Application Form
> - The Consent Form

- Your Service Your Say – HSE Comments and Complaints Policy[25]

The application/consent form includes details on the transfer of medical records, the duration of the home-birth service, and the potential risks faced. By signing the form, the applicant agrees that if a complication is to arise then the management of her care will be transferred to a hospital-based team. The applicant must also agree to an emergency transfer to the nearest or most appropriate hospital if the midwife deems it necessary.[26] Once the form is completed it is to be returned to the Designated Midwifery Officer, who will assess eligibility for the service. If the application is accepted, the home-birth service extends from the date of approval by the HSE until the child is aged 14 days old.

On acceptance of the application, the Designated Midwifery Officer acts to inform the Director of Public Health Nursing, the local Public Health Nurse, the relevant GP, the local health office, and the expectant mother, who is to be provided with a Birth Pack. The eligibility for a home-birth service is to be regularly assessed up until the child is delivered. It is not a once-off assessment, as demonstrated by tables 1–5 in the MoU.

Once the child has been delivered and the home-birth service has ended, the SECM is to send their notes to the designated official along with a request for payment. The notes are reviewed, copied, and transferred to a database for statistics before being returned to the SECM.

8.1.5 Use of a Birthing Pool

A birthing pool can be used for pain relief during labour. It can relax muscles and can reduce the stress experienced during labour. A birthing pool can also pose risks that may not arise with a traditional land-based birth. For instance, a birthing pool can give rise to concerns around infection control, neonatal respiratory distress, cord rupture with neonatal haemorrhage, and neonatal hyponatraemia.[27]

In 2006, a child died after a birthing pool delivery in Cavan General Hospital. Dr Brian Farrell, a Dublin city coroner, accepted

---

[25] Self Employed Community Midwife Agreement (March 2014) 24.
[26] Self-Employed Community Midwife Agreement (March 2014) 8.
[27] Michael Pinette, Joseph Wax, and Elizabeth Wilson, 'The Risks of Underwater Birth' (2004) 190(5) American Journal of Obstetrics and Gynecology 1211.

the view of the pathologist that the child died of a near-drowning event due to aspiration of fresh water with resulting low sodium levels (hyponatraemia) and insufficient levels of oxygen in blood or tissue (hypoxia).[28] The coroner acknowledged that a prenatal hypoxic event could have occurred but that on the balance of probabilities, death was due to an acute near-drowning event. The inquest was informed that the pregnant woman had signed a consent form to give birth in the midwifery-led unit of the hospital but a specific consent form was not signed for a water birth. Instead, verbal consent was relied on for the use of the birthing pool. It is not surprising that the issue of consent was among the recommendations made following a review carried out in the aftermath of this incident. The additional risks posed by a birthing pool underline the importance and need to fully inform the expectant mother of all material risks so an informed decision can be made. Information should be communicated in sufficient time, there should be an opportunity for questions to be raised and answered, and consent should be clearly recorded. The law on patient autonomy and decision-making is outlined in chapter 5 of this text.

8.1.6 The Legal Status of a Birth Plan

A birth plan is a document that identifies a woman's values and preferences for birth. In this way it can provide guidance for midwives, doctors and other healthcare professionals about the type of labour and birth experience that the woman would like to have. The birth plan may include details on the birth environment, birthing position, pain relief, skin-to-skin contact, and caesarean section, among other issues. By considering these issues during the pregnancy, the birth plan can serve as a tool to facilitate and support communication with healthcare professionals. This open channel of communication can help the woman to understand any details, risks or concerns in advance of labour.[29] Appropriate communication at this early stage may result in a more flexible birth plan and could head off potential difficulties that might arise during labour. The case of *Fitzpatrick v National Maternity Hospital*[30] underlines the importance of reviewing the care plan and discussing any controversial elements with the woman in

---

[28] Georgina O'Halloran, 'Birthing Pool Baby Died from Breathing In Water' *The Irish Times* (Dublin, 8 June 2008).
[29] The Royal Australian and New Zealand College of Obstetricians and Gynaecologists, 'Labour and Birth' <https://ranzcog.edu.au/womens-health/patient-information-resources/labour-and-birth> accessed 10 September 2020.
[30] *Fitzpatrick v National Maternity Hospital* [2008] IEHC 62.

sufficient time. The Royal Australian and New Zealand College of Obstetricians and Gynaecologists note that a birth plan will be most useful if it is flexible and went on to state that, 'Labour and birth are not events that you can have total control over even when you do everything in your power to prepare.'[31]

The birth plan is not a contract between the woman and the healthcare professional. If a particular treatment or intervention is requested in the birth plan, consent should not be assumed and the process for informed consent should still be adhered to. Similarly, where a particular intervention is refused in a birth plan, it may still be offered to the patient if judged to be in their best interests. An issue may arise in circumstances where the birth plan is disregarded without a sufficient justification for doing so. It would be wise to record the reasons for any divergence from the birth plan so a clear explanation can be provided.

8.2 Abortion Law in Ireland

As noted in the introduction, the law on abortion in Ireland has been a visible point of contention over the past 40 years. It has been framed by debates on the sanctity of life, reproductive health and human rights. Objections to abortion tend to be grounded in religious, humanitarian, or moral arguments, while supporters of abortion rights tend to emphasise the autonomy of the pregnant woman and her right to control over her body. These divisions are reflected in the simplified 'pro-life' and 'pro-choice' groupings. The focus in this chapter is placed on the legal framework in Ireland. The law has moved from a conservative and restrictive position on abortion to a more liberal position in recent years, as marked by the 36th Amendment to the Constitution, which permitted the Oireachtas to legislate for abortion.

Abortion is defined as the process of ending a pregnancy. Abortion can be carried out in two ways, namely a medical abortion or a surgical abortion. A medical abortion involves taking medications to end the pregnancy. This may take place with a doctor in the community or, if the pregnancy is more advanced, may take place in a hospital. Surgical abortion involves a procedure to remove the pregnancy from the womb by a doctor using a suction method. It follows that surgical abortions are to be carried out in a hospital

---

[31] The Royal Australian and New Zealand College of Obstetricians and Gynaecologists, 'Labour and Birth' <https://ranzcog.edu.au/womens-health/patient-information-resources/labour-and-birth> accessed 10 September 2020.

setting. The Health (Regulation of Termination of Pregnancy) Act 2018 does not use the term 'abortion' and instead refers to a 'termination of pregnancy'.[32] The Act defines this as 'a medical procedure intended to end the life of a foetus'.[33]

8.2.1 The Development of the Law on Abortion

Sections 58 and 59 of the Offences against the Person Act 1861 made abortion a criminal offence in Ireland.[34] The 1861 Act continued to apply in Ireland following independence and the ratification of the 1937 Constitution. Its provisions on abortion were eventually repealed by the Protection of Life During Pregnancy Act 2013. Under the 1861 Act, prosecutions were brought in England and Ireland against persons who performed backstreet abortions. In 1939, the case of *R v Bourne* in England recognised a defence where the abortion is performed to preserve the life of the mother. This included circumstances where the continuance of the pregnancy would make the woman a physical or mental wreck.[35] This defence was not recognised in Ireland and prosecutions continued. The last prosecution for an illegal abortion in Ireland occurred in 1956. The nurse, Mamie Cadden, was sentenced to death by hanging following the death of a patient. Her sentence was subsequently commuted to life imprisonment and she was moved to the Criminal Lunatic Asylum in Dundrum. Mamie Cadden died in 1959.[36]

The passing of the 8th Amendment to the Irish Constitution took place in 1983. This amended the Constitution by inserting Article 40.3.3°:

> The State acknowledges the right to life of the unborn and, with due regard to the equal right to life of the mother, guarantees in its laws to respect, and, as far as practicable, by its laws to defend and vindicate that right.[37]

This amendment represented an attempt to copper-fasten the prohibition on abortion in the State. There was some concern at the time that a privacy-based right to abortion might be accepted by the Irish courts. This concern was tied to the US Supreme Court

---

[32] Health (Regulation of Termination of Pregnancy) Act 2018.
[33] ibid s 2.
[34] Offences against the Person Act 1861, ss 58–59.
[35] *R v Bourne* [1938] 3 All ER 615.
[36] Ray Kavanagh, *Mamie Cadden: Backstreet Abortionist* (Mercier Press 2005).
[37] Bunreacht na hÉireann, Art 40.3.3°.

case of *Roe v Wade*,[38] and the decision of the Irish Supreme Court in *McGee v Attorney General*.[39] In *McGee* the Irish Supreme Court recognised a right to marital privacy, thereby allowing a married couple to import contraceptives for personal use. The decision prompted William Binchy to comment that in the 'foreseeable event of some change in attitudes in this country on the question of abortion ... the privacy concept espoused by that decision provides the key for opening that door in the future'.[40] This served as an impetus to the Pro-Life Amendment Campaign and brought about the passing of the 8th Amendment.

Drawing upon Article 40.3.3°, the Society for the Protection of Unborn Children (SPUC) brought several cases that sought to limit the availability of information about abortion services in Britain. SPUC argued that the provision of such information breached the constitutional right to life of the unborn under Article 40.3.3°, and that the State was failing in its constitutional duty if organisations such as Open Door Counselling and Dublin Wellwoman continued to carry out such activities.[41] Hamilton P granted the declaration sought and granted an injunction. This decision was upheld by the Supreme Court, which also established that there was no implied or unenumerated constitutional right to information about the availability of abortion outside the State. These agencies subsequently brought an appeal to the European Court of Human Rights (ECtHR), which ruled that the ban on abortion information was 'over broad and disproportionate' and constituted a breach of Article 10 ECHR freedom of expression.[42] Prior to the decision of the ECtHR, SPUC also brought a case against officers of students' unions who were engaged in the provision of information. SPUC was again successful in securing court orders against the students, from both the High Court and the Supreme Court.[43]

The interpretation of Article 40.3.3° was of central importance in *Attorney General v X*.[44] The person at the centre of this case was a 14-year old girl, referred to as 'X', who had become pregnant

---

[38] *Roe v Wade* 410 US 113 (1973).
[39] *McGee v Attorney General* [1973] IR 284.
[40] William Binchy, 'Marital Privacy and Family Law: A Reply to Mr O'Reilly' (1977) 66(264) Studies: An Irish Quarterly Review 330, 330.
[41] *Attorney General (SPUC) v Open Door Counselling Ltd* [1988] IR 593; *Open Door Counselling and Dublin Well Woman v Ireland* (1993) 15 EHRR 244.
[42] *Open Door Counselling and Dublin Well Woman v Ireland* (1993) 15 EHRR 244 [74].
[43] *SPUC v Grogan* [1989] IR 753.
[44] *Attorney General v X* [1992] IESC 1; [1992] 1 IR 1.

following a rape. The girl and her parents determined that the best course of action was to travel to England for the purposes of obtaining an abortion. The girl's parents informed the gardaí of their intention to leave the country and raised the possibility of collecting DNA samples from the foetus to support subsequent criminal proceedings for rape. The gardaí sought a legal opinion on the admissibility of such evidence. This led to the Attorney General becoming aware of the matter and obtaining interim injunctions in the High Court to restrain the girl and her parents from interfering with the right to life of the unborn; to restrain the same defendants from leaving the State for nine months; and restraining them from procuring or arranging an abortion within or outside the State. Despite X and her parents being out of the country at the time, they cancelled the arrangements for the abortion and returned to Ireland to contest the injunctions.

The High Court heard evidence that X had expressed a desire to kill herself on several occasions. A clinical psychologist who had met with X commented that she had 'coldly expressed a desire to solve matters by ending her life'.[45] The clinical psychologist believed X to be capable of such an act. Costello J stated that the Court was required to assess the danger to the life of the child and the danger that exists to the life of the mother. He was satisfied that there existed a 'real and imminent danger to the life of the unborn',[46] and noted that if an injunction were granted there is 'a risk that the defendant may take her own life'.[47] Costello J did not consider these risks to be equal, as he stated:

> But the risk that the defendant may take her own life if an order is made is much less and is of a different order of magnitude than the certainty that the life of the unborn will be terminated if the order is not made.[48]

Costello J granted the permanent injunctions sought. On appeal, the Supreme Court discharged the injunctions by a majority of four to one.

In the Supreme Court Finlay CJ set out:

> I, therefore, conclude that the proper test to be applied is that if it is established as a matter of probability that there is a real

---

[45] *Attorney General v X* [1992] 1 IR 1, 8.
[46] ibid 12.
[47] ibid 12.
[48] ibid 12.

and substantial risk to the life, as distinct from the health of the mother, which can only be avoided by the termination of her pregnancy, such termination is permissible, having regard to the true interpretation of Article 40, s. 3, sub-s. 3 of the Constitution.[49]

For Finlay CJ the risk of self-destruction was a real and substantial risk to life and could only be avoided by the termination of the pregnancy. The decision in *Attorney General v X* meant that a person was entitled to a lawful abortion in Ireland where the pregnancy constitutes a real and substantial threat to her life. This included the threat of suicide. For many this was a controversial interpretation of the law and it went on to be a central point in subsequent referenda.

The issues raised in the X case resulted in the Government putting three constitutional amendments to the people in November 1992. These were intended to modify Article 40.3.3°. The first of these amendments sought to exclude the risk of suicide as a ground for lawful abortion: 34.65 per cent voted in favour of the amendment, while 65.35 per cent rejected it. The other two amendments were passed. The second amendment guaranteed the freedom to travel abroad:

> This subsection shall not limit freedom to travel between the State and another state.

The third amendment to Article 40.3.3° related to the provision of information on services lawfully available in other states:

> This subsection shall not limit freedom to obtain or make available, in the State, subject to such conditions as may be laid down by law, information relating to services lawfully available in another state.

This effectively reversed previous decisions of the Supreme Court on the provision of information on abortion services and allowed for this to be regulated by law.[50] This was subsequently addressed by the Regulation of Information (Services Outside the State for Termination of Pregnancies) Act 1995.

---

[49] ibid 53–54.
[50] *Attorney General (SPUC) v Open Door Counselling Ltd* [1988] IR 593; *SPUC v Grogan* [1989] IR 753.

A third referendum on abortion took place in March 2002. This again sought to limit the effect of the X case by excluding the threat of suicide as a risk to life. The amendment was narrowly defeated by 50.42 per cent (No) to 49.58 per cent (Yes). It was clear from case law both before and after the referendum that the law on abortion was far from settled.[51] Subsequent cases included *D v Ireland*[52] and *D (A Minor) v District Judge Brennan, the Health Services Executive, Ireland and the Attorney General*.[53]

In 2005, a woman 'D' brought a case to the ECtHR. She claimed that her inability to obtain an abortion in Ireland constituted a breach of her human rights.[54] The applicant had been pregnant with twins. After fourteen weeks of pregnancy D discovered that one of the twins had died in the womb and the other had a fatal foetal abnormality, Edwards Syndrome. D did not consider bringing legal proceedings in Ireland at that point; instead, she made arrangements to travel to the United Kingdom for an abortion. The ECtHR found the application to be inadmissible as she 'did not comply with the requirement to exhaust domestic remedies as regards the availability of abortion in Ireland in the case of fatal foetal abnormality'.[55] A domestic legal remedy was, in principle, available to her and this should have been pursued at the time. The ECtHR also suggested that there existed 'a feasible argument … that the constitutionally enshrined balance between the right to life of the mother and of the foetus could have shifted in favour of the mother when the "unborn" suffered from a abnormality incompatible with life'.[56]

In May 2007, a 17-year-old girl, Miss D, brought a case against the HSE as it tried to prevent her travelling to Britain for an abortion. Miss D was in State care and was four months pregnant at the time of the hearing. The foetus had anencephaly, which is normally fatal within three days of birth. The HSE refused her permission to leave the State and notified the gardaí. The High Court ruled that there was no law or constitutional impediment that would prevent Miss D from travelling for the purpose of terminating

---

[51] See *A and B v Eastern Health Board, Judge Mary Fahy and C, and the Attorney General (the C Case)* [1998] 1 IR 464.
[52] *D v Ireland* App No 26499/02 (ECtHR, 28 June 2006).
[53] *D (A Minor) v District Judge Brennan, the Health Services Executive, Ireland and the Attorney General* (HC 9 May 2007).
[54] *D v Ireland* App No 26499/02 (ECtHR, 28 June 2006). Arguments based on Articles 1, 3, 8, 10, 13 and 14 of the European Convention on Human Rights.
[55] *D v Ireland* App No 26499/02 (ECtHR, 28 June 2006) [103].
[56] ibid [90].

the pregnancy. Miss D was not suicidal and the question of her having an abortion in Ireland was not raised.

The issue of abortion in Ireland came before the ECtHR once more in the case of *A, B and C v Ireland*.[57] This case involved three women, A, B and C, each of whom unintentionally became pregnant and who travelled to the UK for an abortion. The women argued that their rights under the ECHR were violated when they were forced to terminate their pregnancies outside of the State. In its judgment of 16 December 2010, the Grand Chamber of the ECtHR refused the applications of A and B. Despite this, the Court held that there had been a violation of Article 8 in respect of C.

Prior to the abortion, C had undergone three years of chemotherapy for a rare form of cancer. The cancer was in remission when she became pregnant. She was not aware of the pregnancy when she underwent a series of tests for cancer. Upon learning of the pregnancy, she spoke with her GP and several medical consultants. C alleged that, due to the Irish legal framework, she received insufficient information as to the impact of the pregnancy on her health and life and of her prior tests for cancer on the foetus. Owing to the uncertainty she travelled to England for an abortion. On returning to Ireland, C suffered complications, including prolonged bleeding and infection. She alleged that doctors provided inadequate medical care.

The ECtHR rejected the State's argument that an individual's right to a lawful abortion could be established during medical consultation and/or through litigation before the domestic courts.

> The Court considers that the uncertainty generated by the lack of legislative implementation of Article 40.3.3°, and more particularly by the lack of effective and accessible procedures to establish a right to an abortion under that provision, has resulted in a striking discordance between the theoretical right to lawful abortion in Ireland on grounds of a relevant risk to a woman's life and the reality of its practical implementation.[58]

The ECtHR concluded:

> ... the authorities failed to comply with their positive obligation to secure to the third applicant effective respect for

---
[57] *A, B, and C v Ireland* App No 25579/05 (ECtHR, 16 December 2010).
[58] ibid [264].

her private life by reason of the absence of any implementing legislative or regulatory regime providing an accessible and effective procedure by which the third applicant could have established whether she qualified for a lawful abortion in Ireland in accordance with Article 40.3.3 of the Constitution.[59]

In response to the ECtHR decision in *A, B and C v Ireland*, an expert group was convened to recommend a series of options on how to implement the judgment of *A, B and C v Ireland*. The eventual legislative response took the form of the Protection of Life during Pregnancy Act 2013. The 2013 Act did not represent a radical change but amounted to a codification of the law. It provided for a termination of pregnancy where there is a risk of loss of life from physical illness, or a risk of loss of life from suicide.[60] In the case of the latter, there was considerable medical oversight required. This included further conditions for the obstetrician and psychiatrists who could be involved in such a decision.

The enactment of the Protection of Life during Pregnancy Act 2013 did not signal the end of the debate on abortion in Ireland. The experience of Ms Y underlined the challenges that still existed in securing access to a termination. Ms Y had sought asylum in Ireland. She discovered she was pregnant during a routine medical exam. This pregnancy resulted from a rape prior to her arrival in Ireland. The comments and behaviour of Ms Y made it clear that she did not want to carry the pregnancy to full term. Delays at various points in her care meant that an abortion was not carried out, but instead the child was delivered early by caesarean section.[61]

The case of *Mellet v Ireland*[62] was a further indication that the law on abortion was not satisfactory from a human rights perspective. Amanda Mellet became pregnant in 2011. In the twenty-first week of her pregnancy, she was informed that her foetus had congenital heart defects. Further examinations resulted in a diagnosis of trisomy 18. The child would likely die in utero or shortly after birth. Staff in the hospital advised her that she could 'travel' but no further information was provided. A family planning clinic provided her with assistance to travel to Liverpool Women's Hospital for a termination. Twelve hours after the delivery she

---

[59] ibid [267].
[60] Protection of Life During Pregnancy Act 2013, ss 7–9.
[61] Kitty Holland, 'Timeline of Ms Y case' *The Irish Times* (Dublin, 4 October 2014).
[62] *Mellet v Ireland* Comm No 2324/2013, UN Doc CCPR/C/116/D/2324/2013 (2016).

travelled back to Ireland, while still feeling weak and bleeding. She could not afford to stay any longer in the UK, and no financial assistance was available for women who terminate pregnancies abroad. Upon her return to Dublin, she did not receive any aftercare in the hospital, and bereavement counselling in the hospital was not available to her. Amanda Mellet claimed to be a victim of violations by Ireland of her rights under Articles 2(1), 3, 7, 17, 19 and 26 of the International Covenant on Civil and Political Rights.

The United Nations Human Rights Committee found that Ms Mellet was subjected to cruel, inhuman and degrading treatment. The Committee noted that Ms Mellet's 'wanted pregnancy was not viable, that the options open to her were inevitably a source of intense suffering and that her travel abroad to terminate her pregnancy had significant negative consequences for her, ... that could have been avoided if she had been allowed to terminate her pregnancy in Ireland, resulting in harm contrary to article 7'.[63] In addition, the Committee found that Ireland violated her right to privacy, and discriminated against her by failing to provide her with the services that she required. The UN Human Rights Committee directed that the State was to provide Ms Mellet with 'adequate compensation and to make available to her any psychological treatment she needs'.[64] Furthermore, there was an obligation on Ireland to take steps to prevent similar violations in the future. On this point, the Committee recommended:

> the State party should amend its law on the voluntary termination of pregnancy, including if necessary its Constitution, to ensure compliance with the Covenant, ensuring effective, timely and accessible procedures for pregnancy termination in Ireland, and take measures to ensure that health-care providers are in a position to supply full information on safe abortion services without fearing they will be subjected to criminal sanctions ...[65]

The Irish Government subsequently made an offer of financial compensation and indicated that Ireland's abortion laws would be considered by the Citizens' Assembly.

The Citizens' Assembly was established in 2016. The first issue considered by the Assembly was the 8th Amendment of the

---

[63] ibid 16.
[64] ibid 17.
[65] ibid 17.

Constitution. Evidence was given by a range of invited experts and stakeholders. The Assembly considered the topic across five weekends, with recommendations being voted on in the final weekend. The clear position emerging was that members wanted to remove Article 40.3.3° from the Constitution, and to replace it with a provision that would make it clear that the termination of pregnancy, any rights of the unborn, and any rights of the pregnant woman are matters for the Oireachtas.[66] The Assembly's final report and recommendation were subsequently considered by a Joint Committee of both Houses of the Oireachtas. This Committee delivered its report in December 2017 and recommended the repeal of Article 40.3.3°.[67]

A bill to repeal the 8th Amendment was put to a referendum in May 2018. The amendment was passed with 66.4 per cent voting in favour, and 33.6 per cent voting against the change.[68] Accordingly, Article 40.3.3° now states that:

> Provision may be made by law for the regulation of termination of pregnancy.

This provided the basis for the enactment of the Health (Regulation of Termination of Pregnancy) Act 2018.

8.2.2 Health (Regulation of Termination of Pregnancy) Act 2018

The Health (Regulation of Termination of Pregnancy) Act 2018 defines the circumstances and processes within which abortion can be legally provided in the State.[69] It was signed into law by President Michael D Higgins on 20 December 2018 and commenced on 1 January 2019. This section will outline the key provisions in this legislation, including s 9 termination based on risk to life or health; s 10 termination based on risk to life or health in an emergency; s 11 where there is a condition likely to lead to the death of the foetus; s 12 termination where the pregnancy has not exceeded 12 weeks; s 22 conscientious objection; and s 23 offences.

The NMBI's *Code of Professional Conduct and Ethics* was reviewed in advance of the enactment of the Health (Regulation of Termination

---

[66] The Citizens' Assembly, *First Report and Recommendations of the Citizens' Assembly: The Eighth Amendment of the Constitution* (29 June 2017).
[67] ibid.
[68] 'Abortion Referendum: Yes Secures Landslide Victory' *The Irish Times* (Dublin, 26 May 2018).
[69] Health (Regulation of Termination of Pregnancy) Act 2018.

of Pregnancy) Act 2018. The NMBI made no revision to the Code at the time. Instead, an addendum was added on 19 December 2018, which set out, 'It is not a breach of any part of this Code for nurses and midwives to provide services under the Health (Termination of Pregnancy) Act 2018 once enacted.'[70]

Section 9 Risk to Life or Health

The law provides for a termination of pregnancy where two medical practitioners, having examined the pregnant woman, are of the reasonable opinion formed in good faith that:

> (a) there is a risk to the life, or of serious harm to the health, of the pregnant woman,
>
> (b) the foetus has not reached viability, and
>
> (c) it is appropriate to carry out the termination of pregnancy in order to avert the risk referred to in paragraph (a).[71]

Section 9(2) requires that one of the medical practitioners be an obstetrician and the other shall be an appropriate medical practitioner.

Section 10 Risk to Life or Health in Emergency

Section 10 of the 2018 Act provides for a termination of pregnancy where one medical practitioner, having examined the pregnant woman, is of the reasonable opinion formed in good faith that:

> (a) there is an immediate risk to the life, or of serious harm to the health, of the pregnant woman, and
>
> (b) it is immediately necessary to carry out the termination of pregnancy in order to avert that risk.[72]

Section 11 Condition Likely to Lead to Death of Foetus

Section 11(1) of the Health (Regulation of Termination of Pregnancy) Act 2018 provides:

---

[70] Nursing and Midwifery Board of Ireland, *Code of Professional Conduct and Ethics for Registered Nurses and Registered Midwives* (NMBI 2014).
[71] Health (Regulation of Termination of Pregnancy) Act 2018, s 9(1).
[72] ibid s 10(1).

> A termination of pregnancy may be carried out in accordance with this section where 2 medical practitioners, having examined the pregnant woman, are of the reasonable opinion formed in good faith that there is present a condition affecting the foetus that is likely to lead to the death of the foetus either before, or within 28 days of, birth.[73]

Section 11(2) requires that one of the medical practitioners be an obstetrician and the other shall be a medical practitioner of a relevant specialty.

Section 12 Early Pregnancy

Section 12 of the 2018 Act provides for a termination in cases where the pregnancy has not exceeded 12 weeks as certified by a medical practitioner.

> A termination of pregnancy may be carried out in accordance with this section by a medical practitioner where, having examined the pregnant woman, he or she is of the reasonable opinion formed in good faith that the pregnancy concerned has not exceeded 12 weeks of pregnancy.[74]

Under this section a termination is not to be carried out unless a period of not less than 3 days has elapsed from the date of certification.

Section 22 Conscientious Objection

The question of conscientious objection was a particularly fraught topic during the debates on the legislation. Conscientious objection was provided for under the Protection of Life During Pregnancy Act 2013.[75] It continues to be provided for under the Health (Regulation of Termination of Pregnancy) Act 2018. Section 22(1) of the 2018 Act sets out that:

> … nothing in this Act shall be construed as obliging any medical practitioner, nurse or midwife to carry out, or to participate in carrying out, a termination of pregnancy in accordance with section 9, 11 or 12 to which he or she has a conscientious objection.[76]

---

[73] ibid s 11(1).
[74] ibid s 12.
[75] Protection of Life During Pregnancy Act 2013, s 17.
[76] Health (Regulation of Termination of Pregnancy) Act 2018, s 22(1).

However, this sub-section is not to affect any duty to participate in a termination of pregnancy where it is provided under s 10, risk to life or health in an emergency.[77] In all other cases, if a person has a conscientious objection they are to 'make such arrangements for the transfer of care of the pregnant woman concerned as may be necessary to enable the woman to avail of the termination of pregnancy concerned'.[78]

The NMBI's *Code of Professional Conduct and Ethics* addresses conscientious objection under Principle 2: Professional Responsibility and Accountability. The standards of conduct reflect the provisions set out in s 22 of the 2018 Act.

> Standard of conduct 7: 'If you have a conscientious objection based on religious or moral beliefs which is relevant to your professional practice, you must tell your employer and, if appropriate, tell the patient as soon as you can. If you cannot meet the patient's needs because of this objection, you must talk with your employer and, if appropriate, talk to the patient about other care arrangements.'[79]

> Standard of conduct 8: 'Even if you have a conscientious objection, you must provide care to a patient in an emergency where there is a risk to the patient's life.'[80]

Section 23 Offences

Under s 23(1) it is an offence for a person to intentionally end the life of a foetus otherwise than in accordance with the provisions of the Health (Regulation of Termination of Pregnancy) Act 2018. Section 23(2) sets out that it shall be an offence for a person:

> to prescribe, administer, supply or procure any drug, substance, instrument, apparatus or other thing knowing that it is intended to be used or employed with intent to end the life of a foetus, or being reckless as to whether it is intended to be so used or employed, otherwise than in accordance with the provisions of this Act.[81]

---

[77] ibid s 22(2).
[78] ibid s 22(3).
[79] Nursing and Midwifery Board of Ireland, *Code of Professional Conduct and Ethics for Registered Nurses and Registered Midwives* (NMBI 2014) 17.
[80] ibid.
[81] Health (Regulation of Termination of Pregnancy) Act 2018, s 23(2).

Sub-sections (1) and (2) do not apply to a pregnant woman in respect of her own pregnancy.[82]

Section 23(4) provides that it is an offence for a person 'to aid, abet, counsel or procure a pregnant woman to intentionally end, or attempt to end, the life of the foetus of that pregnant woman otherwise than in accordance with the provisions of this Act'.[83] Under s 23 a person found guilty of an offence shall be liable to a fine and/or a term of imprisonment of up to 14 years.[84]

8.2.3 Abortion and the Young Person

The Child Care Act 1991, the Children Act 2001 and the Mental Health Act 2001 define a child as a service user under the age of 18 years, other than a service user who is or has been married. Section 23(1) of the Non-Fatal Offences Against the Person Act 1997 sets out:

> The consent of a minor who has attained the age of 16 years to any surgical, medical or dental treatment which, in the absence of consent, would constitute a trespass to his or her person, shall be as effective as it would be if he or she were of full age; and where a minor has by virtue of this section given an effective consent to any treatment it shall not be necessary to obtain any consent for it from his or her parent or guardian.[85]

As such, a 16- or 17-year-old may consent to surgical, medical or dental treatment in the same way an adult can. It follows that, if a person aged 16 or 17 has sufficient capacity to understand the nature of the procedure, she may give a valid consent for a termination of pregnancy. Nonetheless, the HSE's *Guide to Medical Abortion* suggests that people aged under 18 should be encouraged to involve their parents or another supportive adult.[86]

Ireland has not traditionally accepted the idea of a 'mature minor' whereby valid consent can be provided by a person under the age of 16. The concept of a 'mature minor' focuses on the child's level of maturity and ability to understand what is being proposed.[87]

---

[82] ibid s 23(3).
[83] ibid s 23(4).
[84] ibid s 23(5).
[85] Non-Fatal Offences Against the Person Act 1997, s 23(1).
[86] Health Service Executive, *Your Guide to Medical Abortion* (HSE 2019) 25.
[87] *Gillick v West Norfolk and Wisbech Area Health Authority and another* [1986] 1 AC 112.

However, it is recognised that there may be circumstances in which a person under the age of 16 can give consent to treatment. On the topic of age of consent, the HSE's *National Consent Policy* sets out the following:

> This policy acknowledges that in health and social care practice it is usual to involve parent(s)/legal guardian(s) and seek their consent when providing a service or treatment to a minor under 16. However, the minor may seek to make a decision on their own without parental involvement or consent. In such circumstances it is best practice to encourage and advise the minor to communicate with and involve their parent(s) or legal guardian(s). It is only in exceptional circumstances that, having regard to the need to take account of an objective assessment of both the rights and the best interests of the person under 16, health and social care interventions would be provided for those under 16 without the knowledge or consent of parent(s) or legal guardian(s).[88]

For persons under the age of 16, the *Guide to Medical Abortion* acknowledges that the child may wish not to involve an adult and the doctor can offer an abortion if there are exceptional circumstances and an assessment has been completed. In such exceptional circumstances, the *National Consent Policy* states that an assessment must be made as to whether:

- the minor has sufficient maturity to understand the information relevant to making the decision and to appreciate its potential consequences;
- the minor's views are stable and a true reflection of his or her core values and beliefs, taking into account his or her physical and mental health and any other factors that affect his or her ability to exercise independent judgement;
- the nature, purpose and usefulness of the treatment or social care intervention;
- the risks and benefits involved in the treatment or social care intervention, and
- any other specific welfare, protection or public health considerations, in respect of which relevant guidance and protocols such as the 2011 Children First: National Guidelines for the Protection and Welfare of Children

---

[88] Health Service Executive, *National Consent Policy* (HSE 2019) 54.

(or any equivalent replacement document) must be applied.[89]

Under the Criminal Law (Sexual Offences) Act 2006 the legal age of consent is 17 years. A report must be made where the child is 14 or under and has engaged in sexual activity; where the child is 15 or 16 and is engaging in sexual activity with someone who is at least two years older; or where the healthcare professional suspects that the child is at risk of sexual abuse or harm or that the child has been sexually abused or harmed.[90]

8.3 Treatment Refusal During Pregnancy

Chapter 5 addressed patient autonomy, informed consent, and the right to refuse treatment. The chapter did not specifically address the rights of a pregnant person to consent or refuse medical treatment. Although a pregnant person enjoys the same right of autonomy as anyone else, the manner in which such autonomy is exercised has been the subject of considerable scrutiny. This is particularly true in circumstances where a refusal of treatment could impact negatively on the foetus. Mills and Mulligan suggest, 'The most acute conflict between the rights of the mother and foetus occurs when the woman refuses consent to caesarean section, because in that case the foetus is well past the point of viability and fully capable of independent life.'[91]

The discussion on abortion in section 8.2.1 highlighted the challenge of applying Article 40.3.3° prior to the 36th Amendment of the Constitution. This provision stated:

> The State acknowledges the right to life of the unborn and, with due regard to the equal right to life of the mother, guarantees in its laws to respect, and, as far as practicable, by its laws to defend and vindicate that right.[92]

The duty of the State was not limited to abortion and extended to other cases in which the right to life of the unborn was threatened. In effect, a refusal of treatment by a pregnant woman raised issues of autonomy, the right to life, bodily integrity, and privacy.

---

[89] ibid.
[90] Health Service Executive, *Your Guide to Medical Abortion* (HSE 2019) 25; see also Children First Act 2015.
[91] Simon Mills and Andrea Mulligan, *Medical Law in Ireland* (3rd edn, Bloomsbury Professional 2017) 131.
[92] Bunreacht na hÉireann, Art 40.3.3°.

Moreover, it raised difficult questions about balancing the interests and rights of the parties affected. The case of *HSE v B* was the first reported case on caesarean section refusal in Ireland.[93] Although the law has since changed, this case may provide an indication of how subsequent cases may be approached.

HSE v B involved an application by the HSE for an order to force a pregnant woman to have a caesarean section against her will in order to vindicate the right to life of the unborn child. Ms B had had three previous caesarean sections. A vaginal delivery therefore posed a risk of her uterus rupturing, which could lead to the death of the child and Ms B. Expert medical advice suggested there was a '1 in 10 chance of Ms. B's uterus rupturing and a consequent risk of serious injury, even death, to the foetus and Ms. B, if she were to proceed with a natural birth'.[94] It was also stated that if uterine rupture was avoided during a natural delivery, it could still require an emergency caesarean section, which would entail greater risks than an elective procedure. Ms B resisted the claim of the applicant and insisted on delivering the child naturally. Twomey J described the issue in the case as 'not whether the Court agrees or not with Ms B, but rather whether she can be forced, against her will, to submit to a surgical procedure in her interest and in the interests of her unborn child'.[95]

The HSE raised the question of Ms B's capacity to make the decisions. Twomey J referred to the presumption of capacity under *Fitzpatrick v FK*, and determined that this presumption was not rebutted by the evidence. Further, Twomey J stated that if the matter only involved Ms B's health she would be entitled to refuse to follow medical advice, however, this decision was complicated by Article 40.3.3°. To resolve the competing rights, Twomey J relied on the line of reasoning set out in *North Western Health Board v HW and CW*:

> … the right of the Courts to intervene in a parent's decision in relation to an unborn child could not be any greater than the Court's right to intervene in relation to born children. Accordingly, the principles laid out in the *HW and CW* case regarding the right to the Courts to intervene in a parent's decision are equally applicable in this case.[96]

---

[93] *HSE v B* [2016] IEHC 605; [2016] 2 IR 350.
[94] *HSE v B* [2016] IEHC 605 [3].
[95] ibid 605 [8].
[96] ibid 605 [15].

On this basis, the intervention of the Court in the parent's decision could only be justified in extreme and exceptional circumstances.

Twomey J did not understand why Ms B was refusing to follow medical advice but determined that an intervention was not appropriate in the circumstances:

> … this Court does not believe that the increased risk which she is undertaking for her unborn child is such as to justify this Court in effectively authorising her to have her uterus opened against her will, something which would constitute a grievous assault if it were done on a woman who was not pregnant.[97]

The case demonstrates that even under Article 40.3.3° the standard to be satisfied for there to be an intervention was particularly high. This position is unlikely to have relaxed in light of the constitutional changes that have since taken place. The amendment to Article 40.3.3° may even place slightly greater weight on maternal autonomy.

---

[97] ibid 605 [19].

CHAPTER 9
Legal Aspects of End-of-Life Treatment and Care

Introduction 239
Care of the Older Person 240
    Standards for Care of the Older Person............ 243
    Elder Abuse....................................... 247
    The Use of Restraint.............................. 250
Autonomy and Medical Treatment....................... 253
    The Withdrawal of Medical Treatment 254
The Provision of Palliative Care...................... 261
    Pain Management 262
Euthanasia and Assisted Suicide....................... 267
    Responding to a Request for Euthanasia or
    Assistance in Suicide 271
Do Not Attempt Resuscitation Orders.................. 273
The Definition of Death............................... 277
    Certification and Registration of Death........... 279
The Role of the Coroner 280
    Post-Mortem Practice............................. 284
    Inquests.. 285
Wills... 287

9.0 Introduction

In 'Aubade' the poet Philip Larkin wrote, 'Most things may never happen: this one will'.[1] Death cannot be avoided and is a reality that is to be accepted. Nevertheless, developments in medicine and technology place ever greater pressure on healthcare professionals as expectations of treatment and care continue to rise. In this respect, the medicalisation of death has been highlighted and discussed in books such as *The Way We Die Now* by Seamus O'Mahony[2] and *Being Mortal* by Atul Gawande.[3]

---

[1] Philip Larkin, 'Aubade' in Harold Pinter, Godbert Godbert and Astbury Astbury (eds), *100 Poems by 100 Poets* (Methuen 1986) 93.
[2] Seamus O'Mahony, *The Way We Die Now* (Head of Zeus 2016).
[3] Atul Gawande, *Being Mortal* (Profile Books 2014).

In keeping with other chapters, it is to be recognised that the nurse's role in end-of-life treatment and care of the older person has expanded and has grown increasingly complex. This is illustrated by the development of master's programmes in gerontological nursing, palliative care nursing, and end-of-life healthcare ethics.

The starting point for this chapter is care of the older person. It addresses human rights, elder abuse, and the use of restraints. Further sections outline autonomy and medical treatment, the provision of palliative care, euthanasia and assisted suicide, do not attempt resuscitation (DNAR) orders, the definition of death, the role of the coroner, and the drafting of wills. However, an aging population combined with the diversity of settings where end-of-life issues arise mean that nurses will be presented with legal issues not covered by this text. In such cases, nurses should keep detailed records, and engage with clinical ethics committees or legal professionals as required. Moreover, the nurse should strive to treat the patient with dignity and aim to protect and promote the individual's human rights as fully as possible.

9.1 Care of the Older Person

The number of older people in the European Union is projected to peak at 149.2 million inhabitants in 2050, and their relative share of total population is expected to reach 28.5 per cent in the same year.[4] Older people are defined as those aged 65 years or over by the Eurostat report.[5] World Population Prospects 2019 suggests that 1 in 6 people in the world will be over the age of 65 by 2050. The figure in 2019 is 1 in 11.[6] These are dramatic changes and will place greater pressure on state finances, long-term care, and healthcare systems.

Ireland is also experiencing this demographic shift. Census 2016 indicated that the population of Ireland has continued to grow older since the 1980s with 637,567 people over 65 years. This represents an increase of 19.1 per cent since Census 2011.[7]

---

[4] Eurostat, *Ageing Europe: Looking at the Lives of Older People in the EU* (Publications Office of the European Union 2019) 8.
[5] ibid 9.
[6] United Nations, Department of Economic and Social Affairs, *World Population Ageing 2019* (2020).
[7] Central Statistics Office, 'Census of Population 2016 – Profile 3 An Age Profile of Ireland' <https://www.cso.ie/en/releasesandpublications/ep/p-cp3oy/cp3/agr/> accessed 26 June 2020.

A population-focused analysis of current and future needs was undertaken by the Health Service Executive and resulted in the publication of a report titled *Planning for Health: Trends and Priorities to Inform Health Service Planning 2017*.[8] The HSE report set out that adults 65 years and over will increase by up to 21 per cent (131,000) by 2022. Moreover, it included projections that there will 16,100 additional people aged 85 years and over by 2022.[9] Further figures are provided by the Department of the Taoiseach in a report titled *National Risk Assessment 2019*.[10] This report stated, 'The share of population aged 65 and over is projected to increase from one in eight to one in six by 2030, and the number of people aged 85 and over is projected to almost double.'[11]

Older persons tend to account for a greater number of interactions with healthcare professionals. It follows that an increase in older persons as a percentage of total population will result in increased pressure on health and social services in the State. In responding to these various challenges, it is important that the human rights of the older person be recognised and protected across policy, planning and practice.

Human Rights, Dignity, and the Older Person

Human rights have a fundamental role in shaping the care and treatment provided to people. Older persons are entitled to the same rights protection as anyone else in society. The legal framework does not discriminate against the older person and neither should policy or clinical practice.

The first human rights treaty to specifically protect the general rights of the older person was the European Social Charter. This Council of Europe treaty was adopted in 1961 and revised in 1996. It places specific emphasis on the protection of vulnerable persons such as the older person, children, people with disabilities, and migrants. Article 23 provides for the right of elderly persons to social protection and seeks to enable elderly persons to remain full members of society for as long as possible through the provision of adequate resources and appropriate information about services

---

[8] Breda Smyth and others, *Planning for Health: Trends and Priorities to Inform Health Service Planning 2017* (HSE 2017).
[9] ibid 6.
[10] Department of the Taoiseach, *National Risk Assessment 2019* (Government of Ireland 2019) 40.
[11] ibid.

and facilities.[12] Article 23 also requires measures 'to guarantee elderly persons living in institutions appropriate support, while respecting their privacy, and participation in decisions concerning living conditions in the institution'.[13]

The rights of the older person are also provided for by Article 25 of the EU Charter of Fundamental Rights. Article 25 states, 'The Union recognises and respects the rights of the elderly to lead a life of dignity and independence and to participate in social and cultural life.'[14] The European Union is required to act and legislate in line with the Charter. It is applicable to the Institutions of the European Union and Member States when implementing EU law. The scope of interpretation is addressed by Article 52 of the Charter and this provides that rights which overlap with the European Convention on Human Rights (ECHR) are to have the same meaning and scope as those laid down by the ECHR. This does not prevent Union law from providing more extensive protection.[15]

The legal framework for human rights protection in Ireland is composed of many different elements. It is shaped by the Irish Constitution, legislation, guidance documents, the ECHR, and treaties such as the International Covenant on Economic, Social and Cultural Rights.

The Irish Constitution, Bunreacht na hÉireann, recognises a number of fundamental rights. These rights are found in Articles 40–44 of the Constitution, and include rights to equality before the law, freedom of expression, freedom of religion, and the right to bodily integrity. Constitutional recognition of these rights underlines their status and protects from political interference. The Constitution is at the top of the hierarchy for domestic sources of law. Other domestic sources of law therefore depend on the Constitution for their validity.

The ECHR was incorporated into Irish law by way of the European Convention on Human Rights Act 2003. This approach provided for the incorporation of the Convention at a sub-constitutional level, thereby maintaining the supremacy of the Irish Constitution. The European Convention on Human Rights was drafted by the Council of Europe in 1950 and establishes a legal obligation on

---

[12] European Social Charter, Art 23.
[13] ibid.
[14] Charter of Fundamental Rights of the European Union, Art 25.
[15] ibid Art 52(3).

States to protect certain civil and political rights. Section 3 of the ECHR Act 2003 requires that 'every organ of the State shall perform its functions in a manner compatible with the State's obligations under the Convention provisions'.[16] Organs of State include bodies such as the Health Information and Quality Authority (HIQA) and the Health Service Executive (HSE). These bodies must therefore carry out their functions in a way that is compatible with the obligations placed on the State. Individuals who feel their rights under the Convention have been violated by the State can ultimately bring a case to the European Court of Human Rights (ECtHR), provided that domestic remedies have first been exhausted.

Like anyone else in society, the older person is entitled to have their rights under the ECHR protected. The following rights are likely to be of particular relevance to the older person:

- Article 2, Right to life
- Article 3, Prohibition of torture
- Article 5, Right to liberty and security
- Article 8, Right to respect for private and family life
- Article 9, Freedom of thought, conscience and religion
- Article 10, Freedom of expression
- Article 14, Prohibition of discrimination

The infringement of human rights may not always be intentional but can come about due to deficiencies in service delivery, the poor provision of information, resource limitations, and inconsistencies in clinical practice. The manner in which care and treatment is structured can have a considerable impact on the way in which human rights are protected and realised within a jurisdiction. In effect, the abstract nature of the rights contained in the legal framework come to be reflected and embedded in everyday practice and in the interactions between the nurse and the older person. It follows that the manner in which the older person experiences and participates in their medical care and treatment reflects both strengths and weaknesses in the relationship between clinical practice and the law.

9.1.1 Standards for Care of the Older Person

Both the Nursing and Midwifery Board of Ireland (NMBI) and HIQA have published standards that shape and define the standard of care to be expected by the older person. The NMBI

---

[16] European Convention on Human Rights Act 2003, s 3.

has published a guidance document titled *Working with Older People, Professional Guidance*.[17] This was originally published in 2009 and reissued in 2015. It acknowledges that registered nurses care for older people in all healthcare settings, and it is designed to form the basis for the drafting of local protocols and policies that reflect the various contexts of practice. The NMBI guidance standards are clustered around the themes of nursing practice and nursing quality. The standards provide a framework and outline the essential elements and competencies required by nurses in caring for the older person. The guidance standards can be read alongside other national standards and guidelines, such as the HIQA's *National Standards for Residential Care Settings for Older People in Ireland*.[18]

The NMBI guidance standards are generic in nature and are broadly framed so as to reflect the diverse settings and roles in which nurses' practice. It is recognised that each care environment will differ, but the standards are intended to define the expected levels of performance. The guidance standards are set out below.

Standards of Nursing Practice

- Standard 1 Person-Centred Holistic Care: Comprehensive person-centred nursing care is provided within the organising framework of assessment, identification of needs, planning, implementation and evaluation.
- Standard 2 Therapeutic Relationship: Therapeutic relationship is developed with the older person that maximises the older person's self-esteem and quality of life.
- Standard 3 Care Environment: A therapeutic safe care environment is promoted and maintained which supports dignity, respect, privacy and independence for the older person
- Standard 4 End of Life Care: The older person receives comprehensive, compassionate, end-of-life care that is person-centred and responds to the older person's unique needs and respect for his/her wishes.

---

[17] Nursing and Midwifery Board of Ireland, *Working with Older People, Professional Guidance* (NMBI 2015).
[18] Health Information and Quality Authority, *National Standards for Residential Care Settings for Older People in Ireland* (HIQA 2016).

Standards of Nursing Quality

- Standard 5 Quality of Care: The nurse caring for the older person evaluates and enhances the quality and effectiveness of his/her nursing care and practice
- Standard 6 Professional Development: The nurse acquires and maintains current knowledge to improve the quality of life and nursing care of the older person

A supporting rationale is outlined for each standard. In addition, competencies for the standards are supported by indicators, which are to be interpreted in accordance with the practice setting and may require further development.

HIQA, National Standards for Residential Care Settings for Older People in Ireland

HIQA is an independent organisation. It was established in the wake of the Leas Cross scandal[19] and was provided for under the Health Act 2007.[20] HIQA has responsibility for setting and monitoring compliance with standards for health and social care services. HIQA also has responsibility for the registration and inspection of 'designated centres' for older people and people with disabilities, as defined by the Health Act 2007. This involves using National Standards, legislation and regulations to decide whether services are providing safe and effective care for the residents. Of particular relevance for the care of the older person are the *National Standards for Residential Care Settings for Older People in Ireland*.[21] The standards were first published in March 2009, and revised in 2016. Key changes include a stronger focus on quality of life and a person-centred approach to care for all residents. These standards apply to residential and residential respite services for the older person, whether they are operated on a public, private or voluntary basis. The standards are not only directed towards the service provider but provide people living in residential care with a guide as to what they should expect from residential services. Section 11 of the Health Act 2007 provides that such standards are also admissible in court proceedings.[22]

---

[19] Desmond O'Neill, *Review of the Deaths at Leas Cross Nursing Home 2002–2005* (2006); Commission of Investigation (Leas Cross Nursing Home), *Final Report* (Department of Health and Children 2009).
[20] Health Act 2007.
[21] Health Information and Quality Authority, *National Standards for Residential Care Settings for Older People in Ireland* (HIQA 2016).
[22] Health Act 2007, s 11.

Under the Health Act 2007, any person carrying on the business of a residential service and/or a residential respite service can only do so if the centre is registered under the 2007 Act and the person is its registered provider. The provider must satisfy the chief inspector that they are fit to provide the service, and that the service is in compliance with the Act, the Regulations and relevant standards.

The monitoring of compliance is a continual process. This ensures that an appropriate standard of care continues to be provided. In circumstances where a designated centre does not meet the required standards and/or the provider fails to address the specific areas of non-compliance, appropriate enforcement action is taken to either control or limit the nature of the service provided, or, to cancel a centre's registration and prevent it from operating. This underlines the fundamental importance of adhering to HIQA standards.

The standards contained in the *National Standards for Residential Care Settings for Older People in Ireland* are presented under eight themes:

Theme 1: Person-Centred Care and Support

Theme 2: Effective Services

Theme 3: Safe Services

Theme 4: Health and Wellbeing

Theme 5: Leadership, Governance and Management

Theme 6: Use of Resources

Theme 7: Responsive Workforce

Theme 8: Use of Information

The themes relate to the dimensions of quality and safety and to the dimensions of capacity and capability. There are 35 standards under these themes, and each standard defines a specific outcome the service is to meet. This is referred to as the 'standard statement' and describes the high-level outcome required to deliver quality residential services and residential respite services for people. In turn, each standard statement has 'features', which give examples of what the residential service may consider in order to meet the standard and achieve the required outcome.

Services for older people are monitored against these standards, in addition to the requirements of other relevant HIQA standards. To support compliance, service providers will be assisted by HIQA guidance, which promotes quality improvement. HIQA have published guidance on supporting autonomy,[23] intimacy and sexual relationships,[24] guidance for designated centres,[25] and guidance on restrictive practice,[26] all of which is intended to promote the care of the individual and ensure a high standard of service provision.

9.1.2 Elder Abuse

Every adult is entitled to live a life free from abuse. The HSE's *Safeguarding Vulnerable Persons at Risk of Abuse, National Policy and Procedures* sets out, 'It is the responsibility of all service providers, statutory and non-statutory, to ensure that, [sic] service users are treated with respect and dignity, have their welfare promoted and receive support in an environment in which every effort is made to promote welfare and to prevent abuse.'[27] This policy applies to all HSE and HSE-funded services, and defines principles intended to promote the welfare of vulnerable people and safeguard them from abuse.

Elder abuse is described as the abuse of a person aged 65 and over. HIQA defines abuse as:

> any act, or failure to act, which results in a breach of a vulnerable person's human rights, civil liberties, physical and mental integrity, dignity or general wellbeing, whether intended or through negligence, including sexual relationships or financial transactions to which the person does not or cannot validly consent, or which are deliberately exploitative.[28]

---

[23] Health Information and Quality Authority, *Supporting People's Autonomy: A Guidance Document* (HIQA 2016).
[24] Health Information and Quality Authority, *Intimacy and Sexual Relationships* (HIQA 2014).
[25] Health Information and Quality Authority, *Guidance for the Assessment of Centres of Older People* (HIQA 2017).
[26] Health Information and Quality Authority, *Guidance on Promoting a Care Environment that Is Free from Restrictive Practice* (HIQA 2019).
[27] Health Service Executive, *Safeguarding Vulnerable Persons at Risk of Abuse: National Policy and Procedures* (HSE 2014).
[28] Health Information and Quality Authority, *National Standards for Residential Services for Children and Adults with Disabilities* (HIQA 2013) 107; Report of the Working Group on Elder Abuse, *Protecting Our Future* (Stationery Office 2002) 25: 'Elder Abuse is a single or repeated act, or lack of inappropriate

While this definition concentrates on abuse by individuals, abuse can also occur due to inappropriate or inadequate care or programmes of care.[29] Elder abuse may take different forms, and an older person may experience more than one form of abuse at a time. Types of abuse include:

> *Physical abuse* includes hitting, slapping, pushing, kicking, misuse of medication, restraint or inappropriate sanctions.
>
> *Sexual abuse* includes rape and sexual assault, or sexual acts to which the vulnerable person has not consented, or could not consent, or into which he or she was compelled to consent.
>
> *Psychological abuse* includes emotional abuse, threats of harm or abandonment, deprivation of contact, humiliation, blaming, controlling, intimidation, coercion, harassment, verbal abuse, isolation or withdrawal from services or supportive networks.
>
> *Financial or material abuse* includes theft, fraud, exploitation, pressure in connection with wills, property, inheritance or financial transactions, or the misuse or misappropriation of property, possessions or benefits.
>
> *Neglect and acts of omission* includes ignoring medical or physical care needs, failure to provide access to appropriate health, social care or educational services, the withholding of the necessities of life such as medication, adequate nutrition and heating.
>
> *Discriminatory abuse* includes ageism, racism, sexism, that based on a person's disability, and other forms of harassment, slurs or similar treatment.
>
> *Institutional abuse* may occur within residential care and acute settings including nursing homes, acute hospitals and any other in-patient settings, and may involve poor standards of care, rigid routines and inadequate responses to complex needs.[30]

---

action, occurring within any relationship where there is an expectation of trust, which causes harm or distress to an older person or violates their human and civil rights.'

[29] Health Service Executive, *Safeguarding Vulnerable Persons at Risk of Abuse: National Policy and Procedures* (HSE 2014) 8.

[30] ibid 9.

These forms of abuse may occur in a range of settings, including in residential or day-care settings, in hospitals, home support services, or in public places. It follows that there is a wide range of people who could potentially be abusive, such as family members, friends, carers, and healthcare professionals.

Nurses have a duty of care to intervene in a situation where an older person is being abused or abuse is suspected.[31] Under the 'Safeguarding Vulnerable Persons at Risk of Abuse' policy, there is a requirement that all services must have a publicly declared 'no tolerance' approach to any form of abuse. Each organisation must have effective procedures in place for assessing and managing risks with regard to safeguarding.

A culture of safeguarding is also promoted by the Health Act 2007 (Care and Support of Residents in Designated Centres for Persons (Children and Adults with Disabilities) Regulation 2013 and the Health Act 2007 (Care and the Welfare of Residents in Designated Centres for Older People) Regulations 2009. Both require measures to be put in place to protect a person from all forms of abuse, and require notification to the chief inspector of any allegation, suspected or confirmed, of abuse of any resident.

The topic of confidentiality was discussed in chapter 6 and underlines its importance in the context of the nurse–patient relationship. However, the effective safeguarding of a vulnerable person may require the disclosure of otherwise confidential information. Under the Criminal Justice (Withholding of Information on Offences against Children and Vulnerable Persons) Act 2012 it is an offence to withhold information on certain offences against children and vulnerable persons from An Garda Síochána.[32] An offence is committed when a person knows or believes that an offence has been committed by another person against a child or vulnerable person, and the person has information, which he or she knows or believes might be of material assistance in securing the apprehension, prosecution or conviction of that other person for that offence, and fails without reasonable excuse to disclose that information as soon as it is practicable to do so to a member of the Garda Síochána.

---

[31] Nursing and Midwifery Board of Ireland, *Working with Older People, Professional Guidance* (NMBI 2015); Appendix 2, 'Reporting Allegations of Elder Abuse' (HSE 2007).
[32] Criminal Justice (Withholding of Information on Offences against Children and Vulnerable Persons) Act 2012.

9.1.3 The Use of Restraint

The use of restraint is a controversial practice, not least because it can significantly impinge on an individual's human rights. The Health Act 2007 (Care and Welfare of Residents in Designated Centres for Older People) Regulations 2013 defines restraint as 'the intentional restriction of a person's voluntary movement or behaviour'.[33] HIQA describes a restrictive practice as something that:

- Limits an individual's movement, activity or function
- Interferes with an individual's ability to acquire positive reinforcement
- Results in the loss of objects or activities that an individual values or
- Requires an individual to engage in a behaviour that the individual would not engage in given freedom of choice.[34]

Restraint may take a variety of forms including physical, environmental, or chemical. It can also arise from inaction. For instance, the care and support needed by a person in order to partake in normal daily activities may not be forthcoming within a reasonable timeframe.

Physical restraint is any manual method or physical or mechanical device, material or equipment attached or adjacent to the resident's body that the individual cannot easily remove that restricts freedom of movement or normal access to one's body.[35] The use of bed rails is a relatively common restrictive practice that arises under this heading. Use of physical restraint has also been used to aid positional support,[36] prevent self-injury,[37] and to prevent the removal of tubes and catheters.[38]

---

[33] Health Act 2007 (Care and Welfare of Residents in Designated Centres for Older People) Regulations 2013, art 2.

[34] Health Information and Quality Authority, *Guidance for Designated Centres, Restrain Procedures* (HIQA October 2014, updated April 2016) 4.

[35] Department of Health, *Towards a Restraint Free Environment in Nursing Homes* (2011, updated July 2019) 6.

[36] Róisín Gallinagh and others, 'The Use of Physical Restraints as a Safety Measure in the Care of Older People in Four Rehabilitation Wards: Findings from an Exploratory Study' (2002) 39(2) International Journal of Nursing Studies 147; see also Health Information and Quality Authority, *Literature Review – Restrictive Practices* (HIQA 2017) 3.

[37] Wayne Fisher and others, 'Direct and Collateral Effects of Restraints and Restraint Fading' (1997) 30(1) Journal of Applied Behavior Analysis 105.

[38] Merav Ben Natan and others, 'Physically Restraining Elder Residents of Long-Term Care Facilities from a Nurse's Perspective' (2010) 16(5)

Chemical restraint is the intentional use of medication to control or modify a person's behaviour or to ensure a patient is compliant or not capable of resistance, when no medically identified condition is being treated; where the treatment is not necessary for the condition; or the intended effect of the drug is to sedate the person for convenience or for disciplinary purposes.[39]

Environmental restraint is the intentional restriction of a resident's normal access to their environment, with the intention of stopping them from leaving, or denying a resident their normal means of independent mobility, means of communicating, or the intentional taking away of ability to exercise civil and religious liberties.[40]

The legal framework for restraint is shaped by legislation, policy documents, national standards, and human rights under the Irish Constitution and the European Convention on Human Rights. As recognised by HIQA, much of the material relating to restraint arises in the context of mental health services. Section 69 of the Mental Health Act 2001 addresses bodily restraint and seclusion:

> A person shall not place a patient in seclusion or apply mechanical means of bodily restraint to the patient unless such seclusion or restraint is determined, in accordance with the rules made under subsection (2), to be necessary for the purposes of treatment or to prevent the patient from injuring himself or herself or others and unless the seclusion or restraint complies with such rules.[41]

As indicated above, s 69(2) of the Act requires the Mental Health Commission to make rules providing for the use of seclusion and mechanical means of bodily restraint on a patient.[42] The *Code of Practice on the Use of Physical Restraint in Approved Centres* was operational in 2010 and it addresses the use of physical restraint, including resident dignity and safety, recording the use of physical restraint, clinical governance, and staff training.[43] Although this is mainly of relevance to mental health services, it may also be

---

International Journal of Nursing Practice 499; Julie Benbenbishty, Sheila Adam, and Ruth Endacott, 'Physical Restraint Use in Intensive Care Units Across Europe: The PRICE Study' (2010) 26(5) Intensive and Critical Care Nursing 241.

[39] Department of Health, *Towards a Restraint Free Environment in Nursing Homes* (2011, updated 12 July 2019) 6.
[40] ibid.
[41] Mental Health Act 2001, s 69.
[42] ibid s 69(2).
[43] Mental Health Commission, *Code of Practice on the Use of Physical Restraint in Approved Centres* (2009).

applicable in the context of services for older people or people with disabilities.

Restrictive procedures are addressed in the Health Act 2007 (Care and Support of Residents in Designated Centres for Persons (Children and Adults) with Disabilities) Regulations 2013, and the Health Act 2007 (Care and Welfare of Residents in Designated Centres for Older People) Regulations 2013. In general, these regulations require service providers to have written policies and procedures on the use of restraint; to ensure the use of restraint is in accordance with national policy and evidence-based practice; to use the least restrictive procedure, for the shortest duration; to consider alternative measures; to support the resident in managing challenging behaviour; and to notify HIQA of the use of restraint.

Guidance and policy documents on restraint have been published by a range of bodies in Ireland, the main policy document being the Department of Health's *Towards a Restraint-Free Environment in Nursing Homes*, published in 2011. Additional documents include:

> Health Information and Quality Authority, *Guidance for Designated Centres – Restraint Procedures* (HIQA 2016)
>
> Health Service Executive, *Policy on the Use of Physical Restraints in Designated Residential Care Units for Older People* (HSE 2011)
>
> Irish Nurses Organisation, *Guidelines on the Use of Restraint in the Care of the Older Person* (INO 2003)

The overarching framework is provided by the Irish Constitution and the ECHR. The Supreme Court has recognised a right to bodily integrity as an unenumerated right under Article 40 of the Constitution.[44] Article 3 of the ECHR provides: 'No one shall be subjected to torture or to inhuman or degrading treatment or punishment.'[45] Based on both the Constitution and the ECHR, the Department of Health outlined the following principles for restraint:

> 1. Use of restraint on another person is, on its face, an interference with the person's constitutional right to bodily integrity/personal liberty.

---

[44] *Ryan v Attorney General* [1965] IR 294.
[45] European Convention on Human Rights, Art 3.

2. Interference with a person's right to bodily integrity/personal liberty may be permissible, if necessary to protect another constitutionally related right.

3. The extent of the restraint used must be proportionate to the risk of harm or injury.

4. From a European Convention on Human Rights perspective, in the absence of detention in a criminal or similar context, the use of restraint (physical or chemical) can only be justified if it is a medical or therapeutic necessity. The standard of proof required to establish this is high.

5. The use of restraint beyond what is necessary to meet this purpose may be found to be inhuman and degrading treatment of a resident and constitute a violation of the resident's human rights under Article 3 of the European Convention on Human Rights.[46]

These principles underline the importance of adhering to defined policy and procedures. Yet it would seem that this does not always occur in practice. In research by Drennan et al, 8.5 per cent of respondents had observed the restraining of a resident beyond what was needed on one or more occasions, and 2.4 per cent of respondents indicated that they had committed such an act on one or more occasions.[47] Such behaviour represents a violation of an individual's human rights and dignity. The use of restraint should be a measure of last resort where there is an imminent risk of serious harm. It is not a long-term measure and should always be in the least restrictive form and used for the least amount of time necessary.[48]

9.2 Autonomy and Medical Treatment

The concept of patient autonomy and decision-making was set out in chapter 5. This involved discussion of informed consent, the right to refuse treatment, and demands for medical treatment. Through this discussion, the basis for autonomy in common

---

[46] Department of Health, *Towards a Restraint-Free Environment in Nursing Homes* (2011, updated July 2019) 4.
[47] Jonathan Drennan and others, *Older People in Residential Care Settings: Results of a National Survey of Staff-Resident Interactions and Conflicts* (NCPOP/UCD 2012).
[48] Department of Health, *Towards a Restraint-Free Environment in Nursing Homes* (2011, updated July 2019) 2.

law, constitutional provisions, the ECHR, and the Charter of Fundamental Rights was set out. The cases discussed in chapter 5 largely concentrated on an individual's right to refuse treatment as illustrated by *Re a Ward of Court*,[49] *JM v The Board of Management of St Vincent's Hospital*,[50] and *Fitzpatrick v FK*.[51] The discussion did not directly address circumstances in which a person lacks capacity and a decision about treatment withdrawal is to be made. The treatment decision may range from the relatively minor to more serious decisions about the withdrawal of life-sustaining treatment. Although it is rare that such matters come before the courts in Ireland, this is not to suggest that these decisions do not occur on a more regular basis in practice.

9.2.1 The Withdrawal of Medical Treatment

The withdrawal of treatment was at issue *In re a Ward of Court*, *PP v HSE*[52] and *In re SR*.[53] In this section, reference will also be made to the withholding of medical treatment as was considered in *Health Service Executive v JM A Ward of Court*.[54] The first case to address the withdrawal of treatment was *Re a Ward of Court*, the facts of which were set out in chapter 5. Both the High Court and the Supreme Court accepted that artificial nutrition and hydration could be withdrawn. Statements were subsequently issued by the Irish Medical Council and An Bord Altranais.[55] An Bord Altranais reaffirmed the Code of Professional Conduct, since updated, and stated: 'In this specific case, a nurse may not participate in the withdrawal and termination of the means of nutrition and hydration by tube. In the event of the withdrawal and termination of the means of nutrition and hydration by tube the nurse's role will be to provide all nursing care.'[56] Despite this statement, nurses tend to have a greater role in these decisions and this will be formalised to some extent by the commencement of the Assisted Decision-Making (Capacity) Act 2015. Current NMBI guidance states that: 'In end-of-life care, you should support the person to

---

[49] *In Re a Ward of Court* [1996] 2 IR 79.
[50] *JM v The Board of Management of St Vincent's Hospital* [2003] 1 IR 321.
[51] *Fitzpatrick v FK* [2008] IEHC 104.
[52] *PP v HSE* [2014] IEHC 622.
[53] *SR (a Minor and a Ward of Court): An Irish Hospital v RH and J McG* [2012] 1 IR 305.
[54] *Health Service Executive v JM A Ward of Court* [2017] IEHC 399.
[55] 'Statements of the Medical Council and An Bord Altranais on the Ward Case' (1995) 1(2) Medico-Legal Journal of Ireland 60.
[56] ibid.

die with dignity and comfort.'[57] For patients lacking capacity, the Code recommends that nurses should:

- take into account the person's previous directions and wishes, if known;
- discuss the case with appropriate family members, carers or guardian;
- discuss the case with other members of the healthcare team;
- take into account (if possible) the expressed views of the person who lacks capacity in making a treatment or care decision. (Standards of Conduct 4 and 5 in Principle 4 – Trust and Confidentiality – discussing personal information – are linked with this standard.)[58]

Re a Ward of Court

As noted in chapter 5, the woman at the centre of this case was described as being in a near-persistent vegetative state and had no prospect of recovery. The woman was made a ward of court and an application was made by the family for the withdrawal of life support consisting of medication as well as artificial nutrition and hydration. In the High Court, Lynch J held that artificial nutrition and hydration could be withdrawn from the ward. In arriving at this decision, Lynch J stated, 'The Court should approach the matter from the standpoint of a prudent, good and loving parent in deciding what course should be adopted.'[59] Lynch J also described the best interests of the ward as the 'acid test' but suggested that the Court could take account of the ward's wishes if she had 'a momentary lucid and articulate period in which to express them'.[60] Lynch J's decision was appealed to the Supreme Court, which upheld the High Court's decision by a 4:1 majority.

The majority judgments in the Supreme Court were grounded in an assessment of the best interests of the ward but there was no one single approach adopted. Hamilton CJ was satisfied by the approach adopted by Lynch J in assessing the best interests of the ward and noted:

---

[57] Nursing and Midwifery Board of Ireland, *Code of Professional Conduct and Ethics for Registered Nurses and Registered Midwives* (NMBI 2014) 12.
[58] ibid 13.
[59] *Re a Ward of Court* [1996] 2 IR 79, 99.
[60] ibid 98.

He had regard to the condition of the ward, to the fact that the treatment was intrusive and burdensome and of no curative effect, to the fact that the ward had only minimal cognitive function, had been in that condition for twenty-three years, to the wishes of the mother and other members of the family, to the medical evidence and to the submissions by all the parties to the proceedings.[61]

Denham J adopted a broad approach to the assessment of best interests and indicated that the 'totality of the ward's situation must be considered'.[62] Factors addressed in the body of Denham J's judgment included:

1. The ward's current condition.

2. The current medical treatment and care of the ward.

3. The degree of bodily invasion of the ward the medical treatment requires.

4. The legal and constitutional process to be carried through in order that medical treatment be given and received.

5. The ward's life history, including whether there has been adequate time to achieve an accurate diagnosis.

6. The prognosis on medical treatment.

7. Any previous views that were expressed by the ward that are relevant, and proved as a matter of fact on the balance of probabilities.

8. The family's view.

9. The medical opinions.

10. The view of any relevant carer.

11. The ward's constitutional right to –

    (a) Life; (b) Privacy; (c) Bodily integrity; (d) Autonomy; (e) Dignity in life; (f) Dignity in death.

---

[61] ibid 128.
[62] ibid 166.

12. The constitutional requirement that the ward's life be (a) respected, (b) vindicated, and (c) protected.

13. The constitutional requirement that life be protected for the common good. The case commences with a constitutional presumption that the ward's life be protected.

14. The burden of proof is on the applicants to establish their application on the balance of probabilities, taking into consideration that this Court will not draw its conclusions lightly or without due regard to all the relevant circumstances.[63]

The condition of the woman was described as a near-persistent vegetative state. Since this decision, our understanding of disorders of consciousness has become more nuanced. The minimally conscious state (MCS) is the most recently identified disorder of consciousness and is defined as 'a condition of severely altered consciousness in which minimal but definite behavioural evidence of self or environmental awareness is demonstrated'.[64] Lombard described the situation as follows:

The MCS is not a single level of minimal consciousness but encompasses a broad spectrum of consciousness ranging from borderline vegetative state to higher levels of consciousness and sensory awareness. An accurate assessment of the level of consciousness is particularly difficult. Accordingly, it is not always clear when treatment may result in a positive outcome and, in turn, this makes an assessment of medical futility and the application of the decision-making framework especially challenging.[65]

This challenge was apparent in early MCS cases that came before the courts in England. In Ireland, the question of withholding treatment from a person diagnosed as being in an MCS state arose in *Health Service Executive v JM A Ward of Court*.

---

[63] ibid 167.
[64] Joseph T Giacino and others, 'The Minimally Conscious State: Definition and Diagnostic Criteria' (2002) 58(3) Neurology 349, 350–51; Royal College of Physicians, 'Prolonged Disorders of Consciousness: National Clinical Guidelines' (2013); Mélanie Boly and others, 'Perception of Pain in the Minimally Conscious State with PET Activation: An Observational Study' (2008) 7(11) The Lancet Neurology 1013.
[65] John Lombard, 'Navigating the Decision-Making Framework for Patients in a Minimally Conscious State' (2016) 22(2) Medico-Legal Journal of Ireland 78, 78.

Health Service Executive v JM A Ward of Court

In *JM* the Court was asked to consent to the withholding of an increase in ventilator support in the event of respiratory deterioration of a patient who was in an MCS and unable to give his consent. Furthermore, in the case of a clinical deterioration, authority was sought to withhold CPR and other therapies identified. As the man's parents would not consent, the applicant deemed it necessary to seek the consent of the Court. Kelly P described this as 'the equivalent of asking the court to give what is commonly called a "do not attempt resuscitation" (DNAR) or "do not attempt cardio-pulmonary resuscitation" (DNACPR) direction'.[66]

In determining the test to be applied, Kelly P cited *Re a Ward of Court*, Lord Goff in *Airedale NHS Trust v Bland*, and the comments of Baroness Hale in *Aintree University Hospital's NHS Foundation Trust v James*. Baroness Hale stated:

> The question is not whether it is in the best interests of the patient that he should die. The question is whether it is in the best interests of the patient that his life should be prolonged by the continuation of this form of treatment ...
>
> Hence, the focus is on whether it is in the patient's best interests to give treatment, rather than whether it is in his best interests to withhold or withdraw it. If the treatment is not in his best interests, the court will not be able to give its consent on his behalf and it will follow that it will be lawful to withhold or withdraw it. Indeed, it will follow that it will not be lawful to give it. It also follows that (provided of course that they have acted reasonably and without negligence) the clinical team will not be in breach of any duty towards the patient if they withhold or withdraw it.[67]

It follows that the assessment is framed by the patient's best interests. On the standard of proof, Kelly P ultimately favoured an approach based on evidence that is clear and convincing. The assessment was to be informed by the fourteen factors identified by Denham J (see previous). Kelly P also cited the shorter, non-exhaustive list of considerations outlined by Kearns P in *Re SR (A Ward of Court)*. In addition, the Court could also take account of relevant clinical or ethical guidelines as well as any previous

---

[66] *Health Service Executive v JM A Ward of Court* [2017] IEHC 399, [84].
[67] *Aintree University Hospital's NHS Foundation Trust v James* [2013] UKSC 67, [21]–[22].

views expressed by the person. Kelly P granted the desired relief to the applicant. At a minimum it demonstrates that treatment can be withheld from a patient in an MCS state and this will be guided by a best-interests assessment. It is, however, unlikely that this would be the final case on this matter and further applications may well come before the courts in the future.

Re SR (A Ward of Court)

Hospital authorities in the case of *SR* sought a declaration that would permit the non-resuscitation of a six-year-old boy were he to experience an acute deterioration requiring invasive treatment.[68] The boy was a ward of court and had suffered a near drowning accident when he was just under two years old. The accident resulted in a cardiac arrest and extensive, irreversible brain damage. The child also developed severe spastic quadriplegic cerebral palsy, was blind, incontinent, and could not communicate, although he was able to cry out at times. The child appeared to feel pain and had no prospect of recovery. His condition continued to worsen owing to respiratory tract infections and chronic lung disease. As a result, it was necessary to consider the question of resuscitation.

Kearns P indicated that once the matter is brought before the court then the decision is solely one for the court, although the judge did note that the views of the child's parents and the doctors must be taken into account in determining the correct course of action.[69] The Court recognised the presumption in favour of life-saving treatment, but this is a rebuttable presumption, which can be deviated from in exceptional circumstances. The best interests of the child were recognised as the principal consideration by the judge. In assessing the best interests, Kearns P sought to balance a range of factors such as 'the pain, suffering that the child could expect if he survives; the longevity and quality of life that the child could expect if he survives; the inherent pain and suffering involved in the proposed treatment and the views of the child's parents and doctors'.[70] Kearns P subsequently cited the comments of Lord Donaldson MR in *In re J (Wardship: Medical Treatment)*[71] that the 'proper test' is to 'ask what the ward would

---

[68] *SR (a Minor and a Ward of Court): An Irish Hospital v RH and J McG* [2012] 1 IR 305.
[69] ibid 323.
[70] ibid.
[71] *In re J (Wardship: Medical Treatment)* [1991] Fam 33.

choose if he were in a position to make a sound judgment'.[72] In applying this approach, the decision-maker is not to impose his own views regarding the quality of life the child would enjoy but is to determine the best interests of the child subjectively. The approach set out in *SR* was subsequently followed in the case of *An Irish Hospital v RF*.[73]

Assisted Decision-Making (Capacity) Act 2015

The Assisted Decision-Making (Capacity) Act 2015 is discussed in chapter 5 of this text. The term 'best interests' is not used in the Act as it provides for a principles-based approach to decision-making in circumstances where the patient lacks capacity. In this respect, s 8 of the Act outlines guiding principles, which are intended to apply before and during an intervention in respect of a relevant person. While the principles were outlined earlier in this text, it is worth highlighting the role of the nurse and allied health professionals. The regular close contact a nurse may have with a patient means that their input is valuable in shaping the nature of the intervention. Section 8(8) of the ADMC Act 2015 sets out:

> The intervener, in making an intervention in respect of a relevant person, may consider the views of –
>
> (a) any person engaged in caring for the relevant person,
>
> (b) any person who has a bona fide interest in the welfare of the relevant person, or
>
> (c) healthcare professionals.[74]

Consultation with these persons is not mandatory and the subject of the consultation is not specifically stated. Donnelly suggests that the focus may be placed on the will and preferences/beliefs and values of the relevant person but notes that 'it would have been preferable if this had been clearly stated'.[75] Further guidance on the interpretation of this legislation is likely to be drafted in the near future.

---

[72] *SR (a Minor and a Ward of Court): An Irish Hospital v RH and J McG* [2012] 1 IR 305, 323.
[73] *An Irish Hospital v RF* [2015] 2 IR 377.
[74] Assisted Decision-Making (Capacity) Act 2015, s 8(8).
[75] Mary Donnelly, 'The Assisted Decision-Making (Capacity) Act 2015: Implications for Healthcare Decision-Making' (2016) 22(2) Medico-Legal Journal of Ireland 65, 71.

9.3 The Provision of Palliative Care

Palliative care has expanded in recent years and has moved from the margins to a more central role in healthcare. It raises a mix of legal and ethical issues, which are not solely of relevance to nurses who pursued a specialism in palliative care. Palliative care is provided at different levels and in a range of settings, including hospices, hospitals, long-term care facilities, and in a person's own home. Issues such as healthcare decision-making, patient autonomy, the withholding and withdrawal of treatment, and patient confidentiality are all applicable to palliative care provision but are addressed in separate sections within this work. This section will, however, touch on human rights and will address pain management in palliative care and some of the challenges that can arise.

Multiple definitions of palliative care have been advanced over the years. Lombard suggested that these 'definitions have evolved in line with clinical developments but also reflect a practice that is attempting to negotiate and characterise its role in the care of the patient'.[76] A commonly cited definition of palliative care is that proposed by the World Health Organization (WHO). The WHO define palliative care as:

> ... an approach that improves the quality of life of patients and their families facing the problems associated with life-threatening illness, through the prevention and relief of suffering by means of early identification and impeccable assessment and treatment of pain and other problems, physical, psychosocial and spiritual. Palliative care:
>
> - provides relief from pain and other distressing symptoms;
> - affirms life and regards dying as a normal process;
> - integrates the psychological and spiritual aspects of patient care;
> - offers a support system to help patients live as actively as possible until death;
> - offers a support system to help the family cope during the patient's illness and in their own bereavement;
> - uses a team approach to address the needs of patients and their families, including bereavement counselling, if indicated;

---

[76] John Lombard, *Law, Palliative Care and Dying* (Routledge 2018) 4.

- will enhance quality of life, and may also positively influence the course of illness;
- is applicable early in the course of illness, in conjunction with other therapies that are intended to prolong life, such as chemotherapy or radiation therapy, and includes those investigations needed to better understand and manage distressing clinical complications.[77]

This definition indicates that palliative care is not to be limited to the end stages of an illness. The principles underpinning palliative care can be applied at an early stage in a disease trajectory. It follows that there are different levels of palliative care: namely, the palliative care approach, general palliative care, and specialist palliative care. It is specialist palliative care that is most closely associated with issues of pain management and the boundaries of palliative care. Dixon et al described it as follows:

> Specialist palliative care is provided by multi-disciplinary teams that can include consultants in palliative medicine, nurse specialists, specialist social workers and experts in psychological care. Such staff are specifically trained to provide, and advise on, symptom control and pain relief and other forms of psycho-social and spiritual support.[78]

9.3.1 Pain Management

The understanding of pain experienced at the end of life has developed considerably in recent decades. It is often multi-dimensional and may include a range of suffering that requires a careful response on the part of the nurse. As such, medication may not always be the appropriate response. For instance, questions have arisen about the appropriateness of using palliative sedation for patients who are experiencing forms of existential distress near the end of life.[79] Nonetheless, in cases where the patient

---

[77] World Health Organization, 'WHO Definition of Palliative Care' <http://www.who.int/cancer/palliative/definition/en/> accessed 30 June 2020; Cecilia Sepúlveda and others, 'Palliative Care: The World Health Organization's Global Perspective' (2002) 24(2) Journal of Pain and Symptom Management 91, 94.
[78] Josie Dixon and others, *Equity in the Provision of Palliative Care in the UK: Review of Evidence* (London School of Economics 2015) 16.
[79] Tatsuya Morita and others, 'Terminal Sedation for Existential Distress' (2000) 17 American Journal of Hospice Palliative Care 189; Paul Rousseau, 'Existential Suffering and Palliative Sedation: A Brief Commentary with a Proposal for Clinical Guidelines' (2001) 18 American Journal of Hospice Palliative Care 151.

is experiencing refractory symptoms it may be necessary to administer a high level of sedative drug.

Palliative sedation has been defined by the European Association for Palliative Care as:

> the monitored use of medications intended to induce a state of decreased or absent awareness (unconsciousness) in order to relieve the burden of otherwise intractable suffering, in a manner that is ethically acceptable to the patient, family and health-care providers.[80]

Palliative sedation is a broad concept and may refer to mild sedation, respite sedation or deep sedation.[81] It is deep sedation that is most controversial. In particular, a tension exists between palliative sedation and euthanasia. This tension stems from the suggestion that palliative sedation effectively ends a person's biographical life and could potentially hasten their death. The drugs used for sedation have changed over the years and literature reviews have indicated that appropriate use and administration of sedation is not associated with the shortening of life.[82] Nonetheless, the suggestion that palliative sedation is a form of 'slow euthanasia' persists.[83] The doctrine of double effect may therefore be called upon as an ethical justification for the administration of palliative sedation.

The Doctrine of Double Effect

The doctrine of double effect can be traced back to Thomas Aquinas in his discussion on self-defence.[84] Aquinas set out:

---

[80] Nathan I Cherny, Lukas Radbruch and The Board of the European Association for Palliative Care, 'European Association for Palliative Care (EAPC) Recommended Framework for the Use of Sedation in Palliative Care' (2009) 23(7) Palliative Medicine 581.

[81] Alexander de Graeff and Mervyn Dean, 'Palliative Sedation Therapy in the Last Weeks in Life: A Literature Review and Recommendations for Standards' (2007) 10 Journal of Palliative Medicine 67, 73–74.

[82] Nigel Sykes and Andrew Thorns, 'The Use of Opioids and Sedatives at the End of Life' (2003) 4 The Lancet Oncology 312, 312; Marco Maltoni and others, 'Palliative Sedation Therapy Does Not Hasten Death: Results from a Prospective Multicenter Study' (2009) 20 Annals of Oncology 1163.

[83] J Andrew Billings and Susan Block, 'Slow Euthanasia' (1996) 12 Journal of Palliative Care 21.

[84] Thomas Aquinas, *Summa Theologica* (Fathers of the English Dominican Province tr, Benziger Brothers 1947) II–II, Qu 64, Art 7; See also Joseph T Mangan, 'An Historical Analysis of the Principle of Double Effect' (1945) Theological Studies 41.

> Nothing hinders one act from having two effects, only one of which is intended, while the other is beside the intention. ... Accordingly, the act of self-defence may have two effects: one, the saving of one's life; the other, the slaying of the aggressor.[85]

Acts such as this can be justified in circumstances where there is an element of proportionality. To rely on the doctrine of double effect, it is necessary that all relevant criteria are satisfied. The criteria for double effect can be described as follows:

> 1. The act must be morally good, or, at a minimum, it should be neutral.
>
> 2. The bad effect should not be the means through which the good effect is achieved.
>
> 3. The bad effect is foreseen and tolerated whereas it is the good effect which is directly intended.
>
> 4. The reasons for carrying out the good act must exceed the unintended bad effect.[86]

There can be a considerable subjective element in the application of these criteria as their application is shaped by the overarching framework being applied. Moreover, palliative sedation is a challenging practice for the application of the doctrine. It is complicated by the patient's condition, the intention of healthcare professionals, the availability of resources for pain management, and a range of additional physiological and pharmacological factors. Lombard has argued that the criteria can be satisfied where the perceived bad effect is the hastening of death.[87]

In short, the act of pain relief can be interpreted as being morally good, thereby satisfying the first criterion. As for the second criterion, the death of the patient is not how the beneficial outcome is achieved. However, the reduction of consciousness is a fundamental element of palliative sedation and it can be difficult to describe this as an unintended side-effect. The third

---

[85] ibid 1471.
[86] John Lombard, 'Sedation of the Terminally Ill Patient: The Role of the Doctrine of Double Effect' (2015) 21(1) Medico-Legal Journal of Ireland 22, 24.
[87] John Lombard, *Law, Palliative Care and Dying* (Routledge 2018) 57. Note that the value of the doctrine is somewhat limited where the perceived harm is the reduction in consciousness.

criterion requires that it is the good effect that is directly intended, whereas the bad effect is foreseen and tolerated. Intention may often be ambiguous, but it need not be assessed in a vacuum. This would involve the examination of patient charts, consideration of surrounding circumstances, and engagement with the multidisciplinary team. The fourth and final criterion is based on proportionality. Lombard commented as follows:

> The administration of palliative sedation is unlikely to be the first sedative administered to the patient. The control of pain will have progressed through several stages, will have gradually increased over time, and may have been informed through use of sedation scales. On this basis, the careful titration of the sedative drug until there is adequate relief from the refractory symptoms could be considered proportionate.[88]

The doctrine of double effect may serve as a form of ethical shorthand when confronted with a complex ethical dilemma, but it is somewhat precarious owing to the range of possible interpretations. In any case, palliative sedation can be provided in this jurisdiction and it is likely that a prosecution would only occur where there was a clear intention on the part of the healthcare professional to end the life of the patient.

A Requirement to Provide Appropriate Palliative Care

A failure to provide appropriate palliative care may breach professional standards and could result in a violation of a patient's human rights. Under 'Respect for the dignity of the person', the NMBI's *Code of Professional Conduct and Ethics* sets out, 'In end-of-life care, you should support the person to die with dignity and comfort.'[89] Palliative care is addressed by the HIQA in the *National Standards for Residential Care Settings for Older People in Ireland*. Standard 2.4 stipulates, 'Each resident receives palliative care based on their assessed needs, which maintains and enhances their quality of life and respects their dignity.'[90] The related features address the philosophy of care, referrals to specialist palliative care, the inclusion of palliative care in care plans, and staff training.

---

[88] ibid 66.
[89] Nursing and Midwifery Board of Ireland, *Code of Professional Conduct and Ethics for Registered Nurses and Registered Midwives* (NMBI 2014) 12.
[90] Health Information and Quality Authority, *National Standards for Residential Care Settings for Older People in Ireland* (HIQA 2016) 13.

Palliative care engages a range of rights, including autonomy, bodily integrity, and protection from inhuman or degrading treatment. In relation to the latter, laws on opioid availability, the access to medical care at the end-of-life, and inadequate prescribing guidelines could result in the engagement of this right. Protection from inhuman and degrading treatment is provided for under the ECHR,[91] the Charter of Fundamental Rights,[92] the Universal Declaration of Human Rights, and as an unenumerated right in the Irish Constitution.[93] A violation of Article 3 ECHR can arise due to a naturally occurring illness as in *D v United Kingdom*.[94] This decision demonstrates that the potential of being denied appropriate medical care was sufficient to engage Article 3. *L v Lithuania* summarised this position as follows: 'if the source is a naturally occurring illness, the treatment for which could involve the responsibility of the State but is not forthcoming or is patently inadequate, an issue may arise under this provision'.[95]

The link between palliative care and the protection from inhuman or degrading treatment has been highlighted outside of the ECHR. The United Nations Special Rapporteur (SR) on Torture and other Cruel, Inhuman or Degrading Treatment or Punishment, Professor Nowak, stated that 'the de facto denial of access to pain relief, if it causes severe pain and suffering, constitutes cruel, inhuman or degrading treatment or punishment',[96] and 'all measures should be taken to ensure full access and to overcome current regulatory, educational and attitudinal obstacles to ensure full access to palliative care'.[97] Furthermore, the SR on the Right to Health and the SR on Torture wrote a joint letter to the Chairperson of the Commission on Narcotic Drugs in December 2008 in which it was stated: 'The failure to ensure access to controlled medicines for the relief of pain and suffering threatens fundamental rights to health and to protection against cruel inhuman and degrading

---

[91] European Convention on Human Rights, Art 3.
[92] Charter of Fundamental Rights of the European Union, Art 4: 'No one shall be subjected to torture or to inhuman or degrading treatment or punishment.'
[93] *State (C) v Frawley* [1976] 1 IR 365.
[94] *D v United Kingdom* (1997) 24 EHRR 423; application of Art 3 to medical treatment first recognised in *X v Denmark* (1992) 15 EHRR 437. See also *Keenan v United Kingdom* (2001) EHRR 913; *Bensaid v United Kingdom* (2001) ECHR 82.
[95] *L v Lithuania* App no 27527/03 (ECtHR, 11 September 2007) [46].
[96] Report of the Special Rapporteur on Torture and other Cruel, Inhuman or Degrading Treatment or Punishment; Manfred Nowak, 'Promotion and Protection of all Human Rights, Civil, Political, Economic, Social and Cultural Rights, including the Right to Development' A/HRC/10/44 (14 January 2009) 23.
[97] ibid.

treatment.'[98] There is a high threshold for relying on this right and it would effectively require an abdication of responsibility on the part of healthcare professionals. Nonetheless, it underlines the human rights dimension of palliative care and illustrates the importance of monitoring the condition of the patient and ensuring that appropriate palliative care is available.

9.4 Euthanasia and Assisted Suicide

The term euthanasia stems from the Greek *eu thanatos*, which means 'good or easy death'.[99] Euthanasia is often referred to in a generic manner, which may not accurately reflect the specific practice being discussed. In particular, it is important to distinguish between euthanasia and physician-assisted suicide as these terms are often confused. *Black's Medical Dictionary* defines euthanasia as 'a deliberate act or omission whose primary intention is to end another person's life'.[100] This is a broad definition and captures many forms of euthanasia. In most cases euthanasia can be understood as referring to a situation where a doctor acts to bring about the death of a person and is acting on a clear request from that person. In contrast, physician-assisted suicide occurs where a doctor intentionally assists a person to end their own life; it may involve the provision of drugs for self-administration and is based on the person's voluntary and competent request. In recent years, the laws prohibiting euthanasia and assisted suicide have been the subject of challenge in several jurisdictions. This has resulted in greater liberalisation of the law surrounding physician-assisted suicide. However, the practices of euthanasia and physician-assisted suicide remain illegal in this jurisdiction.

A healthcare professional who performs euthanasia on a patient will have committed an offence and may be prosecuted for murder. The elements of a murder charge include the *actus reus* and *mens rea*. The *actus reus* refers to the conduct of the defendant and what they did or failed to do in the circumstances. As noted in chapter 4, an omission may be punishable where there is a legal duty to act. In addition to the act, it must be shown that the person had

---

[98] Letter from Manfred Nowak, Special Rapporteur on Torture, and Anand Grover, Special Rapporteur on the Right to the Highest Attainable Standard of Health, to Her Excellency Ms Selma Ashipala-Musavyi, Chairperson of the 52nd Session of the Commission on Narcotic Drugs, Ref G/SO 214 (53–21) (10 December 2008) 4.
[99] Margaret Otlowski, *Voluntary Euthanasia and the Common Law* (Oxford University Press 1997) 4.
[100] Harvey Marcovitch (ed), *Black's Medical Dictionary* (41st edn, A & C Black Publishers 2005) 252.

the requisite intention, referred to as *mens rea*. This is the mental element of a crime and it may be a specific intention to end the life of another person. This mental element for a charge of murder is set out by s 4 of the Criminal Justice Act 1964:

> 1. Where a person kills another unlawfully the killing shall not be murder unless the accused person intended to kill, or cause serious injury to, some person, whether the person actually killed or not.

> 2. The accused person shall be presumed to have intended the natural and probable consequences of his conduct; but this presumption may be rebutted.[101]

In the absence of a clear statement, intention is to be ascertained by considering a person's actions as well as the surrounding circumstances. This may involve 'consideration of the patient's medical history, notes made on the patient's chart, or conversations with other healthcare professionals regarding the treatment and care of a patient'.[102]

Suicide is no longer a crime in this jurisdiction, but it is an offence to assist another person in committing suicide.[103] Section 2(2) of the Criminal Law (Suicide) Act 1993 provides that:

> A person who aids, abets, counsels or procures the suicide of another, or an attempt by another to commit suicide, shall be guilty of an offence and shall be liable on conviction on indictment to imprisonment for a term not exceeding fourteen years.

The wording of s 2(2) demonstrates that no actual suicide or attempted suicide is necessary for an offence to be committed. Furthermore, no proceedings will be brought except by or with the consent of the Director of Public Prosecutions. This provision faced greater scrutiny in recent years and was challenged in the case of *Fleming v Ireland*.

Fleming v Ireland

Marie Fleming, the plaintiff, brought a challenge against the prohibition on assisted suicide in Ireland. At the time of the High

---

[101] Criminal Justice Act 1964, s 4.
[102] John Lombard, *Law, Palliative Care and Dying* (Routledge 2018) 56.
[103] Criminal Law (Suicide) Act 1993, s 2(1).

Court challenge, Marie Fleming was 59 years old and had suffered from multiple sclerosis since the age of 35. She was unable to walk or to use her lower or upper limbs. She was confined to a wheelchair and was described as requiring 'assistance with all aspects of her daily living'.[104] She was able to communicate but this was becoming increasingly difficult. Furthermore, she had experienced choking episodes, which were exhausting and distressing. She also suffered from significant and frequent pain, which was intense and sometimes almost unbearable. The disease had not impaired her cognitive functions and she had no underlying mental illness that affected her decision-making capacity.

In the High Court, the plaintiff sought orders declaring that s 2(2) of the Criminal Law (Suicide) Act 1993 was invalid as it was incompatible with the Irish Constitution, as well as the ECHR. Alternatively, Ms Fleming sought an order directing the DPP to publish guidelines as to the different prosecution considerations when dealing with a person who had assisted another in committing suicide. Her action was unsuccessful in both the High Court and Supreme Court.

The High Court case was heard by three judges. This is referred to as a divisional High Court. The Court recognised that her decision to seek the assistance of others to take active steps to end her own life was in principle engaged by the right to personal autonomy. Yet, the Court recognised 'powerful countervailing considerations', which justified the Oireachtas in enacting legislation such as the 1993 Act for the purpose of making the assistance of suicide a criminal offence.[105] The Court was mindful of their role and suggested that it may be possible for the Oireachtas to identify a solution that would allow for the liberalisation of the law while ensuring effective safeguards were implemented.

Ms Fleming argued that the law effectively discriminated against her as her disability meant that she was prevented from taking her own life. The Court accepted that Article 40.1 was engaged but was of the opinion that such treatment is 'amply justified by the range of factors bearing on the necessity to safeguard the lives of others'.[106] The Court also emphasised the profound distinction between the law permitting an adult to take their own life on the one hand and sanctioning another to assist that person to that end

---

[104] *Fleming v Ireland* [2013] IESC 19, [59].
[105] ibid 2, [53].
[106] ibid 2, [122].

on the other. As for the claim under the ECHR, the Court rejected the claim to a declaration of incompatibility.

The final argument rested on the issuance of guidelines by the Director of Public Prosecutions. Such guidelines had been issued in England and Wales after the House of Lords decision in *R(Purdy) v DPP*.[107] These guidelines provided some modicum of clarity on the points that would be considered in determining whether a prosecution for assisting in a suicide was warranted. However, the High Court considered the issuance of such guidelines to be impermissible under Irish law. The Court determined that it would amount to forcing the DPP into adopting a role that would in effect override statutory measures laid down by the Oireachtas. The claim for DPP guidelines on assisted suicide was dropped on appeal to the Supreme Court.

The appeal was heard by seven Supreme Court judges and a single judgment was delivered. It was noted that while suicide has ceased to be a crime this does not mean that a constitutional right has been established. Such a right would have to be found as part of an expressed right or in an unenumerated right. The Court concluded that 'there is no constitutional right which the State, including the courts, must protect and vindicate, either to commit suicide, or to arrange for the termination of one's life at a time of one's choosing'.[108] It follows that no disability discrimination consideration arose. In relation to the arguments grounded on the ECHR, the Court drew on cases such as *Pretty v United Kingdom* where the ECtHR held that it was for the Member States to assess the likely consequences of a relaxation of assisted suicide legislation with the introduction of exceptions. The issue had therefore been determined in Ireland with the passage of the Criminal Law (Suicide) Act 1993. Accordingly, the appeal for a declaration of incompatibility failed.

Prosecution of Gail O'Rorke

The first prosecution under s 2(2) of the Criminal Law (Suicide) Act 1993 did not occur until 2015. Gail O'Rorke was prosecuted for attempting to assist in the suicide of her friend, Bernadette Forde. There were three charges of helping to procure the suicide of Ms Forde. These involved assisting in making funeral arrangements prior to her death, the ordering of barbiturates, and attempting to organise travel to Dignitas in Zurich.

---

[107] *R(Purdy) v DPP* [2009] UKHL 45.
[108] *Fleming v Ireland* [2013] IESC 19, [114].

The plan to travel to Dignitas was not proceeded with as gardaí intervened and informed Ms O'Rorke that it was an offence to assist in a suicide. Ms Forde subsequently purchased pentobarbital from Mexico. At the request of Ms Forde, Gail O'Rorke organised a money transfer but did not know until later that this payment was for the pentobarbital. McCartan J ordered the jury to acquit Ms O'Rorke of ordering the barbiturates and directed the jury to find Ms O'Rorke not guilty of procuring Ms Forde's suicide by helping to organise her funeral. The jury deliberated for seven hours on the third charge before acquitting Ms O'Rorke.

9.4.1 Responding to a Request for Euthanasia or Assistance in Suicide

It is unlikely that *Fleming v Ireland* represents the last challenge to the prohibition on assisted suicide in Ireland. The topics of euthanasia and assisted suicide are perennial topics for student dissertations, journal articles and, significantly, social debate. Regardless of the legal status, patients may still ask a nurse or other healthcare professional for assistance in hastening their death. While this may place the nurse in a difficult personal situation, the legal position is clear. A nurse may not assist a person in committing suicide, and to do so would result in criminal and professional sanctions. When faced with such a request, nurses are expected to act in an ethically and legally sound manner.

The Royal College of Nursing (RCN) has published guidance on this issue that may prove helpful for nurses in Ireland.[109] The RCN group their recommendations under three headings: stop and think; approach; and reflect and discuss. Under 'stop and think' it is set out:

> A request for assisted suicide should prompt a discussion to draw out the reasoning behind the request through a non-judgemental assessment of needs. This may help uncover previously unrecognised or unmet needs, enabling the ongoing care planning to evolve as the patient's needs become clearer or change.[110]

---

[109] Royal College of Nursing, *When Someone Asks for Your Assistance to Die: RCN Guidance on Responding to a Request to Hasten Death* (2nd edn, RCN 2016).
[110] ibid 13.

This is an important point and is grounded in good open communication with the patient. As noted earlier in this chapter, there are many forms of pain that can arise at the end of life and these can be best treated when healthcare professionals have a clear picture of the patient's experience. In this respect it is to be remembered that pain is an inherently subjective experience.

'Approach' outlines twelve suggested actions that are based on existing best practice or available evidence. Examples of these actions include:

- Listen very carefully to what is being said (and what is not said).
- If the patient is asking specifically for your help with assisted suicide it is essential that you acknowledge the request and resist the inclination to 'ignore' or abandon the conversation.
- Your tone of voice is important as it can denote seriousness, compassion and caring.
- As part of this process you can offer to arrange support or expert help for the patient so they may explore further their fears or concerns or expectations, and their understanding of their diagnosis, disease, or impact of multiple conditions.
- Acknowledge the patient's feelings and concerns regarding their illness, and gently probe for more details about their perceptions of their illness, prognosis, death and dying.
- You should ensure you document all conversations, and share any insights with colleagues and other members of the multidisciplinary team.

The third and final point of guidance is 'reflect and discuss'. This recognises that these discussions raise a host of challenging questions. This is not just confined to ethical and legal issues but also raise strong emotions. Although nurses provide care for patients it is essential that they also look after their own emotional wellbeing. The guidance recommends assistance in identifying support networks or clinical supervision that can help the nurse deal with addressing such feelings.

There are of course differences in the legal framework between Ireland and England and Wales. Nonetheless, the RCN guidance may be a valuable tool for nurses in this jurisdiction. In addition to responding to a direct request to hasten death from a patient, it also outlines the response to receiving a direct request from a patient's family or carer.

9.5 Do Not Attempt Resuscitation Orders

The COVID-19 pandemic placed a spotlight on the decision-making process surrounding DNAR orders. There was concern about the manner in which DNARs were being utilised. In particular, it was feared that patients were often being excluded from these conversations. As should be clear from this text, patient involvement in healthcare decision-making is essential and cannot be bypassed simply because it will result in uncomfortable or emotionally painful discussions.

A DNAR order is a written directive, which states that there should be no attempt to perform cardiopulmonary resuscitation on a patient. The provision of CPR may be viewed as futile and may not be in the best interests of the patient. The decision is normally led by a senior healthcare professional, however, there may be disparity across healthcare facilities. Decisions about DNAR orders are largely framed by policy developed and implemented at a local level. In 2009, the Association of Anaesthetists of Great Britain and Ireland published a guidance document on DNACPR in the perioperative period.[111] More recently, updated guidance has been included as part of the HSE's *National Consent Policy*.[112] This guidance will be set out along with case law from England and Wales, and Ireland.

R (on the application of Tracey) v Cambridge University Hospitals NHS Foundation Trust

Janet Tracey was 63 years old and had metastatic lung cancer with a prognosis of nine months. She was involved in a road traffic accident and was made the subject of a DNACPR order shortly after admission to the hospital. This order was not discussed with Mrs Tracey and was removed after her family became aware of it and objected to it. Subsequently, and after discussions with the family, a second DNACPR notice was imposed. Mrs Tracey died without attempted CPR.

---

[111] Association of Anaesthetists of Great Britain and Ireland, *Do Not Attempt Resuscitation (DNAR) Decisions in the Perioperative Period* (2009).
[112] Health Service Executive, *National Consent Policy* (HSE 2019).

Her family brought a claim against Cambridge University Hospitals NHS Foundation Trust for a breach of Mrs Tracey's rights under Article 8 ECHR. Moreover, a claim was brought against the Secretary of State for a breach of Mrs Tracey's Article 8 rights by failing to publish appropriate national guidance. The claim against the Secretary of State was dismissed on the basis that it would represent an unjustified intrusion into healthcare policy. The claim against the Trust succeeded in part. The Court of Appeal held that there had been an unlawful failure to involve Mrs Tracey in the DNACPR decision and it amounted to a breach of Article 8 ECHR. On the clinicians' obligation to involve the patient in a DNACPR decision, the Court noted:

> … since a DNACPR decision is one which will potentially deprive the patient of life-saving treatment, there should be a presumption in favour of patient involvement. There need to be convincing reasons not to involve the patient.[113]

> … it is inappropriate (and therefore not a requirement of article 8) to involve the patient in the process if the clinician considers that to do so is likely to cause her to suffer physical or psychological harm. … If however the clinician forms the view that the patient will not suffer harm if she is consulted, the fact that she may find the topic distressing is unlikely to make it inappropriate to involve her.[114]

The Court also recognised that if the clinician forms the view that CPR would be futile there exists an obligation to involve the patient. This would allow the patient the opportunity to seek a second opinion. However, the Court went on to accept that if the patient's multi-disciplinary team all take the view that attempting CPR would be futile, the team is not obliged to arrange for a further opinion.

Tracey underlines the necessity for consulting the patient and ensuring that they are involved in these decisions. It encourages openness in communication between the healthcare professional and the patient and demonstrates that it is only in rare circumstances that a non-disclosure could potentially be justified. On the question of communication, Dimond suggests that it is vital that the nurse be involved in discussions surrounding DNAR orders and the patient's prognosis. This ensures the nurse

---

[113] *R (on the application of Tracey) v Cambridge University Hospitals NHS Foundation Trust* [2014] EWCA Civ 822, [53].
[114] ibid 822, [54].

is familiar with the likely outcome and the reasons for the medical practitioner's decision.[115]

Winspear v City Hospitals Sunderland NHS Foundation Trust

The extent to which the principles emerging from *Tracey* are to apply in circumstances where the patient lacks capacity was the subject of consideration in *Winspear v City Hospitals Sunderland NHS Foundation Trust*.[116] Blake J stated: 'There is nothing in the case of *Tracey* or the Strasbourg case law to suggest that the concept of human dignity applies any the less in the case of a patient without capacity.'[117] Accordingly, Blake J accepted that the core principle of prior consultation before a DNACPR decision is put into place on the case file applies in cases both of capacity and absence of capacity. *Winspear* also highlighted the relevance of the Mental Capacity Act 2005, which sets out when and with whom a decision-maker must consult. Blake J was not satisfied that it was other than practicable and appropriate to have attempted to speak with Ms Winspear prior to the DNACPR notice being affixed to her son's records. The Court held that there was a procedural breach of Article 8(2) ECHR.

Health Service Executive v JM A Ward of Court

This case was discussed earlier in this chapter in the context of treatment withdrawal. In *JM* the Court was asked to consent to the withholding of an increase in ventilator support in the event of a clinical or respiratory deterioration of the patient, who was in an MCS and unable to give his consent. As the man's parents would not consent, the applicant sought the consent of the Court. Kelly P described this as 'the equivalent of asking the court to give what is commonly called a 'do not attempt resuscitation' (DNAR) or 'do not attempt cardio-pulmonary resuscitation' (DNACPR) direction'.[118]

In determining the test to be applied, Kelly P cited *Re a Ward of Court*, Lord Goff in *Airedale NHS Trust v Bland*, and the comments of Baroness Hale in *Aintree University Hospital's NHS Foundation Trust v James*. It follows that the assessment was framed by the patient's best interests. Kelly P granted the desired relief to the

---

[115] Richard A Griffith and Iwan Dowie, *Dimond's Legal Aspects of Nursing: A Definitive Guide to Law for Nurses* (8th edn, Pearson 2019) 712.
[116] *Winspear v City Hospitals Sunderland NHS Foundation Trust* [2015] EWHC 3250 (QB).
[117] ibid [45].
[118] *Health Service Executive v JM A Ward of Court* [2017] IEHC 399, [84].

applicant. The case does not substantially advance the legal framework for DNARs in Irish healthcare but, at a minimum, it does suggest judicial approval for their use in practice.

HSE National Consent Policy

Guidance on the use of DNAR orders is contained in Part 4 of the HSE's *National Consent Policy*. It addresses issues relating to CPR and DNAR orders within the broader context of consent. It stipulates that it 'is not intended as guidance for technical and practical considerations relating to resuscitation procedures'.[119] Moreover, the policy is intended to be read in conjunction with the Irish Medical Council's *Guide to Professional Conduct and Ethics for Registered Medical Practitioners*, and the NMBI's *Code of Professional Conduct and Ethics*. The policy is divided into several sub-sections, which address general principles, when CPR and DNAR decisions should be considered, presumption in favour of CPR, balancing the benefits and risks of providing CPR, DNAR decisions and children, documenting and communicating CPR/DNAR decisions, and reviewing DNAR orders.

Under general principles, it is set out that decisions about CPR must be made on the basis of an individual assessment and should not be based on 'age, disability, the subjective views of healthcare professionals regarding the individual's quality of life or whether he/she lives in the community or in long-term care'.[120] The individual is best placed to judge their own quality of life and can define their overall goals and preferences for their treatment and care. In addition to these points of consideration, decisions on CPR and DNAR orders should be made in the context of the likelihood of success and the potential risks. The nature of the decision means that there should be on-going communication between all parties, including the patient, those close to them, and healthcare professionals.

Advance care planning is recognised as an important part of good clinical care for persons at risk of cardiorespiratory arrest and is preferable to making decisions after a crisis has occurred. It is suggested that the likelihood of cardiorespiratory arrest be considered when determining how, when and if to consider the need for CPR/DNAR discussions or decisions for an individual. The policy describes three groups that can be identified based on the foreseeability of cardiorespiratory arrest: cardiorespiratory

---

[119] Health Service Executive, *National Consent Policy* (HSE 2019) 98.
[120] ibid 100.

arrest is considered unlikely; cardiorespiratory arrest, as a terminal event, is considered inevitable; and cardiorespiratory arrest is considered possible or likely.

Decisions about CPR should be clearly and accurately documented in the individual's healthcare record. Details of how the decision was made along with the date of the decision, the rationale for it, and who was involved should be included in the record. A DNAR order is not an unalterable statement but should be reviewed depending on the patient's condition, preferences for CPR change, return of decision-making capacity, or change in clinical responsibility.

9.6 The Definition of Death

In this jurisdiction there is no statutory definition of death. There were moves towards adopting a legislative definition as demonstrated by the Draft Proposals for the General Scheme of the Human Tissue Bill 2009 but this did not materialise.[121] This does not mean that the determination of death is solely a clinical issue. Instead it is important that the nurse and other healthcare professionals recognise the cultural and social factors that may frame the definition applied. Moreover, the definition can influence the time of death which, in turn, may be relevant for rules of inheritance or claims permitted under an insurance policy. It is therefore worth taking the time to consider whether a cardiopulmonary or neurological criteria-based determination is most appropriate in the circumstances.

The definition of death has evolved over time and has been shaped by developments in medicine. The cardiopulmonary standard is the traditional basis for the determination of death. This standard concentrates on vital functions such as respiration and heartbeat. However, the cardiopulmonary standard fails to accommodate heart transplants as well as other transplant related procedures. In addition, advancements in technology now mean that respiratory and circulatory bodily functions can be performed artificially or mechanically.[122] The first heart transplant was performed in December 1967 and this signalled a new wave of discussion on the signs of death. Early engagement was seen in 1968 with the publication of a paper by the Ad Hoc Committee of Harvard Medical School. This paper aimed to provide greater guidance on

---

[121] John Lombard, 'The Definition of Death' (2012) 11 Hibernian Law Journal 63.
[122] Stephen Westaby, *Fragile Lives* (HarperCollins 2018).

the definition of death, not only for healthcare professionals but also the legal profession. This paper was the subject of detailed commentary by the President's Commission Study on Brain Death, which recommended confirmatory tests as well as a 24-hour observation period for patients with anoxic brain damage.

In Ireland, the diagnosis of brain death was described in a memorandum published by the Working Party on Brain Death in 1988. The working party was composed of doctors, anaesthetists, and specialist surgeons. This memorandum stemmed from the expansion of critical care units around Ireland, the development of organ transplantation, and the need to respond to medical advances so that an accurate definition was established. This memorandum subsequently provided the framework for the Intensive Care Society of Ireland (ICSI) guidelines on the diagnosis of brain death.[123] A distinction exists between the various neurological criteria-based approaches to defining death. This distinction is best set out in a medical rather than a law text. At a minimum it can be stated that the approach in Ireland is grounded in the cessation of brainstem function. It is the 'irreversible loss of the brainstem and cerebral functions responsible for consciousness and cognition'.[124]

The ICSI guidance provides that a diagnosis of brain death based on clinical tests should not be made unless there is proof that the condition of the patient is due to irreversible structural brain damage and the exclusion of reversible causes of coma. It then outlines the process for formal clinical testing for brainstem reflexes and outlines situations where a diagnosis of brain death is not possible using clinical criteria alone. If organ donation is being considered then it is essential that the formal clinical tests be repeated within a 'reasonable' period of time. No minimum time period has been recommended. The document specifies that the apnoea test is the final test to be carried out and, if positive, the patient should be declared dead and time and date recorded. In situations where organ transplantation is not to take place, a time should be set for the withdrawal of ventilation. Family members may wish to be in attendance at this time and, it is suggested, 'Privacy and religious or other ceremonies should be facilitated as much as possible during this time.'[125]

---

[123] R Dwyer and others, *Diagnosis of Brain Death in Adults: Guidelines* (ICSI 2016).
[124] Stuart J Youngner and Edward T Bartlett, 'Human Death and High Technology: The Failure of the Whole-Brain Formulations' (1983) 99(2) Annals of Internal Medicine 252, 256.
[125] R Dwyer and others, *Diagnosis of Brain Death in Adults: Guidelines* (ICSI 2016) 8.

The issue of brain death arose in *PP v HSE*.[126] PP was the father of a pregnant woman referred to as NP. NP had been admitted to hospital and subsequently suffered brainstem death. As she was pregnant at the time, the hospital intended to artificially sustain NP for the course of her pregnancy. NP was being supported by mechanical ventilation and was fed by nasogastric tube. In addition, she was receiving high doses of medication for pneumonia, fungal infections, high blood pressure, fluid build-up and fluctuations in the production of urine. NP was also receiving physiotherapy twice daily. Her father considered these measures to be unreasonable and sought a declaration from the Court that the treatment be discontinued. This case was heard prior to the repeal of the 8th Amendment, therefore a central concern for healthcare professionals and the Court was the child's constitutional right to life. The medical evidence presented in the case was described as going one way only, and 'that is to establish that the prospects for a successful delivery of a live baby ... are virtually non-existent'.[127] The Court was satisfied that the best interests of the unborn child would be served by agreeing to the withdrawal of medical treatment. The Court did not question the legitimacy of a brain-based determination of death and accepted the clinical determination of brainstem death as was made on 3 December.

9.6.1 Certification and Registration of Death

It is a legal requirement that every death in the State be recorded and registered. These records are held by the General Register Office, which functions as the central civil repository for records relating to births, stillbirths, adoptions, marriages, civil partnerships, and deaths.

Section 42 of the Civil Registration Act 2004 provides that on the death of a person following an illness, a registered medical practitioner who attended the deceased shall complete and sign a certificate stating to the best of his or her knowledge and belief the cause of the death. This document is the Death Notification Form. Part 1 of this form can only be completed by a medical practitioner who attended the person and is not to be completed by a nurse. The registered medical practitioner must then give the Death Notification Form to a person capable of acting as a qualified informant. The qualified informant will normally be a relative or partner of the deceased. This person must then

---

[126] *PP v HSE* [2014] IEHC 622.
[127] ibid 622, [46].

complete and sign Part 2 of the Death Notification Form. Upon completion, the qualified informant is to submit the form to any Registrar of Deaths and this should occur within three months from the date of the death.

The medical certification of the cause of death is distinct from the pronouncement of death. Registered nurses may pronounce death in defined circumstances. This process should be informed by the National Policy for Pronouncement of Expected Death by Registered Nurses Working Group.[128] This policy is for use in HSE residential, HSE long-stay and HSE specialist palliative care services only. This may be supported by policy developed at the local level that articulates specific communication arrangements between the doctor(s), coroners, and the local HSE service site.

Specific reporting requirements are in place for early neonatal deaths[129] as well as stillbirths that occur in hospitals.[130] Where an early neonatal death occurs, the attending registered medical practitioner is required to provide details to the Superintendent Registrar. If a stillbirth occurs in a hospital, then details will be provided to the local registration authority.

Deaths that occur due to causes other than an illness, or where the medical practitioner had not attended the person prior to the death, are to be referred to the coroner, who will determine if a post-mortem is to be held. Under s 41 of the Civil Registration Act 2004 the death is automatically registered where an inquest or post-mortem is held at the request of the coroner. Prior to an inquest or while awaiting the post-mortem report, the coroner may provide an Interim Certificate of the Fact of Death. This form can assist in administrative tasks that may need to be completed such as engaging with banks, insurance companies, or other relevant institutions.

9.7 The Role of the Coroner

A coroner is an independent official with responsibility for the investigation of sudden and unexplained deaths. The coroner acts independently of the medical profession, the gardaí, the State, and any other interested parties. The principal legislation that defines

---

[128] Health Service Executive, *National Policy for Pronouncement of Expected Death by Registered Nurses Working Group* (HSE 2017).
[129] Civil Registration Act 2004, s 42A (as amended by Civil Registration (Amendment) Act 2014).
[130] ibid s 30.

the role and function of the coroner is the Coroners Act 1962 and this has been reshaped by the Coroners (Amendment) Act 2019.

The role of the coroner is somewhat of a hybrid nature. This is illustrated by the professional qualifications required for appointment to the post. Under s 14 of the Coroners Act 1962 a coroner or deputy coroner should be a practising barrister or solicitor of at least five years' standing or a registered medical practitioner who has been registered or who has been entitled to be so registered for at least five years.[131] The coroner aims to establish the facts relating to an unexplained death, namely the who, when, where, and how the death occurred. This role will arise in the case of sudden, unexplained, or violent deaths. The facts may emerge through a post-mortem examination and, if necessary, may be followed by an inquest. The details of post-mortem and inquest procedures are set out below.

The Coroners Act provides that the coroner shall appoint a deputy coroner, subject to approval by the local authority.[132] The deputy coroner may act for the coroner by whom he was appointed in the case of illness, absence, or in cases where the principal is disqualified from conducting an inquest. Disqualification from certain inquests is set out by s 35 of the Coroners Act 1962. A coroner may not conduct an inquest where they have attended the person as a registered medical practitioner in the month prior to the person's death. Furthermore, a coroner may not hold an inquest, or inquire into the death of, any person if he has drawn up, or assisted in the drawing up of, and benefits under, any testamentary disposition made by that person.[133] The same rules of disqualification also apply to the deputy coroner.

Coroners are organised by district and s 8 of the Coroners Act 1962 provides that there shall be a coroner for every coroner's district.[134] The coroner is to be appointed and paid by the local authority by whom he is appointed. There are 39 coroner districts as of July 2019, with larger counties such as Cork being divided into districts such as Cork City, Cork North, Cork South, and Cork West. Districts can be altered over time and may be amalgamated based on a scheme developed by the local authority.

---

[131] Coroners Act 1962, s 14.
[132] ibid s 13(1).
[133] ibid s 35(2)(a).
[134] ibid s 8(1).

In general, a coroner will not be required in cases where a person passed away due to a natural illness or disease and where the person was attended by a doctor within one month of their death. The doctor may then certify the cause of death allowing for the death to be registered and the death certificate to be obtained. However, sudden, unnatural, violent or unexplained deaths must be reported to the coroner. This responsibility may rest with persons including doctors, funeral directors, and persons in charge of an institution or premises where the person was residing at the time of death. The Coroners (Amendment) Act 2019 includes a schedule setting out deaths reportable to the coroner. These include but are not limited to the following:

1. Any death that may be murder, manslaughter or infanticide.

2. Any death that appears to be connected with a crime or suspected crime.

3. Any death, whether or not accidental, caused wholly or partly by stabbing, drowning, poisoning, hanging, electrocution, asphyxia or a gunshot wound.

4. Any death where the deceased person is dead on arrival at a hospital.

5. Any death which may be by suicide.

6. Any death where the body of the deceased person is unidentified.

7. Any death where no family member of the deceased person can be traced within a reasonable time of the death.

8. Any death where the body of the deceased person is found or recovered in circumstances that indicate that the death may have occurred a considerable period of time previously.

9. Any death (other than in circumstances to which paragraph 8 applies) in respect of which the date of death may not be ascertainable.

10. Any death caused wholly or partly by any of the following: (a) an incident, whether or not accidental, resulting in any

physical injury, including a cut, fracture or contusion; (b) a fall; (c) self-neglect; (d) an eating disorder; (e) exposure or hypothermia; (f) burns.

11. Any death which may be by assisted suicide.

12. Any death caused wholly or partly by any of the following: (a) an accident arising out of the use of a vehicle in a public place; (b) an incident occurring on a railway; (c) an incident arising on a train, aircraft, ship or other vessel.

13. Any death caused wholly or partly by any of the following: (a) a notifiable disease or condition that is, under provisions in that behalf in any other enactment, required to be notified to a Minister of the Government, a Department of State or a statutory body or to an inspector or other officer of a Minister of the Government, a Department of State or a statutory body; (b) an adverse reaction to any drug; (c) a drugs overdose or the presence of toxic substances; (d) in the case of an infant death, maternal drug addiction; (e) an infection contracted as a result of previously contaminated blood product administration; (f) a lack of care or neglect; (g) starvation or malnutrition.

14. Any death which may be due to a prion disease.

15. Any death caused wholly or partly by an accident at work or due to industrial or occupational injury or disease.

16. Any death occurring in a hospital or other health institution – (a) that is unexpected, (b) within 24 hours of presentation or admission, whichever is the later, or (c) of a person transferred from a nursing home.

17. Any maternal death or late maternal death.

18. Any death of a stillborn child, death intrapartum or infant death.

19. Any death occurring in a hospital or other health institution that is directly or indirectly related to a surgical operation or anaesthesia (including recovery from the effects of anaesthesia) or to any other medical, surgical or dental procedure, regardless of the length of time between the procedure and death.

20. Any death which may be due to any healthcare acquired infection.

21. Any death where an allegation is made or a concern has been expressed regarding the medical treatment provided to the deceased person or the management of his or her healthcare.

22. Any death which may be as a result of an unconventional medical procedure or treatment.

23. Any death occurring in – (a) an institution for the care and treatment of persons with a physical or mental disability, or (b) any public or private institution for the care of elderly or infirm persons, including a nursing home.

24. Any death where the deceased person was at the time of his or her death, or immediately before his or her death, in State custody or detention.

25. Any death of a child in care.[135]

9.7.1 Post-Mortem Practice

A post-mortem may be requested by either a coroner or a doctor. The coroner may request that a post-mortem be performed in order to ascertain the cause of death. As it is the coroner's legal duty to investigate the cause of death, they are not required to seek permission from the family or next of kin, whereas such consultation would normally be required from a doctor. The post-mortem is to be conducted by a registered medical practitioner. The coroner may permit one other medical practitioner to provide assistance if it is considered necessary. The post-mortem involves a detailed examination of the body and organs in order to establish the cause of death. As such, there may be a subsequent inquest at which the findings of the post-mortem are relied upon. If the post-mortem concludes that death was due to natural causes then an inquest is not required and a Coroner's Certificate can be issued. The death can then be formally registered and a death certificate obtained.

---

[135] Coroners (Amendment) Act 2019, Sch.

9.7.2 Inquests

An inquest is an official, public enquiry into the cause of a sudden, unexplained or violent death. Section 17 of the Coroners Act 1962 defines the general duty to hold an inquest as follows:

> Subject to the provisions of this Act, where a coroner is informed that the body of a deceased person is lying within his district, it shall be the duty of the coroner to hold an inquest in relation to the death of that person if he is of opinion that the death may have occurred in a violent or unnatural manner, or unexpectedly and from unknown causes or in a place or in circumstances which, under provisions in that behalf contained in any other enactment, require that an inquest should be held.[136]

The Coroners (Amendment) Act 2019 provides that an inquest is to be held where the deceased was in State custody or detention at the time of or immediately before his/her death. It also requires an inquest in cases of maternal or late maternal death.[137] An optional power to hold an inquest is provided by s 18 of the 1962 Act. If the coroner is satisfied that further investigation is not required, then the medical practitioner can be directed to complete part 1 of the Death Notification Form. An inquest may also be ordered by the Attorney General. This is provided for by s 24 of the Coroners Act 1962 and arises where the Attorney General has reason to believe that a person died in circumstances that would make the holding of an inquest advisable.

An inquest is usually held in a courthouse but can take place in other settings such as a hotel. The family of the deceased is entitled to attend the inquest, but there is no legal requirement to do so. The family does not need independent legal representation but if subsequent legal action is envisaged then a solicitor may be engaged to attend and take notes.

Evidence at an inquest can be submitted in a written or verbal form. The coroner can summon witnesses to give evidence at the inquest where their testimony would be of assistance.[138] This may involve testimony relating to the circumstances and cause of death. The coroner has final say on the witnesses at an inquest although

---

[136] Coroners Act 1962, s 17 (as amended by Coroners (Amendment) Act 2019, s 10).
[137] ibid s 10(1)(c).
[138] Coroners Act 1962, s 26.

they may be influenced by input from interested persons.[139] The coroner may examine the witnesses at an inquest on oath.[140] A failure to take an oath legally required by the coroner, or a refusal to answer any question to which the coroner may legally require an answer, will be a contempt of court and will be dealt with by the High Court. It follows that a 'witness at an inquest shall be entitled to the same immunities and privilege as if he were a witness before the High Court'.[141]

The coroner has the option of holding the inquest with or without a jury under s 39 of the Coroners Act 1962. Where there is a coroner's jury, it is to consist of not less than six and not more than twelve persons.[142] The discretion of the coroner to empanel a jury is limited where he/she becomes of the opinion:

(a) that the deceased came by his death by murder, infanticide or manslaughter, or

(b) that the death of the deceased occurred in a place or in circumstances which, under provisions in that behalf contained in any other enactment, require that an inquest should be held, or

(c) that the death of the deceased was caused by accident, poisoning or disease of which, under provisions in that behalf contained in any other enactment, notice is required to be given to a Minister or Department of State or to an inspector or other officer of a Minister or Department of State, or

(d) that the death of the deceased occurred in circumstances the continuance or possible recurrence of which would be prejudicial to the health or safety of the public or any section of the public.[143]

---

[139] Parties to be considered by the coroner may include: spouses/former spouses, partners/former partners, including same sex partners; next of kin of the deceased; personal representatives of the deceased; representatives of the Board or Authority in whose care the deceased was at the time of death, e.g. hospital, prison or other institution; those responsible for the death in any way; representatives of insurance companies; properly interested persons under the provisions of the Safety, Health and Welfare at Work Act, 1989; and other persons arising from the circumstances of the particular case.
[140] Coroners Act 1962, s 38 (as amended by Coroners (Amendment) Act 2019, s 24).
[141] ibid.
[142] Coroners Act 1962, s 41.
[143] ibid, s 40 (as amended by Coroners (Amendment) Act 2019, s 26).

If a jury has been empanelled, then it is the jury rather than the coroner who delivers the verdict. If a unanimous verdict is not agreed on by the jury then a majority verdict shall be accepted by the coroner, or if this is not possible then the coroner shall discharge the jury and hold a new inquest.[144] The inquest does not find persons guilty or innocent, and civil or criminal liability is not considered or investigated. Furthermore, s 31 of the Coroners Act 1962 sets out, 'Neither the verdict nor any rider to the verdict at an inquest, nor any findings made at an inquest, shall contain a censure or exoneration of any person.'[145] A range of verdicts are open to the Coroner or jury and include accidental death, death by misadventure including medical misadventure, suicide, an open verdict, natural causes, and unlawful killing. In addition, a recommendation of a general character can be appended to the verdict. Such a recommendation is intended to prevent further fatalities but has no legal force. As Mills and Mulligan stated, 'the coroner cannot compel action to achieve the ends stipulated in her recommendation, but they do satisfy the coroner's role as a servant of the public interest'.[146]

As the inquest is a public enquiry, it is possible to obtain documentation relating to the proceedings. This may include the post-mortem report, any depositions taken at the inquest, and a copy of the verdict. These documents are only made available once the inquest has concluded and access requires the payment of a small fee. Once the inquest is completed the coroner will then issue a certificate so that the death can be properly registered.

9.8 Wills

Patients in long-term care settings and other healthcare facilities may indicate a desire to arrange their affairs and draw up a will. Arrangements should be made to contact the patient's solicitor and have him or her attend the patient. In such a case the person making a will is referred to as the testator. The nurse should not be involved in the drafting of the will and should leave the matter to the patient and their solicitor. Solicitors are aware of the common challenges to wills drafted in such circumstances. For instance, a question may be raised about the capacity of the patient to draw up a will or it may be alleged that the will was shaped by undue influence. The nurse may play an important role

---

[144] Coroners Act 1962, s 44.
[145] ibid, s 31 (as amended by Coroners (Amendment) Act 2019 s 19).
[146] Simon Mills and Andrea Mulligan, *Medical Law in Ireland* (3rd edn, Bloomsbury 2017) 530.

where the will is challenged on either of these grounds. Nursing records should give an indication of the patient's condition and could be supplemented with additional information on occasions where a patient meets with their solicitor. Such records may also prove useful in circumstances where the nurse is subjected to cross-examination on the patient's capacity or factors indicating undue influence.

There are strict rules surrounding the execution of the will and errors or an irregularity could result in the will being declared invalid.[147] At a minimum the testator must be over 18 years old although if a person is or has been married they can be under 18. The person should also be of sound mind, the will should be in writing, and the will must be appropriately signed or marked at the end of the document and this should occur in the presence of two witnesses. The witnesses are prevented from being a beneficiary under the will and this extends to their spouses or civil partners. As such, if a person intends to give a gift to a healthcare facility or nursing staff then no one from that facility should be involved in the drafting or witnessing of the will. To do so could invalidate the gift on the basis of undue influence.

The testator may subsequently decide to change their will and they may do so by adding a codicil to the document. The codicil must satisfy the same requirements as noted above. If a person wishes to make substantial changes to their will the simplest option may be to have a new will drawn up that incorporates the changes while revoking the earlier will. The law on probate is a complex and nuanced area, which means the drafting of a will requires thought and expertise. It is therefore essential that a solicitor be consulted to ensure the legitimacy and validity of the will.

---

[147] Succession Act 1965.

CHAPTER 10
Clinical Research Ethics

Introduction 289
The Role of the Nurse/Midwife in Research 290
Conduct of Clinical Trials 293
    Randomised Controlled Trials 295
    The Use of Placebos 296
International Codes of Ethics 297
    The Nuremberg Code 298
    The Declaration of Helsinki 301
The Regulation of Research in Ireland 302
    Clinical Trials Regulation 303
    NMBI *Ethical Conduct in Research: Professional Guidance* 304
    Research Ethics Committees 306
Vulnerable Research Participants 313
Consent to Participation in Research 315
Confidentiality 325

10.0 Introduction

Nurses and midwives design and lead research projects, assist in research and clinical trials, and engage with published research as part of continuous professional education and the delivery of professional care. Research is embedded in nurse education and continues into the workplace in a variety of forms. The first section in this chapter will outline the broad spectrum of ways in which nurses engage with research. As part of this, the emerging role of the clinical research nurse and clinical research midwife will be outlined.

This chapter will go on to outline the conduct of clinical trials including randomised controlled trials and the use of placebos. As will be seen, much of the legal framework for research is underpinned and informed by international ethical codes. The Nuremberg Code and the Declaration of Helsinki are set out in section 3. The fourth section addresses the regulation of research in Ireland. This lays out regulations on research, professional guidance, and proposed legislation. Furthermore, the function and work of Research Ethics Committees (RECs) will be set out in this section. The ethics approval process requires close scrutiny of

290 | *Nursing Law in Ireland*

the proposed research. The REC stage should ensure that ethical issues in the research have been comprehensively considered and adequately addressed by the researcher. Particular attention is to be given to the protection of vulnerable research participants, ensuring informed consent has been obtained, and upholding confidentiality and data protection.

10.1 The Role of the Nurse/Midwife in Research

The place of research in nursing practice is reflected in the Nursing and Midwifery Board of Ireland (NMBI) *Code of Professional Conduct and Ethics for Registered Nurses and Registered Midwives*. Principle 3, quality of practice, sets out values and standards linked to research. The relevant values state:

- Nurses and midwives use evidence-based knowledge and apply best practice standards in their work.
- Nurses and midwives value research. Research is central to the nursing and midwifery professions. Research informs standards of care and ensures that both professions provide the highest quality and most cost-effective services to society.[1]

Under standards of conduct it is set out that:

- You should deliver safe and competent practice based on best available evidence and best practice standards.
- If you are involved in research, you should refer to the Board's guidance on the ethical conduct of nursing and midwifery research and the ethical policies and procedures you are required to follow. You must ensure that the rights of patients are protected at all times in the research process.[2]

These values and standards of conduct illustrate how research is to improve standards of care, and to shape evidence-based practice. This envisages the nurse/midwife engaging with research in a variety of ways. The NMBI's *Ethical Conduct in Research: Professional Guidance* identifies the nurse/midwife as researcher, research assistant, research facilitator, research subject, and as a

---

[1] Nursing and Midwifery Board of Ireland, *Code of Professional Conduct and Ethics for Registered Nurses and Registered Midwives* (NMBI 2014) 20.
[2] ibid 21.

consumer of research.[3] The nurse/midwife may occupy several of these roles at a time. In recent years, a distinct position that encapsulates these roles has emerged in the form of the clinical research nurse/midwife (CRN/M).

Clinical Research Nurse/Midwife

Hastings defines clinical research nursing as:

> nursing practice with a specialty focus on the care of research participants. In addition to providing and coordinating clinical care, clinical research nurses have a central role in assuring participant safety, ongoing maintenance of informed consent, integrity of protocol implementation, accuracy of data collection, data recording and follow up.[4]

This presents an image of a role with multiple responsibilities and duties. It can therefore be difficult to definitively define the parameters of the CRN/M role. This is reflected in the findings of the 2008 *Report on the Role of the Nurse or Midwife in Medical-led Clinical Research*.[5] Additional challenges identified in the report related to employment status, lack of visibility, and limited opportunities for professional development.[6] A 2019 study by Schilling and Hyland sought to describe the CRN/M workforce in Ireland.[7] It was a comprehensive examination of this role and demonstrates that the challenges identified by the earlier report are, for the most part, still unresolved.

The responsibilities of the CRN/M can be categorised under headings such as clinical duties, managerial or administrative duties, and educational and training responsibilities. The study by Schilling and Hyland identified the tasks and responsibilities most commonly undertaken by CRNs in Ireland, namely: participant recruitment 85.5 per cent; informed consent process 78 per cent; adverse event management 78 per cent; study visits 77.3 per cent; site file management 77.3 per cent; case report form completion

---

[3] Nursing and Midwifery Board of Ireland, *Ethical Conduct in Research: Professional Guidance* (NMBI 2015) 13.
[4] Clare Hastings, 'Clinical Research Nursing' <https://clinicalcenter.nih.gov/nursing/crn/crn_2010.html> accessed 22 July 2020.
[5] National Council for the Professional Development of Nursing and Midwifery, *Report on the Role of the Nurse or Midwife in Medical-led Clinical Research* (NCNM 2008).
[6] ibid 57-60.
[7] Carole Schilling and Deirdre Hyland, '"Count me in" Study Report: The Irish Research Nurses Network National Clinical Research Nurse/Midwife Workforce Survey' (IRNN 2019).

73.8 per cent; sample processing 70.9 per cent; study set-up 69.5 per cent; staff orientation/training 65.2 per cent; project management 48.2 per cent; ethics application 47.5 per cent; IMP management 44 per cent; study development 39 per cent; and research site management 34 per cent.[8] Understandably, the tasks undertaken by the CRN were influenced by the setting and the nature of research being conducted. Roles such as project management were primarily the responsibility of CRNs employed at Clinical Nurse Manager and Director of Nursing grade. However, the study noted that these roles were occasionally performed by a CRN employed at staff nurse level.[9] In addition to the tasks and responsibilities set out above, Hyland and Clarke Moloney suggest that the core responsibility of the CRN/M is patient advocacy. This responsibility is ingrained in the legal framework and requires the nurse to advocate for the research participant.[10]

The Schilling and Hyland study also provided a snapshot of the type of research that CRNs were working on. In excess of 60 per cent of CRNs were involved in clinical trials of investigational medicinal products, and some nurses worked on two or more types of study.[11] The majority of respondents indicated that they worked across several areas of practice. Areas of research included clinical trial of an investigational medicinal product, biobanking, interventional research, clinical investigation of a medical device, and patient registry.

The lack of visibility for CRN/Ms has raised questions about how many people are employed in such roles. An exploration of this question formed part of a 2018 Irish Research Nurses Network survey[12] and was a primary objective in the Schilling and Hyland research. In total 141 CRNs were included in the data analysis by Schilling and Hyland. This represented three times the number of CRNs that were identified in previous studies and surveys.[13] The role of research nurse/midwife will undoubtedly become more visible in the future and might yet be recognised as a division in the NMBI Register.

---

[8] ibid 23.
[9] ibid.
[10] Deirdre Hyland and Mary Clarke Moloney, 'Spotlight on Clinical Research Nursing' (2016) 24(3) WIN 52.
[11] Schilling and Hyland (n 7) 23.
[12] Smith and others, '2017/2018 Irish Research Nurses Network Survey on Research Nurses/Midwives in Ireland (Initial Report)' <https://irnn.ie/wp-assets-irnn/uploads/2018/03/Initial-Report-from-the-2017-2018-Irish-Research-Nurses-Network-Survey-on-Research-Nurses-Midwives.pdf> accessed 22 July 2020.
[13] Schilling and Hyland (n 7) 17.

10.2 Conduct of Clinical Trials

Prior to a medicinal product being authorised for use, it must be put through the clinical trials process. This ensures that the product is effective and safe for use.[14] In Ireland, the Health Products Regulatory Authority has responsibility for the assessment of clinical trials with medicinal products.

As part of a clinical trial, participants receive specific interventions in accordance with the research protocol established by the researchers. Regardless of the type of study, clinical trials usually follow a defined research pathway in which there are three fundamental phases. A fourth phase may also take place after the medicine has been licenced.

Clinical trials include a mix of therapeutic and non-therapeutic elements, although this distinction can be blurred at times. Therapeutic research involves a potential benefit for the research participant. In contrast, non-therapeutic research is not intended to offer such a benefit and may be used to test the safety of a medicinal product prior to subsequent trial phases. A claim that research is therapeutic should be carefully examined. There is a temptation to emphasise the positive attributes of a medicinal product in an attempt to encourage the enrolment of participants, including those who lack capacity.[15] Furthermore, the therapeutic attributes of a treatment may not always be evident and it is in some ways counterintuitive to make such positive claims. As Jackson noted, 'To say that a trial is therapeutic implies that it is known in advance that subjects will benefit from participation.'[16]

The search for a COVID-19 vaccine has placed a spotlight on the clinical trials process internationally. It has illustrated the detailed and lengthy procedures involved in developing and testing a new vaccine before it can be successfully licensed and brought to market. It has also underlined the importance of good research practice at all phases of the clinical trials process.

---

[14] Health Products Regulatory Authority, 'Clinical Trials' <http://www.hpra.ie/homepage/medicines/regulatory-information/clinical-trials> accessed 22 July 2020.

[15] Emily Jackson, *Medical Law* (Oxford University Press 2019) 517; Lars Noah, 'Informed Consent and the Elusive Dichotomy between Standard and Experimental Therapy' (2002) 28(4) American Journal of Law and Medicine 361.

[16] ibid.

Phase I

In the first phase of a clinical trial, a new medicinal product is normally given to a small group of healthy volunteers. However, if the medicine is a treatment for a terminal illness such as cancer then it may be tested on volunteers who have been diagnosed with the condition. This stage commences with small doses of the drug before slowly increasing, referred to as dose escalation studies. The researchers examine any side effects and monitor participants in order to identify a suitable dose.

The principal objectives of this phase are to ensure that the medicinal product is not a safety risk, to ascertain whether it can reach the targeted area, and gather preliminary data as to whether it could be of therapeutic value or prevent the disease or illness. It follows that phase one is non-therapeutic, whereas subsequent phases will aim to demonstrate a therapeutic benefit for research participants.

Phase II

Not all medicinal products will progress to phase two trials. This phase involves a larger number of participants, including persons who have been diagnosed with the condition that the medicinal product is targeting. Phase two aims to explore the effectiveness of the medicinal product in treating or preventing the condition. It should also lead to more accurate information on the appropriate dose to be administered, more detail about potential side effects and how best to control for them.

Phase III

Phase three of a clinical trial involves a larger group of research participants and may expand to include international research. This phase is carried out over a longer period of time and will involve comparison with the best available treatment to determine effectiveness. Most phase three trials are randomised, a process outlined below. If the medicinal product continues to demonstrate positive results at the conclusion of phase three then regulatory approval may be sought so the medicinal product can ultimately be brought to market.

Phase IV – Post Licensing

The licensing of a new drug does not signal the end of the research process. Instead, monitoring of the product will continue. This includes actively reviewing the safety of the drug, collecting feedback from patients, and reports from prescribers. It explores the administration of the drug outside standard research protocols and can involve patients who are not normally included in clinical trials. It is a 'real world' examination of the medicinal product, which can gather data on the long-term risks and benefits.

10.2.1 Randomised Controlled Trials

A majority of phase three trials are randomised as are some phase two trials. A randomised controlled trial has at least two distinct treatment groups. The treatment received by the members of each group will vary in order to provide a comparator to determine the effectiveness of the new medicinal product. Research participants are assigned a group at random, and may be placed in the control or active arm of the trial. Persons enrolled in the active arm will receive the new medicinal product, while persons in the control group will receive the standard treatment as though they were not enrolled in the clinical trial. Although, if no standard treatment is available then it may be necessary to administer a placebo. The condition of some persons receiving the standard treatment is likely to improve. The randomised controlled trial, therefore, aims to measure the scale of improvement in the active versus the control arm of the trial. In this way it can be determined whether the new drug being trialled is truly effective.

The randomised trial is a way in which researcher bias can be diminished if not eliminated. Researchers undoubtedly seek to identify the most accurate data but the interpretation of results could potentially be influenced by forms of unconscious bias. The randomised trial seeks to control for such bias and allow for analysis that is not prejudiced by extraneous considerations. This takes the form of a double-blind trial. As part of a double-blind trial neither the researcher nor the participant knows which group is enrolled in the active or control arms of the study.

Conducting a randomised controlled trial poses a number of ethical challenges, the first of which is the potential conflict faced by a healthcare professional in determining whether a patient should be enrolled in a clinical trial. If a healthcare professional believes that a certain treatment is best for the patient, then enrolling that patient in a randomised controlled trial may breach their duty to place the interests of the individual ahead of scientific interests. Accordingly, there must be 'equipoise' for a randomised controlled trial to be considered ethical. This concept means that there must be genuine uncertainty among healthcare professionals as to whether a medicinal product or treatment will be beneficial.

During the clinical trial it may be evident that the new medicinal product offers considerable benefits. This will raise the question as to whether the trial must be stopped. Depending on the data, the state of equipoise that underpinned the running of the trial may no longer be tenable. At such a point, persons assigned to the control group could be offered the new treatment. While such a positive outcome is to be welcomed, it is a difficult decision to end a trial earlier than anticipated. Such a move reduces the scope of data collection, and may limit knowledge on the short- versus long-term impact of the treatment.

A further ethical challenge relates to securing informed consent from potential research participants. The nature of the randomised control trial is such that significant information is necessarily kept from the participant. For instance, the participant should not know whether they are assigned to the active or control arms of the study. In such circumstances, it may be difficult to describe the consent as fully informed. However, it has been argued that the participant gives informed consent to the nature of the randomised controlled trial and the general manner in which the trial is to be conducted. This consent may be at a more general level but is deemed sufficient.

10.2.2 The Use of Placebos

In limited circumstances, research participants enrolled in the control arm of a randomised controlled trial may receive a placebo rather than a form of medical treatment. A placebo is intended to be indistinguishable in appearance from a tablet or drug. As such, participants should have no indication that they are not in the active arm of the trial. The use of a placebo in a randomised controlled trial should only occur where a standard treatment is not available. A research participant should not be deprived of treatment that they would have received if they were not part of the trial. In this way the clinical trial should not disadvantage a participant from receiving appropriate medical care. It would be inappropriate to design a clinical trial in a way that deprives participants of medical treatment and it would be unlikely that such a study would be approved by a research ethics committee.

The use of placebos in clinical research was addressed in the Declaration of Helsinki. The general position adopted by the

Declaration is that the new intervention should be tested against the best proven intervention. This benefits the research participant but also ensures that the benefits, risks, burdens, and effectiveness are rigorously demonstrated. The Declaration does, however, acknowledge that there are limited exceptions where a placebo or no intervention may be administered:

> 33. The benefits, risks, burdens and effectiveness of a new intervention must be tested against those of the best proven intervention(s), except in the following circumstances:
>
>> Where no proven intervention exists, the use of placebo, or no intervention, is acceptable; or
>
>> Where for compelling and scientifically sound methodological reasons the use of any intervention less effective than the best proven one, the use of placebo, or no intervention is necessary to determine the efficacy or safety of an intervention and the patients who receive any intervention less effective than the best proven one, placebo, or no intervention will not be subject to additional risks of serious or irreversible harm as a result of not receiving the best proven intervention.
>
> Extreme care must be taken to avoid abuse of this option.[17]

10.3 International Codes of Ethics

International codes of ethics have been developed in response to the unethical treatment and gross abuse of often unwilling or unknowing research participants. The international ethics codes are aimed at protecting research participants and define principles that are intended to ameliorate research standards. As will be seen in section 10.4, the principles enunciated in these codes have ultimately shaped the regulation of research at a national level.

The research abuses that occurred during World War II resulted in the first international code of research ethics, the Nuremberg Code, discussed at section 10.3.1. This did not, however, mark the end of abusive research practices. An infamous violation of ethical principles and breach of fundamental human rights took place in the Tuskegee Syphilis Trial.

---

[17] World Medical Association, Declaration of Helsinki [33].

Tuskegee Syphilis Trial 1932–72

In 1932 the Public Health Service in the US began working with the Tuskegee Institute on a study to record the natural history of syphilis. The study involved 600 black men, 399 with syphilis and 201 who did not have the disease. Researchers told the men they were being treated for 'bad blood' but the men did not receive appropriate treatment to cure the illness. The men had not given informed consent to be part of this study and had not been sufficiently informed of the study's true purpose. The study continued for 40 years until an Associated Press story led to a public outcry. At that point, the study ended, congressional hearings took place, and a class-action lawsuit was filed. In 1997 President Bill Clinton apologised on behalf of the United States. The last research participant in this study died in January 2004.[18]

10.3.1 The Nuremberg Code

The Nuremberg Code, formulated in August 1947, has been described as 'the most important document in the history of the ethics of medical research'.[19] The principles set out in the Code grew out of the 'Doctor's Trial' conducted in the aftermath of World War II.[20] The trial was conducted by the Allied Powers, and three US judges sat for the trial.[21] Twenty doctors and three bureaucrats were prosecuted for their role in organising and participating in war crimes and crimes against humanity in the form of medical experiments and medical procedures inflicted on prisoners and civilians.

Among the experiments and other 'medical' crimes were: high-altitude experiments; freezing experiments; malaria experiments; mustard gas experiments; sulfanilamide experiments; bone,

---

[18] Centers for Disease Control and Prevention, 'U.S. Public Health Service Syphilis Study at Tuskegee' <https://www.cdc.gov/tuskegee/timeline.htm> accessed 22 July 2020.
[19] Evelyne Shuster, 'Fifty Years Later: The Significance of the Nuremberg Code' (1997) 337(2) The New England Journal of Medicine 1436, 1436; George J Annas and Michael A Grodin (eds), *The Nazi Doctors and the Nuremberg Code: Human Rights in Human Experimentation* (Oxford University Press 1992).
[20] *United States of America v Karl Brandt et al*, 21 November 1946–20 August 1947.
[21] Walter Beals, Presiding Judge (Chief Justice of Supreme Court of State of Washington); Johnson Crawford, Member (former District Court Judge, Oklahoma); Harold Sebring, Member (Associate Justice of Supreme Court of Florida); Victor Swearingen, Alternate Member (former Special Assistant to US Attorney General).

muscle, and nerve regeneration, and bone transplant experiments; seawater experiments; epidemic jaundice experiments; typhus and other vaccine experiments; poison experiments; incendiary bomb experiments; sterilisation experiments; skeleton collection; the imprisonment or killing of Polish nationals alleged to have tuberculosis; and euthanasia.[22]

Sixteen defendants were found guilty, seven of whom were sentenced to death by hanging. Eight defendants were imprisoned for periods of time ranging from life imprisonment to ten years. Seven of the accused were acquitted by the Court.

In part of the judgment, the Court turned to consider the nature of permissible medical experiments. It was stated, 'All agree ... that certain basic principles must be observed in order to satisfy moral, ethical and legal concepts.'[23] At this point, the Court outlined the key principles that form the Nuremberg Code:

> 1. The voluntary consent of the human subject is absolutely essential.
>
>> This means that the person involved should have legal capacity to give consent; should be so situated as to be able to exercise free power of choice, without the intervention of any element of force, fraud, deceit, duress, overreaching, or other ulterior form of constraint or coercion; and should have sufficient knowledge and comprehension of the elements of the subject matter involved as to enable him to make an understanding and enlightened decision. This latter element requires that before the acceptance of an affirmative decision by the experimental subject there should be made known to him the nature, duration, and purpose of the experiment; the method and means by which it is to be conducted; all inconveniences and hazards reasonably to be expected; and the effects upon his health or person which may possibly come from his participation in the experiment.

---

[22] Telford Taylor, 'Opening Statement of the Prosecution, 9 December 1946' (US Government Printing Office 1949); Arthur L Caplan (ed), *When Medicine Went Mad: Bioethics and the Holocaust* (Humana Press 1992).

[23] Trials of War Criminals before the Nuernberg Military Tribunals (vol II, US Government Printing Office, October 1946–April 1949) 181.

The duty and responsibility for ascertaining the quality of the consent rests upon each individual who initiates, directs or engages in the experiment. It is a personal duty and responsibility which may not be delegated to another with impunity.

2. The experiment should be such as to yield fruitful results for the good of society, unprocurable by other methods or means of study, and not random and unnecessary in nature.

3. The experiment should be so designed and based on the results of animal experimentation and a knowledge of the natural history of the disease or other problem under study that the anticipated results will justify the performance of the experiment.

4. The experiment should be so conducted as to avoid all unnecessary physical and mental suffering and injury.

5. No experiment should be conducted where there is an *a priori* reason to believe that death or disabling injury will occur; except, perhaps, in those experiments where the experimental physicians also serve as subjects.

6. The degree of risk to be taken should never exceed that determined by the humanitarian importance of the problem to be solved by the experiment.

7. Proper preparations should be made and adequate facilities provided to protect the experimental subject against even remote possibilities of injury, disability, or death.

8. The experiment should be conducted only by scientifically qualified persons. The highest degree of skill and care should be required through all stages of the experiment of those who conduct or engage in the experiment.

9. During the course of the experiment the human subject should be at liberty to bring the experiment to an end if he has reached the physical or mental state where continuation of the experiment seems to him to be impossible.

10. During the course of the experiment the scientist in charge must be prepared to terminate the experiment at any stage, if he has probable cause to believe, in the exercise of the good faith, superior skill, and careful judgment required of him,

that a continuation of the experiment is likely to result in injury, disability, or death to the experimental subject.[24]

This seminal document has had a marked impact on the development of human rights and medical ethics. It has been influential in shaping international ethical guidelines and has defined the centrality of informed consent in medical research. In examining the significance of the Code, Shuster noted that it 'focuses on the human rights of research subjects'.[25] This stands in contrast to the Declaration of Helsinki, which 'focuses on the obligations of physician-investigators to research subjects'.[26]

10.3.2 The Declaration of Helsinki

In June 1964 the Declaration of Helsinki was adopted by the 18th World Medical Association (WMA) General Assembly in Helsinki. The WMA is an international organisation that represents physicians and was founded in 1947. The Declaration has been amended and revised on multiple occasions, most recently at the 64th WMA General Assembly in 2013. The Declaration is not legally binding but its ethical principles have shaped the legal framework for the regulation of medical research in many jurisdictions.

The Declaration has expanded in scope since first being adopted. The 1964 Declaration was composed of 11 sections, whereas the most recent Declaration includes 37 sections. This has allowed the Declaration to respond to emerging ethical and social concerns.[27] Nonetheless, the development and expansion of the Declaration has resulted in controversy at times.[28]

Under the heading of 'General Principles' the Declaration states:

> 9. It is the duty of physicians who are involved in medical research to protect the life, health, dignity, integrity, right to self-determination, privacy, and confidentiality of personal

---

[24] ibid 181–82.
[25] Shuster (n 19) 1440.
[26] ibid.
[27] World Medical Association, Declaration of Helsinki, Principle 11: 'Medical research should be conducted in a manner that minimises possible harm to the environment.'
[28] Howard Wolinsky, 'The Battle of Helsinki: Two Troublesome Paragraphs in the Declaration of Helsinki Are Causing a Furore over Medical Research Ethics' (2006) 7(7) EMBO Reports 670; Antonia-Sophie Skierka and Karin B Michels, 'Ethical Principles and Placebo-Controlled Trials – Interpretation and Implementation of the Declaration of Helsinki's Placebo Paragraph in Medical Research' (2018) 19(1) BMC Medical Ethics 24.

information of research subjects. The responsibility for the protection of research subjects must always rest with the physician or other health care professionals and never with the research subjects, even though they have given consent.

10. Physicians must consider the ethical, legal and regulatory norms and standards for research involving human subjects in their own countries as well as applicable international norms and standards. No national or international ethical, legal or regulatory requirement should reduce or eliminate any of the protections for research subjects set forth in this Declaration.[29]

The Declaration of Helsinki also addresses the following points:

- Risks, Burdens and Benefits
- Vulnerable Groups and Individuals
- Scientific Requirements and Research Protocols
- Research Ethics Committees
- Privacy and Confidentiality
- Informed Consent
- Use of Placebo
- Post-Trial Provisions
- Research Registration and Publication and Dissemination of Results
- Unproven Interventions in Clinical Practice[30]

10.4 The Regulation of Research in Ireland

Clinical research in Ireland is framed by EU Directives, legislation, and professional guidance. Human rights also have an integral role in shaping the conduct of clinical research. The research participant is entitled to have their rights protected at all stages of the research process. This includes respect for the individual's autonomy, respect for bodily integrity, and the avoidance of inhuman or degrading treatment. In this section the clinical trials regulations will be outlined along with the NMBI's *Ethical Conduct in Research: Professional Guidance* and the proposed legislation for the National Research Ethics Committee.

---

[29] World Medical Association, Declaration of Helsinki, Principle 9 and 10.
[30] World Medical Association, Declaration of Helsinki.

10.4.1 Clinical Trials Regulation

Clinical trials in Ireland are currently governed by the European Communities (Clinical Trials on Medicinal Products for Human Use) Regulations 2004.[31] These Regulations transposed the provisions of Directive 2001/20/EC, the Clinical Trials Directive.[32] This Directive sought to harmonise the conduct of clinical trials and investigational medicinal product manufacture in EU Member States. The 2004 Regulations were subsequently amended by SI 878/2004[33] and SI 374/2006.[34] Among the points addressed by the 2004 Regulations were the establishment, recognition and monitoring of ethics committees; the authorisation procedure for clinical trials; obligations of good clinical practice; pharmacovigilance; and the manufacture and importation of investigational medicinal products.

The implementation of the Clinical Trials Directive resulted in some discrepancies between EU Member States and did not deliver the high level of harmonisation that had been hoped for. A new clinical trials regulation was adopted on 16 April 2014.[35] As it is a Regulation rather than a Directive it is directly binding on Member States without the need for transposing legislation. This will aid the creation of a uniform framework for the authorisation of clinical trials. However, the new EU Clinical Trials Regulation is not yet in effect.

The EU Clinical Trials Regulation provides for the establishment of a single EU Clinical Trial Portal and Database. The European Medicines Agency is tasked with establishing both the portal and database.[36] The EU portal is to be a 'single entry point for the

---

[31] European Communities (Clinical Trials on Medicinal Products for Human Use) Regulations 2004, SI 190/2004. Subsequent amendments include European Communities (Clinical Trials on Medicinal Products for Human Use) (Amendment) Regulations 2004, SI 878 of 2004; European Communities (Clinical Trials on Medicinal Products for Human Use) (Amendment No 2) Regulations 2006, SI 374 of 2006.

[32] Directive 2001/20/EC of the European Parliament and of the Council of 4 April 2001 on the approximation of the laws, regulations and administrative provisions of the Member States relating to the implementation of good clinical practice in the conduct of clinical trials on medicinal products for human use [2001] OJ L121, 1.5.2001, 34.

[33] European Communities (Clinical Trials on Medicinal Products For Human Use) (Amendment) Regulations 2004, SI 878/2004.

[34] ibid (Amendment No 2) Regulations 2006, SI 374/2006.

[35] Regulation (EU) No 536/2014 of the European Parliament and of the Council of 16 April 2014 on clinical trials on medicinal products for human use, and repealing Directive 2001/20/EC.

[36] ibid Arts 80, 81.

submission of data and information relating to clinical trials'.[37] The database will contain all data and information submitted by way of the portal. These resources are intended to aid the application for clinical trials authorisation, particularly for multinational clinical trials. Unfortunately, technical difficulties with the development of IT systems significantly delayed the development of the portal and, accordingly, delayed the application of the EU Clinical Trials Regulation. Other measures introduced as part of the EU Clinical Trials Regulations are intended to improve transparency on clinical trials data and to simplify the rules on safety reporting for trials running in the EU.

10.4.2 NMBI *Ethical Conduct in Research: Professional Guidance*

Ethical Conduct in Research: Professional Guidance was originally published in January 2007 and was re-issued in November 2015. The purpose of this guidance is 'to provide nurses and midwives with general guidance on ethical matters relating to research and to ensure the protection of the rights of all those involved in research'.[38] The guidance document addresses the role of the *Code of Professional Conduct and Ethics for Registered Nurses and Registered Midwives*, ethical principles, considerations when undertaking research, ethical conduct and the research process, the use of records in research, and clinical trials.

The guidance document identifies specific ethical principles that serve as a framework to guide the researcher through the research process and its subsequent use. These principles are:

- Respect for persons/autonomy
- Beneficence and non-maleficence
- Justice
- Veracity
- Fidelity
- Confidentiality
- Informed Consent[39]

Autonomy and healthcare decision-making are set out in chapter 5 of this work. In the context of research, the principle of autonomy is adhered to by respecting the participants' right to self-determination, ensuring that appropriate information

---

[37] ibid Art 80.
[38] Nursing and Midwifery Board of Ireland, 'Ethical Conduct in Research: Professional Guidance' (NMBI 2015) 4.
[39] ibid; Owen Doody and Maria Noonan, 'Nursing Research Ethics, Guidance and Application in Practice' (2016) 25(14) British Journal of Nursing 803.

is made available, and facilitating the right of withdrawal from research.

Beneficence seeks to do good and should represent a benefit for research participants and society as a whole. This requires a close examination of potential and perceived benefits associated with a piece of research. The concept of beneficence can be subjective, as Doody and Noonan note: 'Beneficence of any action can be extremely personal and may differ between individuals, where what benefits one person might not benefit another.'[40] The researcher must also take care to acknowledge and respond to potential risks. In this respect, the researcher has a responsibility to safeguard and protect participants at all stages of the research process. Appropriate safeguards may allow more people to benefit from the research.

Non-maleficence is closely linked to beneficence. This principle seeks to avoid the imposition of harm. Care must therefore be taken to protect research participants and reduce the likelihood of injury or harm occurring. Doody and Noonan rightly draw attention to the fact that the protection of the researcher is an 'often overlooked' factor in the research process.[41] In considering the risks to the participant, the researcher may fail to adequately examine the risks that they themselves face. Accordingly, any such risk should be identified and mitigated in so far as is possible.

The NMBI professional guidance describes the principle of justice as being 'synonymous with fairness and equity'.[42] Participants are to be treated fairly and equitably at all stages of the research study. Potential benefits and risks should be distributed as evenly as possible. It follows that 'certain individuals, groups or communities should neither bear an unfair share of the burden nor be unfairly omitted/excluded from the potential benefits of participation'.[43]

Veracity involves the concepts of truth and the absence of deception. Individuals have the right to be told the truth and not to be deceived about any aspect of the research. The researcher must explain the research project in sufficient detail and make every effort to ensure that participants understand the implications throughout the study. The information letter for participants is an

---

[40] Doody and Noonan (n 39) 804.
[41] ibid 805.
[42] Nursing and Midwifery Board of Ireland, *Ethical Conduct in Research: Professional Guidance* (NMBI 2015) 8.
[43] Doody and Noonan (n 39) 805.

opportunity to provide considerable detail about the nature of the research, associated risks and benefits, and an explanation of the participant's rights. The NMBI note that this principle of veracity is linked with respect for autonomy.[44]

Fidelity involves the concept of trust. Research participants place considerable trust in researchers and this requires a commitment to protect them. The researcher must ensure that the participant has a clear understanding of the risks, and can thereby foster a trusting relationship. Fidelity in the researcher–participant relationship is a shared principle. The participant should also be truthful in detailing their experience and responding to questions that form part of the research. This can improve the accuracy of the data gathered and strengthens the validity of the research.

The final two principles set out by the NMBI are confidentiality and informed consent. These will be discussed at sections 10.6 and 10.7 in this chapter.

10.4.3 Research Ethics Committees

The HSE describes research ethics committees (RECs) as 'the acknowledged international best practice structure for overseeing the conduct of ethical standards in healthcare research'.[45] Approval from a REC is often a necessary first step before research can commence. It is the responsibility of the principal investigator to apply for REC approval and ensure that the study remains within the parameters set out in the ethics application. If the principal investigator is not sure whether REC approval is needed then it would be advisable to consult with the Chairperson of an appropriate REC.

RECs can be described as having a protection, advice, and a research quality function. The work of a REC can contribute to safeguarding both the participant, the researcher, and institutional reputation.[46] Advice can be given on REC procedures and whether a research ethics review is required for a study. The committee acts to examine the proposed research for sources of harm or injury and will provide feedback on steps that should be taken to

---

[44] Nursing and Midwifery Board of Ireland, *Ethical Conduct in Research: Professional Guidance* (NMBI 2015) 8.
[45] Health Service Executive, 'Research Ethics Committees' <https://www.hse.ie/eng/services/list/5/publichealth/publichealthdepts/research/rec.html> accessed 20 July 2020.
[46] Nursing and Midwifery Board of Ireland, *Ethical Conduct in Research: Professional Guidance* (NMBI 2015) 11.

mitigate the risk. RECs also promote research quality by ensuring research is carefully planned. The time invested in preparing a REC application may be viewed by some as burdensome and time-consuming. In reality, the REC application provides a form of ethical quality assurance for the research study.[47] It can therefore promote good practice, and can provide the researcher with a roadmap for how the research will be conducted and what safeguards are required at all stages.

As previously mentioned, not every research project or study will need to go through the REC approval process. Examples of such activities that do not usually require REC review have been set out by the HSE and include:

- Research utilising existing publicly available documents or data
- Observational studies in public places in which the identity of the participant remains anonymous
- Case study of one patient with the proviso that written informed consent has been obtained from the relevant study subject/participant
- Quality assurance studies
- Clinical audits
- Service evaluations[48]

Conversely, activities that require REC review include:

- Clinical trials involving human participants
- Testing of new treatment or interventions or medical devices
- Observational clinical research
- Research involving human remains, cadavers, tissues, discarded tissue (e.g. placenta), biological fluids
- Testing innovative practices in health and disability services
- Qualitative research involving access to personal information by means of questionnaires, interviews or focus groups

---

[47] ibid: 'When applying to ethics committees for approval, all the ethical issues must be identified clearly in the written proposal and the researcher must demonstrate how these will be addressed in the conduct of the research study.'

[48] Health Service Executive, 'Research Ethics Committees' <https://www.hse.ie/eng/services/list/5/publichealth/publichealthdepts/research/rec.html> accessed 20 July 2020.

- Research involving the secondary use of data (use of data not collected for that research purpose), if any form of identifier is involved and/or if personal health information pertaining to individuals is involved
- Physiological studies
- Comparing an established procedure, whether therapeutic, non-therapeutic or diagnostic, with other procedures which are not recognised as established by virtue of their recent development, discovery or use in a new or unfamiliar way
- Research conducted by students, which include all activities that meet the definition of research with human participants.
- Case studies, when a series of subject observations allow possible extrapolation or generalisation of the results from the reported cases and when there is an intent to publish or disseminate data[49]

RECs in Ireland have traditionally developed from local institutional initiatives rather than stemming from a national policy. This type of development has resulted in 'several kinds of RECs with different jurisdictions and scopes of operation'.[50] A 2012 HIQA survey identified 72 RECs,[51] while a Regulatory Impact Analysis document from July 2019 relied on anecdotal evidence to suggest that there are more than 80 RECs currently operating across the country.[52] These include RECs in third-level institutions, hospitals, voluntary community organisations, government agencies, and professional organisations. These RECs vary greatly in the type of research applications that they can review. This can prove challenging for researchers, and in the context of national health projects, can result in a fragmented, costly, and slow REC approval process.[53]

Clinical Trials

Regulation 10 of the European Communities (Clinical Trials on Medicinal Products for Human Use) Regulations 2004 provides:

---

[49] ibid.
[50] 'Regulatory Impact Analysis on the General Scheme of the National Research Ethics Committee Bill 2019' <https://assets.gov.ie/22010/e30aa5cfff9a42b0853bab696b6db2dc.pdf> accessed 20 July 2020.
[51] Health Information and Quality Authority, 'International Review of Research Ethics Structures' (HIQA 2012) 17.
[52] 'Regulatory Impact Analysis on the General Scheme of the National Research Ethics Committee Bill 2019' <https://assets.gov.ie/22010/e30aa5cfff9a42b0853bab696b6db2dc.pdf> accessed 20 July 2020.
[53] ibid.

A person shall not conduct, commence or cause a clinical trial to be commenced unless –

> (a) an ethics committee has issued a favourable opinion in relation to the clinical trial;
>
> (b) the Board has granted an authorisation in respect of the clinical trial; and
>
> (c) the sponsor of the clinical trial, or the person authorised to act on his or her behalf in relation to the trial, is established in the Community.[54]

Before any clinical trial can get underway it must have received authorisation from the Health Products Regulatory Authority (HPRA). The HPRA reviews the medical and scientific elements of an application. In this way, the risks and benefits can be weighed up and a decision arrived at. A positive opinion must also be issued by an ethics committee prior to the commencement of a clinical trial.

Under Regulation 6(1) of SI 190/2004 the Minister for Health is the Ethics Committees Supervisory Body and has responsibility for recognising and monitoring ethics committees. Of the RECs currently operating in Ireland, 12 are recognised institutional RECs for the purpose of reviewing applications for clinical trials of medicinal products. The 2004 Regulations provide for a single ethical opinion from a recognised ethics committee for investigational medicinal products, although it appears that this process is not functioning as effectively as intended.[55]

The composition of a recognised ethics committee is defined by Schedule 2 of SI 190/2004. Under the new Clinical Trials Regulation, the establishment and organisation of ethics committees will remain a matter for the Member State to determine. As it stands, the ethics committee is to be established by appointing authorities and is to consist of expert and lay members.[56] There are to be no more than 21 members, of which

---

[54] European Communities (Clinical Trials on Medicinal Products for Human Use) Regulations 2004, SI 190/2004, Reg 10.

[55] 'Regulatory Impact Analysis on the General Scheme of the National Research Ethics Committee Bill 2019' <https://assets.gov.ie/22010/e30aa5cfff9a42b0853bab696b6db2dc.pdf> accessed 20 July 2020.

[56] European Communities (Clinical Trials on Medicinal Products for Human Use) Regulations 2004, SI 190/2004, Schedule 2, 1(1): 'expert member' means a member of an ethics committee who is a healthcare professional

at least one-third shall be lay members and at least half of those lay members should not be and have never been a healthcare professional. Positions such as the chairperson, vice-chairperson, and an alternate vice-chairperson are appointed by the appointing authority. The legislation requires that a quorum be achieved when the opinion of an ethics committee in relation to a clinical trial is to be determined.[57] This requires the chairperson and at least six other members to be present, including at least one lay member and one expert member.

The legislation sets out that an ethics committee should give an opinion within 60 days of receiving a valid application. This time limit is suspended where the applicant is asked to provide additional information to aid the work of the ethics committee.[58] A longer period of time is provided for in clinical trials involving a medicinal product for gene therapy or somatic cell therapy, or a medicinal product containing a genetically modified organism. The time limit does not apply for a clinical trial involving a medicinal product for xenogeneic cell therapy. The new Clinical Trials Regulation requires that a single decision be issued within 60 days or it will result in tacit approval. This will prove challenging in this jurisdiction but its purpose is 'to ensure that timelines are adhered to'.[59]

Regulation 13(6) of SI 190/2004 sets out that the ethics committee shall consider the following matters in preparing its opinion:

(a) the relevance of the clinical trial and its design;

(b) whether the evaluation of the anticipated benefits and risks as required under paragraph 1 of Part 2 of Schedule 1 is satisfactory and whether the conclusions are justified;

---

or who has professional qualifications or experience relating to the conduct of, or use of statistics in, clinical research, unless the said qualifications or experience relate only to the ethics of clinical research or medical treatment; 'lay member' means a member of an ethics committee who is not an expert member and who is not and never has been a registered medical practitioner or registered dentist and who does not in the course of his or her employment or business provide medical, dental or nursing care or participate in the promotion or conduct of clinical research.

[57] European Communities (Clinical Trials on Medicinal Products for Human Use) Regulations 2004, SI 190/2004, Schedule 2.
[58] ibid Reg 13.
[59] Regulation (EU) No 536/2014 of the European Parliament and of the Council of 16 April 2014 on clinical trials on medicinal products for human use, and repealing Directive 2001/20/EC, (8).

(c) the clinical trial protocol;

(d) the suitability of the investigator and supporting staff;

(e) the investigator's brochure;

(f) the quality and adequacy of the facilities for the trial;

(g) the adequacy and completeness of the written information to be given and the procedure to be followed for the purpose of obtaining informed consent to participation in the trial;

(h) if the subjects are to include persons who because they are minors are incapable of giving informed consent, whether the research is justified having regard to the conditions and principles laid down in Part 4 of Schedule 1;

(i) if the subjects are to include persons who are adults and who are incapable by reason of physical or mental incapacity of giving informed consent, whether the research is justified having regard to the conditions and principles laid down in Part 5 of Schedule 1;

(j) the arrangements for the recruitment of subjects;

(k) the provision made for indemnity or compensation in the event of injury or death attributable to the clinical trial;

(l) any insurance or indemnity to cover the liability of the investigator and sponsor;

(m) the amounts and, where appropriate, the arrangements for rewarding or compensating investigators and trial subjects;

(n) the terms of any agreement between the sponsor and the owner or occupier of the trial site which are relevant to the arrangements referred to in subparagraph (m).[60]

This can serve as a useful checklist in the development and submission of the ethics application. The preparation of an ethics application is normally associated with a higher level or management function. Nonetheless, 48.2 per cent of CRN/Ms in

---

[60] European Communities (Clinical Trials on Medicinal Products for Human Use) Regulations 2004, SI 190/2004, Reg 13(6).

the 2019 Schilling and Hyland study indicated that this formed part of their responsibilities.[61]

Review of 'Other' Research

RECs are not only of relevance for clinical trials but they also review many other types of research, a point mentioned earlier in this chapter. Academic and non-interventional research is most often reviewed by a local REC. This may be an REC based in a third-level institution or a hospital-based REC. While there is no specific legislation governing RECs in this area, they must be careful to comply with the broader legal framework. This includes data protection legislation, Health Research Regulations, the Freedom of Information Act 2014, and professional standards and guidelines.

General Scheme of the National Research Ethics Committees Bill

In July 2019, the General Scheme of the National Research Ethics Committees Bill was published. The aim was to establish a National Research Ethics Committee mixed model framework that would encompass all human health research with clear lines on what would be reviewed by the National RECs and the institutional RECs. Under this Bill, a number of National RECs would be established, starting with one in the area of clinical trials of medicinal products. These single-opinion national committees would be supported by staff in a National Office for Research Ethics Committees. This Office has since been established and is hosted by the Health Research Board.

National Research Ethics Committee COVID-19

A National Research Ethics Committee (NREC) was established by the Minister for Health on a temporary basis in 2020. This formed part of Ireland's response to the COVID-19 pandemic. The function of this NREC was to deliver an expedited review process for COVID-19-related research studies. Consequently, the NREC COVID-19 was to prioritise the review of the following study types:

- All COVID-19 clinical trials, including Clinical Trials of Investigational Medicinal Products (CTIMPs) and trials of medical devices, observational trials and all COVID-19 intervention studies;

---

[61] Schilling and Hyland (n 7) 23.

- Cross-institutional COVID-19 studies;
- COVID-19 studies carried out at national level, for example in multiple settings including but not limited to large cohort studies;
- International COVID-19 studies, including CTIMPs and registries, in which Ireland is a participant;
- COVID-19 studies involving linkage of datasets;
- COVID-19 studies that will, directly or indirectly, result in the establishment of, or expansion of, a biobank;
- Other COVID-19-related health research where, following consideration between the applicant and their local REC (or in the absence of an obvious local REC), they feel review by the NREC COVID-19 would best support expedited review.[62]

The aim of the NREC COVID-19 was to respond with a decision within seven days of confirmation of a validated application. It was the intention that responsibility for REC review would transition back to the existing distributed REC system once the peak volume of applications has been processed and projects are underway. The three-month tenure of the NREC COVID-19 was extended until August 2020. A standing sub-committee of the NREC COVID-19 was then put in place, on approval from the Department of Health, to review applications for amendments to studies receiving ethics approval from the NREC COVID-19.

10.5 Vulnerable Research Participants

In designing a research study, it is essential that measures be taken to identify and protect any vulnerable research participants. This can be a challenging process as the concept of vulnerability has been described as being vague.[63] Principles 19 and 20 of the Declaration of Helsinki address 'Vulnerable Groups and Individuals':

> 19. Some groups and individuals are particularly vulnerable and may have an increased likelihood of being wronged or of incurring additional harm.

---

[62] Health Research Board, 'NREC COVID-19' <https://www.hrb.ie/covid-19-ethical-review/nrec-covid-19-overview/> accessed 20 July 2020.

[63] Bracken-Roche and others, 'The Concept of "Vulnerability" in Research Ethics: An In-Depth Analysis of Policies and Guidelines' (2017) 15(8) Health Research Policy and Systems.

> All vulnerable groups and individuals should receive specifically considered protection.
>
> 20. Medical research with a vulnerable group is only justified if the research is responsive to the health needs or priorities of this group and the research cannot be carried out in a non-vulnerable group. In addition, this group should stand to benefit from the knowledge, practices or interventions that result from the research.[64]

As Principle 20 indicates, if someone is described as being vulnerable this does not mean that they should be automatically excluded from the research. Instead, the researcher should develop the ethical practices needed to promote the involvement of such persons and minimise any risks they may be exposed to. This may require additional measures to be taken for participant recruitment, the use of appropriate terminology/language, appropriate information and supports for informed consent, garda vetting of researchers, including breaks and rest periods in the research process, allowing for the presence of a third-party such as a family member or friend of the participant, and access to appropriate supports after the research has been concluded. These measures should be carefully tailored to the research project and will be a key point for any REC in examining an ethics application.

The issue of vulnerability is addressed in the NMBI's *Ethical Conduct in Research: Professional Guidance*:

> Individuals who are the recipients of nursing and midwifery care/intervention may be vulnerable because of patient and client status and require additional protection because of their vulnerability. Likewise children and certain groups of adults such as unconscious patients, the terminally ill, some elderly people and those with mental health problems may be viewed as vulnerable participants. Potentially vulnerable groups should not be chosen simply because they are readily available. They may lack insight and competence to make an informed decision to participate in a research project. It is vital that the nurse and midwife, irrespective of their role in the research process, protect vulnerable individuals and respect their right to self-determination and autonomy.[65]

---

[64] World Medical Association, Declaration of Helsinki, [19]–[20].
[65] Nursing and Midwifery Board of Ireland, *Ethical Conduct in Research: Professional Guidance* (NMBI 2015) 11–12.

Groups with potentially vulnerable persons include:

- Patients
- Those who are disabled, physically, intellectually, socially and emotionally
- Those who are hearing or visually impaired
- Persons who reside in institutions and residential settings
- Pregnant women
- The unborn
- Children and adolescents
- Elderly
- Prisoners
- Students
- Those whose first language is not English.[66]

The protection of several of these groups will be discussed in the next section, which outlines the informed consent process.

10.6 Consent to Participation in Research

Chapter 5 of this text is titled 'Patient Autonomy and Decision-Making'. The introduction to chapter 5 noted that the patient now has much greater involvement in their healthcare and this has changed the responsibilities and duties of the healthcare professional. The same is true in research, namely that the participant's informed consent is of fundamental importance and this has altered the responsibilities and duties of the researcher.

Valid informed consent requires the sufficient disclosure of information; the prospective participant should have adequate capacity to consent; and the decision should be made voluntarily. The purpose of informed consent is to ensure that the prospective research participant has sufficient information on which to base a decision about their participation so the decision can be an accurate reflection of their will and preferences. It follows that the prospective participant should be given adequate time to consider the information and be given an opportunity to ask further questions prior to making a decision.[67]

---

[66] ibid 12.
[67] Health Service Executive, *National Consent Policy* (HSE 2019) 67: 'Special consideration must also be given to the timing of the consent process. Prospective research participants should be given enough time to fully consider their participation and to ask questions.'

Under the Clinical Trials Regulation 2014, informed consent is defined as

> a subject's free and voluntary expression of his or her willingness to participate in a particular clinical trial, after having been informed of all aspects of the clinical trial that are relevant to the subject's decision to participate or, in case of minors and of incapacitated subjects, an authorisation or agreement from their legally designated representative to include them in the clinical trial[68]

This definition indicates that children and individuals lacking capacity can potentially be included in research studies, including clinical trials. The consent process and requisite safeguards for these groups are discussed later in this section.

Informed consent is addressed by Principles 25–32 of the Declaration of Helsinki. Principles 25 and 26 are as follows:

> 25. Participation by individuals capable of giving informed consent as subjects in medical research must be voluntary. Although it may be appropriate to consult family members or community leaders, no individual capable of giving informed consent may be enrolled in a research study unless he or she freely agrees.

> 26. In medical research involving human subjects capable of giving informed consent, each potential subject must be adequately informed of the aims, methods, sources of funding, any possible conflicts of interest, institutional affiliations of the researcher, the anticipated benefits and potential risks of the study and the discomfort it may entail, post-study provisions and any other relevant aspects of the study. The potential subject must be informed of the right to refuse to participate in the study or to withdraw consent to participate at any time without reprisal. Special attention should be given to the specific information needs of individual potential subjects as well as to the methods used to deliver the information.

> After ensuring that the potential subject has understood the information, the physician or another appropriately

---

[68] Regulation (EU) No 536/2014 of the European Parliament and of the Council of 16 April 2014 on clinical trials on medicinal products for human use, and repealing Directive 2001/20/EC, Art 2(21).

qualified individual must then seek the potential subject's freely-given informed consent, preferably in writing. If the consent cannot be expressed in writing, the non-written consent must be formally documented and witnessed.

All medical research subjects should be given the option of being informed about the general outcome and results of the study.[69]

The practical measures to be taken in securing informed consent are also set out by Article 29 of the Clinical Trials Regulation. The information provided to the prospective participant or their legally designated representative shall:

> 2(a) enable the subject or his or her legally designated representative to understand:
>
>> i. the nature, objectives, benefits, implications, risks and inconveniences of the clinical trial;
>>
>> ii. the subject's rights and guarantees regarding his or her protection, in particular his or her right to refuse to participate and the right to withdraw from the clinical trial at any time without any resulting detriment and without having to provide any justification;
>>
>> iii. the conditions under which the clinical trial is to be conducted, including the expected duration of the subject's participation in the clinical trial; and
>>
>> iv. the possible treatment alternatives, including the follow-up measures if the participation of the subject in the clinical trial is discontinued;
>
> (b) be kept comprehensive, concise, clear, relevant, and understandable to a layperson;
>
> (c) be provided in a prior interview with a member of the investigating team who is appropriately qualified …;
>
> (d) include information about the applicable damage compensation system …

---

[69] World Medical Association, Declaration of Helsinki, [25]–[26].

> (e) include the EU trial number and information about the availability of the clinical trial results …
>
> 3. The information referred to in paragraph 2 shall be prepared in writing and be available to the subject or, where the subject is not able to give informed consent, his or her legally designated representative.
>
> 4. In the interview referred to in point (c) of paragraph 2, special attention shall be paid to the information needs of specific patient populations and of individual subjects, as well as to the methods used to give the information.
>
> 5. In the interview referred to in point (c) of paragraph 2, it shall be verified that the subject has understood the information.
>
> 6. The subject shall be informed that the summary of the results of the clinical trial and a summary presented in terms understandable to a layperson will be made available in the EU database …[70]

Both the Declaration of Helsinki and the Clinical Trials Regulation 2014 illustrate the level of detail required for informed consent for research purposes. The requirements are more prescriptive than consent in other healthcare situations and reflect the increased level of choice that a participant may have. For instance, participation in a research study may offer no obvious therapeutic benefit yet the participant may still be exposed to risks they would otherwise not encounter. This underlines the importance of ensuring appropriate informed consent procedures are implemented from the outset. This includes asking who should seek consent.

Part three of the HSE's *National Consent Policy* provides, 'The person obtaining consent should have sufficient knowledge about the research and be capable of answering questions from prospective participants.'[71] It is also necessary to consider the relationship between the person obtaining consent and the prospective participant. This relationship may give rise to concerns about data protection or the potential for undue

---

[70] Regulation (EU) No 536/2014 of the European Parliament and of the Council of 16 April 2014 on clinical trials on medicinal products for human use, and repealing Directive 2001/20/EC, Art 29.
[71] Health Service Executive, *National Consent Policy* (HSE 2019) 71.

influence. In circumstances where the researcher does not have direct access to the prospective participant(s) it may be necessary to include a gatekeeper. On this point the *National Consent Policy* states, 'best practice and data protection considerations require that the service provider should act as a gatekeeper and make the initial contact with the prospective participant and provide him/her with the contact details of the research team'.[72] This will normally require the researcher to take some additional steps to ensure the proposed gatekeeper is sufficiently informed about the proposed research.

In healthcare research, the researcher may be involved in providing care and support to the prospective participant. The patient may feel obliged to partake in the research and feel they cannot refuse. This gives rise to the concern that the informed consent may be negated by undue influence. This risk may be lessened to some degree by the involvement of a third party. On this point, the *National Consent Policy* states:

> There may be situations where the researcher is also directly involved in providing care or support to the individual. Where this is the case, it is essential that any conflict of interest that might arise as a result of the original relationship be acknowledged and that any possibility that the individual might feel obliged to participate be averted. This might be achieved by having the consent either obtained or witnessed by a person who is independent of the research.[73]

Taking such measures encourages a robust informed consent process and can provide a solid foundation for the subsequent research.

Informed Consent and Children

The HSE's *National Consent Policy* states that a person over the age of 16 can consent on his/her own behalf for a clinical trial. For all other research, the person must be over the age of 18 in order to give consent.[74] As mentioned previously, this does not mean that

---

[72] ibid.
[73] ibid; World Medical Association, Declaration of Helsinki, [27]: 'When seeking informed consent for participation in a research study the physician must be particularly cautious if the potential subject is in a dependent relationship with the physician or may consent under duress. In such situations the informed consent must be sought by an appropriately qualified individual who is completely independent of this relationship.'
[74] ibid 72; see also the Department of Children and Youth Affairs, *Guidance for Developing Research Projects Involving Children* (DCYA 2012).

children cannot take part in research. The wholesale exclusion of children from research would be detrimental to research on childhood illnesses. Such research will necessarily involve children for both therapeutic and non-therapeutic components of the research.

The *National Consent Policy* outlined principles that should be adhered to when conducting research involving children:

- The research should only include children where the relevant knowledge cannot be obtained by conducting research involving adults
- The purpose of the research is to generate knowledge about the health or social care needs of children
- The research does not pose more than minimal risk unless there is a prospect of direct benefit for the participants
- The research has been designed to minimise pain, discomfort, fear and any other foreseeable risk to the child or his/her stage of development
- Consent to the child's participation must be obtained from a parent/legal guardian
- Whenever s/he has sufficient competence to provide it, the child's assent must be sought in a child-appropriate manner; and
- A child's refusal to participate or continue in research should be respected.[75]

The consent policy goes on to outline the concept of 'minimal risk' in research. This concept requires that 'the probability and magnitude of the possible harms posed by participating in research are no greater than those encountered by participants in their everyday life or during the performance of routine physical or psychological examinations or tests'.[76]

The consent of one parent/legal guardian is sufficient to permit the child's participation in the research, although the REC may stipulate that the consent of both parent(s)/legal guardian(s) is required. The decision is not solely one for the parents as there is a recognition of the growing maturity and developing capacity of the child. This is also reflected in the Clinical Trials Regulation 2014. Information should be presented in a manner the child can understand, so that they can consider assent. It should also be

---
[75] ibid.
[76] ibid 73.

explained to the child that they can elect to withdraw from the research if they are uncomfortable with continuing.

Clinical trials on minors is addressed by Article 32 of the Clinical Trials Regulation 2014. This provides that a clinical trial on a minor may only be conducted where the following conditions are satisfied:

> (a) the informed consent of their legally designated representative has been obtained;
>
> (b) the minors have received the information referred to in Article 29(2) in a way adapted to their age and mental maturity and from investigators or members of the investigating team who are trained or experienced in working with children;
>
> c) the explicit wish of a minor who is capable of forming an opinion and assessing the information referred to in Article 29(2) to refuse participation in, or to withdraw from, the clinical trial at any time, is respected by the investigator;
>
> (d) no incentives or financial inducements are given to the subject or his or her legally designated representative except for compensation for expenses and loss of earnings directly related to the participation in the clinical trial;
>
> (e) the clinical trial is intended to investigate treatments for a medical condition that only occurs in minors or the clinical trial is essential with respect to minors to validate data obtained in clinical trials on persons able to give informed consent or by other research methods;
>
> (f) the clinical trial either relates directly to a medical condition from which the minor concerned suffers or is of such a nature that it can only be carried out on minors;
>
> (g) there are scientific grounds for expecting that participation in the clinical trial will produce:
>
>> i. a direct benefit for the minor concerned outweighing the risks and burdens involved; or
>>
>> ii. some benefit for the population represented by the minor concerned and such a clinical trial will pose only minimal risk to, and will impose minimal burden on,

the minor concerned in comparison with the standard treatment of the minor's condition.

2. The minor shall take part in the informed consent procedure in a way adapted to his or her age and mental maturity.[77]

The 2014 Regulations give greater weight to a child's refusal to participate than the 2004 Regulation. The researcher is to respect the decision of a child to refuse participation in, or to withdraw from, a clinical trial where the child is capable of forming an opinion and assessing the relevant information. This allows for developments in a child's maturity and understanding over the course of a clinical trial. In this respect, the Regulation also requires informed consent to be given where the minor reaches the legal age of competence during the clinical trial.[78]

Informed Consent and Adults Lacking Decision-Making Capacity

The functional approach to capacity was outlined in chapter 5 of this text. It provides that capacity assessment is time- and issue-specific. An individual may have sufficient capacity to make smaller decisions but a more complex decision may be beyond their capacity at that time. A decision to participate in research that poses a potentially serious risk to health is likely to require a high level of capacity. The *National Consent Policy* recommends: 'In such cases, researchers must ensure that efforts are made to assist people in reaching their decision and that they are provided with the appropriate tools to maximise their decision-making ability.'[79] Information should be provided in a way that is comprehensible and the prospective participant should be informed of the right to withdraw from the research at any time without there being any negative repercussions.[80]

If an adult lacks decision-making capacity they may still be included in the research. As with research involving children, measures must be taken to safeguard their rights and interests. The *National Consent Policy* outlines principles to be adhered to

---

[77] Regulation (EU) No 536/2014 of the European Parliament and of the Council of 16 April 2014 on clinical trials on medicinal products for human use, and repealing Directive 2001/20/EC, Art 32.
[78] ibid Art 32(3): 'If during a clinical trial the minor reaches the age of legal competence to give informed consent as defined in the law of the Member State concerned, his or her express informed consent shall be obtained before that subject can continue to participate in the clinical trial.'
[79] Health Service Executive, *National Consent Policy* (HSE 2019) 76.
[80] ibid.

when conducting research involving adults lacking decision-making capacity:

- The research should only be undertaken if the required knowledge cannot be obtained by conducting research involving adults with decision-making capacity
- The research is expected to provide a direct benefit to the participants or to provide knowledge about the cause or treatment of the impairing or similar condition. Where there is no prospect of direct benefit for participants, the risks involved should be no more than minimal
- Consent for participation must be sought from the person's legal representative
- A REC must approve the participation of adults lacking decision-making capacity in research taking all of the above factors into consideration
- The explicit wish of a participant to refuse participation in or to be withdrawn from the study should be respected.[81]

The consent policy also notes that, outside of clinical trials, there is no legal framework for a person who lacks decision-making capacity to participate in research. The policy recommends that 'as a matter of best practice the same principles should apply to both clinical trials and other forms of research'.[82] Article 31 of the Clinical Trials Regulation 2014 sets out the provisions for clinical trials on incapacitated subjects. It provides that a clinical trial may be conducted where the following conditions are met:

(a) the informed consent of their legally designated representative has been obtained;

(b) the incapacitated subjects have received the information referred to in Article 29(2) in a way that is adequate in view of their capacity to understand it;

(c) the explicit wish of an incapacitated subject who is capable of forming an opinion and assessing the information referred to in Article 29(2) to refuse participation in, or to withdraw from, the clinical trial at any time, is respected by the investigator;

---

[81] ibid.
[82] ibid 77.

(d) no incentives or financial inducements are given to the subjects or their legally designated representatives, except for compensation for expenses and loss of earnings directly related to the participation in the clinical trial;

(e) the clinical trial is essential with respect to incapacitated subjects and data of comparable validity cannot be obtained in clinical trials on persons able to give informed consent, or by other research methods;

(f) the clinical trial relates directly to a medical condition from which the subject suffers;

(g) there are scientific grounds for expecting that participation in the clinical trial will produce:

> i. a direct benefit to the incapacitated subject outweighing the risks and burdens involved; or
>
> ii. some benefit for the population represented by the incapacitated subject concerned when the clinical trial relates directly to the life-threatening or debilitating medical condition from which the subject suffers and such trial will pose only minimal risk to, and will impose minimal burden on, the incapacitated subject concerned in comparison with the standard treatment of the incapacitated subject's condition.[83]

The legally designated representative has a significant role in protecting the rights and interests of the individual lacking capacity. The legally designated representative is defined as 'a natural or legal person, authority or body which, according to the law of the Member State concerned, is empowered to give informed consent on behalf of a subject who is an incapacitated subject or a minor'.[84] Despite their significance, it is clear that the prospective research participant should be involved in the informed consent process as far as possible.[85] This promotes the rights of the person and indicates respect for their dignity.

---

[83] Regulation (EU) No 536/2014 of the European Parliament and of the Council of 16 April 2014 on clinical trials on medicinal products for human use, and repealing Directive 2001/20/EC, Art 31.
[84] ibid Art 2(20).
[85] ibid Art 31(3).

10.7 Confidentiality

The NMBI's *Ethical Conduct in Research: Professional Guidance* document states:

> The researcher is responsible for ensuring confidentiality and privacy of the research participants and the data obtained from them. Personal information obtained by the researcher must not lead to identification of research participants and this information should not be made available to others without their consent. There are exceptional circumstances where information may have to be disclosed without the permission of participants, thus breaching confidentiality. These circumstances include public interest and safety and when the researcher believes that there may be a risk in non-disclosure. The researcher must have clear justification for the disclosure of information and should seek support from the research supervisor, ethics committee and other relevant persons. The decision should be clearly documented.
>
> Personal information obtained through group research needs vigilance from both the researcher and research participants to maintain confidentiality.
>
> Researchers can ensure that confidentiality is maintained by assigning an identification number to each participant, so that identifying information is effectively secured and that identifying information is not entered on a computer system or other potentially accessible database.[86]

There is a distinction between confidentiality and anonymity, as underlined by Doody and Noonan.[87] True anonymity is often not possible in research and instead it is most appropriate to emphasise confidentiality. A number of practical steps can be built into the research process in order to effectively protect participant confidentiality. These measures relate to the access and storage of data, the use of unique identifiers, as well as password protection and computer encryption. The Irish Research Nurses Network identify the following steps:

- Data should be stored in a secure room
- Data must be locked away if unattended

---

[86] Nursing and Midwifery Board of Ireland, *Ethical Conduct in Research: Professional Guidance* (NMBI 2015) 8.
[87] Doody and Noonan (n 39) 806.

- No one should access subject data unless authorised to do so by research personnel and/or data protection officer.
- Research subject confidentiality should be maintained by the use of initials and/or research numbers as unique identifiers on research material
- Electronic data must be password protected
- Personal data that could potentially identify research subjects should be kept in a secure place, separate from research files.[88]

As already touched on in this chapter, researchers must also comply with General Data Protection Regulation (GDPR) requirements. These requirements are contained in the Data Protection Act 2018 and the Data Protection Act 2018 (s 36(2)) (Health Research) Regulations 2018 (HRR). Regulation 3 of the HRR defines the mandatory measures for the processing of personal data for the purposes of health research.[89] Among the requirements stipulated by Regulation 3 the following processes and procedures relating to the management and conduct of health research are to be in place:

(i) the carrying out of an assessment of the data protection implications of the health research;

(ii) where the assessment carried out under clause (i) indicates a high risk to the rights and freedoms of individuals, the carrying out of a data protection impact assessment;

(iii) measures that demonstrate compliance with the data minimisation principle in Article 5(1)(c);

(iv) controls to limit access to the personal data undergoing processing in order to prevent unauthorised consultation, alteration, disclosure or erasure of personal data;

(v) controls to log whether and by whom personal data have been consulted, altered, disclosed or erased;

(vi) measures to protect the security of the personal data concerned;

---

[88] Irish Research Nurses Network, *IRNN Clinical Research Nurse and Midwife Orientation Pack* (IRNN 2019) 29.
[89] Data Protection Act 2018 (s 36(2)) (Health Research) Regulations 2018, SI 314/2018, Reg 3.

(vii) arrangements to anonymise, archive or destroy personal data once the health research has been completed;

(viii) other technical and organisational measures designed to ensure that processing is carried out in accordance with the Data Protection Regulation, together with processes for testing and evaluating the effectiveness of such measures.[90]

The concept of 'health research' is defined broadly under the HRR and is likely to capture much of the research undertaken by nurses and midwives, including those in a CRN/M role. Regulation 3(2) of the HRR sets out that 'health research' means any of the following scientific research for the purpose of human health:

(i) research with the goal of understanding normal and abnormal functioning, at molecular, cellular, organ system and whole body levels;

(ii) research that is specifically concerned with innovative strategies, devices, products or services for the diagnosis, treatment or prevention of human disease or injury;

(iii) research with the goal of improving the diagnosis and treatment (including the rehabilitation and palliation) of human disease and injury and of improving the health and quality of life of individuals;

(iv) research with the goal of improving the efficiency and effectiveness of health professionals and the health care system;

(v) research with the goal of improving the health of the population as a whole or any part of the population through a better understanding of the ways in which social, cultural, environmental, occupational and economic factors determine health status.[91]

The GDPR requirements will also extend to any action taken to establish whether an individual may be suitable for inclusion in research.[92]

---

[90] ibid Reg 3(1)(c).
[91] ibid Reg 3(2).
[92] ibid Reg 3(2)(b).

Index

Abortion
  Citizen's Assembly 229–30
  Code of Professional Conduct and Ethics 230–1
  condition likely to lead to death of foetus 231–2
  conscientious objection 232–3
  definitions 221, 222
  early pregnancy 232
  emergency provisions 231
  generally 210, 221–2
  human rights issues 226, 228–9
  information on services 223, 225
  law in Ireland 221–2
    development of 222–30
  legislation 230–4
  medical abortion 221
  outside the State 223–9
  privacy concept 222–3
  referenda 225, 226, 230
  risk to life/health 231
  s.23 offences 233–4
  suicide risk 224–5, 228
  surgical abortions 221–2
  young persons 234–6
Abuse *see* Elder abuse
Academic commentary 23
Administration of medicines *see* Prescribing and administration of medicines
Advance healthcare directives 135–40
An Bord Altranais
  generally 35, 36
  renaming of 36
  see also Nursing and Midwifery Board of Ireland
Aquinas, Thomas 263–4
Assisted decision-making
  decision-making assistant 127, 128–9
  generally 127–9
  withdrawal of medical treatment 260
  see also Decision-making

Assisted suicide *see* Euthanasia and assisted suicide
Attorney General 31–2
Audi alteram partem principle 53
Autonomy
  advance healthcare directives 135–40
  assisted suicide and 100
  conceptions of autonomy 96–8
  consent issues *see* Consent
  constitutional right 99
  decision-making *see* Decision-making
  demand for medical treatment 120–2
  Dworkin on 97
  ECtHR and 100
  elevation of 95–101
  end-of-life care 253–60
  generally 94–5
  Kantian view 96
  legal recognition of 98–100
  liberal perspective 97–8
  medical treatment and 253–60
  Millian view 96, 97
  older people and 253–60
  patient autonomy 94–101
  patient-centred care 93, 103, 115
  Principles of Biomedical Ethics 96
  professional autonomy 76, 77
  professional guidelines 100–1
  refusal of treatment 117–20

Barristers 30
Birth environment
  birth plan, legal status of 220–1
  birthing pools 219–20
  generally 212
  home birth services
    accessing 218–19
    Agreement for Home Birth Services 215–18
    Clinical Indemnity Scheme 215–16

330 | Index

Birth environment (*continued*)
   Memorandum of
      Understanding 215–18
   right to 212–15
   self-employed community
      midwife (SECM) 215–17, 218, 219
  National Maternity Strategy 209, 212
  regulation of midwifery 210–21
Bodily integrity, right to 14–15
Brain death 278–9
Bunreacht na hÉireann
  amendments 12, 17
  autonomy, right to 99
  confidentiality 144
  constitutional interpretation 16
  Council of State 13–14
  courts 14, 24
  European Union law and 12
  executive powers 13
  fundamental rights 14–15, 242
  generally 12–13
  institutions of the State 13–14
  Irish language 13
  limits on Constitutional rights 16
  Oireachtas 13, 17
  privacy right 148–9
  referenda 12

Canon law 23
Capacity
  assessment of 105, 107–11
  consent issues *see* Consent
  decision-making *see* Decision-making
  disclosure of information 152
  enduring power of attorney 133–5
  functional assessment of 125
  functional model 106–7, 110
  meaning of 105
  models of 106–7
  presumption of 106
  refusal of treatment 118, 237
Causation
  burden of proof 82–3
  division of liability 87–8
  factual causation test 82, 83
    'but for' test 83–4
      material contribution test 84–5
  generally 70, 82–3
  legal causation test 82, 86

  foreseeability 86–7
  novus actus interveniens 82, 86–7
  recklessness 87
  see also Negligence
Central Midwives Board 34, 35
Childbirth *see* Birth environment
Children
  access to records pertaining to 172–5
  consent issues 151–2, 319–22
  disclosure of information 151–2
  participation in clinical research 319–22
  withdrawal of medical treatment 259–60
Circuit Court 25–6
Civil actions 11
Civil law systems 8–9
Clinical Indemnity Scheme (CIS) 215–16
Clinical research
  anonymity 325
  beneficence/non-maleficence principle 305
  clinical research nurse/midwife 291–2
  conduct of clinical trials 293–7, 308–12
  confidentiality 325–7
  consent to participation 315–19
    adults lacking capacity 322–4
    children 319–22
    Nuremberg Code 299–300
  Declaration of Helsinki 296–7, 301–2, 313–14, 316, 318
  fidelity principle 306
  generally 5, 289–90
  international codes of ethics 297–302
  NMBI *Ethical Conduct in Research* 290–1, 304–6, 314, 325
  Nuremberg Code 298–301
  phases of clinical trials 294–5
  placebos 296–7
  randomised controlled trials 295–6
  RECs *see* Research ethics committees
  Regulation *see* Clinical Trials Regulation
  role of nurse/midwife 290–2

Tuskegee Syphilis Trial 1932-72 298
veracity principle 305–6
vulnerable participants 313–15
war crimes 298–9
Clinical Trials Regulation
  children 320–2
  ethics committees 309–12
  generally 303–4
  incapacitated subjects 323–4
  informed consent 316, 317–18
Close connection test, vicarious liability 92
Co-decision-making 129–31
  see also Decision-making
Code of Professional Conduct and Ethics
  abortion 230–1
  aims of 43
  complaints and 43, 51
  confidentiality 145–6, 155, 178
  disclosure of information 155, 156
  generally 42–4
  international conventions and 44
  non-compliance with 43, 51
  open disclosure 178
  palliative care 265
  principles 43–4
  professional misconduct 49
  purpose of 42–3
  research in nursing practice 290–1
  see also Standards of practice
Collaborative Practice Agreement (CPA) 194–5
Commencement orders 18
Common law
  doctrine of precedent 8–9, 18
  generally 18–19
  law reports 18–19
  systems of 8–9
Complaints
  alcohol addiction 51
  conviction for offence triable on indictment 52–3
  drug addiction 51
  failures in compliance
    codes of professional conduct 43, 51
    conditions 51–2
    legislative provisions 52
    Regulations 52
    supply of drugs 52
  undertakings 52
  FTPC *see* Fitness to Practise Committee
  generally 46–8
  grounds 46–7
  medical disability 51
  poor professional performance 47, 50–1
  PPC *see* Preliminary Proceedings Committee
  process 46–66
  professional misconduct 47, 48–50
Confidentiality
  clinical research 325–7
  Code of Professional Conduct and Ethics 145–6, 155, 178
  consent to disclosure 151–2
  Constitutional rights 148–9
  contractual obligation 147–8
  court orders 152–3
  data protection *see* Data protection
  demographic information 143
  elder abuse and 249
  equitable basis for 148
  European Convention on Human Rights 144, 149–50
  exceptions to duty 150–1
    consent to disclosure 151–2
    disclosure required by law 152–4
    interests of society 159–60
    patient's best interests 154–5
    risk of harm to another 156–9
  freedom of information
    access to records 169–70
    children's records 172–5
    legislation 169–77
    medical/psychiatric records 171–2
    personal information 171
    posthumous protection 175–7
    restrictions 170–2
  generally 4, 142–4
  infectious diseases 154
  meaning of confidential information 142–3
  open disclosure *see* Open disclosure
  posthumous protection of information 175–7

Index | 331

Index

Confidentiality (*continued*)
  professional codes of conduct 144–7
  research participants 325–7
  social media 181
Consent
  advance healthcare directives 135–40
  birthing pool 220
  capacity
    assessment of 105, 107–11
    disclosure of information 152
    functional model 106–7, 110
    meaning of 105
    models of 106–7
    presumption of 106
    research participants 322–4
  children 151–2, 319–22
  civil and criminal liability 101–3
  disclosure of appropriate information 111–13
  disclosure of information 151
    children 151–2
    fluctuating capacity 152
    next of kin 152
  DNAR orders 273–7
  duress 105
  emergencies 103–4
  express consent 102
  fluctuating consent 152
  generally 93–4
  HSE's *National Consent Policy* 104, 105, 106, 107
    research participants 318–20, 322–3
  implied consent 103
  informed consent 97, 101
    capacity, role of 105–11
    Clinical Trials Regulation 316, 317–18
    research participants 315–24
    risk disclosure 113–16
    therapeutic privilege 116–17
  negligence and 102
  patient autonomy and 94, 95, 98, 100–1
  research participants 315–19
    adults lacking capacity 322–4
    children 319–21
    Clinical Trials Regulation 316, 317–18

  Nuremberg Code 299–300
  risk disclosure 111–16
  therapeutic privilege 116–17
  undue influence 105
  voluntary consent 104–5
  written consent 102–3
Constitution of Ireland *see* Bunreacht na hÉireann
Continuing Education Units (CEUs) 41
Coroner
  deputy coroner 281
  districts 281
  inquests 285–7
  post-mortem practice 284
  professional qualifications 281
  reportable deaths 282–4
  role of 280–7
Council of the European Union 20
Court of Appeal 26–7
Courts
  Circuit Court 25–6
  Court of Appeal 26–7
  criminal prosecutions 10–11
  decisions 8–9, 18–19
  District Court 9, 24–5
  doctrine of precedent 9
  European Court of Human Rights 22, 28–9
  European Court of Justice 28
  High Court 26
  judicial activism 15
  Labour Court 28
  Special Criminal Court 28
  structure of courts system 23–9
  Supreme Court 9, 27
COVID-19 research 312–13
Criminal prosecutions 10–11

Data protection
  data breach 169
  freedom of information
    access to records 169–70
    children's records 172–5
    legislation 169–77
    medical/psychiatric records 171–2
    personal information 171
    posthumous protection 175–7
    restrictions 170–2
  GDPR 161–2

breach of 169
personal data 161–2, 164–6
principles 161, 162
generally 161–2
personal data
access 166
definition 161
processing of 162, 164–6
special categories 161
privacy notice 163–4
rights of data subject 166–8
access to personal data 166
automated processing/profiling 168
data portability 168
erasure 167
objection 168
rectification 166
restriction of processing 267–8
transparency 162–4
see also Confidentiality; Disclosure of information; Open disclosure
Death
brain death 278–9
brainstem death 279
certification of 280
coroner's role 280–7
definition of 277–80
gross negligence manslaughter 68–9
registration of 279–80
Decision-making
advance healthcare directives 135–40
assisted decision-making 127–9, 260
capacity, assessment of 125
co-decision-making 129–31
decision-making assistant 127–9
decision-making representatives 131–3
Director of the Decision Support Service 123–5
enduring power of attorney 133–5
generally 3, 127–9
guiding principles 125–7
intervener's responsibilities 126–7
legislation 122–40, 260
supports 127–33
Declaration of Geneva 145

Declaration of Helsinki 296–7, 301–2, 313–14, 316, 318
Demand for medical treatment 120–2
Director of Public Prosecutions (DPP) 31
Disclosure of information
consent issues 151
children 151–2
fluctuating capacity 152
next of kin 152
court orders 152–3
infectious diseases 154
interests of society 159–60
legal requirement 152–4
patient's best interests 154–6
risk of harm to another person 156–9
see also Confidentiality; Data protection; Open disclosure
District Court 9, 24–5
Do not attempt resuscitation orders (DNAR orders)
case law 273–6
generally 273
HSE *National Consent Policy* 276–7
Double effect, doctrine of 263–5
Duty of care
generally 70, 71–3
nursing and 72–3
proximity of relationship 72
reasonable foreseeability 72
test for 72
see also Negligence
Dworkin, Ronald 97

Education and training
continued professional development 41
NMBI's duties 40–1
programmes of 40
Eggshell skull rule 88–90
Elder abuse
confidentiality and 249
definition 247
forms of 248–9
generally 247–9
see also End-of-life care
Emergencies
abortion 231
childbirth 211
informed consent 103–4

Emergencies (*continued*)
  prescriptions 200–1
End-of-life care
  abuse *see* Elder abuse
  assisted decision-making 260
  autonomy and 253–60
  demographic issues 240–1
  dignity 241–3, 265, 275
  DNAR orders 273–7
  human rights 241–3
  palliative care *see* Palliative care
  restraint, use of 250–3
  standards for care 243–7
  wills 287–8
  withdrawal of medical treatment 254–60
Enduring power of attorney 133–5
Enterprise liability, healthcare facilities 91
European Commission 20
European Convention on Human Rights (ECHR)
  confidentiality 144, 149–50
  generally 22–3
  older people's rights 242
  restraint, use of 252
European Court of Human Rights (ECtHR) 22, 28–9, 100
European Court of Justice (ECJ) 28
European Social Charter 241–2
European Union
  Bunreacht na hÉireann and 12
  Council of the European Union 20
  European Commission 20
  European Parliament 20
  generally 19–21
  institutions 19–20
  national sovereignty and 19
  treaties 19, 20–1
Euthanasia and assisted suicide
  advance healthcare directives 135–40
  autonomy and 100
  case law 268–70
  definitions 267
  DNAR orders 273–7
  doctrine of double effect 263–5
  generally 267–8
  murder charge 267–8
  palliative sedation 262–3
  prosecution 270–1

  responding to request for 271–3
  withdrawal of medical treatment 254–60
Expected standards test 48

Fenwick, Ethel 34–5
Fitness to Practise Committee (FTPC)
  administrative/procedural concerns 53–4
  appeals 64
  complaints referred to by PPC 47, 57
  confirmation of decisions 65
  conflicts of interest/bias 58–9
  evidence 60–1
  generally 37
  High Court 65
  inquiries 52, 58–62
  membership of 39, 58–9
  mitigating factors 64
  notice of referral 59–60
  notification of decisions 65
  proceedings 60
  restoration of registration 66
  sanctions 62–6
  ultra vires actions 54
  undertakings to 61
  witnesses 60–1
  written report 62
Fluoridation of water supply 14–15
Freedom of information
  access to records 169–70
  children's records 172–5
  legislation 169–77
  medical/psychiatric records 171–2
  personal information 171
  posthumous protection 175–7
  restrictions 170–2
French Code de la Santé Publique (Code of Public Health) 9
Fundamental rights
  bodily integrity 14–15
  Bunreacht na hÉireann 14–15, 242
  privacy in marital affairs 15
  unenumerated rights 14–15

Gawande, Atul 239
General Nursing Council 34, 35
Gross negligence manslaughter 68–9
Guide to Professional Conduct and Ethics

autonomy 100–1
confidentiality 145

Health Information and Quality
 Authority (HIQA)
 generally 205, 206, 207
 standard for care of older people
  245–7
Health Protection Surveillance
 Centre (HPSC) 154
High Court 26, 57–8, 65
Hippocratic Oath 144
Home birth service *see* Birth
 environment
Human rights
 abortion 226, 228–9
 confidentiality 144, 149–50
 older people 241–3
 palliative care 266
 restraint 252–3

Infectious diseases 154
Inquests 285–7
 see also Coroner
International Code of Medical Ethics 145
International law 21–2

Judges 30–1
Judicial activism 15

Kant, Immanuel 96

Labour *see* Birth environment
Labour Court 28
Larkin, Philip 239
Law reports 18–19
Legal framework
 academic commentary 23
 canon law 23
 civil actions 11
 civil law systems 8–9
 commencement orders 18
 common law 18–19
 common law systems 8–9
 concept of law 8–11
 Constitution of Ireland *see*
  Bunreacht na hÉireann
 courts *see* Courts
 criminal law 10–11
 European law 19–21
 generally 2–3

institutions of the State 13–14
international law 21–3
legal principles 8–9
legislation 17–18
nursing and midwifery in Ireland
 34–7
Oireachtas 13, 17
prescriptive authority of nurses/
 midwives 185–91
private Acts 17
private law and public law 9–10
public general acts 17
referenda 12
secondary legislation 17–18
solicitors 29–30
sources of law 11–23
statutory instruments 17–18
Legal profession
 Attorney General 31–2
 barristers 30
 Director of Public
  Prosecutions 31
 judges 30–1

Manslaughter, gross negligence
 manslaughter 68–9
Marital affairs, right to privacy in 15
Medical treatment
 advance healthcare directives
  135–40
 assisted decision-making 260
 autonomy and 253–60
 demand for 120–2
 end-of-life care 253–60
 palliative care *see* Palliative care
 refusal of 117–20
  advance healthcare directives
   135–40
  capacity 118, 237
  DNAR orders 273–7
  in pregnancy 139, 236–8
 withdrawal of 120–1, 254–60
Medicines
 controlled drugs 188–90, 199, 200,
  201
 covert administration 205–6
 medication errors 206–7
  open disclosure 207
  professional accountability
   207–8
 self-administration 205

Medicines (*continued*)
   see also Prescribing and administration of medicines
Mill, JS 96, 97
Misconduct see Professional misconduct
Moral turpitude test 48

National Maternity Strategy 209, 212
National Research Ethics Committees (NRECs)
   Bill 312
   COVID-19 312–13
   see also Research ethics committees
Negligence
   causation see Causation
   civil actions 11
   close connection test 92
   consent and 102
   direct liability 90–1
   duty of care 70, 71–3
   eggshell skull rule 88–90
   enterprise liability 91
   generally 3, 67–8
   gross negligence manslaughter 68–9
   harm 88–90
   healthcare facilities 90–2
   law of torts 69
   professional negligence 74–8
   res ipsa loquitur principle 70
   standard of care see Standard of care
   strict liability 69
   tort of 70
   vicarious liability 91–2
Nemo judexi in causa sua principle 53
Nightingale, Florence 144–5
Nuremberg Code 298–301
Nurses Rules 2010/2013 37–8
Nursing and Midwifery Board of Ireland (NMBI)
   the Board 38–9
   committees/sub-committees 39
   complaints see Complaints
   confidentiality 145–6
   education and training duties 40–1
   establishment of 36
   Ethical Conduct in Research 290–1, 304–6, 314, 325
   fees 41
   FTPC see Fitness to Practise Committee
   functions of 37
   generally 33, 37–8
   Guide to Fitness to Practice 57
   members of 38–9
   Nurses and Midwives Act 2011 35–7
   Nurses Rules 2010/2013 37–8
   object of 37
   PPC see Preliminary Proceedings Committee
   Register of Nurses and Midwives in Ireland 39–40
   registration fee 41
   social media use 181
   standard for care of older people 243–5
   standards of practice 41–5

Oireachtas 13, 17
Older people see End-of-life care
O'Mahony, Seamus 239
Open disclosure
   apologies 177, 178, 180
   civil liability legislation 179–80
   Code of Professional Conduct and Ethics 178
   culture of candour 178
   definition 177
   ethical basis 178–9
   generally 177–81
   HSE staff 179
   medication errors 207
   meetings 180
   patient safety incident 179–81

Palliative care
   definitions 261–2
   doctrine of double effect 263–5
   generally 261–2
   human rights 266
   older people 261–7
   pain management 262–7
   requirement to provide 265–7
   sedation 262–3
   see also End-of-life care
Patient autonomy see Autonomy
Patient-centred care 93, 103, 115
Physical restraint see Restraint
Placebos 296–7

Policy, procedures, protocols or guidelines (PPPGs) 195–6, 203, 204
Post-mortem practice 284
see also Coroner
Practice Standards for Midwives
   core values 45–6
   generally 44–6
   principles 44
   the Standards 45
Precedent, doctrine of 8–9, 18
Pregnancy
   advanced healthcare directives 139
   death of mother 279
   generally 4, 209
   National Maternity Strategy 209, 212
   refusal of treatment 139, 236–8
   regulation of midwifery 210–21
   see also Abortion; Birth environment
Preliminary Proceedings Committee (PPC)
   administrative/procedural concerns 53–4
   case officer 55
   case worker 54
   conflicts of interest 55
   consideration of complaint 55–6
   expert reports 56
   generally 36–7, 47, 54–7
   immediate suspension of registration 57–8
   membership of 39, 55
   no further action 56
   referral of complaint to FTPC 47, 57
   responses to complaint 56–7
   role of 47
   ultra vires actions 54
   withdrawal of complaint 56
   see also Complaints
Prescribing and administration of medicines
   clinical decision-making process 197–9
   clinical governance 194–6
   Collaborative Practice Agreement 194–5
   controlled drugs 188–90, 199, 200, 201
   covert administration 205–6
   data collection system 191–2
   Department of Health 191–2
   emergency prescribing 200–1
   exempt medicinal products 201–3
   generally 4, 183–4, 197
   Health Service Executive 191–2
   legal framework for prescriptive authority 185–91
   medication errors 206–8
   medication protocols 204–5
   nurse prescribing programmes 193–4
   nurses rules 190–1
   off-label prescribing 201–3
   policy, procedures, protocols or guidelines (PPPGs) 195–6, 203, 204
   Practice Standards and Guidelines 196–7
   prescribing consultation 199
   prescription practices and limitations 199–205
   registration as nurse/midwife prescriber 192–4
   repeat prescribing 200
   for self, family, significant others 200
   self-administration 205
   separation of responsibilities 203–4
   writing of prescriptions 199
Principles of Biomedical Ethics 96
Professional competence 40–1
Professional misconduct
   expected standards test 48
   generally 47, 48–50
   meaning of 48–9
   moral turpitude test 48
   standard of proof 49–50

Randomised controlled trials 295–6
Referenda 12
   abortion issue 225, 226, 230
Refusal of treatment
   advance healthcare directives 135–40
   autonomy and 117–20
   capacity 118, 237
   DNAR orders 273–7
   in pregnancy 139, 236–8
Register of Nurses and Midwives in Ireland 39–40

Register of Nurses and Midwives in Ireland (*continued*)
  registration fee 41
  restoration to 41
Registration
  restoration of 66
  suspension of 57–8, 63
Research ethics committees (RECs)
  clinical trials 308–12
  function 306–7
  generally 306–8
  National Research Ethics Committees Bill 312
  COVID-19 312–13
  review of other research 312
  see also Clinical research
Restraint
  chemical restraint 251
  environmental restraint 251
  human rights 252–3
  physical restraint 250
  use of 250–3
Roll of Midwives 34

Secondary legislation 17–18
self-employed community midwife (SECM) 215–17, 218, 219
Social media
  confidentiality and 181
  NMBI guidance 181
Solicitors 29–30
Sources of law *see* Legal framework
Special Criminal Court 28
Standard of care
  differences of opinion 79, 82
  Dunne 78–80
  equal specialisation 80–1
  general and approved practice 79, 80
    deviation from 78–9, 81–2
  generally 70, 73–8
  inherent defects 82
  medical treatment 74
  nursing education 75–8
  professional negligence 74–8
  reasonable person 73
  reasonable skilled nurse 75
  see also Negligence
Standards of practice
  generally 41–2
  NMBI's function 41–5
  Nurses and Midwives Act 2011 41–2
  see also Code of Professional Conduct and Ethics; Practice Standards for Midwives
Statutory instruments (SIs) 17–18
Strict liability 69
Suicide
  abortion and 224–5, 228
  assisted *see* Euthanasia and assisted suicide
Supreme Court 9, 27
Suspension of registration 57–8, 63

Torts
  forms of 69
  intentional 69
  law of 69
  negligent *see* Negligence
  strict liability 69
Training *see* Education and training
Tuskegee Syphilis Trial 1932-72 298

Ultra vires actions 54
Unenumerated rights 14–15

Vicarious liability
  close connection test 92
  healthcare facilities 91–2

Wills 287–8
Withdrawal of medical treatment 120–1, 254–60